/658.408
GRA

BOOK NO: 1867897

KU-052-335

Corporate Social Opportunity!
Seven Steps to Make Corporate Social Responsibility Work for Your Business

David Grayson and Adrian Hodges

UNIVERSITY OF WALES, NEWPORT
LIBRARY
AND
INFORMATION
SERVICES
ALLT-YR-YN

DAVID GRAYSON (www.davidgrayson.net) is a former managing director of Business in the Community and remains a part-time director where he particularly focuses on small businesses and CSR, as chairman of the UK Small Business Consortium. He is the founder Principal of the BLU — the world's first virtual 'corporate university' for small business development professionals. He speaks, writes and advises regularly on business, society and entrepreneurialism, for businesses, media and business schools around the world. David sits on the board of the Strategic Rail Authority (www.sra.gov.uk) where he particularly champions disability access. He was the first chairman of the UK's National Disability Council and is now a patron of the disability charity Scope (www.scope.org.uk); and an ambassador for the National AIDS Trust (www.nat.org.uk). He is also a trustee of the Responsibility in Gambling Trust (www.rigt.org.uk). He was co-founder/director of Project North East — an innovative British NGO which has now worked in 40 countries (www.pne.org).

dgrayson@bitc.org.uk

ADRIAN HODGES is managing director of the International Business Leaders Forum. He specialises in issues of corporate responsibility as they relate to international business strategy and practice, and has provided counsel to many executives on how to successfully integrate social, ethical and environmental concerns into management processes. He also works with leaders from civil society seeking to forge partnerships with business, and is a regular speaker on the impacts of globalisation and the contribution of business to sustainable development. He has worked in business, local government and non-governmental organisations, and has held the positions of worldwide Head of Corporate Communications for the retailer Body Shop International and Director of Communications and Marketing at Business in the Community. Adrian has lived in Ecuador and the United States and has worked extensively across the Americas. He is currently resident in London.

adrian.hodges@iblf.org

RWE Thames Water and Pfizer Inc. kindly provided sponsorship to support the research and development of this book.

CORPORATE SOCIAL OPPORTUNITY!

7

UNIVERSITY OF WALES, NEWPORT
LIBRARY AND INFORMATION SERVICES
ALLT-YR-YN

steps

to make
CORPORATE SOCIAL RESPONSIBILITY
work for your business

Greenleaf
PUBLISHING

2 0 0 4

© 2004 Greenleaf Publishing Limited

Published by Greenleaf Publishing Limited
Aizlewood's Mill
Nursery Street
Sheffield S3 8GG
UK

Printed on paper made from at least 75% post-consumer waste
using TCF and ECF bleaching.
Printed in Great Britain by William Clowes Ltd, Beccles, Suffolk.
Cover by LaliAbril.com.

All rights reserved. No part of this publication may be reproduced,
stored in a retrieval system, or transmitted, in any form or by any
means, electronic, mechanical, photocopying, recording or
otherwise, without the prior permission in writing of the
publishers.

British Library Cataloguing in Publication Data:
A catalogue record for this book is available from the British Library.

Hardback: ISBN 1874719845
Paperback: ISBN 1874719837

Contents

How to use this book

The structure of this book is built around a seven-step analytical process. This process enables managers to assess the implications of corporate social responsibility on their overall business strategy. It describes how to interpret the resulting analysis to spot business opportunities — what we call *corporate social opportunities*. It provides a methodology to show how to generate revised or potentially new business strategies to capitalise on those opportunities. And it shows how to consider associated (subsequent) governance and operational implications.

The seven-step process is repeated twice, in Part I and Part II. In Part I, the seven steps are introduced chapter by chapter. Key concepts and analytical techniques are described for each step. Information on relevant trends is presented, along with explanations of how practical diagnostic tools can be applied. Throughout, real-company examples and illustrations are provided.

In Part II we repeat the seven steps, but this time in the structure of a series of analytical process forms, supported by explanatory notes. The format of the forms creates a disciplined and methodical approach to considering the impact of corporate social responsibility on business strategy. The forms provide a framework to draw down the learning from the information provided in Part I, and capture outputs — data, views and opinions — gleaned from applying the seven-step process to a company. Populating the forms with relevant information leads to the identification of ideas for new or revised business strategies, which are then explored and tested further. Governance and operational implications are also identified.

Rather than describe the analytical process forms in the abstract, in Part II we illustrate the application of the seven steps along with inputs for the forms by capturing the deliberations from the senior management of a hypothetical business — 'Advent Foods' — as they work through the seven steps at an imaginary management retreat. Food is one industry sector that everyone can relate to, as we all are consumers of its products, even if we have little direct expertise of management issues in the sector. The food business has been much in the news recently as the media have extensively reported concerns from a number of quarters on rising levels of health-related problems due to obesity, poor nutrition and a decline in levels of physical activity. The causes of obesity are complex, but some campaigners have focused their attention on claiming a direct link between the products and marketing activities of food and soft drinks companies. As a consequence, companies in this sector have had to work out their response to intense scrutiny from the media, pressure groups, consumer groups and governments. This scenario provides a topical focus for describing the application of the seven steps. We have supported the completed forms with a corresponding narrative that gives insight into the conversations and thinking that took place at the retreat around this theme.

You can use the book in a number of ways:

- As a survey of CSR-related trends and their implications for business strategy and a guide to management techniques that will help not only manage associated risks but also nurture associated opportunities

- For preparatory reading and then a reference and source book when applying the seven-step process to your own business or business unit

For the latter option, a set of blank forms can be downloaded directly from www. greenleaf-publishing.com/catalogue/csoforms.htm or via links on www.iblf.org and www.bitc.org.uk. The questions and issues prompted by the process forms can be used as the basis for debate and discussion with colleagues, and resulting thoughts and ideas can be captured on the forms for further analysis and sharing across the business.

For those who would like to apply the seven-step process with assistance from the authors and team who developed the analytical process forms, there are seminars, presentations and assisted workshops are available. See page 377 for details.

Introduction

Corporate social responsibility (CSR) is now firmly on the business agenda for a significant number of firms. Some 2,000 international companies regularly report on their environmental and social impacts, and in some countries, such as France and Australia, reporting is mandatory. It is increasingly common for Fortune 500 companies to have a designated manager or department that has oversight of CSR. Many of these same companies retain management and public relations consultants selected from a growing pool of professional services firms offering CSR advice.

These observations reflect how, over the last decade, CSR has shifted from the margins to the mainstream of business practice. However, behind this apparently positive picture lie two problems that create an impediment to companies in realising the potential benefits of CSR. The first problem arises from the fact that one of the greatest drivers causing business leaders to adopt CSR is 'fear', with the emphasis on avoiding trouble rather than looking for opportunities. The second problem is that CSR is too often a 'bolt-on' to business operations rather than 'built-in' to business strategy, resulting in CSR becoming a distraction and hindrance to business purpose and objectives, rather than a help.

▶ The fear factor

As we all know, the fear of getting hurt is an important influence on how we behave. In a business context one of the biggest drivers behind the increasing attention given by management to CSR has been the 'fear' factor. Business leaders fear that their company could be a target of the next high-profile campaign by a non-governmental organisation, with allegations that the company is party to poor labour practices at its overseas suppliers; they may fear the consequences of a class action lawsuit filed against them, with litigants claiming discrimination in the workplace; or they may fear that a government, under pressure to demonstrate its 'green credentials', will pass legislation requiring adherence to even higher environmental standards, necessitating further non-revenue-earning investment.

Given that fear is a key driver, it is perhaps not surprising that CSR is increasingly associated with the business discipline of risk management, in which the objective is the avoidance of potential hazards and reduction of potential threats. As advocates for CSR we, like many others, have framed our arguments for why businesses should adopt good CSR practices in the vocabulary of risk management, highlighting the potential dangers to corporate and brand reputation, or the negative impact on efforts to recruit and retain the most talented employees, or the loss of the 'licence to operate' if the company gets the management of CSR wrong.

The promotion of CSR on a risk management platform has led to some success in shifting it from the margins to the mainstream of corporate practice. However, we observe that an over-emphasis on linking CSR to risk mitigation is somewhat hazardous in its own right. The consequence is that business leaders are being conditioned to regard CSR as synonymous with cost, burden, obligation and duty rather than associate it with possibilities of market growth, product or service differentiation and new business opportunities. To many business leaders, the language and tone of CSR has become earnest and dull. Therein lies the challenge. If the prevailing interpretation of CSR as essentially negative and limiting is left to dominate corporate thinking, it will serve only to define minimum expectations of business behaviour and performance.

After all, not many successful companies we know have achieved their success in an extremely competitive marketplace simply because they were particularly attentive to risk management (apart, perhaps, from firms in the insurance sector). Sound risk management may have helped a company *retain* a market leadership position, but not *earn* it. The driver for successful business is entrepreneurialism, opportunity and the competitive instinct, not fear. It is a willingness to take risks in order to attain goals and achieve objectives. It is a willingness to look for creativity and innovation from non-traditional areas — including CSR.

While sound and effective CSR policies and practices are very much needed, we are concerned that too many business leaders and managers regard them as the end game. Yet CSR can and should be much more than that. It has the potential to be an extremely positive force that can fuel the engine of business growth and development and contribute to social and environmental sustainable development.

▶ Bolt-on or built-in?

A second concern we have is the way in which CSR is integrated into companies. In our previous book, *Everybody's Business*,[1] we focused on the why of CSR. Feedback we received from managers around the world indicated that there is still a considerable gap between the corporate CSR rhetoric and actual practice on the ground because of difficulties in making it operational: 'Yes, we understand what it

---

1   D. Grayson and A. Hodges, *Everybody's Business* (London: Dorling Kindersley, 2001).

is. Our company has even made a public commitment to CSR. But how do we do it? How do we integrate CSR into our mainstream operations?'

A typical response to this challenge, and one we ourselves have advocated, is to segment the relevant CSR issues as they impinge on particular business operations and suggest changes in policies and practices accordingly. This is fine, to a point, but it is this approach that is leading to increasing dissatisfaction among business leaders and managers alike, who complain of 'bolt-on' rather than 'built-in' CSR. Rather than helping to integrate CSR into core processes, this approach can lead to a proliferation of initiatives and projects that become a distraction to primary business purpose and a drag on performance. All too often, CSR has consequently been seen as adding further layers of bureaucracy. As a result, it has been hard to find traction with busy middle managers preoccupied with keeping head counts low, reaching sales targets and contributing to next-quarter earnings.

The solution to this problem lies in integrating CSR not into operations but into business strategy. Because business operations serve strategy, not the other way round, this approach will help to determine which are the appropriate CSR policies and practices for the business, and which are potentially superfluous. CSR becomes 'built-in' not 'bolt-on'.

Putting it another way, all our life experiences suggest that, by and large, 'form' should follow 'purpose'. Business operations — purchasing and supply, manufacturing, marketing, etc. — are the means by which a company achieves its business purpose. That purpose is articulated in terms of business strategies and objectives. Hence it is perhaps not surprising that, if changes are made to business operations without reference to business strategies and objectives, divergence results.

▶ Seven steps to integrating CSR into business strategy and generating corporate social opportunities

In light of these concerns, how then can a business leader or manager build CSR into business strategy and, while not ignoring potential risks, exploit associated opportunities? And what are those opportunities?

We describe a seven-step analytical process which shows how the implications of CSR on business strategy can be considered and illustrates how it can be factored into decision-making at a point when new business strategies are being explored or existing strategies updated. In this way the repercussions of CSR for business operations can be considered and the pros and cons of alternative policies and practices weighed up. Final decisions are subsequently taken on the basis that form (business operations) serves purpose (business strategies and objectives).

As the book title suggests, we believe that, given the right approach, CSR can be made to work *for* a business. If companies can advance from regarding CSR as primarily a risk minimisation process and learn how to integrate CSR into future business strategy, they will, we suggest, be able to capitalise on *corporate social opportunity* (CSO).

Here are three short descriptions of examples of CSO in practice.

> Technicians in the research laboratories of IBM worked with colleagues from their community relations department in a collaborative project with SeniorNet, an American NGO promoting access to technology for senior citizens. As a result of the partnership, IBM created new technology to transform readability of web pages, and was able to utilise the technology in other web-based products and in support for Internet service providers. In addition, IBM was consequently well placed to respond to new US regulations on media accessibility.

> The Bank of America has funded some $4 billion-worth of mortgages in recent years thanks to borrowing arranged by community activists in low-income areas in US inner cities. One community partnership — the Neighbourhood Assistance Corporation of America — has some $10 billion-worth of commitments from Bank of America and Citigroup combined. The banks reach new untapped markets that they otherwise would have difficulty reaching. Low-income families are advised by those they already know and can trust.

> In emerging markets and less-developed countries, international food company Nestlé has a policy of investing over the long term in capacity-building for local suppliers, as a way of ensuring the quantity and quality of the supplies it requires. In Brazil the company provides technical assistance and loans supporting over 300,000 farmers in the dairy industry, with no accompanying conditions obliging farmers to sell to Nestlé. Local communities have seen significant rises in standards of social and economic development in areas where Nestlé operates these policies.

We see individual corporate social opportunities (CSOs) as commercially viable activities which also advance environmental and social sustainability. These tend to be based on one or more of the following: innovations in developing new or improved products and services; serving under-served or creating new markets; or organising the business differently in a new business model: for example, in how it conceives and develops the new products and services, or how they are financed, marketed and distributed (see Figure 1). The goal is to be able to create an environment where numerous CSOs are possible. When that starts to happen, you might also then use corporate social opportunity to describe the corporate culture, the mind-set, 'the way we do business round here'.

One company is, in fact, using the terminology of CSO to describe its approach to CSR. Speaking at the launch of Procter & Gamble's 2002 *Corporate Sustainability Report*, Paul Polman, President of P&G Western Europe, said:

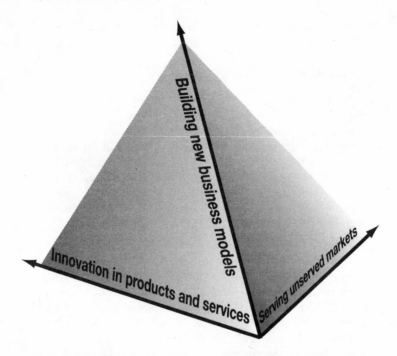

Figure 1 **The three dimensions of corporate social opportunity**

We can never lose sight of our responsibility to the outside world and our employees. But to be really sustainable in the long term, companies need to link business opportunity to sustainable development. By harnessing their creativity and innovation, companies can find new products, new services, new initiatives, develop new markets and business models that can deliver a better quality of life to all, for now and for the future. We need to move beyond Corporate Social Responsibility to embrace our Corporate Social Opportunity.[2]

▶ Characteristics of a corporate social opportunity corporation

How might we recognise a CSO corporation? How does a company get there from where it is today to become a CSO corporation? What are the critical success factors

2   Paul Polman, President of P&G Western Europe, speaking at the Euro-Environment Conference, Aalborg, 2–3 October 2002.

that will help ensure it builds on a 'have-to-do' CSR compliance-based approach to foster a 'want-to-do' CSO mentality?

In summary, the answer lies in achieving alignment of business values, purpose and strategy with the social and economic needs of customers and consumers, while embedding responsible and ethical business policies and practices throughout the company.

The individual corporate social opportunity examples listed above all reflect this concept of alignment. But achievement of this in a consistent way across a large international organisation over a sustained period of time is quite a challenge. As with most things in life, it is the journey that is as important as arriving at the ultimate destination: this book is designed to be a practical guide for the journey from CSR to CSO.

Our exploration of the nature and potential of the concept of CSO began with interviews during 2003 with a number of chairmen and CEOs. It struck us how quickly — and unprompted — many of them started talking about their own personal values and about the values of the company in order to explain the company's approach to social, ethical and environmental issues.

- Crispin Davis CEO at publisher Reed Elsevier explained how he had personally championed the articulation of the Reed Elsevier corporate values (see pages 145-46).

- David Varney at telecommunications firm mmO$_2$ referred back to the 'O$_2$' values (to be bold, open, clear and trusted) in order to explain why they had taken the approach they had to a particular business issue — that of children gaining unsupervised access to the Internet via mobile phones (see page 53).

- Hank McKinnell, chairman and CEO of Pfizer, talked about how corporate responsibility and citizenship were core elements of the pharmaceutical company's stated values and approach to doing business.

- Jeremy Pelczer, president and CEO of the largest private water company in the US, American Water (part of RWE Thames Water), stated his belief that adherence to their professed corporate values should be the critical test when making business decisions.

Informed by these perspectives, the issue of corporate values tops our list of defining characteristics for a CSO company (see Box 1).

▶ How to achieve corporate social opportunity?

It is important to note that in suggesting that companies aim for CSO we are not for a moment proposing that a sound understanding and compliance with CSR requirements are not still crucial. On the contrary, CSR is the foundation for learning and

Key characteristics of a corporate social opportunity company

1 The organisation aligns and articulates explicitly its purpose, vision and values consistent with responsible business practice. It is believed that a sense of shared ownership and commitment will be easier when purpose, vision and values are co-created by people throughout the organisation rather than being imposed from the top leadership.

2 The leadership and senior management team fully believes in and lives those values and purpose—and demonstrably so.

3 Purpose, vision and values are intensely and continuously communicated throughout the organisation and beyond.

4 Purpose, vision and values are constantly reinforced through culture, processes and rewards. This includes their incorporation into:
   - Recruitment and induction
   - Management and staff training
   - Performance objectives
   - Appraisal, reward and recognition structures
   - Promotion considerations
   - Procurement criteria and processes
   - Due diligence procedures for assessing business partners

5 In addition, there are effective mechanisms for whistle-blowing on any 'values gaps'—that is, gaps between values espoused and values lived.

6 There are effective tools and processes for scoping and then prioritising risks and opportunities associated with corporate social responsibility and a framework for deciding how to reach decisions and to check for consistency with corporate values.

7 There are decision-making processes at the top of the organisation (in the board, board sub-committee and so on) for oversight and effective decision-making throughout the organisation and there is a means of capturing and codifying knowledge to ensure continuous improvement.

8 There are effective stakeholder engagement processes to seek proactively any corporate social opportunities and to build trust, openness and empathy, which encourage such opportunities to emerge.

9 There is an ethical code governing relations with stakeholder partners to determine the fair share of risks and rewards (e.g. in relation to intellectual property rights) in exploiting corporate social opportunities and opportunities for entrepreneurialism and creativity — a set of opportunities that is widened by the spirit of openness and by the culture of enlightened curiosity.

10 There is appropriate measurement and reporting of the company's performance as well as processes for rectifying gaps and learning from the emergence of gaps.

Box 1 **Key characteristics of a company or organisation taking corporate social opportunities**

attaining the necessary competences through which CSO can be achieved. Most business leaders with whom we work accept and understand that minimum standards of environmental and social performance are necessary to reduce risks. Indeed, most believe these standards are also simply the 'right thing to do'. They are happy to fulfil their duty in ensuring that sound CSR policies and practices are in place. Much of the practical guidance we give in this book is about how to better integrate CSR into the business en route to CSO.

It will be of no surprise to the reader that we would strongly support a contention that a company should commit to CSR at the highest corporate level. But we understand that for most companies this commitment is the result of cumulative experiences over time of actions taken at the level of individual business units. We are confident that, when the consequences of CSR-informed and CSO-inspired business strategies are considered, the conclusion will be reached that they are unlikely to succeed without commitment within the organisation from the top. On the other hand, if the start-point *is* top-level commitment, then managers through the business are going to need to know how to translate it into decision-making at many levels of the firm — which again is where the seven-step process is useful.

The CSO approach we advocate is based on more than 40 years' experience between us, working with companies from many sectors and in many parts of the world. This is not always a story of black and white, of what is social, ethically or environmentally acceptable, what is right or what is wrong. Often it embraces apparently conflicting demands that require the application of judgement, guided by a clear sense of overall direction and corporate purpose. This book is designed to act as a compass for aiding navigation through such dilemmas and complex decisions.

In addition to providing diagnostic tools, we also aim to show where business leaders and managers can go for CSO inspiration and ideas: for example, to non-traditional sources of business know-how such as not-for-profit organisations, or to entrepreneurs who run small and medium-sized businesses and who can be an ongoing source of innovation for many larger corporations.

▶ Our world — everybody's world

This book is written first and foremost with the purpose of helping to improve business performance, because business is, after all, the principal motor for growth and development in the world today. We believe that a situation where companies adhere to best practice in CSR and take advantage of possibilities inherent in corporate social opportunity is good for shareholders, customers, employees and communities.

We do not shy away from focusing on business benefits, both short-term and long-term. We do not give equal space to identifying community needs or environmental challenges, not because we are unaware, unconcerned or insensitive to these issues, but because this is a book focused on business development, not community development. We happen to believe that getting many more sustainably successful businesses is the best route to optimising the contribution that business can make to sustainable development and to some of the world's seemingly intractable social, economic and environmental challenges of poverty, inequality and disease. We would argue that the creative flair and can-do entrepreneurialism of business can best be harnessed for positive social and environmental impact by demonstrating the case for engagement rather than dragging a reluctant business kicking and screaming to the table with more regulations and mandatory CSR reporting.

The people we meet, by and large, want to do the right thing — to do what is fair and equitable: fair to their customers, fair to their co-workers and to their investors, as well as to the communities in which they operate. Increasing numbers are also becoming increasingly aware of the need for sustainable development. A sustainable business is a business that people value: its employees value it as a great place to work; its customers and suppliers value it as a great business to do business with; the community values it as a great neighbour (and, like good neighbours anywhere, they look out for you as you look out for them); and, as a result, investors and financiers value it as a business into which it is worth putting their money.

This book is for business people who take such a view. We are not attempting to address the issue of the minority of businesses and business people who don't care. Our very conscious purpose is to inspire a more 'can-do' approach — and share further and faster what seems to be working.

This is a fast-moving subject — so we very much welcome feedback, new insights and further examples from readers around the world.

David Grayson and Adrian Hodges
London, June 2004

dgrayson@bitc.org.uk
adrian.hodges@iblf.org

Part I
From corporate social responsibility to corporate social opportunity in seven steps

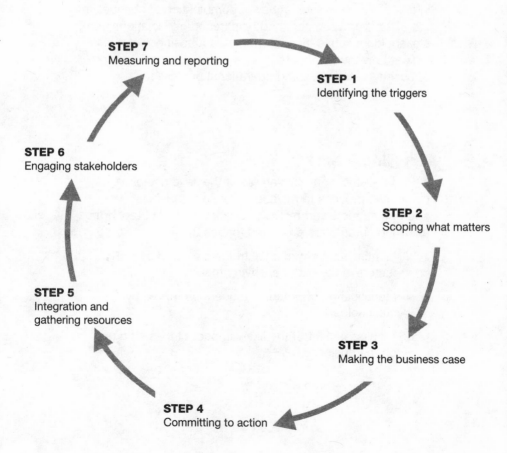

STEP 7
Measuring and reporting

STEP 1
Identifying the triggers

STEP 6
Engaging stakeholders

STEP 2
Scoping what matters

STEP 5
Integration and gathering resources

STEP 3
Making the business case

STEP 4
Committing to action

Step 1
Identifying the triggers

Focus

In this chapter, we look at how a combination of changes in the external environment and heightened expectations from stakeholders cause triggers that impact business. We also look at how these triggers can pave the way for a revision of business strategies and operational practices.

Applying Step 1

In Part II — the worked example of the seven steps — the completed process forms show how, by applying appropriate tools and techniques selected from Step 1, the following outputs are produced (pages 272ff.)

- Identification of potential triggers caused by CSR factors in the external environment

- Identification of potential triggers prompted by stakeholders

- An assessment of the likely impact of these triggers on the business

NIKE NOW HAS STRINGENT REQUIREMENTS ABOUT PAY AND working conditions in its suppliers' third-world factories. It has invested heavily in verification systems to ensure that these conditions are being met. This came about because of highly publicised NGO (non-governmental organisation) and media campaigns about the poor conditions in suppliers' factories. Shell is now committed to sustainable development and to triple-bottom-line reporting against environmental and social as well as business performance. These are now integral to Shell's business principles and strategy. Shell's commitments were the result of an intense, worldwide examination, led by top management, of the changing expectations that stakeholders had of a global business such as Shell. This examination was prompted by the Greenpeace-led campaign against the company's plans to dispose of the Brent Spar platform in the North Sea which generated media and political pressure, as well as criticism of a perceived low-level response to the execution of Nigerian activist Ken Sara-Wiwa; and — probably most significantly — to Shell employees consequently expressing concerns about the company's values and behaviour. The world-famous De Beers diamond house supported an industry-wide 'mine to finger' certification system — now known as the Kimberley Process — to answer a media and NGO campaign against 'blood diamonds', which alleged that income from diamond mining was being siphoned off to finance bloody civil wars in Africa: allegations which, if allowed to fester, might have threatened consumer demand for diamonds (see Step 2, page 99).

▶ Understanding triggers

All of these high-profile and significant changes of corporate strategy were *triggered* by political, economic, social, technological and environmental changes — what we call 'global forces for change'; and by the resulting heightened expectations of stakeholders about corporate behaviour. For every high-profile example, there are many more unpublicised changes in the strategies of individual businesses — such as the discovery by a small website design business of a new market niche in designing websites that would be accessible to blind and partially sighted users, which was *triggered* by one customer specifying that his new website had to be more widely accessible.

A trigger can act as a much-needed catalyst for stimulating internal discussion and debate about threats and opportunities in the market. More than that, a trigger can be the device whereby the win–win seven-step model kick-starts a company's journey from corporate social responsibility to corporate social opportunity.

Through the examples and evidence presented in this chapter we hope to:

● Encourage companies to take a wide-angle view of the forces at work in the external environment and concurrent changing stakeholder expectations

● Help business leaders to identify the resulting CSR-related factors in their industry and company

- Ask companies to consider the potential triggers in their company and industry and to estimate the impact these triggers may have on current and future business strategies

Before we look in more detail at the causes of triggers, the stakeholders involved and the impact of triggers, it is first useful to look at the various forms that triggers can take.

▶ Types of triggers

A trigger can take many forms. A trigger may be a threatened or actual consumer boycott, as in the Nike case. It could be an NGO or media campaign as with Greenpeace's campaign against Shell over Brent Spar; or De Beers and 'blood diamonds'. It might be pressure from a government such as a recent UK government request to the tobacco giant BAT to withdraw from operations in Burma (Myanmar) because of that country's abusive human rights record — a request that contributed to BAT's decision to eventually disinvest. A trigger may be prompted by the loss of key staff or customers — or, more positively, the result of proposals put forward by staff. Equally, a trigger may be a root-and-branch review instigated by a new CEO. It may be information gleaned from the process of due diligence during a merger or acquisition. For a new enterprise, it may be a very basic question about 'what's the way that we want to do business?' What are the values that the founders want to inculcate from the outset? Pohjoisranta is a small Finnish PR company we met at a Danish business conference. Pohjoisranta's founders were committed from the outset to an open-books policy; to a strong learning ethos for all staff; and to putting something back into the community through *pro bono* assignments. Other triggers might be a pollution or a health and safety incident; queries from investors; lawsuits from disgruntled employees over allegations of discrimination; a badly handled product recall; or the stimulus of another company's problems with poor environmental or social performance.

In the hurly burly of everyday business life, it is not surprising that these triggers are usually regarded as bad news. They expose problems, often require intensive and extensive management time to respond to and often cost money to rectify. But the price of ignoring triggers can be much higher. All of the examples given below can lead to one or more of the following: fines, boycotts, critical media coverage, disaffected staff and wary potential recruits, difficult questions from institutional investors, damaged reputation amongst consumers, loss of clients, more expensive insurance and capital, and damaged share price.

We suggest that rather than seeing triggers as risks to be managed in a climate of fear, they should be seen as timely early warning signs of potential systemic problems or issues that are or will be material to the performance of the business, which require thoughtful analysis rather than a knee-jerk reaction. As David Varney, chairman of mmO$_2$, told us, 'one of the skills of leadership is how quickly you can pick up on the weak signals'. In this chapter, we hope to help the reader to learn how to do just that.

We can see that a complex array of forces causes triggers to happen. Developments in communications and technology, the ongoing globalisation of markets, shifts in demographics and shifts in values held by different publics — our 'global forces for change' — act both independently and interdependently to influence the business operating environment. One of many outcomes for business from these forces is a set of social, ethical and environmental factors that have repercussions for business — we call them 'CSR factors'.

These CSR factors may take many forms, such as an increase in the prominence of particular issues: how a business handles pollution and waste or how it treats its staff; whether diversity is not just accepted but expected; how a company interacts with the local community where it has a significant presence. Previously, some of these issues were referred to dismissively as 'soft management issues', but are rapidly becoming today's 'hard management issues' — hard to predict, hard to control and hard for the business to deal with when they go wrong.

CSR factors may also take the form of particular businesses processes that previously were regarded as marginal to effective management but that now have gained recognition as being fundamental to business performance. Here, we are referring to processes that ensure sound ethical business practice and good corporate governance systems and that embrace accountability and transparency.

The recent string of corporate scandals in the USA and Europe, where companies such as Enron WorldCom, Parmalat and Ahold have become associated with a culture of executive greed and poor management oversight, has caused a growing deficit of trust and have spurred a general climate of increased scrutiny, tighter rules and legislation. Whether emerging management issues or business processes, these CSR factors impact companies through events or incidents — what we call triggers.

In addition, a concurrent set of forces in the form of changing stakeholder expectations also lead to trigger events or incidents, ranging from boycott campaigns to investors voting on CSR-related issues at corporate annual general meetings. The interaction between a company and its stakeholders is now so critical to a business being able to fulfil its purpose and to achieve its corporate goals that the consideration of triggers specifically from the perspective of stakeholder expectations is a crucial additional filter for businesses.

In summary, triggers are a combination of events and incidents that impact business as a result of global forces for change and changing stakeholder expectations. Decisions taken in response to triggers can be tactical and short-term sticking plasters, or they can lay the foundations for a forward-thinking systemic change in operational behaviour or corporate strategy.

A positive approach in assessing the impact of triggers is necessary if a company wishes to turn the burden and obligation of managing corporate responsibilities into the benefits that typify the management of corporate social opportunities. What we are describing in this chapter, therefore, is what *could*, if used creatively, be triggers for systemic transformation — causing what we call a 'Brent Spar moment', the moment when a company reacts positively to a trigger.

▶ The 'Brent Spar moment'

The 'Brent Spar moment' will vary from company to company and from sector to sector and may arrive at a different point for different people even in the same company. Take, for instance, the case of Shell International, from which we take our phrase the 'Brent Spar moment'. In Shell, this moment may have occurred for some when they first saw pictures live on television of the Greenpeace protesters on the Brent Spar platform. For others, it may have occurred when the then German Chancellor, Helmut Kohl, entered the debate, criticising Shell and spurring a consumer boycott of Shell's service stations; or when children of Shell employees in Germany were criticised at school because their parents worked for the company. For a few, the moment may have arrived only some 18 months later when they read the results of a global multi-stakeholder dialogue on the role of business which demonstrated heightened societal expectations of business behaviour.[1]

What is unarguable is that at any given moment, somewhere on our planet, some shareholders will be asking critical questions of a company; some NGOs will be calling for a boycott of a company's products or services; some consumers will be rewarding or punishing corporate behaviour of which they particularly approve or disapprove; some talented young graduates will be choosing which company to work for on the basis that they can identify more with the values of one business over another. Indeed, *all* of those things may be happening to *each* of the world's largest companies somewhere every day.

Why do businesses respond to some of these triggers and not to others? Sometimes there is no choice: the investor, the customer, the newspaper or the politician raising the concerns may be just too powerful to ignore; the sheer volume of concerned voices cumulatively cannot be silenced; or the issue may be so high-profile and the potential fallout so great that there is no option but to respond. But those are the 'no brainers'.

More often it is serendipity: the trigger is the result of a number of seemingly unconnected inputs. A manager reads some consumer reports, does a field-visit with one of the sales force, spots a couple of magazine articles in the trade press and then — all of a sudden — a pattern emerges, when he or she has a chance conversation with a stranger in the next seat on an aeroplane.

In his book, *The Tipping Point* — about how ideas and fashions take off — Malcolm Gladwell draws analogies with how viruses and diseases spread.[2] A key conclusion from the book is that ideas and fashions spread thanks to the existence of people whom Gladwell calls connectors, mavens and salespeople. Connectors naturally put people together all the time — it is second nature to them; *maven* is a Yiddish word for collectors and assemblers of information — people who able to make sense of it; and 'salespeople' are able to communicate that sense to others. Essentially, in this

---

1 For an insider's account, see the then Chairman of Shell's Committee of Managing Directors, Cor Herkströter's speech, 'Dealing with Contradictory Expectations: The Dilemmas Facing Multinationals' (The Hague, 11 October 1996).

2 Malcolm Gladwell, *The Tipping Point: How Little Things Can Make a Big Difference, How Ideas and Fashions Spread* (Boston, MA: Little, Brown, 2000).

book we are inviting you to be 'connectors', 'mavens' and 'salespeople', to view triggers more systematically.

Jeremy Pelczer, President and CEO of American Water, describes his personal trigger as follows: [3]

> The trigger for me in understanding the need for a planned approach to CSR came from a combination of events and information. I went on a visit to Jakarta where our local managers took me to see some poor communities desperate for a supply of clean water. I attended a meeting organised by IBLF [International Business Leaders Forum] and UNDP [United Nations Development Programme] where I noticed that there was common ground between business and NGOs; it wasn't adversarial: there was a desire for partnership and collaboration. And I came to the conclusion that as one of the largest water companies in the world, we needed to think through the role we were going to play in addressing the fundamental issue of access to water. That's when we initiated a search for a professional CSR manager.

▶ Triggers and their causes: global forces for change

In this section we focus on the causes of triggers. First, we look at triggers in the context of the external environment and global forces for change.

There may be a tendency for managers wishing to take the path towards CSO to 'cut corners' at this stage, but the broad and expansive approach described in the following section creates the chance to spot links and synergies previously regarded as unconnected. To make these connections, we look at changes in the external operating environment through a fairly wide-angle lens in order to take in a broad range of those CSR factors that may have material consequences and implications for business.

> Everything about our world is changing: its economy, its technology, its culture, its way of living. If the twentieth century scripted our conventional way of thinking, the twenty-first century is unconventional in almost every respect.
>
> *Prime Minister Tony Blair, 2004*[4]

---

3 Jeremy Pelczer, now President and CEO of American Water, part of the RWE Group, in an interview with the authors, October 2003. At the time of interview he was COO of the sister international water company, RWE Thames Water.

4 Website of 10 Downing Street (www.number-10.gov.uk), Prime Minister's speech on Global Security, 5 March 2004.

Business does not operate in a vacuum. Business opportunities have always been the result of a complex interaction of advances in technology and science, of political, economic and social developments and of innovation, inspiration and risk-taking. In this section, to make this dynamic, multi-dimensional interplay 'digestible', we organise these forces for change into four categories:

- The revolution of technology and communications

- The revolution of markets

- The revolution of demographics and development

- The revolution of values

There are many aspects of each of these forces which impact and are impacted by business in different ways. Below (pages 24-34), we give a sample of the types of impacts and, in Boxes 2–13, show how they create CSR factors which in turn lead to triggers. We use the example of a hypothetical food and beverage company, in keeping with the sector of the hypothetical company described in Part II.

For the reader interested in seeing further data and examples of how global forces for change are impacting business and producing CSR factors and their associated triggers, we direct the reader to our book *Everybody's Business*, particularly to Section 1 of that book.[5]

The revolution of technology and communications

> All of the communications that we saw in the entirety of 2000 will be delivered in no more than a few seconds in 2025. Annually, we now generate as much knowledge about science as has been created throughout human history to around 1950. The entire output of the world in 1900 is matched by two weeks' production in 2000 and, on trend, will be surpassed by the product of a single working week in 2015 and that of a few days in 2025.
>
> *Dr Oliver Sparrow, 2003*[6]

A revolution of communications and technology permits automation, customisation, subcontracting, global supply chains, homeworking, manufacturing and extraction in remote areas and back offices across the world. Companies can move operations to lower-wage economies — often countries with less advanced environmental, health and safety and labour standards and regulation. More businesses will find themselves involved in remote locations impacting sensitive environments and/or indigenous people. But the communications revolution also means easier global access to information about companies and no hiding places. It is harder to keep secrets nowadays than it was in the Cold War era. Via the Internet and other

5   D. Grayson and A. Hodges, *Everybody's Business* (London: Dorling Kindersley, 2001).
6   O. Sparrow, 'Challenge! Forum Scenarios to 2025', www.chforum.org.uk (2003).

new media, vigilante consumers, concerned citizens and activist NGOs can mobilise powerful campaigns against corporate behaviour of which they disapprove. Activist NGOs can now spread information and co-ordinate global campaigns against business behaviour — fast, using the Internet.[7] There were 600 million Internet users worldwide in 2002 (up from less than 60 million in 1996) — and this figure is predicted to rise to 965 million by 2005.[8] The futurist Don Tapscott shows some of the websites where a company such as Wal-Mart might feature (see Figure 2).

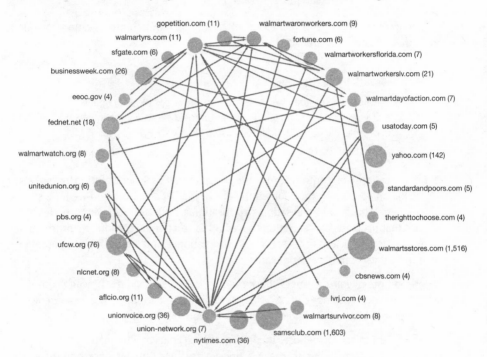

Figure 2 **Wal-Mart's web of commentary**

Source: from a presentation by Don Tapscott at The Conference Board, February 2003: 'CGI (formerly Digital 4Sight)'. The image was generated using Govcom.org's *Issue Crawler* software

As the distinguished *New York Times* writer Thomas Friedman observes:

> What's even more dangerous is that the Internet, because it has the aura of technology around it, also has a totally undeserved aura of instant credibility. People now say, 'It must be true — I read it on the Internet'. The fact that it was conveyed in this high-tech manner somehow adds authority to what is conveyed, when in fact the

7   Howard Rheingold argues that technology is empowering new 'self-organising' networks of citizens; see H. Rheingold, *Smart Mobs: The Next Social Revolution* (New York: Perseus Books, 2002).
8   These figures are provided by Pyramid Research, quoted in *The Economist Yearbook 2004*, p. 107.

Internet is a global conveyor of unfiltered, unedited, untreated information. It is not only the greatest tool we have for making people smarter quicker. It's also the greatest tool we have for making people dumber faster. Rumours published on the Internet now have a way of immediately becoming facts. This is particularly true among less well-educated people who might not themselves have access to the Internet but hear a piece of news or gossip from one of the elites around them who [does] have access.[9]

The implications of the revolution of technology and communication for our hypothetical company are listed in Box 2.

The revolution of markets

We have to see that we have a life in other people's imagination, quite beyond our control. Globalisation means that we are involved in dramas we never thought of, cast in roles we never chose.

Rowan Williams, 2002[10]

Since the collapse of Communism at the end of the 1980s, in a revolution in markets three billion consumers have joined the global market economy and we have seen a relentless process of liberalisation, privatisation and globalisation. In turn, this has meant that privatised organisations have had to create new corporate cultures and employee loyalty. More firms are 'going international' and are having to operate in culturally diverse markets. For example:

● In Cote d'Ivoire, farmers check cocoa prices directly on the Chicago commodities exchange through village cell phones, no longer being dependent on the biased price indications of local traders.

● In Ethiopia, a farmer uses the Internet to sell goats to Ethiopian taxi drivers in New York eager to make a present to their families back home for traditional celebrations.

Welcome to the new world economy!

Contrary to the views of anti-globalisation campaigners, such as Naomi Klein in her book *No Logo*,[11] the dramatic growth in the reach and value of brands makes them more vulnerable to media attacks and consumer boycotts. In part, this is because business is a larger part of society and a greater proportion of the economy in liberalised and privatised economies. In turn, this means that business is more in the public eye. It also results in more businesses wanting to raise funds on international financial markets where funders will assess risks to the value of their

---

9 Thomas L. Friedman, *Longitudes and Attitudes: Exploring the World after September 11* (New York: Farrar, Straus & Giroux, 2003).

10 Rowan Williams, Archbishop of Canterbury, reflecting on being in New York on 9/11, in *Writing in the Dust: Reflections on 11th September and its Aftermath* (London: Hodder & Stoughton, 2002).

11 N. Klein, *No Logo, No Space, No Choice, No Jobs* (London: Flamingo, 2000).

Technology and communication: potential triggers

External forces

- Increased quantity and quality of Internet connectivity
- Availability of more powerful and cheaper computer power, including to consumers
- Growth in 'e-commerce'
- Increased outsourcing of functions
- Developments in agriculture, food technology and genetics (e.g. in terms of added nutrition or use of genetically modified organisms [GMOs])
- Improvements in production and mass manufacturing processes and packaging (e.g. the availability of technology to allow the production of small batches)
- Improvements in transportation (e.g. leading to fewer damaged goods and giving better refrigeration)
- Consolidation of media ownership, with the fragmentation of alternative media outlets with poor editorial oversight

CSR factors

- The '24/7' world (active 24 hours a day, 7 days a week) intensifies the culture of overwork, increases pressure on staff and contributes to a loss of traditional, day-to-day family occasions, such as meal times together
- Retailers' stock control systems are more accurate and are able to predict order requirements and to anticipate the need for just-in-time (JIT) deliveries, leading to impacts on delivery schedules, on traffic congestion and on pollution and emissions
- Internet ordering and direct sales have an impact on the volume of local deliveries
- 'Online brands' (those sold via the Internet) are vulnerable to attack
- The use of outsourcing firms and subcontractors means that authorities have less direct control over hygiene and the possible exploitation of workers
- A greater use of outsourcing may create concerns over job losses for existing in-house employees

Potential triggers

- There may be increased employee absenteeism because of stress
- Companies may not be able to market products to the whole family at what used to be traditional family meal times, increasing advertising spend
- Business logistics may be blamed for traffic congestion or accidents, causing bad press
- Legal action or industrial action may be taken by workers at outsource or supplier firms, producing bad press
- Product withdrawals or recalls may be necessary because of contamination during production
- Employees in domestic production plants may take industrial action over possible future loss of jobs to locations abroad
- Lawsuits may be filed on behalf of workers in the developing world, alleging company liability for the use of dangerous chemicals and pesticides by those workers
- There may be an increase in the level of customer enquiries regarding genetically modified products

Box 2 **The revolution of technology and communication: forces, factors and triggers impacting a hypothetical company in the food and beverage sector** (continued over)

Technology and communication: potential triggers
(continued)

CSR factors (cont.)

- Intensive farming techniques put pressure on water resources, and use of pesticides can endanger workers who do not wear the necessary protective clothing or who are not made aware of and encouraged to follow safety procedures

- Customers may be unwilling to accept food produced with use of new technology, such as products containing or derived from GMOs

- Producers are able to produce larger portions of food at marginal extra cost

- Mass-produced goods receive 'mixed reviews' from consumers

- There is the possibility for less waste of material in packages and for more sophisticated recycling of materials

- The ability to source produce and materials from further afield and to maintain production 365 days a year stretches companies' ability to manage their supply chains

- Companies face risk to their reputation because there is 'no place to hide' as news and views (sometimes unsubstan-tiated) travels fast

Potential triggers (cont.)

- Activists may target companies that market large portions of food and drink to children, or that market to children food and drink that is regarded as unhealthy (e.g. foods high in sugar, salt and fat, and drinks high in sugar), claiming irresponsible marketing

- Recycling of waste produces positive press for the company

Box 2 (continued)

investment or loan on a range of factors, which increasingly include environmental and social issues.

J.F. Rischard characterises four features of the new world economy:[12]

- It is bent on speed (Bill Gates calls it 'velocity'), so you have to be agile.

- It flows across national boundaries, so you must be 'plugged in' and good at networking internationally.

- It is highly knowledge intensive, so you must be good at constantly learning. If you stand still, you fall back.

- It is hyper-competitive, so you must be 100% reliable or business will shift to someone else.

The implications of the revolution in markets for our hypothetical company in the food and soft drinks industry are listed in Box 3.

The revolution of demographics and development

> The developed world's interest in global poverty is 'near a low point', according to James Wolfensohn, president of the World Bank.[13]

The revolutions in communications and technology and in the markets have been happening alongside a revolution in demographics and development. Europeans are living longer and having fewer children: without immigration, the population of the now 25 member-states of the European Union will drop from about 450 million now to fewer than 400 million in 2050.[14] Also, ageing populations in the West mean changes in company personnel practices and assumptions about what staff can achieve at different ages, physically and mentally. In addition, after the terrorist attacks on the USA on 11 September 2001 (9/11) and the US-led war on Iraq, the increasing Muslim population in many industrialised countries heightens the need to manage cultural diversity — and the population of the 49 least developed countries is expected to grow from today's 668 million people to 1.7 billion by 2050.[15] According to *The Economist*, AIDS (acquired immunodeficiency syndrome) has become 'arguably the biggest threat to life and prosperity in the developing world':[16] 40 million people are now infected with HIV (human immunodeficiency virus) worldwide, 2.5 million of whom are children.[17] In a global, connected society pandemics will threaten business stability and capacity to operate if businesses are

12   J.F. Rischard, *High Noon: 20 Global Problems; 20 Years to Solve Them* (New York: Basic Books, 2002).

13   Richard McGregor in *Financial Times* (www.FT.com), 25 May 2004, quoting Wolfensohn speaking ahead of the opening of a conference in Shanghai to look at new approaches to the problem.

14   These figures were quoted by UN Secretary-General, Kofi Annan, *Financial Times*, 29 January 2004.

15   Syed Mohamed Ali, *Daily Times*, Pakistan, 4 June 2004.

16   *The Economist*, 'AIDS: A Mixed Prognosis', 29 November 2003.

17   Figures are reported in the 2003 annual report of UNAIDS, 'AIDS Epidemic Update 2003', www.unaids.org/Unaids/EN/Resources/publications.asp.

Markets: potential triggers

External forces

- Increasing numbers of overseas suppliers vying for business, including from greater numbers of emerging markets with lower cost bases

- Increase in opportunities in overseas markets, either directly or via joint ventures

- Need for an adequate supply base for overseas manufacturing and processing

- Increase in competition in the home market as a result of low-cost-base competitors

- An increasingly higher brand visibility overseas

- Increasing opportunities for business-to-business (B2B) markets as a result of privatisation of services (such as in the provision of school and hospital meals)

CSR factors

- A lower cost base may also mean poor workplace conditions and may prove difficult to monitor

- Operating in new markets requires sensitivities to local cultural and social norms, behaviour and consumer tastes

- Joint ventures share costs and risks but weaken direct control over how products are distributed and the conditions in which they are sold

- Capacity-building (such as raising standards and the transfer of technology) in the local supply base carries costs

- There is increased vulnerability to pressure for 'facilitation payments and bribes' at customs and so on

- Increased brand visibility could lead to association with anti-Western or anti-globalisation causes and thus to security risks

- The privatised provision of meals in institutions may lead to the introduction of canteen-like services, with wide 'popular' menu choice

Potential triggers

- The company may be the subject of exposés of poor labour conditions or poor hygiene in supplier factories in less-developed countries

- A lack of appreciation of local cultural sensitivities could lead to inappropriate advertising, causing offence

- 'Sharp' (illegal) local selling practices may give a brand a bad name

- The pressure to make 'facilitation' payments may lead to employees being accused of paying bribes against OECD guidelines

- There may be a threat of or an actual attack on the workforce or on physical assets

- Parents at schools may complain about the menu on offer in a canteen-style service

Box 3 **The revolution of markets: forces, factors and triggers impacting a hypothetical company in the food and beverage sector**

in danger of losing core staff. Likewise, visible, global inequalities — more visible still because of 24 hour satellite TV and the Internet — threatens business stability and operations.

The implications of the revolution of demographics and development for our hypothetical company are listed in Box 4.

The revolution of values

> Campaigns against corporations have led them to take greater care that their goods are not produced under unacceptable working conditions for starvation wages. All of us, by the decisions we make about how we live and work and travel and consume help to shape an environment. To think and act morally, to do what is right because it is right, influences others; it begins to create a climate of opinion; good, like evil, is infectious. We do not have to accept the unacceptable. The only thing that makes social or economic trends inevitable is the belief that they are. The unfolding drama of the Twenty-First Century is one of which we are the co-writers of the script.
>
> *Chief Rabbi Jonathan Sacks*[18]

Last, but not least, we are in the midst of a revolution in values (for the implications of this revolution on our hypothetical company, see Box 5). Significant increases in wealth, choice and education mean that for the first time in history large numbers of people across the globe are free to express their own values and often do so in unstructured, unpredictable and spontaneous ways. This flowering of diversity undercuts authoritarianism and conformity — we see a decline of deference. In such a world, trust has to be earned and constantly re-earned. A range of studies have confirmed a growing reluctance to defer to so-called experts whether on childhood vaccinations or food safety.

This has particular consequences for businesses, especially after the well-publicised corporate scandals of the past couple of years, and brings with it broader concerns over the remuneration of top executives, particularly in cases where remuneration is seen as 'reward for failure'. The meeting of the World Economic Forum (WEF) in Davos, Switzerland, held in January 2004, explored this loss of trust. Research produced for this gathering by the international PR firm Edelman found that US multinationals were trusted far less by the public in Europe than by the US public. Attitudes were most negative in Britain, where only 28% said they trusted US companies. Edelman concluded that foreign affiliates of companies from countries with a poor image abroad were likely to face problems when hiring local staff and dealing with governments on issues such as regulation. Also, although the survey found that public trust in governments and companies had recently begun to

---

18   J. Sacks, *The Dignity of Difference: How to Avoid the Clash of Civilizations* (London: Continuum), page 86.

Demographics and development: potential triggers

External forces

- Ageing population in industrialised world
- Food consumption patterns and associated issues (i.e. there are differences within the developed markets and between the developed markets and the developing world regarding the incidence of obesity, diabetes and malnutrition)
- Trends in adherence to faiths, with different dietary requirements
- Geopolitical issues and their impact on disparate sourcing, as well as on transportation routes and costs
- Pressure on scarce water resources for use in agriculture
- Access to adequate physical infrastructure and pool of educated employees for overseas operations
- Use of migrant labour in agriculture
- Quality of the regulatory regime (e.g. regarding environment, health and safety, and food safety) overseas

CSR factors

- There is a trend toward greater use of shopping via the Internet and home delivery
- There is an increase in the number of people in care, with a corresponding increased role for care providers and care institutions with regard to shopping and choice of foods consumed
- There is a need for packaging that is easy to open and reseal
- Food companies are held responsible for the endemic of obesity in Western markets and, increasingly, in emerging markets; they are also being criticised for high levels of salt and sugar in products, for increased portion sizes and for marketing such products to children
- New product developments allow the addition of vitamins and extra nutritional quality
- The cost of water is increasing
- There are costs to providing roads and other infrastructure directly and for establishing remedial training
- The legal status of migrant workers and the quality of workplace conditions have to be considered in overseas operations
- There may be a risk of a poor-quality product or health and safety dangers as a result of poor regulatory oversight

Potential triggers

- Complaints may be raised about traffic and pollution
- Institutional purchasers can join together to negotiate discounts
- Consumer groups may criticise the company for the poor accessibility of packaging
- Research reports by consumer groups may be reported in the media, blaming food companies for obese children
- Health services say the cost of treating obesity is high, and make links to the food sector
- Funding agency may offer to support the development of foods that have added nutrition
- Business may find itself in the middle of local 'water wars' regarding the use of this scare resource
- Use of illegal migrant workers may be exposed and poor company employment practices revealed
- An outbreak of food poisoning may be traced to a company product

Box 4 **The revolution of demographics and development: forces, factors and triggers impacting a hypothetical company in the food and beverage sector**

Values: potential triggers

External forces

- Loss of trust in both private-sector and public-sector authorities over issues such as BSE (bovine spongiform encephalopathy) and foot and mouth
- The rising importance of NGOs and civil society worldwide
- Rising concerns over healthy eating and diets
- Pressure on business to actively contribute to alleviating poverty and hunger
- Rise in standards and codes of conduct in business behaviour
- Anti-Western and anti-globalisation sentiment
- Planning-gain requirements

CSR factors

- Informing consumers and others of facts and opinions is difficult for food companies as there is an inherent lack of trust
- The requirement to know and monitor views of relevant NGOs is greater
- There is a need to consider whether product formulations and marketing messages are contributing to unhealthy eating
- There is a need to be responsive to calls for product donations and to implement social investment programmes
- Signing up to appropriate codes of conduct may require changes in policies and practices and capacity-building of staff
- Added security measures may be necessary for overseas staff and plant
- There may be a need to accept that the ability to expand plant may require additional investment in local social or recreational facilities

Potential triggers

- The benefits of new products require high marketing costs in order for the product to penetrate the market
- Business may be caught off guard by a critical campaign launched by an NGO
- A consumer group may identify a company product as being high in salt and having poor labelling
- The plant manager may refuse to make a donation to a good cause, which leads to bad press
- Adherence to external code of conduct in overseas plant may be shown by an NGO investigation to be poor
- Campaigners may target the company as a symbol of Western capitalism

Box 5 **The revolution of values: forces, factors and triggers impacting a hypothetical company in the food and beverage sector**

recover in the USA and Europe after a steep decline, still only about 20% of those questioned expressed confidence in the credibility of corporate CEOs.[19]

In the United Kingdom, a MORI poll commissioned by the *Financial Times* revealed a deep distrust of business leaders, with 80% of UK adults saying that top company directors cannot be trusted to tell the truth. On 30 June 2003 MORI chairman Robert Worcester was quoted as saying that 'these findings strike at the heart of corporate Britain, and are a measure of the scepticism, even cynicism, of the public toward business leaders'. In *The Observer*, on 6 July 2003, Mike Emmott, head of employee relations at the Chartered Institute of Personnel and Development, argued that there is a deep irony in the fact that while companies make ever-more high-flown claims of environmental and corporate responsibility, at a much more basic level their employees and customers do not trust them.

Two major surveys provide evidence of the state of and decline in trust. According to Environics International (now Globescan)'s 2002 survey of 47,000 adults across 47 countries (titled 'Voice of the People'):[20]

- 48% of the global public have little or no trust in large companies, with only 39% with some trust of global companies. The only group less trusted globally than business is politicians. The most trusted are the armed forces and NGOs.

- The public are most trusting of business in Indonesia, Nigeria, India and Sweden and least trusting in Argentina, Spain, South Korea and Britain.

In the 2003 MORI Trust Monitor, carried out on behalf of the BMA (British Medical Association), it was found that:

- 60% of British adults do not trust business leaders to tell the truth.

- Only 25% trusted that the profits of large companies help to make things better for everyone who uses their products and services, compared with 52% in 1983.

- About 50% of those that had heard about the case of Enron or WorldCom in 2002 said that it had had a negative impact on their trust in large companies, with 24% that had heard of the case saying that they trust companies much less as a result, and a further 24% saying that they trust companies a little less as a result, showing that recent corporate scandals have undermined trust in business even further.

Business is clearly facing a trust crisis.

---

19 Details of this report, 'The Fifth Annual Edelman Trust Barometer', may be found in *Financial Times*, 12 January 2004, and in an Edelman press release, 'Trust in Business on the Rise in Europe, According to Edelman', www.edelman.be/published_news/Trust_in_Business_on_the_Rise_in_Europe.pdf.

20 Quoted in the Business in the Community (BITC) Research Review, Number 1 (March 2004); see www.bitc.org.uk.

Synthesis

A few weeks ago, one of us was sitting in a video-conference suite just off Trafalgar Square in central London. We were lecturing live to an audience of several hundred managers in a hotel in Rio de Janeiro, 6,000 miles away, about the global forces for change and what these might mean for the managers in the Rio hotel — who all worked for CVRD — one of Brazil's largest companies.

The event itself was a microcosm of the global forces for change that we have outlined above:

- The revolution of communications and technology made possible high-quality interactivity, with the Powerpoint slides accompanying the live lecture having been e-mailed overnight from London to ensure maximum topicality and the video cameras showing individual questioners in the audience when they spoke.

- The audience from CVRD illustrated the revolution of markets. CVRD was privatised in 1997 and is now operating in several other countries, including Norway, France and China. One of the drivers for its interest in sustainability and corporate responsibility concerns the requirements of the international financial markets in which it is raising funds.

- The revolution in demographics and development was reflected in some of the topics under discussion, such as CVRD's response to Brazil's anti-poverty and education drives.

- Finally, as the debate from the floor showed, the CVRD managers were already experiencing the revolution in values in the form of heightened demands from a range of different stakeholders.

In sum, the impact on business, and on other parts of society, of these global forces is immense and complex. We are concerned here with focusing only on the social, ethical and environmental factors that arise. Some factors are generic to all businesses and some are peculiar to particular industry sectors. Some factors impact *what* the business does — what is technically, physically and commercially feasible. Some factors affect *how* the business goes about doing what it does — hence the inclusion of issues such as sourcing, labour practices and environmental impacts. Some factors concern the way in which business is expected to govern itself and measure and report on what it does and how it does so. Finally, some factors are generated by the concerns of stakeholders — what is permissible, desired or valued by (often conflicting) expectations of different constituencies.

▶ Triggers and their causes: stakeholders

The external forces described above are both impacted by and influence the social, ethical and environmental concerns of a company's stakeholders, either reinforcing the external environmental triggers identified above or leading to additional triggers.

Stakeholders are those who have an interest or 'stake' of some sort in the company and, traditionally, they include primary stakeholders, such as customers, employees and investors, and secondary stakeholders, such as government and the wider community — though each business needs to determine which is which depending on the nature of the business and the level of 'stake' in the company.[21]

In considering potential stakeholder-related triggers, it is helpful to consider stakeholders' needs and motivations, the expectations they have traditionally had of business and then the more contemporary expectations within a CSR agenda. It is these contemporary expectations that prompt potential triggers.

Such stakeholder expectations, and how they are expressed, will depend on the business sector, the history and success or otherwise of the company and so on. To help the reader make a start in considering how they affect their business we have mapped generic corporate responsibility concerns, likely stakeholder expectations and possible triggers that might emerge.

We have mapped out stakeholder triggers under the following headings:

- Employees

- Investors

- Consumers

- Business partners and suppliers

- Non-governmental organisations and media campaigns

- Governmental, intergovernmental organisation and regulatory pressures

- Community and society

In Part II of this book we will be applying the seven-step model to a hypothetical food and beverage manufacturer. The International Business Leaders Forum, in its publication *Food for Thought: Corporate Social Responsibility for Food and Beverage Manufacturers* (2002), has produced a summary diagram of the influence of various stakeholders for the food and beverage sector (see Figure 3), including, in addition to the above-named stakeholders, competitors, rural producers, trade unions, executives and retailers.

Employee concerns

There is a growing body of evidence showing that prospective and current employees are concerned not only about pay, conditions, the level of interest of the work and opportunities for advancement but also about reputation, the social and environmental impacts of their employer and the way the company helps or hinders employees in balancing life–work considerations. Companies with a poor track

---

21   The AA1000 Standard for stakeholder engagement defines stakeholders as 'People (individuals or categories) who: Can influence or are affected by the activities of the organisation; Have an explicit or implied contract with the organisation; Possess information, resources and expertise needed for strategy formulation and implementation' (www.accountability.org.uk).

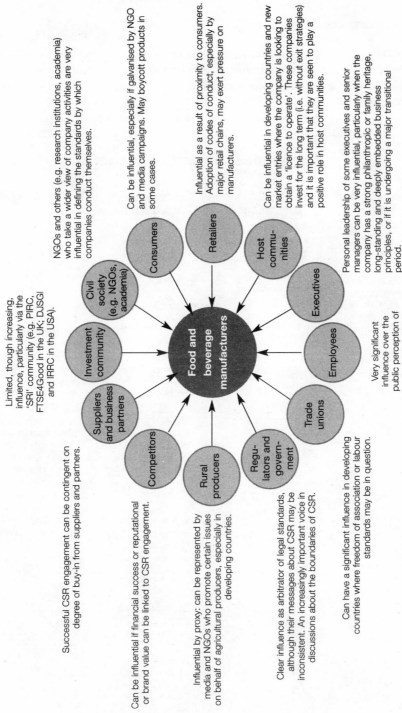

Figure 3 **Stakeholder corporate social responsibility (CSR) pressures in the food and beverage sector**

Source: International Business Leaders Forum, *Food for Thought: Corporate Social Responsibility for Food and Beverage Manufacturers* (2002)

CSR = corporate social responsibility; DJSGI Dow Jones Sustainability Group Index; IRRC = Investor Responsibility Research Center; NGO = non-governmental organisation; PIRC = Pensions Investment Research Consultants Ltd; SRI = socially responsible investment

record in these areas will have difficulty recruiting employees compared with their more advanced counterparts and, in the 'war for talent', a growing number of those joining the company will ask searching questions of its attitudes and CSR-related performance.

Potential triggers relating to employees are described in Box 6.

Employees: potential triggers

Expectations of business	Traditional expectations	Contemporary CSR expectations	Potential triggers
• To provide labour, knowledge and services • To provide jobs, reward and recognition	• Fair remuneration • Fair working conditions • Job security • Job satisfaction • Pension	• Employees expect to work for an employer they can trust and with values that mirror their own • Employees expect to receive respect for family responsibilities and help with their work–life balance • Employees expect to receive adequate contributions to health, well-being and pension needs • Employees expect to be given opportunities for life-long learning and opportunities to invest in future employability • Employees expect to work for a socially and environmentally responsible employer that puts 'back' into the communities from which it collects its profits • Employees expect to work for a company that shares their own social interests • Employees expect to work for a company that respects the right to privacy at work and home	• High turnover could indicate employees do not value the company they work for, and vice versa • Low demand for job places may suggest a bad company reputation • Employees may look to their employers to support volunteering and charitable fund-raising activities • Pay negotiations may break down because of 'bad blood' caused by the inflated pay levels of senior management • Unions may threaten industrial action if job losses arising from outsourcing continues at some current rate

Box 6 **Employee concerns: expectations for the business and potential trigger events**

Investor concerns

Pressure from investors over corporate approaches to CSR-related issues is leading to trigger incidents for publicly listed companies. For example, pharmaceutical company GlaxoSmithKline received a letter from Sean Harrigan, President of CalPERS (California Public Employees' Retirement System), the world's largest pension fund, on the issue of how it and other companies in the sector were responding to pressure over licensing arrangements for HIV/AIDS drugs in emerging and developing markets. In the letter, Harrigan wrote, 'We [at CalPERS] feel that the pharmaceutical industry faces very specific risks with regard to reputation, and this is particularly true with regard to AIDS.' He went on to say, 'How the company handles this risk is important to long-term shareholders.'

Concern expressed by CalPERS echoed that of various European-based investment institutions as outlined in a so-called 'framework of good practice' for the pharmaceutical sector in response to the public health crises in emerging markets. As at CalPERS, those institutions also believe that the sector's response to the crisis 'could impact on shareholder value in the long-term'.[23]

With pressure like this — CalPERS alone has an approximately 1% stake in the company — GSK was bound to listen. The letter and the report are examples of potential triggers from the investment community, as they put pressure on a number of industry sectors over issues that they regard as potentially being 'material' to corporate performance.

Potential triggers relating to investors are described in Box 7.

Consumer concerns

The loss of trust in corporations is acute among consumers, as shown clearly by the findings of various surveys, as highlighted above in the section on changing values (see pages 31, 33-34). Paradoxically, this trend is taking place when there is evidence that consumers are demonstrating a growing desire to be reassured by companies on a range of CSR issues. The US-based organisation Business for Social Responsibility (BSR) identifies a number of key issues that consumers are concerned with:[24]

- The integrity of product manufacturing and quality, covering, for example:
    - The use of genetically modified organisms (GMOs)
    - Food health and safety
    - Workplace practices, including, for instance, issues of sweatshop conditions

22   Harrigan, in a letter to GSK, quoted in G. Dyer, 'GSK urged to evaluate AIDS drug licensing', *Financial Times*, 16 April 2003.

23   This framework, titled 'Investor Statement on Pharmaceutical Companies in the Public Health Crisis in Emerging Markets', and produced in March 2003 by ISIS Asset Management and Universities Superannuation Scheme, was supported by, among others, Legal & General Investment Management and Schroders & Morley Fund Management.

24   Authors' example. For more details, see BSR (Business for Social Responsibility) 'Overview of Business and Marketplace', BSR White Papers, www.bsr.org (2003).

Investors: potential triggers

Expectations of business	Traditional expectations	Contemporary CSR expectations	Potential triggers
• To provide capital • To provide a return on investment	• Maximisation of return • Provision of financial information that is material to the performance of the business • To show financial due diligence in entering into mergers and acquisitions	• The niche market of socially responsible investment (SRI) is looking for a balance between return and the social and environmental impact of company operations and, further, is seeking to 'engage' with the company over areas of concern • The mainstream investment community is concerned with minimising social, ethical and environmental risks, including risks to reputation and operational risks, through the redefinition of 'materiality'; there are new expectations for public reporting of analysis and risk-mitigation processes • The broader concept of due diligence is expected to include CSR issues • Evidence of adequate corporate governance compliance, to the letter and spirit of law and codes, is expected	• A decision to invest or divest may trigger protests from those adversely affected • People may write or call the company to express their concerns or wishing to discuss issues • Difficult questions may be asked at analyst briefings • Shareholder resolutions to alter company practice or policy may be tabled by activist shareholders • Difficult questions may be asked at the annual general meeting • The investment community may indicate its support for changes to governance, reporting requirements and the disclosure of wider social, ethical and environmental associated risk-management criteria and processes

Box 7 **Investor concerns: expectations for the business and potential trigger events**

Consumers: potential triggers

Expectations of business	Traditional expectations	Contemporary CSR expectations	Potential triggers
• To purchase goods and services • To provide safe, reliable and affordable products	• Honest marketing • The provision of basic information on the performance of products • A system of refund or repair if necessary	• A growing number of consumer niches profess purchasing decisions based partially on the social, ethical and environmental 'pedigree' of a product or on the performance of a company behind a product or brand • As a consequence of the above, more detailed information is required on the 'CSR pedigree' of products and brands • Consumers expect privacy rights to be respected regarding data held on their purchasing • Consumers wish (and will respond to) 'cause-related marketing' schemes actively linking money raised from product purchases to contributions to social causes	• Consumers may boycott a product or brand • There may be an increased number of enquiries about the pedigree of a product • Consumers may look for external third-party endorsements or eco-labels on products and displays

Box 8 **Consumer concerns: expectations for the business and potential trigger events**

- – Ethical or fair trade
- – Animal testing

● Disclosure, labelling and packaging, covering, for example:
  - – Health claims
  - – Product contents
  - – Product origins
  - – Waste and recycling

● Marketing and advertising, covering, for example:
  - – Marketing aimed at children
  - – Privacy issues over use of sales and marketing data
  - – Use of stereotyped images in advertisements

● Selling practices, covering, for example:
  - – Predatory lending
  - – Mis-selling of products and services

● Distribution and access, covering, for example:
  - – Access to and differential pricing of medicines
  - – Access for the disabled
  - – Access to insurance in light of developments in genetic screening

Consumers' views may be expressed either individually or collectively through a variety of trigger mechanisms. For example, they may make their views known through product or company boycotts, by letter or e-mail campaigns directed at the company, the company's suppliers or other customers, or by letters or e-mails to politicians and regulators (for examples of triggers related to consumers, see Box 8). Major NGOs often take up, lead or claim to lead consumer campaigns on particular issues (the role of NGO and media campaigns is discussed in more detail below).

Business partner and supplier concerns

Business partners — whether joint-venture partners or business-to-business (B2B) customers — are increasingly vetting their suppliers against various social, ethical and environmental criteria because they are concerned about the threat of damage to their own reputation through an extended supply chain (for examples relating to business partners and suppliers, see Box 9). Corporate reputation can be badly damaged by the actions of suppliers (examples in the apparel industry, such as Nike, are perhaps the most well known),[25] and, as a result of extended supply chains, companies will face increasing pressures to become more responsible for the stewardship of their products and services over the life-cycle of the product or service.

It is now common practice for procurement conditions to be laid down by large corporations to all company suppliers — large or small — specifying adherence to a

25 A brief description of the case of Nike is given above in the section on negative publicity from NGOs and the media (see page 19).

B2B: potential triggers

Expectations of business	Traditional expectations	Contemporary CSR expectations	Potential triggers
• To purchase goods and services • To provide service and components	• To provide products and services on time at the agreed quality and price	• Business customers expect guarantees that goods purchased and services provided do not damage their reputation 'by association'; such a 'guarantee' sometimes requires compliance to specific standards and measures of corporate performance before contracts can be agreed • Other businesses may wish to 'know their customers' before doing substantial business with them	• Questionnaires may be sent from the business customer requesting information about social, ethical and environmental practices • An independent monitoring company may be sent to undertake an audit and to verify compliance to stipulated standards • Tender documents may stipulate the need for evidence of compliance to standards

Box 9 **Business-to-business concerns: expectations for the business and potential trigger events**

Suppliers: potential triggers

Expectations of business	Traditional expectations	Contemporary CSR expectations	Potential triggers
• To provide goods and services • To fulfil orders	• To pay fair prices and to make prompt payment	• Suppliers expect to receive technical support to help them meet new contractual social, ethical and environmental criteria	• The supplier may be unable to meet an order to new specifications and will lose the customer's business • Loss of profit margins as supplier has additional costs to meet new specifications

Box 10 **Supplier concerns: expectations for the business and potential trigger events**

particular set of standards (e.g. in environmental or workplace practices) in many industry sectors (for examples, see Box 10). Some purchasers may require independent verification of compliance, especially if they are pitching the finished goods at the niche market segment for 'ethical consumers'. For example, suppliers to General Motors are required to be certified to the standard of the International Organisation for Standardisation (ISO) regarding environmental management systems (EMSs), ISO 14001, or to an equivalent standard for EMS. The company website explains:

> In July 1998, we [at General Motors] advised our top 600 vehicle parts suppliers (based on sales volume) that we required them to become certified to an environmental management system equivalent to ISO 14001 by the end of 2002. This requirement applies to all supplier facilities that provide parts to [General Motors] and that have a significant environmental impact and to suppliers whose current or future contracts extend, or might extend, beyond 2002.[26]

Chiquita provides a further example.

Chiquita

Chiquita, an international marketer, producer and distributor of fresh fruit, processed fruit and vegetable products, purchases over 50% of its bananas in Latin America from independent growers. The company is working to encourage those growers to achieve certification under the Rainforest Alliance's Better Banana Project, which measures adherence to environmental standards. According to Chiquita's Corporate Responsibility Report, all of Chiquita's growers are now certified to this scheme.

Non-governmental organisations and media campaigns

A while ago, when one of us suggested to the newly appointed CEO of one of the world's largest international companies that NGOs were going increasingly to impinge on the business of business, his response was: 'What is an NGO?' We doubt very much whether we would get a similar response today.

Business has learned the hard way that NGOs are a force to reckon with. NGOs exert an influence on individual companies and groups of companies by acting as self-appointed corporate watchdogs, catalysing consumer boycotts and instigating critical and highly professional media campaigns. They can be protagonists in many of the triggers we have identified. The revolution of information and communications technologies makes NGO and media triggers even more powerful, as NGOs can use e-mail and other Internet tools to co-ordinate global campaigns against business. Maria Eitel, Vice-President for Corporate Responsibility at Nike, speaking at the 2002 Conference Board Corporate Citizenship Conference in New York, expressed

NGOs and media: potential triggers

Expectations of business	Traditional expectations	Contemporary CSR expectations	Potential triggers
• To represent communities of interest • To provide social services • To 'do no harm'	• Companies are expected to donate money and provide in-kind goods and services to charities and community groups and projects • Companies are expected to ensure their business actions cause minimal harm to people, other creatures and the environment	• Companies are expected to make changes to business behaviour and to take action to mitigate any social and environmental impacts • Companies are expected to be transparent and to seek independent verification of any reporting of impacts • Companies are expected to participate in ongoing dialogue and consultation with stakeholders • Companies are expected to enter into partnerships with stakeholders to address social, economic and environmental challenges • Companies are expected to pay penalties for breaking the spirit and letter of the law	• NGOs and consumer groups may run media campaigns to expose alleged harmful behaviour or business impacts • Targeting of companies for boycotts • Stakeholder activists may purchase shares and table shareholder resolutions • Stakeholder activists may demonstrate at outlets and premises • Civil lawsuits may be taken out against the company

Box 11 **Non-governmental organisation (NGO) and media campaigns: expectations for the business and potential trigger events**

vividly the impact of such campaigns: 'We were attacked! It got people's attention real quick!'

However, it would be wrong to categorise the engagement of all NGOs under the one heading. Some NGOs may choose 'constructive engagement' rather than a confrontational approach, whereas other NGOs do not stop at peaceful protest in their preferred method of influence on corporations. Contrast, for example, the constructive engagement tactics of an NGO such as People for the Ethical Treatment of Animals (PETA) with that of some of the militant anti-vivisection campaigners who have used violence and physical intimidation to attack companies such as

Huntingdon Life Sciences in the United Kingdom (general examples are given in Box 11).

Governmental, intergovernmental organisation and regulatory pressures

Governments exert pressures on business in response to a variety of internal and external pressures (for examples, see Box 12). First, governments are increasingly becoming stakeholders in business not so much because they have a legal share in them but, ironically, because they do not! In many countries, rounds of privatisation have left governments owning fewer businesses, making them increasingly reliant on business performance. This is the case for governments in most countries where many previously state-owned businesses have been privatised (e.g. electricity and gas suppliers, the railways, and telecommunications) and where many services previously run by the public sector have been contracted out (e.g. catering and cleaning in hospitals). As business now provides a higher proportion of all jobs and economic activity than in the past, its success affects the potential tax yield and the demand for government-provided welfare.

Second, governments may respond to external influences, such as outside events or pressure from lobbyists:

- The US and UK governments responded quickly to the events surrounding the case of malpractice at Enron and WorldCom, leading to the Sarbanes–Oxley Act in the USA and to the Modernising Company Law Bill in the United Kingdom.[27]

- The amendment to the 1995 UK Pensions Act, 'The SRI Pensions Disclosure Regulation', which came into force in July 2000, and which requires pension-fund trustees to state their attitude to social, ethical and environmental risk assessment, arose from pressure from campaigning NGOs.

- In Japan, nine laws, covering packaging, household appliances, construction materials, food and cars, have been passed since 2000 as a result of pressure from environmentalists. [28]

- Governments may have to act as national signatories to international law (such as the European Human Rights Act) or to multilateral agreements (such as the Kyoto Protocol).

In addition, as a result of pressures from a variety of stakeholders, mandatory requirements for business action in CSR areas are increasing, covering, for example:

- Employment anti-discrimination (e.g. in the European Union)

- Recycling (such as through the EU Environmental Liability Directive)

27 More details on the White Paper on 'Modernising Company Law' can be found in Step 2, page 56.
28 Reported in V. Houlder, 'Industry faces heavy costs of recycling', *Financial Times*, 27 May 2003.

Government: potential triggers

Expectations of business	Traditional expectations	Contemporary CSR expectations	Potential triggers
• To be responsible for national security • To contribute to social welfare • To respect the rule of law • To work within the regulatory framework • To develop infrastructure • To provide public goods • To be part of a thriving private sector	• The company should pay taxes • The company is expected to provide employment • The company is expected to provide goods and services • The company is expected to obey laws • The company is expected to engage in corporate philanthropy • The company is encouraged to contribute to political parties	• The company is expected to adhere to an increasing range of mandatory and voluntary regulation governing social, ethical and environmental behaviour — at the local, national and supra-national levels • The company is expected to play an active role in economic development • The company is expected to engage in public policy formulation • The company is expected to support improvements to public-sector delivery • The company is expected to engage in public–private partnerships	• Companies may be fined for breaking the law • Companies need to keep up to date with and adhere to new legislation, which may be costly if the legislation requires substantial capital investment • The company may be 'named and shamed' for failure to meet social, environmental or ethical standards • The company may be subject to 'informal', behind-doors persuasion • The government may give awards for 'good practice' • The government may provide tax and other financial incentives for improved standards • The company may enjoy reduced regulatory oversight if it can demonstrate a good compliance record • Challenge funding may be available to support mutually beneficial development projects

Box 12 **Governmental, intergovernmental organisation and regulatory pressures: expectations for the business and potential trigger events**

- Product safety (such as the EU Registration, Evaluation and Authorisation of Chemicals [REACH] regulations)

- Product content (as in the case of trans fatty acids in food in the USA)

On these and a wide range of other CSR and governance issues, government exerts pressure on companies through the due process of law, through changes in the regulatory regime, through naming and shaming, through the encouragement of adherence to supposed 'voluntary' norms and as purchasers.

Community and society concerns

Local communities based close to company premises or physically affected by the operations of company sites are increasingly vocal in encouraging 'neighbours of choice' and in fighting 'dangerous intruders'. Airports wishing to expand, logistics companies wanting to build new freight terminals and interchanges, and companies with physical activities deemed dangerous or socially unattractive have all fallen foul

---

Community: potential triggers

Expectations of business	Traditional expectations	Contemporary CSR expectations	Potential triggers
• To serve the local geographical community • To provide employment for local people • To pay local taxes	• People expect the company to provide jobs and training • The company is expected to support local sports, arts and community groups • The company is expected to create minimal environmental damage and pollution	• The company is expected to enter into consultation with the local community on downsizing or upsizing • On building new premises, the company is expected to provide infrastructure or buildings that benefit the local community (to provide 'planning gain') • The company is expected to treat indigenous people fairly • The company is expected to have a positive impact socially and on the community, including in terms of local business development	• There may be local boycotts of company products and services • Local people may protest to planning authorities over expansion plans

---

Box 13 **Community and society concern: implications for a hypothetical company in the food and beverage sector in terms of the role of the business, expectations for the business and potential trigger events**

of increasingly activist and well-organised local communities. We call these communities of geography.

We may equally define the word 'communities' as 'communities of interest' or 'communities of identity':

- Communities of interest may be campaigners for animal welfare or for the relief of third-world debt; they may be informal groups of a few people, or international NGOs with thousands or even millions of members.

- Communities of identity may be African American or Hispanic American employees; and often a business will have to deal with conflicting communities of identity: for example, Disney has gay Americans pushing for 'Gay Disney Days' in its theme parks, while evangelical Christian Americans are opposing.

For examples of community pressures, see Box 13.

Stakeholder mapping

Stakeholder mapping is increasingly being used by companies as a way of understanding the interface between a company's products, services and operations and

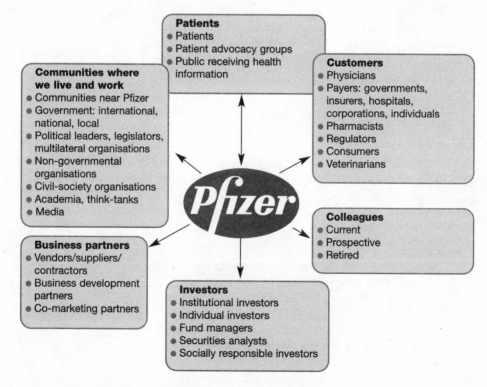

Figure 4 **Pfizer's stakeholder map**

Source: Pfizer

stakeholders. Pharmaceutical company Pfizer has mapped its key stakeholders and divided them into six broad categories (see Figure 4). The company has then articulated what it believes are the 'needs' of those stakeholders from Pfizer, and also the influence they have over Pfizer's 'value' as a business (see Table 1). The process of stakeholder identification and needs analysis is further explored in Step 2. Pfizer goes on to make it clear that expectations of the company and its products and services vary from within the same stakeholder group. These differences can be caused by the precise nature of the relationship and level of contact for those within a group; by differing cultural and personal values; by different socioeconomic characteristics; by sources of information and authority that are accessed or relied on; and by different relationships experienced with other companies apart from Pfizer.

Stakeholder needs and influences

Stakeholders	Their needs from Pfizer	How they determine Pfizer's value
Patients	• Access to medicine • Efficacy of medicines • Affordable medicines	They decide whether to take Pfizer medicines
Customers	• Efficacy of medicines • Quality of service • Access, affordability of medicines	Doctors decide whether to prescribe; government decides whether to reimburse
Colleagues	• Employment • Job satisfaction • Pride in company	They decide whether to work at Pfizer and how productive to be
Business partners	• Code of ethics, integrity • Fair business deals • Timely payments	They decide whether to make Pfizer a partner of choice
Investors	• Good rate of return on investment • Good pharmaceutical 'pipeline'	They decide whether and how much to invest in Pfizer
Communities	• To add value as a good neighbour	Where Pfizer operates, they shape the living and working environment

Table 1   **Pfizer's stakeholders: their needs and the influence they have on the company's value**

▶ Triggers and their impacts

Having identified potential triggers, the next stage is to consider their potential impact on current business strategies or operational practices. The objective is to begin to rank triggers from those that are of no impact, to those of marginal impact, to those that have or may have material and long-term impact on the business. At this stage, such a process is likely to be subjective, but the task is, nevertheless, to make a judgement. If possible, its significance should be expressed in financial terms — and the time-period over which its effects may be felt should be considered. The primary aim is:

- To make quantifiable estimates in terms of degree of loss of revenue, increase in cost of materials etc.

- To differentiate between low-intensity short-term impacts and high-intensity long-term impacts

At a minimum, the aim should be to express impact in broad terms such as low, medium or high.

Because of commercial confidentiality, it is difficult to get accurate examples of the effect that particular triggers have had on specific companies from firms themselves. We referred to some examples at the beginning of this chapter — Nike, Shell and De Beers. However, it is possible to illustrate the nature of potential impacts for some companies by extrapolating from published sources and records (see Table 2); alternatively, it may be possible to determine the industry-wide impacts of a specific trigger (e.g. of legislation; see Table 3).

Trigger impacts on specific companies

Company	Trigger	Business impact	Time-scale of impact
Mattel	Threat of boycott of products[a]	Boycott represented a potential loss of sales	Within 12 months
Eli Lilly	Accident rates at the research laboratories[b]	Health and safety risk led to higher costs because of loss of trained personnel, increased healthcare costs and lower productivity	Now and ongoing

a Analysis based on a reading of 'Sweatshop Wars', The Economist, 27 February 1999
b Analysis based on a reading of GEMI (Global Environmental Management Initiative), 'New Paths to Value Creation', March 2001

Table 2 **Illustrations of analyses of trigger impacts on specific companies: the case of the toy company Mattel and the case of the Eli Lilly research laboratories**

Cost impacts of regulatory triggers

Legislation	Estimated cost	Time-scale of impact
EU REACH Directive	The EU estimates a cost of £22 billion to industry (the trade-body estimate is higher)	Present to 2020
Nine Japanese recycling laws	Costs of recycling are set at ¥53.9 billion (£280 million) for recycling containers and packaging in 2001, up from ¥1.7 billion in 1997	Ongoing

Table 3 **Illustrations of analyses of trigger events on industry-wide costs: the case of the EU REACH (Registration, Evaluation and Authorisation of Chemicals) Directive on the testing of chemicals and the case of nine Japanese laws, passed since 2000, on the recycling of packaging, household appliances, construction materials and cars**

▶ Synthesis of Step 1

The themes and issues described in Step 1 can be seen in the following examples, the first of which describes how changes in the external environment and pressures from stakeholders impacted one particular company — the US-based retailer Staples; and, for contrast, this is followed by a second example of how they are impacting a very different sector —telecommunications.

Triggers at Staples

Staples, the office-supplies giant, faced two years of stakeholder pressure from shareholders, community groups and environmental NGOs involving more than 600 demonstrations at Staples stores across the USA. In addition, tens of thousands of e-mails, letters and calls were made to the CEO. Staples eventually agreed to achieve an average of 30% post-consumer recycled content in all the paper products it sells, to phase out purchases of paper products from endangered forests, to create an environmental affairs division and to report annually on its environmental results.*

* Reported in Ethical Corporation and Nima Hunter Inc., 'The Business of Business: Managing Corporate Social Responsibility: What Business Leaders are Saying and Doing, 2002–2007', www.ethicalcorp.com (2003).

Triggers in the telecommunications sector

Several processes are evident in this sector. Technological advances make it possible to transmit pictures and video clips to mobile phones, and marketplace changes mean that mobile-phone usage is now widespread throughout the population, including among children. In addition, shifts in values in Western societies mean that material containing adult content is now more readily available and more socially acceptable. These factors in combination mean that children may be able to access pornographic or otherwise explicit images via their mobile phones.

A possible trigger event might therefore come in the form of an increasing stream of complaints from consumers (especially parents), directly to company customer services departments as well as via regulatory bodies covering the telecommunications sector, parliamentarians and the media. Some employees of mobile telecommunications companies might also be uncomfortable with the knowledge that their company is complicit in making such images accessible to children. Societal views may differ between different national markets where the same mobile telephony business has a presence.

Mobile telecommunications companies may identify the trigger of consumer complaints about adult (albeit legal) content as being likely to have a significant impact on the business. On the one hand, a complete ban on the transmission of such material would alienate other customers and lead to a loss of potentially substantial revenues — particularly if other providers did not follow suit. It might also undermine a marketing strategy designed to project a funky, liberated image to the rapidly growing youth market. On the other hand, failure to respond at all to the trigger could harm the marketing strategy to build up 'family package' deals for multi-phone use by a family. It might also lead to regulatory intervention that might restrict the transmission of adult content or ban it entirely.

▶ Moving from Step 1 to Step 2

In this chapter we looked at Step 1 of the seven-step process: identification of potential triggers and their causes, and their likely impact on business. In Step 2 we go on to examine in more detail the causes behind the triggers, whether they present significant commercial or operational risks or create the conditions for corporate social opportunities.

Step 2
Scoping what matters

Focus

In this chapter we describe how to assess the potential impact of key triggers on business strategies. We then discuss how to generate revised strategies.

Applying Step 2

In Part II — the worked example of the seven steps — the completed process forms show how, by applying appropriate tools and techniques selected from Step 2, the following outputs are produced (see pages 287ff.):

- Identification of potential business strategies

- A revision of the strategies in the light of stakeholder impacts and inputs

- Further refinement of the strategies taking into account current market and operational issues

- A ranking of the strategies based on possible importance for the business

AT AN ANNUAL GENERAL MEETING (AGM), A SHAREHOLDER'S provocative question alleging poor working conditions at a second-tier supplier may not pose much of an immediate challenge to an experienced chairman, but gone are the days when those who raise such issues can be dismissed as cranks. The shareholder may be a member of a well-staffed non-governmental organisation (NGO) operating internationally with access to information that the company is not able immediately to verify or deny. Wise investor-relations managers are treating such questions raised at AGMs or through the proxy systems as triggers to open dialogue with their critics in order to ensure the business understands the facts and underlying issues behind individual alleged incidents.

One particular event, taken in isolation, may not appear particularly significant for a large and complex business. The challenge for busy managers is to use it as a trigger — to look beyond the individual incident and to consider whether it is genuinely a one-off or whether, in fact, it reflects a pattern of behaviour that has wider ramifications.

The purpose of Step 2 is to show how trigger events can be used as catalysts to scope changes in the operating environment that might have significant implications for a particular business. In this chapter a number of tools and techniques are introduced to help spot the risks and/or opportunities represented by such changes. Use of these tools and techniques can help lead you to creative thinking about potential future business strategies, whether in terms of market segments or revenue streams or in terms of how markets are being serviced by the organisation. Step 2 calls for an assessment of the potential impact of particular triggers on business strategies that is informed by stakeholders and by current markets and operational practices.

The attitudes or behaviour of key stakeholders may well determine the feasibility of any strategy being proposed. Stakeholders can be a source of intelligence and inspiration or they can present potential obstacles. Mapping how stakeholders might be impacted or might impact strategies is a key process. Arguably, the failure of Monsanto, the US food biotechnology company, to understand the depth of consumer and political concerns in Europe about genetically modified organisms (GMOs) and its perceived unwillingness to debate the merits of these concerns in a proactive way contributed to its subsequent difficulties and eventual takeover in the late 1990s.[1]

In addition, the attractiveness of proposed strategies will be influenced by how well they sit with the firm's current markets and operational practices. Will they cannibalise an existing market segment, or do market trends suggest a new niche waiting to be served? Could they lead to greater economies of scale in production, or will they require bespoke facilities or operators with different expertise? An additional process is, therefore, to highlight the consequences for current markets

1   For an insider reflection on this, see John Elkington's book, *The Chrysalis Economy: How Citizen CEOs and their Corporations Can Fuse Values and Value Creation* (Oxford: Capstone Publishing, 2001). John's consultancy SustainAbility resigned from helping Monsanto on European stakeholder engagement. He later interviewed Monsanto CEO Bob Shapiro for his book.

and business practices. This should help inform the choice of which strategies merit further consideration and development.

Overall, the structured approach of the seven-step model is designed to capture innovative thinking and creative brainstorming about possibilities: what we are calling corporate social opportunities. Nowhere is the concept of 'what might be' more important than in the scoping of what matters in Step 2. It is at this stage that we illustrate examples of how companies are capitalising on the possibilities of corporate social opportunity.

▶ Risks and opportunities for business strategies and operational practices

CSR factors usually have the potential for negative impact if they are not managed effectively. The traditional association of CSR is with avoiding problems and mitigating risk. For the manager open to creative and lateral thinking, those same factors can create positive opportunities. These opportunities might range from saving costs, to providing insights for innovation in products and services; from identifying or creating new markets, to discovering more productive ways of organising the business.

There are several ways to explore the risks and opportunities of CSR factors:

- By considering the rising importance to business of issues such as ecology and environment, health and well-being, human rights and diversity, and community relations

- By tracking the development of other issues on the radar screen

- By considering attitudes and trends in CSR from different stakeholder perspectives

- Through benchmarking against other companies — competitors or industry leaders — or, indeed, against social enterprises

- By considering possible futures through scenario planning

For many companies, a risk assessment of CSR issues is not an optional extra. In Step 1 (page 46ff.) we referred briefly to changes in corporate governance arrangements and corporate law in the United Kingdom that have or will act as triggers for addressing CSR issues. In particular, in July 2002 the UK government published its White Paper, 'Modernising Company Law', in response to the final report of the Company Law Review (CLR). In that White Paper the government gave its support to many of the CLR proposals, including the recommendation that UK companies over a certain size threshold be required to prepare and publish an annual operating and financial review (OFR) to incorporate an assessment of the most 'material' significant environmental and social impacts of the company. The White Paper makes it clear that it will be for directors to decide precisely what information is material to their particular business and thus should be published in their OFR.[2]

In an earlier piece of governance reform, the Turnbull Code of 1999, all companies quoted on the stock exchange in Britain are required to explain their approach to managing and exploiting risk, including that related to social, ethical and environmental issues. In line with our concept of corporate social opportunity, risk is conceived not only as inferring negative consequences but also potential positive impacts. The 'trigger' of the Turnbull Code has led many companies to address CSR risks systematically. For example, prompted by the Turnbull Code, brewer SABMiller has listed 13 risk areas that its board reviewed in 2002, ranging from 'traditional' financial risk areas to broader, 'softer' issues such as organisational change and use of partnerships, stakeholder reputation, HIV and AIDS in Africa, and environmental policy and reporting.[3] The Securities Exchange Commission (SEC) in the USA has had submissions encouraging it to introduce a similar practice.

The application of traditional risk-management tools and processes to such CSR issues is difficult because many of the measurement techniques are undeveloped, and it is not easy to put values on qualitative impacts. Internal audit functions, often responsible for traditional risk-management processes, are beginning to widen their remit to embrace CSR-related risks, where they lead to more robust metrics. In the next section we look at how to scope the risks and opportunities of tough, specific CSR issues.

► Scoping by CSR issue

The CSR agenda is mushrooming. Not even the largest multinational corporation (MNC) can — or should — attempt to predict or manage everything. As Greg Bourne, then Regional President of BP Australasia, observed at New Zealand's Redesigning Resources Conference in 2002: 'BP cannot contribute effectively on fish stock depletion or medical care — but it can on climate change or inner-city pollution.'[4]

It is common sense for companies to consider those CSR issues that affect them most directly in their sector and their markets. They have to recognise, however, that the field is very fluid — it does not necessarily respect easy, traditional industry-sector definitions.

In our book *Everybody's Business*,[5] we identified a short-hand framework to scope potential risks and opportunities through a set of emerging management issues:

2   On 5 May 2004, it was announced that the Operating and Financial Review would be introduced for all publicly quoted companies in the UK requiring boards of directors to report annually on the most significant environmental and social impacts of their business.
3   See South African Breweries plc, 'Annual Report 2002', www.sabmiller.com/results/annual2002/index.htm.
4   Quote taken from personal notes made at the conference.
5   D. Grayson and A. Hodges, *Everybody's Business* (London: Dorling Kindersley, 2001).

- Ecology and environment
- Health and well-being
- Human rights and diversity
- Communities

A summary of each is provided below, with illustrations of some of the main risks and opportunities presented in the accompanying boxes. Then we look at the overall questions posed by transparency, accountability and governance issues.

Ecology and environment

In Box 14 we list some of the risks and opportunities that are raised by ecological and environmental issues. What is a risk for some might be viewed as an opportunity by another. For example, climate change may be seen as the cause of rising insurance premiums in response to the increased incidence of cases of structural damage to buildings and property as a result of extreme weather conditions, such as flooding and high winds; however, it may also be seen as providing product development opportunities. Opportunities presented by concerns over climate change and the destruction of the ozone layer are illustrated by the reinsurance company Swiss Re.

Ecology and environment

Risks

- Fines for breaching pollution regulations
- Expenditure for new equipment required as a result of stringent regulations on emissions
- Increased insurance costs as a result of the effects of global warming
- Rising costs for landfill and disposal
- Costs arising from take-back legislation, specifying producers accept responsibility for disposal and recycling
- Inheritance of environmental liability through merger and acquisition (M&A) activity
- Disqualification from contracts that require adherence to specific standards that the company cannot meet

Opportunities

- Energy savings through use of clean technologies and through measures to conserve energy
- Cost savings through use of new packaging that entails less waste disposal
- Access to a growing market for eco-efficient technologies, products and services
- Market opportunities for market leaders through raised performance standards from regulators and customers
- The chance to become the brand or company of choice for consumers interested in conservation and environmental performance

---

Box 14 **Examples of risks and opportunities presented by ecological and environmental issues**

Swiss Re

The results of changes in weather patterns are being felt in the insurance sector in the form of an increasing number of claims for structural damage to property resulting from, for example, flooding and high winds. Events that used to occur once in 100 years are now occurring more frequently. To offset this change, insurance premiums are being raised, and those living in high-risk areas (e.g. in houses with a high risk of flooding, such as in houses built on a river flood plain) are being refused insurance on their properties.

The re-insurance firm Swiss Re has now developed a sustainable approach to insurance underwriting by presenting commercial opportunities in the form of new risk-specific insurance products (for further information, see www.swissre.com).

Health and well-being

In Box 15 we provide some examples of the risks and opportunities presented by the rise in importance of health and well-being as a management issue.

Companies are now having to look beyond traditional responsibilities for the health and safety of their products and facilities. For example, in many developed economies, stress is an increasingly important issue. It is being caused by a combination of factors, such as increasing workloads for fewer staff (so-called 'job-loading'); a 'long hours' culture; and a 24/7 mentality where a combination of pagers, mobiles and e-mails means more employees feel permanently 'on call'. Further causes of stress may come from increasing individual responsibility for child- and eldercare due to social changes (e.g. more single parents; more families where both partners are working; more geographically extended families; and the demographics of an ageing population). As we explore below, the rise in HIV/AIDS infections and its consequences is slowly being recognised as a business issue and one which companies can impact directly. And, as we go on to consider in Part II, we are also seeing increasing global concerns about obesity and consequent rises in diseases such as diabetes, with direct consequences for the health and well-being of employees and consumers. The World Health Organisation suggests that diabetes (of which type 2 diabetes is linked to diet) has now overtaken AIDS as a cause of death, with three million fatalities a year being attributed to the condition. This is leading to greater interest in the responsibilities of companies — both for products and services that may affect consumers' health and for helping employees to stay healthy, with companies providing employees with gyms or subsidised gym membership, stress-relaxation courses, and healthier options in company canteens.

An increasing health problem faced by companies is that posed by HIV and AIDS. As discussed in Step 1 (page 29), many tens of millions of people's lives are now affected by HIV and AIDS, especially in the developing world, and it is increasingly being seen as an investor concern (see page 73). Despite the scale of the problem, only 21% of the largest 100 multinationals worldwide have policies or programmes

Health and well-being

Risks

- The cost (financial and to reputation) of product recalls
- Damage to reputation as a result of consumer and interest-group action on the health and safety aspects of products
- Potential liability to the company resulting from, for example, the excessive consumption of company food products by consumers (in the case of a food and beverage company)
- Costs of absenteeism or low productivity as a result of employees being overworked and stressed
- Cost of high turnover of trained staff who are unable to achieve a suitable work–life balance, with the possibility they may move to competitors with different policies
- Cost of loss of trained staff and costs of secondary care for employees' families as a result of the HIV/AIDS pandemic
- Cost (financially and in terms of management time) of litigation by employees claiming against work-related illness, injury or permanent disability
- Cost of expensive provision of basic healthcare if the state system is ineffectual

Opportunities

- Access to a growing market for products and services orientated to health and well-being
- The benefit of productive employees and good company morale as a result of the provision of comprehensive employee healthcare and health insurance
- The benefits of high rates of retention of staff because of controlled recruitment and training costs and flexible working practices
- Savings on absenteeism, a problem that decreases when employees are motivated
- Lower rates of sickness because of health promotion via company communication channels
- The benefits of investment in learning, which reduces staff turnover and also leads to less stress-related absenteeism because staff feel better equipped to do their jobs and feel they are supported

Box 15 **Examples of risks and opportunities presented by health and well-being issues**

for AIDS in the workplace.[6] Two companies that do have programmes are the drinks producer Diageo (details are given to illustrate Step 3; see pages 138f.) and the car manufacturer Volkswagen Brazil (for a brief description, see page 122). Another company that has taken a proactive approach to health and well-being is Philips.

Human rights and diversity

In Box 16 we provide some examples of risks and opportunities presented by the rise in importance of human rights and diversity as a management issue.

6   This statistic is taken from a report of the UN Research Institute for Social Development (UNRISD), published in November 2003 and quoted in an IBLF 'Business and Aids' supplement of the *Financial Times* on 1 December 2003.

Philips

The Philips 'Voices In Your Hand' project aims to develop a handset that would extend the reach of public Internet centres (telecentres) and bring the benefits of a simple, low-cost information and communication channel to the rural and urban poor.

In its *Sustainability Report 2002*, Philips explains the possibilities of the technology by imagining a hypothetical user:

> Here's how it would work for someone like Maria, a 19-year-old single mother living in a shantytown in Recife, Brazil. Maria has three children, does not have a regular job and relies on the support of local NGOs for clothes, medicines and general assistance. Her family suffers from malnutrition, and her daughter Rosalie is often sick. Normally, it takes six weeks to get an appointment with a doctor at the medical center in town. But if she had a 'Voices in Your Hand' device, Maria would be able to go to the closest public telecenter to get medical advice. She would simply record her questions in the handset and upload them on the telecenter's PC for quick delivery to a remote advice center. Later, she could download the doctor's reply.

Source: www.philips.com/Assets/Downloadablefile/sustainability-2153.pdf

Human rights and diversity

Risks

- Damage to reputation and loss of consumers or business-to-business (B2B) orders if human rights violations are alleged against the company or its suppliers

- Disqualification from bidding for contracts if specific standards are not met

- Increased costs in replacing employees who leave because of discrimination or a lack of belief in possibilities for personal advancement

- Costs of lengthy litigation cases; if complaints are upheld then there is the possibility of fines, with the risk of class-action suits for discrimination

- Added transaction costs if company actions perpetuate corrupt practices

- Cost of exposure over use of child labour, sweatshop labour and hazardous working conditions in supplier factories in less-developed countries

Opportunities

- Competitive edge gained by attracting and retaining the best employees from a diverse pool of talent if effective policies and practices are in place

- Access to preferred-supplier status if stipulated standards are met

- A higher market share won from concerned consumers because of independent verification of standards

- Familiarity with the needs of diverse minorities, spurring the development of new products and the penetration of minority markets

- Reduced chance of being implicated in scandals surrounding bribery and corruption

Box 16 **Examples of risks and opportunities presented by human rights and diversity issues**

Companies are under scrutiny from a mix of campaigning NGOs on their treatment of stakeholders, and incidents of direct abuses that are counter to recognised international norms enshrined under the Universal Declaration of Human Rights are exposed through reports and the media. Increasingly companies are having to be wary of being accused of 'complicity' in abuses. In other words they may not be responsible for the incident(s) of mistreatment themselves, but if they are seen to have stood by and not taken reasonable action within their power to stop the abuse, they too are being held to account.

Recognition of human rights and diversity may have many benefits. Two companies that have benefited from the opportunities presented by understanding diversity are Investec and Unilever.

Investec

Financial services group Investec expects to generate new business opportunities after having to sell a stake in its South African business as a result of new black empowerment legislation. According to the chief executive Stephen Koseff, quoted in an article in the *Financial Times*, titled 'Black Economic Empowerment in South Africa' (22 May 2003), 'The deal was defensive and business-generating at the same time.' The sale created potential new business opportunities with the owners of the new entity.

Unilever

At Unilever it was recognised that women make 80% of the decisions about buying Unilever products. To reflect this reality in the workforce it was felt that more women should be recruited into senior positions in the business. According to Niall FitzGerald, co-chairman of Unilever, quoted in an article in the *Financial Times*, titled 'Unilever hits at glass ceiling from above' (17 June 2003), 'We want our share of all the talent that's available. If we have to do things in different ways to accommodate that and make it easier, that's what we must do.'

Communities

In Box 17 we provide examples of risks and opportunities presented by the rise in importance of community relations as a management issue.

Scoping in practice

An example of an integrated approach to specific sets of issues is illustrated by Marks & Spencer.

Communities

Risks

- Expensive and time-consuming clashes with antagonistic local communities
- High security costs if the company is operating in physical conflict with local communities
- Adverse effect on expansion or relocation plans if local community is not supportive
- Costs of local remedial education when the state system produces an under-educated workforce
- Pressure from governments to provide low-cost services to unserved or under-served markets
- Danger of community-relations issues becoming a high-profile cause for campaigning NGOs
- Backlash from raising, but not fulfilling, local expectations to provide jobs and social investment

Opportunities

- A bank of goodwill is formed by good community relations, providing early warning signs of potential problems before they become crises
- Where partnerships with local communities are formed, risks are shared, access to information and expertise is gained and the company reputation benefits, especially where the partnerships are of common interest (e.g. in combating breast cancer) or identity (e.g. ethnicity, nationality, age group)
- Influence is gained over the quality of the local labour supply base by sharing good practice and by investing in local training initiatives
- By investing in local economic development programmes, potential client businesses are attracted and an attractive location for employees is ensured
- Dialogue with community mitigates opposition to planning applications
- Better workforce skills are developed when employees volunteer in the community

Box 17 **Examples of risks and opportunities presented by community issues**

Marks & Spencer

When we met David Gregory, Director of Food Technology at Marks & Spencer, and asked what CSR means to him, he stood up, went over to his desk and returned with an A3 sheet of paper. The sheet consisted of 16 photographs, each with a one-word or two-word caption such as 'fish farming', 'pesticides' or 'health'. David and his colleagues had taken the overall Marks & Spencer commitment to CSR and analysed the most important issues within the food division. They had run internal discussions and consulted external experts and stakeholders. They had participated in scenario planning and Delphi panel exercises with the UK government Department for Environment, Farming and Regional Affairs (DEFRA) and the industry trade body, the Institute of Grocery Distribution (IGD). In these exercises, scenarios are built up through progressive iterations, with feedback from panel members being incorporated into each successive iteration. David and his colleagues then refined their list of priorities down to the 16 issues captured in the photographs. Different members of the team are now championing individual issues to determine what the company should do about those issues and in what time-frame.

As a simple device to enable busy people to visualise quickly what practical issues are covered by the responsible business agenda, the approach of the food technology division of Marks & Spencer is hard to beat.

Transparency, accountability and governance issues

As well as looking at specific issues, we need to address the more general issues of transparency, accountability and governance, including corruption and corporate ethics.

In Box 18 we list some examples of risks and opportunities presented by these issues.

Transparency, accountability and governance

Risks

- Costs in terms of time and resources to prepare reports and make assessments of company performance
- Cost to reputation if poor performance is reported
- Reports can be seen as no more than public-relations exercises
- Lax governance may lead to loss of trust of employees and investors

Opportunities

- Reputation benefits if the company is seen to be open, including about its mistakes
- Assessments carried out for reports can reveal business opportunities
- Reputation may benefit if company is seen to take a firm stance on issues such as bribery and corruption
- Reputation enhances opportunities to win customers

Box 18 **Examples of risks and opportunities presented by transparency, accountability and governance issues**

▶ Tracking issues on the corporate radar screen

CSR issues do not stand still. They are in a constant state of flux. What is moving to the centre of the radar screen today may not be such a hot issue tomorrow. In our book *Everybody's Business* we quoted a technique, pioneered by the scenario planners Peter Schwartz and Blair Gibb, for understanding pressures on business specifically in relation to NGOs.[7] We provided our own interpretation of some current developing CSR issues in a European and US context across the spectrum of the state of engagement with those issues, from emerging issues to consultation with NGOs, with 'consultation' suggesting areas of collaboration and joint ventures between NGOs and corporations. A sample of current issues for business to consider is listed in Table 4, with our suggestion as to the state of development.

Looking ahead, some of the issues we see as emerging on the radar screen include:

---

7   P. Schwartz and B. Gibb, *When Companies Do Bad Things: Responsibility and Risk in an Age of Globalisation* (New York: John Wiley, 1999).

- The under-funding of pensions
- Healthy ageing
- Taxes paid in different jurisdictions
- Boundaries of corporate responsibility for the use (and misuse) of products
- Social and environmental performance along the supply chain
- Electronic monitoring of employees

The under-funding of pensions

First, we anticipate that the issue of under-funded pensions will arise, including the broader responsibilities of employers in helping employees to retrain and move towards what could be called a more 'portfolio' lifestyle. On average, people are living longer and are more physically and mentally active to a much older age than they were in the past; we therefore expect that people will hold down work in several paid jobs and voluntary roles at the same time, will have more hobbies and will undertake further studies later in life.

Healthy ageing

Second, and related to the first point, we expect the issue of healthy ageing to be of increasing importance. The revolution of demographics (see Step 1, pages 29, 31-32) sees the population in the West ageing, with fewer young people available for the job market and with older people living longer as a result of advances in medical technology. This will have significant implications for business, both in the market-place and in the workplace. Some businesses, including the pharmaceutical company Pfizer, are already encouraging employees to carry on working beyond the formal age of retirement, and others are hiring older workers. If they have stayed fit and healthy, older workers can enjoy a more active life later into old age than did previous generations. (One manifestation is that specialist holiday companies for older people such as SAGA in the UK are now offering more physically challenging

Pfizer

Pharmaceutical company Pfizer has recognised healthy ageing as a profound challenge to society and a key issue and platform for encouraging research and debate on public policy and private-sector implications. An ageing population would also have significant implications for the pharmaceutical and healthcare sectors. Pfizer's programme on Healthy Ageing is one way the company is aligning itself with society to improve the quality of healthcare. Indeed Chairman and CEO of Pfizer, Hank McKinnell, in addressing the company's consumers, says explicitly: 'Ultimately, *our* goal is *your* healthy ageing' (see www.pfizer.com).

Issues on the corporate radar screen

Emerging ▼	*Consumer debt:* the financial services sector is under attack for encouraging unsustainable levels of debt among its consumers
Campaigning ↓	*Obesity:* health campaigners are alleging that food companies are irresponsibly marketing foods with a high sugar and salt content to children
	CSR implications of outsourcing to India, China etc.: as more companies transfer service jobs such as call centres to India and manufacturing jobs to China, questions of how this relates to being a responsible business will grow (see Step 5)
Codifying ↓	*Stress and work–life balance:* health campaigners and unions are working to define work–life balance indicators for employees and acceptable levels of stress and are campaigning for corresponding legislation
	Corruption: the NGO Transparency International[8] is working to set good-practice codes of conduct regarding bribery and corruption for international firms investing in emerging markets. In Nigeria, for example, a small NGO, Integrity, is championing ethical behaviour and good governance in corporate and public life and is linking into the resources of international organisations such as Transparency International and international donor agencies to extend their reach
Monitoring ↓	*Blood diamonds:* the Kimberley Process is a multi-stakeholder process initiated by campaigning NGOs to monitor the origins of diamonds, revenues from which have been implicated in funding and extending civil wars in Africa (for the role of De Beers, see page 99)
Consulting	*Labour conditions:* Companies such as The Gap and Nike are working with the US-based Fair Labor Association (FLA) and the UK-based Ethical Trading Initiative (ETI) to ensure better labour conditions in suppliers' factories in LDCs

- **Emerging.** These may require research and analysis to gain a greater understanding of the issue
- **Campaigning.** Claims from NGOs may require rebuttal or there may be a need to enter into dialogue with the NGOs
- **Codifying.** This may be throughout an industry group or as part of a multi-stakeholder forum to determine acceptable standards, voluntary or mandatory
- **Monitoring.** This may involve a mixture of self-monitoring, regular inspection by the relevant authorities or independent verification and reporting on progress
- **Consulting.** This may consist of collaborative efforts to address the impacts of key strategic issues

Table 4 Examples of issues raised by non-governmental organisations and the current stage of engagement with those issues

Source: adapted from D. Grayson and A. Hodges, *Everybody's Business* (London: Dorling Kindersley, 2001), p. 231

8   See www.transparency.org. TI has a comprehensive toolkit for people who want to introduce their own codes; see also the Global Corporate Governance Forum website at www.gcgf.org.

and adventurous holidays, such as white-water rafting in Vietnam!) Helping employees to 'age healthily' — by encouraging them to take regular exercise, go for medical check-ups and eat a balanced diet — will become an increasingly important dimension of the CSR agenda, the business rationale being less absenteeism and higher productivity.

Taxes paid in different jurisdictions

Third, the taxes that companies pay in different jurisdictions and the totality of a company's positive or negative impacts on a locality, region or country are set to become emerging issues. Deloitte & Touche estimate that Europe-wide tax dodging is worth almost £100 billion a year. Of course, tax evasion and tax avoidance must not be confused: the first is illegal; the second legal. One means of avoiding the payment of taxes is through transfer pricing, with one academic study estimating that this practice costs the US Treasury US$53 billion per year and has cost well over US$50 billion per year to countries in the global South.[9]

Transfer pricing is the practice where one company reports that it sells products to another company in the same group at a higher or lower price to ensure the profits can be recorded in the company that faces lower tax rates. It is about moving money from one country to another to avoid tax. This practice is not without social consequences, given the poor state of national budgets in many countries in the southern hemisphere and because governments have little option but to shift the tax burden onto labour, raising the costs of employment and reducing take-home wages.[10] These issues of corporate responsibility and transfer-pricing are increasingly being linked to issues of lobbying and responsible corporate lobbying of governments — including questions of transparency and consistency.

In practice, like most of these emerging issues, practical solutions are likely to involve actions by the various different players involved: NGOs, governments, international organisations as well as business. In this case this will probably involve tax treaty and convergence of taxation, rather than telling companies to pay more tax.

Boundaries of corporate responsibility for the use (and misuse) of products

Fourth, the boundaries of corporate responsibility for the use (and misuse) of company products (such as issues of responsible drinking) are being highlighted by a number of CEOs as an emerging trend. Banks are being criticised for encouraging consumers to run up too much debt on their credit cards. Mortgage lenders are criticised for offering large mortgages which borrowers will find hard to maintain if interest rates rise. There are increasing debates about what responsibility food

---

9   See the 2003 Lifeworth Annual Review of Corporate Responsibility (www.lifeworth.net), supported by the New Academy of Business and *The Journal of Corporate Citizenship* (Greenleaf Publishing).

10 *Ibid.*

companies should take for obesity and diet-related illnesses. Companies that are marketing perfectly legal products or services are being held responsible for the misuse or over-consumption — perhaps by those with an addictive personality type — of those services or products. This is seen in the case of Hilton. (For further discussion of the extent of responsibility for misuse of company products, see the discussion in Step 5 on marketing, pages 182ff.)

Hilton

Hilton has recently taken over the gaming business Ladbrokes and has introduced initiatives aimed at the responsible management of gambling. For example, its product management initiatives include a 'self-exclusion' programme for addicted gamblers, staff training in coping with customer contact and the linking up of problem gamblers with support services. It has been involved in developing — and is the first company to be audited and accredited to — a new CSR industry standard in gambling. In the UK, a new industry-supported organisation has been created — 'The Responsibility in Gambling Trust' — to research the extent of 'problem gambling' and develop more effective preventative measures and better treatments for those already addicted (www.rigt.org.uk).

Social and environmental performance along the supply chain

Fifth, there are expectations that big businesses will help companies in their supply chain to meet higher standards of environmental and social performance. Such expectations apply particularly to multinational corporations operating in less-developed countries where weak government makes compliance with standards more difficult to enforce.

Electronic monitoring of employees

Last, electronic monitoring of employees may involve monitoring personal use of corporate e-mail and telephones; hidden cameras; measuring how fast call-centre staff handle telephone calls; or how long staff are away from their desks. The American Civil Liberties Union (www.aclu.org) suggests that 'a fair electronic monitoring policy' would contain the following features:

- A notice to employees of the company's electronic monitoring practices
- Use of a signal to let an employee know when he or she is being monitored
- Employee access to all personal electronic data collected through monitoring
- No monitoring of areas designed for the health or comfort of employees
- The right to dispute and delete inaccurate data

- A ban on the collection of data unrelated to work performance
- Restrictions on the disclosure of personal data to others without the employees' permission

▶ Scoping by stakeholder attitude and behaviour

Understanding the attitudes and behaviour of stakeholders is critical to sustainable business success in the 21st century. This is why stakeholders appear throughout the seven steps described in this book. They are the actors who create specific triggers. They can also potentially play a number of other roles, from enthusiastic partners or compliant allies all the way to obstructive and seemingly narrow-minded opponents, especially when involved in what can be very emotive social and environmental issues.

That is why it is so important at the scoping stage to gauge what impact potential business strategies will have on different stakeholders. To be able to do this, it is necessary to have intelligence on who the key stakeholders are in any given circumstances, what their potential contribution might be and whether this contribution is a perceived help or hindrance. In the following sections, we describe some of the concerns that some generic stakeholder groups may raise, but for each company that undertakes a scoping exercise it will be necessary to verify actual attitudes and motivations through stakeholder surveys and dialogue (techniques for this are described in Step 6). Stakeholder dialogue should be a continuous process.

Employees

Whether as existing or potential employees, the attitude and behaviour of employee stakeholders will be a key influence on the effectiveness of business strategies — as a source of obstruction and opposition or, conversely, as a source of inspiration and innovation. For example, if a company wishes to recruit the very brightest graduates, it needs to be alert to research that is consistently showing that graduates regard a prospective employer's ethical standards as important and as a key determinant in choosing who they will work for. In a special report on 'Graduate Recruitment' reported in the *Financial Times* (24 October 2002), authors from Ernst & Young suggested that 'what we may be seeing is people becoming more wary about the standards of credentials of potential employers'.

Similarly, among existing employees, there is a trend for workers to take a greater level of interest in their company's approach to social, ethical and environmental issues. Employers who ignore employee concerns will find their staff, particularly their most talented staff, leaving for employers that can authentically demonstrate positive values. Where the workforce is highly skilled and therefore mobile, employees will not put up with companies that do not reflect their own values, as the following statistics show:

- In the 2003 Global Campus Monitor conducted by the company Environics International (now Globescan; see www.globescan.com) surveying the views of 1,200 undergraduates across the world's 20 largest economies, it was found that three in five people want to work for a company with values that are consistent with their own.

- There is increasing evidence that the proportion of people wanting to work for a responsible organisation is growing.

- Some 81% of young people have a strong belief in the power of responsible business practice to improve profitability over time.

- Corporate responsibility is increasingly the key factor in attracting and retaining a talented and diverse workforce.

Furthermore, employees are becoming more vocal and more adept at pressing their grievances if they feel they are victims of discrimination. New European-wide legislation on ageism and sex discrimination is likely to increase this trend. For companies to defend such charges is costly in terms of time and money — whether as a result of fines or out-of-court settlements. Employees are also looking for employers to help them respond to changes in working patterns and lifestyles that require them to juggle work and parenting, care for elderly relatives and housework by providing family-friendly workplace practices, such as teleworking and flexitime, and access to employee healthcare benefits.

The level of 'trust' and the loyalty between employee and employer are fragile, intangible quantities. The increasing sophistication and application of electronic monitoring of employees' use of computers and mobile telephones by employers is likely to be a battleground for future conflict.[11]

Investors

Like every other stakeholder group, investors are not a homogenous movement. Nevertheless, we are seeing a distinct trend as a significant number of investors are are seeking to play an increasing role in governance and the strategic direction of the companies in which they invest. To date, this has been most visible in a series of high-profile cases, such as Disney, ITV, Shell and Sainsbury's, where institutional investors have intervened either to block the appointment of a chairman or CEO or to force changes in the top leadership.

The motivations for taking a more proactive interest are many and varied, but for the company the result is a heightened requirement to listen, engage and explain. We do not believe it will take much of a change in the mind-set of such activist investors for them to incorporate CSR more directly in their approaches to

11   In the United Kingdom there is now a government-supported code on workplace monitoring; see www.informationcommissioner.gov.uk.

companies. Indeed, already a number of CSR-related issues — access to medicines, climate change, obesity — have gained high-profile traction with the investment community. Some investors — particularly mainstream investors — are driven by concerns about potential 'material' impact on performance. Others, in the socially responsible investment (SRI) community, have a mandate to encourage responsible business practices.

SRI combines investors' financial objectives with their concerns about social, environmental and ethical issues. There are four main approaches currently used by SRI investors with regard to taking into consideration CSR practices, either separately or in combination (see Table 5).

Approach	Description	Example
Negative screening	Investors exclude companies or sectors on the basis of social, environmental and ethical criteria	Sectors that may be excluded are those involving arms, nuclear power and tobacco products
Positive screening	Investors actively select companies on the basis of social, environmental and ethical performance	Companies that will be favoured include those that show respect for the environment and human rights
Engagement	Investors engage in dialogue to change company behaviour	Dialogue will include the encouragement of the development of policies on the environment (e.g. on climate change) and on questions of human rights (e.g. over operations in countries with a poor human rights record)
Shareholder activism	Shareholders attend AGMs to influence resolutions and so on	Shareholder activists may vote against the annual report and accounts

Table 5 **Socially responsible investment: four approaches**

Source: CSR Europe, Deloitte, and Euronext, *Investing in Responsible Business* (2003; www.csreurope.org/CSRESRISURVEY2003FINAL_pdf_media_public.aspx)

Investment funds are increasingly grouping together to add weight to their efforts to communicate with companies over what they regard as material issues. As reflected by the Carbon Disclosure Project and the Investor Network on Climate Change (see Box 19), global environmental problems are increasingly being seen by investors as being relevant to investment decisions. According to Sarah Murray, writing in the *Financial Times* in an article titled 'New Voices Entering the Fray' (16

Issues raised by investors

Human rights

Eight institutional investors, including Henderson Global Investors, CIS, Isis, Jupiter and Morley, have questioned business involvement in Myanmar (Burma), a country accused of human rights abuses.

Transparency

Insight Investment, a £68 billion fund-management arm of HBOS and covering all business sectors, has taken the initiative of publishing quarterly reports on its lobbying activities. This was done as part of a commitment to invest in a socially responsible way. This initiative can be seen as a step towards transparency in its lobbying activities. CIS (now part of CFS) is consulting on a new, customer-inspired CIS Socially Responsible Investment policy which it aims to introduce in 2005. It also publishes the CIS voting record at corporate AGMs and has committed to exercise its vote on all occasions.

Climate change

Some 35 major institutional investors, such as Connecticut Retirement Plans and Trust Funds (CRPTF), the Credit Suisse Group and the University Superannuation Scheme, representing more than US$4 trillion in assets, have launched the Carbon Disclosure Project (www.cdproject.net) in which they gathered investment-relevant information from the 500 largest companies in the world, by market capitalisation, concerning their greenhouse gas emissions.

Socioeconomic impacts

Communities

Ten big banks, including Barclays Royal Bank of Scotland, Citigroup and WestLB, have endorsed the Equator Principles, applicable to companies working on construction projects (such as dam, pipeline and power-plant projects). These principles were established by the International Finance Corporation (IFC) and are a set of voluntary guidelines allowing investors to consider the impact of pollution, human health and other socioeconomic factors before they offer loans to companies working on such large-scale construction projects (www.equator-principles.com).

Additionally, Citigroup has also developed its own policies, which go beyond the Equator Principles, for financing projects. For example, it will not finance projects that are a risk to 'fragile' or environmentally sensitive habitats. This policy reduces the risk to the financing proposition.

Government revenue

The Extractive Industries Transparency Initiative was announced by UK Prime Minister Tony Blair at the World Summit on Sustainable Development in Johannesburg, September 2002, as a multi-stakeholder effort including ten big investors such as ISIS Asset Management, Jupiter and Schroders. Its aim is to increase transparency over payments by companies to governments and government-linked entities, as well as transparency over revenues by those host-country governments (www.dfid.gov.uk/News/News/files/eiti_guide_b.htm).

Box 19 **Examples of issues raised or initiatives taken by groups of investors**
(continued opposite)

Issues raised by investors (continued)

Health issues in emerging markets

ISIS Asset Management and Universities Superannuation Scheme (USS) Ltd, in consultation with institutional investors, pharmaceutical companies and other informed organisations, has developed the Pharmaproject which focuses mainly on issues relating to access to patented medicines in less-developed countries. It is supported by investors who believe that the sector's response to the crisis could impact on shareholder value in the long term and who therefore want to enhance their understanding of how companies are addressing this issue (www.pharmaproject.org).

Box 19 (continued)

October 2003), 'S&P [Standard and Poor's] [is] reported to be considering cutting credit ratings of 15 Canadian utilities citing amongst other things increasingly unpredictable weather patterns and the Kyoto Protocol.'

Often, a specific event or incident might not be perceived as being material to earnings, but the question is whether it is symptomatic of broader problems. That was the question asked of BP's management by a number of investment funds following a number of specific health and safety problems in BP's Alaskan operations.

Investors use different tactics to interact with companies. These include proposing or supporting shareholder resolutions, publicising areas of disagreement with company management, encouraging reporting and disclosure, and monitoring and assessing company performance. Companies listed in more than one location have to juggle different CSR investment-related requirements. If listed in Australia, the Financial Services Act of 2002 requires disclosure statements on social and environmental issues; in South Africa, the Stock Exchange requires all listed firms to spell out AIDS-related issues; in the UK, the Association of British Insurers has requirements for environmental and social reporting for all its members (representing some 25% of shares traded on the London Stock Exchange). A lack of internationally agreed standards is a challenge for companies and investors alike.

We expect that institutional investors will increasingly take a stewardship approach to their investments and will become more and more attuned to longer-term performance issues rather than taking a short-term quick-fix 'returns-today' approach. Over the next five to ten years, corporations will improve their environmental and social disclosure in response to SRI investor demands. Even now, they are having to invest in personnel and systems to respond to the myriad of questionnaires and queries they receive from various bodies. More than 60% of some 100 top European companies have encountered higher levels of shareholder activism in 2003 and are 'beefing up' their investor-relations departments accordingly.[12] By

---

12   Reported in the January 2004 *Investor Relations Handbook* of *IR* magazine.

2010, CSR and a commitment to principles of sustainable development will be differentiators when a company deals with analysts and investors and one of the key questions that will be asked especially of certain companies in certain industries.

Consumers

As we saw in Step 1, there is a small but vocal and influential segment of 'vigilante' — or at least 'concerned' — consumers who are interested in a business's environmental and social track record. A positive record on CSR has, for these consumers, become a requirement for customer loyalty, provided other things such as price, quality and availability are equal (and, for a small minority, a good CSR record may mean they are willing to pay a price premium: for example, organic and fair-trade buyers).

Much attention with consumers so far has focused on so-called 'cause-related marketing' (defined by the BITC team as 'a commercial activity by which business and charities or causes form a partnership with each other to market an image, product or service to mutual benefit'). We believe that increasingly the emphasis is shifting to core marketing issues: how a product or service is used, disposed of and promoted and its availability. There are some obvious areas where consumer concerns are already having an impact:

- The issue of the use of advertising and the availability of products to specific market segments (e.g. to children)

- There are calls for companies producing alcoholic drinks and for companies promoting gambling to ensure responsible use of the products and services they provide

- Manufacturers and retailers of high-fat, high-sugar and high-salt foods (such as fast food and process foods) are facing claims that they are responsible for obesity

Concerns extend to a broad range of sectors over a wide range of issues. Take, for example, issues surrounding the disposal of discarded products (e.g. cars, white goods and products such as ink-jet laser printers) and of excess packaging. There is a body of research that points to a growing interest by consumers in the social, ethical and environmental performance and impact of corporations. Some report that consumers are willing to pay a premium for products that are 'more ethical'. However, such research is notoriously difficult to back up with comparative sales data, although with the increasing prevalence of supermarket loyalty cards it ought to be possible to generate this data in future.

Evidence of consumer concerns, and the willingness of consumers to act on those concerns, is provided by a survey carried out by Environics International (now Globescan) in G20 countries over the period 1999–2000. Some of the findings from this survey are given in Table 6. It can be seen from this table that a significant minority of consumers take account of a company's record for responsible behav-

Have you ever punished companies seen as being socially irresponsible?			
Response		Year	
	1999	2001	2002
Have done so	25	20	29
Have considered doing so	17	19	20
Have not considered doing so	51	54	44

Table 6 **Evidence of consumer concerns: responses rates (expressed as percentages) to the question 'Have you ever considered punishing companies seen as being socially irresponsible?', as reported in a survey of G20 countries, 1999–2002**

Source: Environics International (now Globescan), *CSR Monitor*, 2003

iour when making purchases. The table also shows a trend towards an increasing tendency to take action or to consider taking action.

In agreement with these findings, a MORI survey in 2003, reported in the *Financial Times* (4 December 2003), found that 17% of adults in the UK had boycotted a product on ethical grounds in the previous year, and 14% had bought a product from a company because of its ethical reputation. MORI says that 15% of the population can be defined as CSR activists — that is, 15% of people regularly act on their beliefs.

Some companies are responding to this expressed consumer interest and are attempting to create positive differentiation in the marketplace by promoting their CSR-related credentials and are engaging in cause-related marketing programmes as a way of appealing to niche consumer market segments. In doing so, however, companies are faced with a dilemma. On the one hand, consumers say they are interested in knowing more about corporate CSR activity, as illustrated by Figure 5(a), but, as highlighted in Step 1 in the section on the revolution of values (page 31), consumers also have serious doubts about the honesty with which companies tell their stories, as illustrated by Figure 5(b).

The view that consumers are interested in the CSR performance of companies is supported by the experience of Walter Dondi, Director of Co-op Adriatica, Italy's largest retailer:

> Our consumers are very sensitive to social and environmental issues
> . . . We have actively engaged with them on these issues in the last
> ten years, and they have become very aware as consumers. They
> especially ask for information on environmental policies, workers'
> rights and product safety.[13]

13   Quoted in CSR Europe, *Stakeholder Report, 2003*.

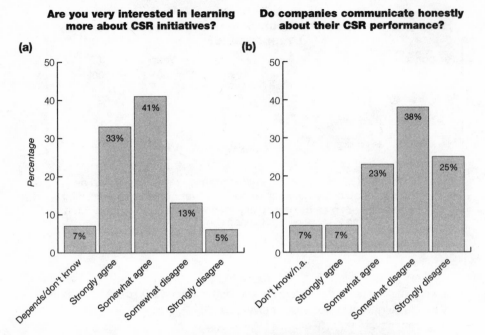

Figure 5 **(a) Response rates to the statement '[I am] very interested in learning more about CSR initiatives' (respondents from 25 countries, 2002); (b) Response rates to the statement 'Companies communicate honestly about their CSR performance' (respondents in G20 countries, excluding Japan, 2003)**

Source: Environics International (now Globescan)

An added dimension of consumer concern has come to the fore as an indirect result of geopolitical events of 9/11, with the terrorist attacks on the USA. Boycotts and attacks on Western companies, particularly US brands such as Coca-Cola and Kentucky Fried Chicken (KFC), are on the increase. In some markets this has led to the introduction of similar products produced by non-Western manufacturers, such as so-called 'Muslim' or 'Mecca' Cola. This has reinforced the need for companies to demonstrate their local credentials and the social and economic benefits that they bring. The Edelman research for the 2004 World Economic Forum — referred to in Step 1 in the section on the revolution of values (see pages 31, 33f.) — also suggests that in Europe there is currently some antipathy to the products of US-head-quartered companies in the aftermath of transatlantic tensions over the recent (2003) Iraq War.[14]

14   See page 34, footnote 19.

Business partners

The pressure for business-to-business (B2B) suppliers to adhere to particular standards of CSR performance, as well as to meet quality, delivery and price specifications, is increasing. We have both worked with major international companies that have been asked by their clients to supply data and information to verify their CSR business practices, from environmental impacts to labour standards. The Global Environmental Management Initiative (GEMI), in a March 2001 report titled 'New Paths to Business Value', noted that companies increasingly are required to be certified to the ISO 14001 standard for environmental management systems (EMSs) or to have an EMS to an equivalent standard:

> Bristol-Myers Squibb, IBM [and] Xerox have encouraged their suppliers to develop environmental systems consistent with ISO 14001. Ford, GM [General Motors] and Toyota have required their suppliers to obtain ISO 14001 certification (p. 7).

A twist in the changing expectations in B2B relationships is the development of a movement known as Know Your Customer. So far, this is focused largely on the financial-services sector — especially in the USA since the 2001 US Patriot Act was passed after 9/11 — where banks are being asked to vet the nature of their clients for security, anti-terrorism and fraud concerns and where lenders are being questioned as to whether recipients of loans are engaged in potentially environmentally or socially damaging infrastructure development projects. We can see this extending to other sectors.

Governments — at the national and local levels — are large purchasers of goods and services. In industrial countries this is estimated as representing 25% of GDP.[15] The scale of government purchasing can have a significant impact on changes to manufacturing processes and product specifications. For example, drawing on various sources, the Worldwatch Institute concluded that requirements by the US government in the early 1990s that federal agencies buy only computer equipment that met the Energy Star programme standards on energy efficiency was the trigger to such computers becoming the industry norm.[16] It was estimated that the US government purchased some 7% of new computers worldwide at the time.

Some firms are now proactively using their purchasing power to encourage changes in the design and manufacturing process as a means of demonstrating their own CSR credentials and commitment to sustainability. Firms purchasing back-office functions and services through outsourcing arrangements are setting social, ethical and environmental standards in tender documents and final contracts. Some, such as Coro Strandberg, previously a director of the Vancouver City Savings Credit Union (VanCity) and now an independent consultant,[17] predict that increased campaigning from NGOs will make companies vulnerable to attacks

15   As reported in OECD, *Greener Public Purchasing: Issues and Practical Solutions* (Paris: OECD, 2001), cited in Worldwatch Institute, 'Purchasing Power', paper 166, July 2003.
16   Worldwatch Institute, 'Purchasing Power', paper 166, July 2003.
17   Quoted in VanCity Savings Credit Union, *The Future of Corporate Social Responsibility* (2002).

brought to bear at their weakest links, which can often show up in their outsourced operations and are difficult to anticipate. This will probably be one of the most important triggers for small businesses — as large businesses put pressure on their business suppliers to demonstrate compliance as part of the tender process, as can be seen from the example of VanCity.

VanCity

Vancouver City Savings Credit Union (VanCity), a Canadian financial-services business, requires all its suppliers to conform to its ethical policy. Each year VanCity places around US$70 million of business with 1,500 suppliers. It has been training employees to apply the policy that commits it to actively seek suppliers that practise progressive employee relations, contribute to the well-being of their communities and respect the environment.

That such pressure is being applied is supported by the findings of a survey of small businesses by AccountAbility, BITC, the British Institute of Directors (IOD) and the British Chambers of Commerce (BCC). They found that in the preceding 12 months:

- 60% of small and medium-sized enterprises (SMEs) had been asked questions about their safety policies and performance by their customers in big business.

- 43% had been asked questions on environmental policies and practices.

- 17% had been asked questions on social and community policies and practices.[18]

However, the degree of control a business customer can exert will vary from market to market and from issue to issue. Some issues, such as child labour, create dilemmas caused by differing cultural values or customs, so the impact of setting 'global' standards needs careful consideration (for a discussion of the dilemmas posed by the issue of child labour, see Box 20).

Non-governmental organisations

There is great diversity in the structure, mode of operation and objectives of NGOs, and part of the challenge for business is to gain the know-how to distinguish between the many varieties and learn how to respond to them. Some NGOs may be campaigning directly to change corporate behaviour; in other instances, the focus may be, for example, to change the regulation of business such as the International Right to Know (IRTK) campaign in the USA.

18   Business in the Community (BITC), 'Engaging SMEs in Community and Social Issues' (2002); downloadable pdf version available at www.bitc.org.uk.

We have always been uncomfortable with a simplistic 'no child labour, full stop!' line. Taking steps to enforce a complete ban on any use of child labour may salve the conscience of Western consumers — but it may not always be the most socially responsible strategy. Both of us have visited projects in Asia, South Africa or South America that have to deal with the consequences of a unilateral imposition on suppliers by Western multinationals of a stipulation of no child labour. Sometimes, children are the main family breadwinner, and so no work can lead to child prostitution or work in the unsupervised and unsafe informal sector. Indeed, as the HIV/AIDS pandemic spreads and more heads of household in countries such as South Africa are minors, this issue is going to need a more nuanced response. Leading NGOs in the field such as Save the Children already recognise this and are championing pragmatic partnerships that combine some work in safe conditions with education and family support.

Box 20 **Supply-chain management dilemmas: child labour**

The International Right to Know (IRTK) campaign

The IRTK campaign includes the American Federation of Labor (AFL)–Congress of Industrial Organisations (CIO), Amnesty International USA, Oxfam America and the Sierra Club. The aim of the 200 groups backing the IRTK campaign is that the USA should extend its right-to-know laws geographically, to cover US corporate activities abroad, and, qualitatively, to also cover important non-environmental issues.

Source: the 2003 *Lifeworth Annual Review of Corporate Responsibility*, supported by the New Academy of Business and *The Journal of Corporate Citizenship* (Greenleaf Publishing); www.lifeworth.net.

Media coverage of the relationship between NGOs and business tends to focus on conflict. In practice there is a spectrum. Some continue to be implacably opposed to business. For such groups, an invitation to partner with business would be akin to putting Dracula in charge of a blood-bank drive! However, interestingly, as NGOs grow in sophistication they can — through collaborative partnerships with business and with intellectual capital of their own — become market makers. They can provide routes and channels to new markets and can share information that leads to product development (for example, Greenpeace and ozone-friendly fridges). They can influence consumer demand, change supply-chain dynamics and prompt new laws. They can even play a role in determining whether a market is feasible — such as in the debate surrounding the use and development of GMOs. Some NGOs are reaching out to business to form partnerships as a way of furthering their own agenda and accessing resources, offering value in the form of market intelligence, networks and brand association. Just as firms can collaborate with another company in one area of commercial activity and compete with it in another, so NGOs may collaborate with, and campaign against, the same company, as was the case with Greenpeace and BP.

In future, we are envisaging some business–NGO collaborations as commercial joint ventures. Most partnerships, so far, remain at the stage of strategic philanthropy or good corporate community investment. Some are further along the spectrum such as in certification of products meeting fair trade, environmental or minimum approved labour standards — such as the Ethical Trading Initiative, the Marine Stewardship Council and the Forest Stewardship Council, and the Fair Labor Association agreements with companies such as The Gap. Some relationships are evolving further into advice and consulting — particularly to well-known multinationals in the public eye and to LDC SMEs — as we discuss with examples such as Starbucks and Conservation International and Cathay Pacific and TRAFFIC-Hong Kong).

Starbucks and Conservation International

Starbucks has worked with CI since 1998 to promote sustainable coffee growing. The NGO's Conservation Coffee programme encourages shade-grown coffee, the traditional method which protects biodiversity. The partnership has developed this approach in Mexico, Colombia and Peru, and made shade-grown coffee available in Starbucks' shops — at a significant price premium which delivers better livelihoods for the farmers.

Starbucks has also loaned $2.5 million to help capitalize CI's Verde Ventures microfinance fund. The fund provides loans to small-scale coffee producers. CI will use the money to address some of the financial challenges facing small-scale coffee producers, providing loans in the run-up to harvest and afterwards to bridge the income gap until cash is received from the sale of the crop. Most of the loans will be distributed in Central and South America.

Cathay Pacific and TRAFFIC-Hong Kong

TRAFFIC-Hong Kong is one of the 22 offices of an NGO network that monitors wildlife trade globally. TRAFFIC-Hong Kong partnered with Cathay Pacific Airways Ltd to improve the airline's ability to stop the smuggling of rare plants and species on its planes. TRAFFIC trained baggage handlers to recognise signs of illegal flora and fauna in luggage and boxes. Halting illegal shipments has helped Cathay Pacific avoid fines and strengthened the airline's environmental reputation.

Nonetheless, we already see some glimpses of more commercial partnerships which we believe will be one of the ways that businesses find and exploit corporate social opportunities in the future. Illustrating this are FedEx and Environmental Defense, and some of the examples of corporate social opportunity quoted later in this chapter (DaimlerChrysler, Shell and Norsk Hydro, page 91; mmO$_2$ and e-San Ltd, page 93). There may be analogies with the evolution over time of the partnerships between business and universities — in that, nowadays, there is a spectrum from charitable donations and corporate sponsorships through to fully commercial relationships to exploit university-derived intellectual property. How responsible businesses handle this putative evolution of some of their relationships with NGOs may well have something to learn from the university analogy — which we discuss further in Step 5.

FedEx and Environmental Defense

Environmental Defense has worked with FedEx to develop a hybrid electric delivery truck that will slash pollution and save fuel. This is part of its work with companies to incorporate environmental considerations into business decisions, creating solutions that make environmental and business sense.

The FedEx project should fundamentally change the environmental profile of FedEx's fleet of 30,000 vehicles. The new vehicle cuts fuel use in half and achieves a 90% reduction in exhaust emissions compared to 2001 performance. The OptiFleet E700 made its debut in May 2003, and FedEx committed to purchase 20 of the hybrid electric vehicles, to begin operation in four US cities over the winter of 2003/2004. Assuming they prove their viability in real operating conditions, FedEx says they could replace the existing fleet over the next ten years.

Telenor Invest, Marubeni Corporation and Gonophone with the Grameen Bank

Grameen Phone (GP) is a commercial venture in Bangladesh. It is a joint venture between Grameen Telecom (GTC) — part of the non-profit Grameen Bank (GB) — and Telenor Invest AS of Norway, Marubeni Corporation of Japan and Gonophone of the USA. GP was granted a nationwide licence for cellular mobile phones in 1996. As a part of its operation, GP establishes the network, and operates and provides telephone connections.

Under the Village Phone programme, GTC provides cellular phones to selected borrowers of GB who then sell phone time to other rural villagers — providing both a vital service in rural areas and much-needed new income through the micro-enterprises.

Governments, intergovernmental organisations, international organisations and regulatory bodies

Individual governments and their regulatory agencies are passing legislation and creating new rules in a myriad of social and environmental areas that have a direct impact on corporations. Tracking and keeping on top of regulatory developments is an expertise that companies have long recognised as a necessity — the breadth and range of issues that are being codified into laws are, however, causing concern that 'red tape' will stifle entrepreneurial drive and growth.

A further trend is for some governments to play a role in actively encouraging CSR:[19]

- The Danish government has created the Copenhagen Centre as a source of good practice in CSR and cross-sectoral partnerships between business and other parts of society.

19 To mark the Italian presidency of the EU, a European conference was held in November 2003 on how public policy could encourage CSR, with individual EU governments talking about the initiatives they were taking.

- In Spain the national and regional governments, politicians from all the political parties, business, unions, civil society and academia are represented on a national taskforce debating how best to stimulate more CSR.

- In the Netherlands, the Dutch government, with eight leading universities, has launched a three-year inquiry into CSR.

- The British government consulted on a proposed international strategy for the promotion of CSR in spring 2004. The recommendations will serve as input for the EU Commission's new policy paper on CSR.[20]

Similarly, commitment is seen at the international level, as shown by the following examples:

- The EU has been running a Multi-stakeholder Forum on CSR that was due to report in the summer of 2004.[21]

- Leaders of overseas development agencies of some seven countries met in Sweden in 2004 to discuss their role in promoting CSR through development assistance.

- At the 1999 World Economic Forum in Davos, Switzerland, Kofi Annan, the UN Secretary-General, launched the Global Compact (www.unglobalcompact.org).

A survey of CEOs in 2002 found that 29% of firms representing 59% of the market capital of the FTSE 100 index have made commitments to one or more international standards, such as the Universal Declaration of Human Rights, the International Labour Organisation (ILO) Tripartite Declaration of Principles concerning Multinational Enterprises and Social Policy, and the OECD Guidelines for Multinational Enterprises (www.oecd.org). Five years previously only a handful had made such commitments. Critics object to the voluntary nature of some of these initiatives and that any company can subscribe, irrespective of its track record. Thus, in its report, *Behind the Mask: The Real Face of Corporate Social Responsibility* (January 2004), Christian Aid argue for a

> framework of international regulation, backed up by national legislation, to ensure the enforcement of real social responsibility on the corporate world. Introducing the threat of prosecution and legal action, with resulting detailed disclosure of company documents, would create a powerful incentive for companies to behave responsibly.

More broadly, the globalisation of markets has prompted many to argue for global governance systems and institutions, either through new mechanisms or strengthened Bretton Wood institutions (e.g. the World Bank and the International

---

20 This consultation document was rejected by a coalition of NGOs; see *Financial Times*, 'Voluntary groups shun DTI initiative', 29 May 2004.
21 http://europa.eu.int/comm/enterprise/csr/forum.htm

Monetary Fund [IMF]). We do not see this as an 'either/or' situation — either regulation or voluntary initiatives. Rather, we believe that internationally, as at the national level, there has to be an intelligent balance between legal regulation and individual voluntary action — action taken by businesses because they believe it is in their own enlightened self-interest.

▶ Benchmarking

One way a company can learn about potential strategies is to compare its own performance and actions with those of other, similar companies by use of benchmarking tools. For example, the company can note, and learn from, how key competitors or industry leaders are managing particular issues or situations.

There are a variety of formal CSR-related benchmarking surveys that companies can sign up to that are run by commercial consultants or by intermediary organisations. The London Benchmarking Group — run by the Corporate Citizenship Company — enables participating companies to measure and compare their corporate community investment expenditure against that of other firms; comparability is assured as the same methodology is used for each firm (www.lbg-online.net).

As mentioned briefly above regarding rating institutions and indexes for use by investors, another initiative is the Corporate Responsibility Index of BITC. The second annual Corporate Responsibility Index, covering 139 firms, was published in March 2004 (www.bitc.org.uk; material from this Index informs our discussion and examples of corporate good practice later in this book; for details of how the Index was constructed, see Step 5, pages 168f.]). Now, an Australian version of the Index is also being run, by the St James's Ethics Centre, Sydney, with support from Ernst and Young, Australia and BITC, as reported in the *Sydney Morning Herald* in an article titled '111 Ways to Make it on to the Ethical Register' (19 February 2004).

Equally helpful can be comparisons drawn up by in-house teams, as highlighted by the example of firms A, B and C in which we benchmark three food and beverage companies and their different responses to issues relating to obesity.

In Step 1 we heard from Jeremy Pelczer, CEO of American Water, on his 'personal trigger' (page 23). He also references the importance of benchmarking in determining good practice. On the impact of benchmarking:[22]

> It had not escaped our notice [at RWE Thames Water] that some oil and gas companies had been getting heavily criticised for alleged failures to understand their social and environmental impact — that was an important benchmark and driver for us to look closely at our own policies and practices.

22   Jeremy Pelczer, President and CEO of American Water, part of the RWE Group, in an interview with the authors, October 2003. At the time of interview he was COO of RWE Thames Water.

**Obesity and the food and beverage sector:
three hypothetical responses**

Firm A

Firm A established an advisory council, commissioned independent research and formed a collaborative partnership with a non-governmental organisation to consider product development options.

Firm B

Firm B sold off to another company the business unit that produces the controversial product line.

Firm C

Firm C committed itself to adhere to an externally monitored code of conduct regarding the marketing of its products to children and agreed to arbitration if dispute should arise.

Box 21 **Obesity and the food and beverage sector: three hypothetical responses**

▶ Scoping the future development of issues: scenario planning[23]

Some businesses use scenarios to help them vision the potential future and to plan responses. In some cases, this involves building their own scenarios from scratch; in other instances, it involves 'borrowing' scenarios already created by another organisation. Scenarios are not predictions of the future but are alternative, internally consistent, pictures of possible futures.

A business wishing to use scenario planning to scope the CSR issues it might face can visit the website of the Challenge! Forum, at www.chforum.org, which is a rich resource for data and scenarios. The director of the Forum, Dr Oliver Sparrow, a former scenario-planner for Shell, explains there that the output of the process for any business is usually the conclusion that to operate in a complex world where there are many stakeholders, with often conflicting views, one needs more than a single business criterion (e.g. profit or zero accidents). Instead, it becomes clear that one is presented with a wide range of desirable outcomes that have to be traded off against and balanced with each other.

Two companies that utilise the scenario-planning tool are Shell and Novo Nordisk.

---

23 This section is adapted and paraphrased from the Challenge! Forum website, at www. chforum.org. All quotes by Dr Oliver Sparrow are taken from this website.

Shell

The oil company Shell has worked with scenarios for decades. The early work was a call to action. The oil industry had changed, former truths were no longer true and previous norms and values no longer worked. The subsequent scenario rounds began to stress the need for complex, coherent values: was Shell to be thought of as existing 'for' the shareholders, or was it to be aimed at satisfying a broader group, not least of them national governments? Latterly, the stress seems to have moved more to consider how Shell fits into the developing transnational culture or cultures, and how to interpret its capabilities to that culture.

Novo Nordisk

Novo Nordisk, the Danish-headquartered diabetes care company, developed its own scenarios in 2002 called Diabetes 2020, which integrate CSR issues with the broader business strategy (see figure, below).

According to Lars Rebien Sørensen, president and CEO of Novo Nordisk, writing in the company's 2002 sustainability report (see www.novonordisk.com):

> Defeating diabetes is not just a business proposition — diabetes is a huge individual and societal problem, the consequences of which the world's leaders are only beginning to understand. As a company we deal with the rapidly growing epidemic of diabetes. We cannot solve the enormous problems of hunger, we cannot overcome illiteracy, or provide housing, sanitation or decently paid work to everyone. But what we can do is to acknowledge these factors and identify where and how we can make a difference.

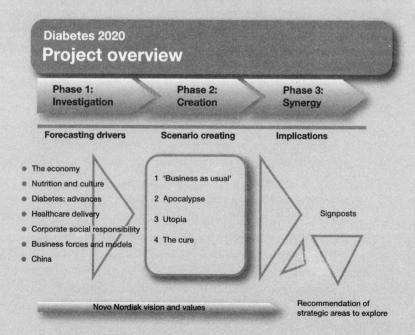

Source: Lise Kingo, EABIS Conference, Copenhagen Business School, September 2003.

▶ Scoping in different circumstances

Naturally, the underlying causes of triggers that matter most for one company or another, and what these causes might mean for it, varies greatly. For example, a company in the midst of a merger or acquisition, undertaking due diligence, will be looking to scope social and environmental contingent liabilities. A company entering a new market in the developing world will be scoping in the context of different cultural values and norms. A start-up business will be able to consider all key business strategies in the light of CSR-related risks and opportunities and the values to which it wants to adhere.

For a merger or acquisition

Firms may need to scope the relevance of triggers and their implications in the context of a merger or acquisition — or indeed, the prospect of a merger or acquisition may be a trigger in its own right. During the writing of this book, one of the largest supermarket chains in the UK, Safeway, was the subject of an intense takeover battle; the 'battle' was eventually won by Morrisons, but the bidding process involved all the other major retailers as well as a legion of corporate financiers, lawyers and PR advisers. We would like to think that environmental and social considerations might have formed part of the due diligence undertaken. Realistically, the probability of that happening in such cases is still some way off. However, some of the CSR issues and questions that might be raised by a takeover of a company such as Safeway or in other mergers and acquisitions, include the following:

- How can any downsizing of staffing at the company headquarters and in stores, branches or offices that are subsequently sold be done responsibly?

- What are the implications for suppliers and to the winning concern in relation to payment and other terms of trade and in relation to balancing different stakeholders (e.g. customers, shareholders and suppliers)?

- How are suppliers that lose their orders in the merged operation to be handled?[24] For example:
  - Are there transitional arrangements in place?
  - If there is to be an upgrading of standards, are programmes to be set up to help suppliers meet the tougher quality standards?

- Is an analysis to be made of existing environmental and social good practice at the firm being taken over, including whether any of these might be appropriate for migration to the new, combined operation?

---

24 At the time of writing, Safeway's Caribbean banana suppliers were lobbying hard to protect their contracts.

- Have opportunities been identified for the new, larger company to generate more positive environmental and social impacts, for example through
diversity training and employment or in the use of environmental packaging?

- Is there a possibility for the 'creative theft' from other companies of good
practice, skills and know-how in CSR-related fields to be applied to the
merged company?

For entrance to a new market in another cultural context

We believe that there is increasing convergence of the major issues of environmental and social impact around the world. Nevertheless, some issues are more
important than others, depending on the country concerned. Issues obviously do
vary across regions and industry sectors. According to Anglo American, a leading
mining and natural resources multinational:

> Clearly the issue of HIV/AIDS and black economic empowerment are
> most pertinent to South Africa. In Latin American and Canada issues
> connected with the rights of indigenous peoples are of significance.
> 'Green/environmental' issues look larger as risks in Europe than
> some of the social risk areas which are of greatest concern in the
> developing countries.[25]

This view is echoed by DHL, a provider of express logistics and freight:

> Clearly issues such as HIV/AIDS and human rights will have more
> impact in some parts of the world than others. Likewise, some
> countries, for example the Nordic area, are much further advanced
> in their response to environmental concerns than others, where
> perhaps the focus is on building efficient infrastructure and dealing
> with poverty. DHL does not have one-size fits all approach and seeks
> to develop an appropriate approach locally, which is guided by global
> values.[26]

Our own experience in South America and South Africa confirms some of these
distinctions. In countries such as Brazil and other parts of Central and South
America we would add issues of basic poverty eradication and the ways in which
business can contribute to improving education as a route out of poverty. In many
emerging markets there are also major issues of good governance — and the role
that business can play both in relation to its own corporate governance and in
relation to good public governance. In China, there are especially issues of labour

---

.25   Quoted in J. Nelson, International Business Leaders Forum and the Kennedy School of Govern-
      ment, Harvard University, 'Values and Value', paper prepared for the World Economic Forum
      in Davos, Switzerland, 2004.
26   *Ibid.*

rights, such as the pressure from employees themselves to be given more overtime. Campaigns such as Publish What You Pay are helping to crystallise these issues.

Publish What You Pay

The Publish What You Pay campaign aims to help citizens of resource-rich developing countries hold their governments accountable for the management of revenues from the oil, gas and mining industries. Natural resource revenues are an important source of income for governments of over 50 developing countries, including Angola, Congo-Brazzaville, Kazakhstan and Venezuela. When properly managed, these revenues should serve as a basis for poverty reduction, economic growth and development. The Publish What You Pay coalition of over 200 NGOs worldwide calls for the mandatory disclosure of the payments made by oil, gas and mining companies to all governments for the extraction of natural resources. This is a necessary first step towards a more accountable system for the management of natural resource revenues in resource-rich developing countries. The campaign was launched by George Soros and founded by Global Witness, CAFOD, Open Society Institute, Oxfam, Save the Children UK and Transparency International UK (www.publishwhatyoupay.org).

For a new business starting operations

Think back to Pohjoisranta — the Finnish PR company discussed in Step 1 (see page 20). For them, the starting point was to determine the values by which the founding owners wanted to run the business and then to determine how to live those values in practice. A further example is the car-leasing business Going Green.

Going Green

A new start-up with which we are familiar, Going Green (www.goingreen.co.uk), has the UK licence for distribution of a new electric car that has been designed and manufactured in Bangalore, India. Apart from the environmental credentials, the founders of Going Green had to satisfy themselves on the labour, health and safety conditions under which the cars are manufactured — and, although it might seem premature, on the recyclable content of the cars. In marketing the cars the company has deliberately tried to avoid an earnest 'save the world' pitch and, instead, make heightened environmental consciousness 'cool'. On the community side, there might be some opportunities in the future to develop educational programmes for schools based on the car, which would also help to build awareness of the car.

Some of the CSR issues facing start-ups include the following:

- Minimise consumption of energy, water and other natural resources, and emissions of hazardous substances; maximise use of recycled and recyclable materials; increase the durability of products; and minimise packaging through effective design ('reduce, re-use and recycle').

- Establish policies to ensure the health and safety of all employees — which should then be known to employees.

- Involve employees in business decisions that affect them and will improve the work environment: for example, through operating 'open-book policies' and helping employees to understand financial statements.

- Provide training opportunities and mentoring so that promotion from within the organisation is maximised; be open to job-splitting, flexitime and other forms of work–life balance and family-friendly policies.

- Make sure that all staff know that there are explicit policies against discrimination in hiring, salary, promotion, training or termination of any employee on the basis of gender, race, age, ethnicity, disability, sexual orientation or religion.

- When hiring, don't just ask friends or work colleagues but think creatively about where to advertise, about the job and person specification, and whether there are any local employability schemes, e.g. run by a local council or big local employer to help find work for the homeless or dis-abled candidates.

- Encourage employee volunteering in the community and back this up with financial contributions and help in-kind; make some of the business's products or services available free or at cost to charitable and community projects; and look for opportunities to make surplus product and redundant equipment available to local schools, charities and community organisations.

▶ Scoping what corporate social opportunities are possible

In the Introduction, we described corporate social opportunities as falling into one or more of three groups:

- New products or services, or innovation in existing products and services

- Providing for unserved or under-served markets

- New ways of organising the business through new business models

Managers can use this categorisation to help focus discussion on potential strategies, stimulating ideas and creating tough, specific questioning:

- Could the strategy help lead to innovation in products and services?

- Could the strategy lead to the servicing of new or under-served markets?

● Does the strategy suggest a different business model?

In this section, we provide some examples of how some companies have found their own corporate social opportunities. The examples we relate contain a mix of product and service innovation, market development and variations on traditional business models, but we have presented them under three main headings for ease of reference.

Innovations in products and services

> In effect, every industrial society enters a race between the rising use of materials and energy and the growing efficiency and effectiveness of its technology. Over time, efficiency and effectiveness tend to win ... At that moment, society as a whole takes a definite tilt toward greenness.
>
> *Peter Schwartz, Global Business Network, 2003*[27]

The most common examples of corporate social opportunity are to be found in the field of environmental innovation, thanks to growing interest in conservation, tough environmental regulation and rapid technological developments. For instance, car manufacturers are investing heavily in developing more efficient vehicles that use traditional fuels as well as hybrid cars, such as Toyota's Prius. Prius® is a hybrid vehicle capable of running on gasoline or electricity. Hybrids are certified to stringent emission levels in the USA — most notably in California.

Also in the area of cleaner transportation, there are some interesting collaborative inter-industry research and development (R&D) projects under way, such as that between DaimlerChrysler, Shell and Norsk Hydro. Environmental drivers were also the trigger for the creation of a new service created by IdleAire Technologies Corporation.

However, product development as illustrated by examples from Procter & Gamble and Unilever, is not driven solely by environmental factors. Social triggers such as healthcare are increasingly driving innovation.

The servicing of new or under-served markets

The benefits of new technology are often slow to penetrate into low-income and developing-world markets. The company Smart Communications has addressed this problem in the Philippines in an initiative to make mobile communications available in rural areas.

However, it would be wrong to think of corporate social opportunities as being appropriate only for low-income and developing-world markets, as illustrated by the examples of Nestlé and mmO$_2$.

---

27 P. Schwartz, *Inevitable Surprises Thinking Ahead in a Time of Turbulence* (New York: Gotham Books, 2003).

DaimlerChrysler, Shell and Norsk Hydro

A Shell-branded hydrogen station has opened in Reykjavik, Iceland. The station refuels DaimlerChrysler fuel cell buses. It uses Norsk Hydro plant to produce hydrogen from water by electrolysis. As with all of Iceland's electricity, the power for this comes from hydro and geothermal. Shell plans to open similar hydrogen stations in Washington DC and Tokyo. Other stations will be built in Hamburg and Berlin. This is part of a wider public–private joint venture in Iceland which has become the first country to undertake a shift to a hydrogen-energy economy. If the project succeeds, the island nation expects to gain complete freedom from dependence on oil or coal by 2030. In doing so, it will also eliminate its main sources of greenhouse gas emissions. Iceland currently produces more greenhouse gas emissions per head than any other country.

Source: *Renewable Energy World*, July/August 2003

IdleAire Technologies Corporation

IdleAire Technologies Corporation is a small business in Knoxville, Tennessee. It has developed a technology that allows long-haul truck drivers to heat and cool their cabs without having to idle their engines. This involves connecting to heat and air units above parking spaces at truck stops. The 1.3 million long-haul trucks operating in the USA currently waste 4.4 *billion* gallons of diesel fuel each year when drivers stop to rest but leave their engine idling (www.idleaire.com).

Procter & Gamble

Procter & Gamble has introduced a new product, Nutristar®, to combat the problem of 'hidden hunger' in developing countries, reflecting Procter & Gamble's vision for its food and beverage business, which is focused on developing foods that provide 'superior health and nutrition benefits on a global scale'.

Tests in Tanzania found that Nutristar® had a measurable impact on the physiques of children who took it. It also led to greater concentration and achievement in school. In the Philippines the 'taller, stronger, smarter' tag was copied by other producers without justification, which confused the market. At the time of writing (March 2004), we interviewed Peter White, Associate Director of Corporate Social Development, and he indicated that Procter & Gamble are reviewing their options for Nutristar® but remain committed to the concept of corporate social opportunities.

Unilever

International consumer marketing firm Unilever has developed a number of product lines that appeal to lower-spending market niches, adding value to the products by enriching them with vitamins and essential minerals. In Ghana, Annapurna salt is fortified with Idokine K-15, supporting preventive healthcare for pregnant women. It is packaged in small portions and is priced accordingly. This was developed as a result of a partnership between the company, UNICEF and the Ghanaian Ministry of Health.

Hindustan Lever

Competitor activity and the traditional behaviour of Indian consumers led Hindustan Lever Ltd, a division of Unilever, to develop the Wheel detergent formula using a reduced oil-to-water ratio, reducing potentially harmful environmental impacts when consumers wash clothes in rivers and public water supplies. The product is manufactured at decentralised factories, distributed by small vendor units — the 'bicycle brigades' — to reach rural areas and sold at low prices, matching consumer spending ability and patterns. According to a report from the *Financial Times*, titled 'Final frontier for shampoo sellers' (20 May 2003), core rural markets generate some 50% of Hindustan Lever's turnover.

Source: Unilever *2002 Social Report*

Smart Communications

In the Philippines, telecommunications operator Smart Communications has created a Buddy e-Load product offer by which small bits of unused airtime can be passed on to those in under-served (often rural) areas through a network of sales agents. According to the *New York Times*, in an article titled 'Cellular phone company gains by thinking small' (17 October 2003), this 'telecommunications in sachets' business model led to a growth of 700,000 users in just two months, so that telecommunications services now reach 11 million out of a population of 76 million.

Nestlé

In institutions such as hospitals and homes for senior citizens there is a concern that patients and residents do not receive food of a sufficiently high nutritional value and may suffer malnutrition as a result. This failing is not necessarily a result of poor catering arrangements as such, but some patients and elderly people may have difficulty eating foods such as fresh fruit and vegetables. Also, in the West, despite good, reasonably priced food being available in most areas, there are still some (predominantly low-income) areas where fresh food is unavailable (e.g. on housing estates where there are no local shops because of problems with crime) or where there is less demand for such food perhaps because of poor health education and so on. Children in these areas may not receive adequate nutrition, and this is a problem that can be addressed through meals provided at school.

The Swiss-based global food company Nestlé has a range of 'branded active ingredients' in some 30 markets worldwide. For example, Caring® in Switzerland and Nutriservices in France are product ranges designed for institutional markets such as hospitals, homes for senior citizens, schools and so on. These products are enriched with proteins, calcium and fibre to ensure those eating the food receive a balanced diet with nutrients they require to maintain or improve health. (For more detail, see the company's 2001 annual report.)

mmO$_2$ and e-San Ltd, Oxford University

British telecommunications company mmO$_2$ is partnering with e-San Ltd of the Department of Engineering Science at Oxford University to look at the possibility of making innovative use of mobile technology to address a health issue very much associated with urban, developed economies and regions — asthma.

For people with asthma, an attack can come at any time and there is no easy way to predict how bad it will be. Many sufferers keep a hand-written, twice-daily record of their breathing. Once every 12 weeks they take this record to their doctor and have their treatment adjusted based on the results. It is not the best way to treat a condition that now affects some 3.4 million people in the United Kingdom alone and is an increasingly serious problem across Europe and the USA.

But what if sufferers could be in touch with their doctor every time a bad attack seemed imminent and get immediate advice on how to prevent it? Mobile technology is making this possible for the first time. mmO$_2$ is working on a one-year trial with 100 asthma sufferers aged between 12 and 55 years in the Thames Valley area of the United Kingdom, where the incidence of asthma is higher than in any other part of the country. Each patient is given an mmO$_2$ xda combined phone and mobile computer. This is fitted with an electronic peak-flow meter, containing reporting and analysis software. When the person breathes into the meter, the xda automatically records the person's condition and the results are transmitted immediately to a computer that charts them against expected trends. Should any readings cause concern then the person's doctor can be notified and can instantly advise that person on how to adjust his or her treatment or if a visit to the surgery is required.

Oxford University's e-San Ltd is exploring how mobiles can improve the self-monitoring and self-management of chronic illnesses. Early results from the trial show that patients are recording their condition more accurately, a key step in pre-empting and preventing acute attacks. There could also be benefits in the treatment of other ailments, such as hypertension and diabetes, where patients also take care of their own treatment. This project will provide mmO$_2$ with useful experience for developing other wireless applications to support health-related services. (For more details, see the July 2003 CSR report from mmO$_2$.)

Use of new business models

We can summarise corporate social opportunities in new business models in terms of how a business is developed, how finance is raised, how products and services are delivered to market, how a business is staffed and how purchasing practices are organised.

Business development

One new business model is based on the idea of where a business looks for sources of innovation and for help in developing new products and services. This may involve working with an NGO either at the initiative of the NGO or of the business — as we saw above at page 90 and with the example of IBM with SeniorNet quoted in the Introduction. Equally, it may be with a social enterprise (see page 98 below) or a university department or an international agency. In the case of Procter & Gamble's PuR® product (below) it involved collaboration with several such partners. The point here is an openness to approaches from, and a willingness to turn to, a more eclectic range of potential collaborators. Where this results in new intellectual property and corporate social opportunities, there will obviously be issues of how to share fairly any resulting profits. We suggested in the Introduction that having a robust process for agreeing up-front such allocation of rewards would be one of the critical success factors for a business moving to CSO. How to handle this is discussed in Step 5, page 240.

A major problem facing the world is the supply of safe drinking water and the provision of sanitation:

- 1.2 billion people lack access to safe drinking water

- 2.4 billion people have inadequate sanitation

The UN Millennium Development Goals include the target to halve by 2015 the proportion of people that lack access to safe drinking water and to halve the number of those without access to adequate sanitation. Currently, the public sector provides 90% of water services worldwide. However, the World Bank predicts that by 2010 1.75 billion people could be serviced by a private-sector water company. Two companies that are addressing this issue in very different ways are RWE Thames Water and Procter & Gamble.

The provision of safe drinking water and sanitation: RWE Thames Water

Private-sector companies such as RWE Thames Water have the expertise to contribute to addressing development challenges. But business risks generally preclude them from operating in the areas of greatest need. Some help can be given on a philanthropic basis, but this will not make a significant impact on such a vast problem. What is needed is a new business model in which risks are reduced to the point at which a low rate of return can be accepted, for the affordable delivery of water and sanitation to those in greatest need. RWE Thames Water is currently investigating such a model, in partnership with two other major businesses and three international NGOs. The partnership aims to establish new ways of providing water and sanitation to the urban poor of the developing world, with each of the partners contributing their particular skills. This will be done using a combination of aid and local funding for infrastructure provision, and in close consultation with the communities who will receive the service.

The provision of safe drinking water: Procter & Gamble

The UN Millennium Development Goals involve, among other things, the delivery of safe drinking water to 125,000 new people every day. Procter and Gamble's PuR® water purifier in a sachet is a commercial product enabling people in the developing world to decontaminate water in their own homes and to store that water safely (for more information, see the company press release of 19 June 2003, www.pghsi.com). When we challenged Peter White, Associate Director of Corporate Sustainable Development, as to why Procter & Gamble has not made PuR® a philanthropic effort, he replied that:

> Philanthropy can be a real limiting factor to sustainability and scale. Sometimes philanthropy is necessary, so we are providing PuR at cost for disaster relief. But, to make this product available to all who need it, on a regular sustainable basis, we need an economic business model so that there is an incentive for everyone in the value chain — from P&G to the seller on the street corner — to distribute it widely. Relying on philanthropy would limit the scale of providing clean water this way: it would only go as far as the funding allows; a sustainable business model will allow the product to reach many more who need it (interview, March 2004).

In a speech on 21 March 2003, his colleague George Carpenter, Director, Corporate Sustainable Development at Procter & Gamble, explained:

> These products and business model innovations can significantly improve lives, and help build our business at the same time. This is not business as usual and it is not philanthropy; it is building social, environmental and economic sustainability into our business in a strategic way.

Business financing

New business models may involve new types of collaborators for innovation and development of new products and services. Equally, they may involve a broader and more eclectic range of sources of finance for the corporate social opportunity. These may be business angels, venture capitalists or institutional investors seeking environmentally and socially sustainable projects in which to invest. It may also involve an openness to putting together a multi-source financing package which includes public funds: for example, from local or regional development agencies and international development funds.

In the section on product innovation (page 90) we provided three examples of companies that are developing 'cleaner' transportation (see the examples of Toyota's Prius®; DaimlerChrysler, Shell and Norsk Hydro; and IdleAire Technologies Corporation). In some cases, however, energy-efficient products have been developed but have still, for various reasons, to penetrate some markets. Securing adequate finance is often a problem. Finance has been found to support efforts to market energy-efficient products by offering price discounts and by education regarding the benefits of these products; this is exemplified by the case of the promotion of fluorescent lighting in Poland through the Global Environmental Facility.

Polish lighting manufacturers

As part of the Global Environmental Facility (www.gefweb.org), which is supported financially by Western donor countries and is administered through the World Bank and UN agencies, four Polish lighting manufacturers have received funding from the International Finance Corporation (IFC) of the World Bank. The project is administered by a Dutch private utility company with support from a Polish energy-efficiency non-governmental organisation.

Between them, the companies have received US$5 million to enable them to sell compact fluorescent lamps (CFLs) and related products at below cost price to Polish consumers and small businesses. The objective is to accelerate the development of the Polish market for energy-efficient lighting technologies to realise global and national environmental benefits. The project is also undertaking pilot demand-side management (DSM) activities at Polish electric utilities that are being privatised, as well as running education programmes to consumers and lighting professionals on efficiency and energy conservation.

Market delivery

Another aspect of a new business model may be about how a business markets and distributes its products and services to consumers — again, involving a willingness to explore new routes to market. It may involve collaboration with a community group such as Bank of America and Citigroup (see the Introduction, page 11) to sell mortgages to low-income neighbourhoods. The Unilever and Procter & Gamble examples above have involved using new, more grassroots-based distribution channels. It may also involve rethinking a conventional business model so that, for example, instead of selling a product, the business believes it is more commercially advantageous as well as environmentally or socially sustainable to lease it. This is the basis of the Going Green start-up company quoted above — and the following examples from Schindler, Interface and Dow.

Schindler

Schindler, a manufacturer of lifts (elevators), would rather not sell you any of its lifts; it would rather lease you a 'vertical transportation service', because it thinks its lifts require less electricity and maintenance than competing lifts do. Schindler aims to capture that benefit for itself by keeping the lift, operating it and by providing to customers only what those customers want, which is the service of moving up and down. So the resource efficiency of the elevator becomes for them not a reduced revenue but a reduced cost and enhanced revenue.

Interface

Interface Incorporated is the world's largest manufacturer of carpet tiles and upholstery fabrics for commercial interiors. It has redesigned its business approach so that as well as selling its products it now offers, as an alternative, a carpet-leasing service. This allows the company to retain ownership of its products and to maximise resource productivity.

In a 2004 KPMG publication titled 'Beyond Numbers', Ray Anderson, CEO of Interface, writes:

> We've found a new way to win in the marketplace . . . one that doesn't come at the expense of our grandchildren or the Earth, but at the expense of the inefficient competitor (quoted at a presentation at the Conference Board, New York, February 2004).

(Environmental concerns extend to its business-to-business contracts, as evidenced in its account with UPS [see Step 3, page 108].)

Dow Chemical Company

In a search for a safer way to deliver chlorinated solvents, the Dow Chemical Company came up with a new business model that involves the company 'renting' its chemicals to customers. Dow now delivers solvents to customers in a safe, environmentally preferable, closed-loop system and then collects them for recycling when they have been used.

Purchasing

In the section above on market delivery we looked at the benefits to the company of selling a service rather than a product. Similarly, there are benefits to the business, as a customer, in purchasing a service rather than a series of products, as illustrated by the chemical management solution chosen by General Motors. The General Motors example also illustrates another facet of the focus on service delivery rather than product delivery — service suppliers are encouraged to focus not on sales volume (which means the use of more raw materials to produce more goods) but on, among other things, the efficiency and recyclability of their products.

Staffing

One further type of new business model involves businesses developing new approaches to how they recruit staff and how they finance and organise pre-recruitment and induction training. A difficulty that companies may face is a lack of relevant skills in the local workforce. This is something addressed by Tesco in a series of regeneration projects in low- and middle-income communities in the UK. A criticism of companies when they move into an area is that they do not provide jobs for local people, bringing their workers from outside areas.

General Motors

To address the problems associated with having numerous chemical suppliers, General Motors has redesigned its chemicals management — forming a partnership with a single supplier that works in conjunction with the General Motors chemicals team to facilitate process innovation. The supplier is not paid for volume sales but, rather, is rewarded for plant performance. Plant performance includes product quality as well as a range of efficiency improvements with cost savings and environmental benefits.

Under a more traditional approach to chemicals management a single facility would have had many different chemical suppliers, resulting in an inefficient use of time, effort, money and chemicals. Hence, there would be no incentive for the supplier to help the plant reduce its usage of chemicals. Under the new system, the facility no longer purchases chemicals. The facility now purchases chemical services. In addition to supplying chemicals, the supplier provides management, analysis and inventory control. The supplier is paid based on production and not on the amount of chemicals used and hence there is no longer an incentive for the supplier to sell volume chemicals.

Tesco

The leading supermarket chain in the UK, Tesco, has initiated 14 regeneration partnerships in low to moderate income communities across the UK. This involves developing new retail stores in under-served areas. Tesco partners with community groups and public-sector and private-sector agencies to put together, finance and deliver appropriate and customised skill training to the local community while the store is being built rather than after it is completed when it requires staffing. Key to the success of the programme is a job guarantee to all those who successfully complete the training — which has necessitated changes to Tesco's internal personnel practices. The provision of jobs to local residents helps to build community support for the stores and community protection in what are often high-crime areas. (For more detail, see the report by AccountAbility and Brody, Weiser & Burns, 'Community-enabled Innovation: An Innovation through Partnership', published September 2003 and sponsored by The Ford Foundation.)

▶ Scoping more eclectically to find corporate social opportunities

A business that is really seeking new opportunities might stretch the above scoping tools. In dialogue with stakeholders it might probe more deliberately for potential opportunities. For example, it might consider being more eclectic about the types of organisation with which to benchmark itself, to include social enterprises[28] and 'for-

28   Social enterprises are defined by the Social Enterprise Unit (SEU) of the UK government Department of Trade and Industry as 'businesses with primarily social objectives whose surpluses are principally reinvested for that purpose in the business or in the community, rather than being driven by the need to maximise profit for shareholders and owners'.

benefit' organisations rather than only with other businesses. Similarly, in scenario planning, it might wish to place more emphasis on emerging insights into new technologies and how these can lead to new, 'out-of-the-box' thinking about how to deliver goods and services to meet currently unmet needs.

▶ Synthesis of Step 2

Here, we show how the response of De Beers to the 'blood diamond' campaign is consistent with the application of Step 2 of our model.

Scoping what mattered at De Beers

For the diamond business De Beers, the triggers referred to in Step 1 (page 19) were a combination of NGO and media campaigns over the emotive issue of 'blood diamonds' — allegations that revenue from some diamond mines were financing rival armies and prolonging some of Africa's bloodiest civil wars.

The company De Beers could have confronted this emerging campaign through a number of possible strategies:

- It could have ignored the campaign and done nothing, working on the principle of not fanning the flames of the campaign, gambling that the enduring allure of diamonds ('diamonds are forever', 'diamonds are a girl's best friend') would be sufficient to overcome any consumer distaste of gems becoming associated with suffering and bloody conflict.
- It could have increased its advertising to consumers and pursued high-profile sponsorships with the hope of 'drowning out' the negative campaigns.
- It could have challenged the veracity of the accusations and fidelity of the campaigners.

However, it chose to take the criticisms seriously and to enter into dialogue with the NGO campaigners.

We don't know what type of decision-making process the company went through, but had it been applying the seven-step method it might have looked at its strategic options in terms of potential impacts on stakeholders and might have concluded, among other things:

- Sufficient numbers of customers, particularly high-net-worth individuals, would have been negatively impacted by the 'blood diamond' campaign, seeing diamonds as the 'new fur' — namely a luxury product that takes on very negative connotations.
- Some business partners might have become nervous about a failure to act.
- As with some other high-profile corporate triggers (such as Brent Spar for Shell, and allegations of poor labour conditions in supplier factories for Nike) a failure to act might have particularly hit the morale of the employees at De Beers.
- Conversely, there may have been some resistance among some governments in conflict zones to De Beers taking an initiative with the NGOs and the media to end the practice of using revenue from diamond mines to fund conflict.

continued ➜

- However, it might have been considered that taking action would be welcomed by the US State Department — particularly as De Beers has faced an unrelated, half-century ban on doing business in the US market over price-fixing charges over industrial diamonds (see the article in *The Times*, titled 'De Beers out to end half-century ban from US', 25 February 2004).

Again, had De Beers been following the approach advocated in this book, then it might have refined its options in the light of:

- The operational and logistical requirements involved in setting up a certification system to validate a diamond from 'mine to finger' and the critical success factors in creating a credible validation system
- The pros and cons of working alone or with others in the industry, and whether collective action might more readily secure government backing

Building still further on this approach, it might have considered turning potentially negative and damaging publicity into a way of reinforcing positive images of diamonds helping to reduce armed conflicts by stopping the flow of illegal funds to finance rival armies.

▶ Moving from Step 2 to Step 3

By the end of Step 2, a business will have scoped a variety of potential risks and opportunities. The next stage, Step 3, is about prioritisation and assessing the business case for action on the chosen priorities.

Making the business case

Focus

In this chapter we show how to build the business case for the proposed business strategies, informed by the marketing mix, organisational considerations and by overall corporate goals and business drivers.

Applying Step 3

In Part II — the worked example of the seven steps — the completed process forms show how, by applying appropriate tools and techniques selected from Step 3, the following outputs are produced (pages 306ff.):

- An analysis of the impact of the proposed strategies on revenues and costs, informed by marketing mix and organisational considerations

- An analysis of the alignment between proposed strategies, key business drivers and corporate goals

- An assessment of how the proposed strategies fit with organisational culture

- A ranking to identify the most attractive strategies

IN MANY RESPECTS, THE ENTIRE SEVEN-STEP PROCESS BUILDS a business case for a proactive approach to responsible business practices led from the highest corporate level. However, as we said in our introduction, our purpose is to show how to integrate corporate social responsibility (CSR) issues into the ongoing and regular business planning and decision-making processes that will be taking place at various places and levels of a company.

Step 3 is therefore focused initially on helping to construct a business case for the individual business strategies and opportunities identified in Step 2. Each of these, because of the nature of the process completed so far, has certain social, ethical and environmental characteristics built in, providing the basis for identifying potential corporate social opportunities (CSOs).

At this stage, managers are encouraged to consider the potential and feasibility of the CSOs that are emerging. For example, will proposed strategies help products reach under-served markets? Will they fill gaps left by other suppliers in particular market segments? Does the strategy lend itself to new brand positioning built around ethical values? What are the price implications for sourcing new materials from fair-trade suppliers? Each question needs to be considered in terms of impacts on revenues and costs, to ascertain viability and attractiveness.

Any proposed strategy will not be delivered in isolation. It needs to be considered in the context of known business drivers and of overall corporate purpose and goals. For example, how does it contribute to drivers such as innovation and reputation? Does it reinforce or detract from stated market goals? Does it fit with organisational commitments to diversity or to sustainable development? Does it demonstrably add to shareholder value?

It is not until all these elements can be considered that a business case can be fully articulated and a judgement made as to its attractiveness. These broader corporate considerations may override or give different weight to an initially unfavourable cost–benefit analysis. As George Carpenter and Peter White of Procter & Gamble state:[1]

> The real business case requires that companies link opportunity to responsibility. If the focus stays limited to just areas of corporate responsibility, the oft-quoted view that sustainability provides long-term value, but short-term costs, will prevail.

The arguments for and against individual business strategies will, we contend, soon lead to the emergence of a broad-based case for an organisation-wide commitment to CSR and indeed to CSO. To support this view, we provide the latest evidence for the link between responsible business practices and overall corporate performance. Separately, we would further argue that there is a business case for collective action and why regional development agencies, groups of businesses taking collective action and similar organisations might find a business case for building clusters of businesses committed to CSR.

---

1   G. Carpenter and P. White, 'Sustainable Development: Finding the Real Business Case', *Corporate Environmental Strategy: International Journal for Sustainable Business* 2.2 (February 2004).

Companies will have different sets of existing processes for determining potential investments and strategies. These can be adapted to take into account the factors that we illustrate in this step. As far as we are aware, few existing processes incorporate CSR issues; an exception is the commercial development process of RWE Thames Water.

RWE Thames Water

RWE Thames Water is integrating CSR into its business case analysis through its Commercial Development Process (CDP) — a numerical assessment framework within which all new business opportunities are considered. The company says that the primary objective of the process is to support the successful management of opportunities from their generation to the conclusion of successful transactions (Richard Aylard, interview with authors, October 2003). The four key stages of the opportunity life-cycle are:

- Opportunity generation
- Opportunity assessment
- Opportunity development
- Deal conclusion and review

Within these stages there are four approval phases:

- Policy approval
- Development approval
- Bid approval
- Implementation approval

The CDP is being amended to ensure that CSR criteria are considered, mainly at the policy and development approval stages. For projects that have a distinct CSR element to them, there are plans to introduce an additional set of measures (e.g. in the way in which environmental and/or social activities contribute to the overall value proposition) that should be considered at each stage but that are not necessarily prerequisites to enable the opportunity to progress.

▶ A marketing approach

Any proposed strategy needs to be considered in the light of its impact on and opportunities provided by market segments and on the classic elements of the marketing mix — product, price, promotion, process and place. Given, as we saw in Step 2, that much of the responsible business agenda is about 'how' a company goes about its business, we suggest there is also a need for a further element to be taken into account, relating to organisational considerations, which we refer to as people concerns.

Each business case will be different, depending on the characteristics of the given business strategy and operating scenario. However, each of the elements of the marketing mix should prompt a series of related questions when viewed within the appropriate part of the seven-step process, and a corresponding calculation of impact on revenue and costs should be made.

In the next seven sub-sections we look at some sample questions and case-study examples in relation to:

- Markets
- Products
- Price
- Promotion
- Process
- Place
- People

It may be helpful to work with marketing colleagues in considering these elements.

Markets

Under 'markets', we ask: Which combination of old and new products and existing and new markets does the strategy involve? 'Market' in this context refers to market segment, which can be defined as the group of buyers and users of any product and service that responds consistently and in the same way to the product, price, promotion, place, people and process offers. Market segments can be grouped within specific geographical areas, in countries or regions. Country markets can, for example, be developed or developing countries. Marketers would suggest that the hierarchy of ease of opportunity would be from A to D, as shown in Table 7. For CSO, it is helpful to consider moving from the supply of existing products to existing markets to additional product/market opportunities.

	Existing markets	New markets
Existing products	A	B
New products	C	D

Table 7 **Matrix of marketing opportunities**

The example of Avis supplying cars to the able-bodied is one of existing products to existing markets. Moving to a new CSO of supplying cars to those with disabilities is new products to new markets (not only is the car different, but access for customers at distribution points will be different, as may booking facilities for the hard of hearing, etc.).

Sample business case questions

- Would the strategy lead to cannibalisation of existing markets?

- Would the strategy create a new market segment or serve a currently unserved or under-served market (e.g. a market applicable to an ethnic minority, people with disabilities or to the elderly)?

- Do those in the existing market segment need information and education regarding a new product or service?

- In business-to-business (B2B) transactions, do clients require information on social, ethical and environmental performance?

Examples

In the USA, Avis Rent A Car Systems Inc. is offering a service tailored to disabled drivers which would correspond to a new product for a new market demonstrated in Table 7. Also in the USA, some banks are offering existing banking services appropriate to the Hispanic population, a new market.

Avis Rent A Car Systems Inc.

According to the *Wall Street Journal* there are estimated to be 54 million disabled people in the USA, spending US$13.6 billion on 31.7 million trips per year. It has been estimated by the Open Doors Organisation in Chicago, which researches services and products for disabled consumers, that this population cohort would spend at least twice as much if travel facilities and services were more accommodating to its needs. In 2003 Avis Rent A Car Systems Inc., part of Cendant Corporation, announced plans to offer free equipment add-ons for its cars, to aid disabled drivers (for more details, see 'Avis plans free add-ons for disabled', *Wall Street Journal*, 18 September 2003).

Bank accounts for the US Hispanic population

There are some 40 million Hispanics in the US market, and numbers are fast increasing. Some 60% are Mexican and half are estimated to lack a bank account. At the same time US-to-Mexico remittances from US-based migrants and their families equalled US$2.4 billion in the first quarter of 2003 alone. A number of US banks are offering cheap remittance services as a way to build relationships, with the goal of transferring remittance customers to full banking services. Bank of America reports that 33% of its remittance customers have opened a current account.

Source: *Financial Times*, 'Banks eyeing green, green cash of home', 5 June 2003

Products

Sample business-case questions

- Would the strategy lead to a new or adapted product range or a new category of service?

- Would the raw materials required for products come from new, fair-trade resources and cost more?

- Is packaging more or less material-intensive? Will there be less or more waste?

- What are the implications for the product specification of environmental life-cycle analysis and extended producer responsibility?

Example

The example of Shields Environmental provides a good example of how small and medium-sized firms can be a source of social opportunities for multinational corporations. It also illustrates how small and medium-sized enterprises in a supply chain can promote CSR to larger firms, rather than pressure always being applied from the other direction in the supply chain.

Shields Environmental

A phenomenon of the past decade has been the rise in the availability and use of mobile, cellular telephones. Some 15 million mobile phones are discarded every year, equating to some 1,500 metric tonnes of potential landfill.

Mobile phones contain a variety of substances, including precious metals and some hazardous materials. In terms of the materials they contain they are completely harmless until they are thrown into a landfill site, where they degrade and can cause serious damage to the environment. However, there is no need for them to end up as landfill—old handsets often can be refurbished and re-used, or their components can be separated and recycled.

Shields Environmental is a medium-sized British business. It was one of the first businesses to achieve certification to a recognised environmental management system (in 1995, to BS 7750, now ISO 14001) and was one of the first businesses to report publicly on its environmental performance.

Confronted with the need to generate new revenue streams, Shields used its own environmental commitment to spot a new market opportunity in forthcoming EU recycling legislation. Shields worked with mobile-phone manufacturers, retailers and networks to develop the Fonebak project to recycle mobile phones and reduce potentially hazardous landfill. Fonebak was launched in September 2002 and involves a number of major networks, retailers and manufacturers. Benefits have included the creation of new revenue streams, improved risk management and enhanced corporate reputation. Over 100 new jobs have been created in an area of high unemployment and a source of waste has been substantially reduced.

Price

Bold pricing strategies that help differentiate a product can be effective elements to marketing-led strategies. For example, many supermarkets charge a premium for organic foods, both reflecting the additional sourcing costs of the produce, but also the willingness of consumers to pay extra for them. One supermarket chain attempted to buck this pricing for organics with disappointing results.

Iceland

In 2000, the UK supermarket chain Iceland (since changed to The Big Food Group) announced with a fanfare a commitment to selling only frozen vegetables that were organic, and at the same price as other supermarkets were selling non-organic vegetables. Traditionally, organic foods had sold at a premium price. The company undertook research that suggested that three out of four consumers would prefer to buy organic food if prices were less than the prevailing high prices at the time. In order to meet expected demand as a result of their price commitment, the BBC reported that the firm bought nearly 40% of the world's organic vegetable crop. Six months after the announcement, the company reported a decline in performance and blamed a drop of like-to-like sales of 0.5% on the decision to push organics. According to Bill Grimsey, CEO, 'Customers are not ready to make the jump' from non-organic to organic and went on to say that the company was reviewing the positioning of organic produce in line with consumer demand.

There are various possible interpretations of the failure of Iceland's bold pricing strategy. The firm may not have invested sufficiently in a marketing campaign to educate the consumer (about look, taste, availability etc. of organics over non-organics) and thus 'prepare' or 'create' the market before the price variable could have had an impact. Or, the market was simply not ready for the product. Either way, the case illustrates that pricing needs to be seen within the context of an integrated marketing approach.

Source: BBC news, 14 June 2000 and 22 June 2001 (www.bbc.com)

Sample business-case questions

- Within the strategy, will the price of the product or service remain the same as before, or could it carry a premium price: for example, because it is ethically sourced or organic?

- Does the strategy require a discount on the product or service to encourage potential customers to sample it?

Promotion

Sample business-case questions

- Does the strategy call for specific promotion to consumers around social, ethical or environmental characteristics?

- Will brand association mean promotional efforts take place in a climate of cynicism or high trust?

- Does the strategy call for own-branded products?

- Does the strategy suggest more below-the-line spending (non-advertising): for example, through associated sponsorships or street marketing?

- Should the strategy be part of a wider strategy to look at stakeholder relations?

- Will the strategy have an impact on employee recruitment (e.g. advertising, choice of publication, images, language)?

Example

The case of UPS illustrates how B2B business can be enhanced by the communication of environmental credentials.

UPS

Courier and logistics firm UPS reported that it gained two accounts, one with carpet firm Interface Incorporated (on the environmental approach of this company, see Step 2, page 97) and one with Patagonia, a clothing company, worth several million US dollars combined, in large part as a result of the inclusion of its environmental credentials in a critical part of its pitch process (see the Summer 2000 issue of *Environmental Quality Management*). UPS has introduced the world's largest fleet of alternative-fuel vehicles as well as the first re-usable packaging, reducing waste. The proactive stance on sustainable development was part of the attraction to UPS for Interface and Patagonia, both companies with reputations in their own right for leading environmental practices.

Process

Sample business-case questions

- Does the strategy require new training systems and processes?

- If new training systems and processes are required, can they be provided in-house or are outside trainers required?

- Does new equipment require new training for handlers?

- Will the strategy require adherence to particular environmental or employment regulations?

Examples

A strategy to increase and stabilise the supply of milk to a milk factory led Hindustan Lever to undertake a capacity-building programme aimed at local farmers. A similar desire to increase the local supply base led ChevronTexaco and Citibank, in partnership with the United Nations Development Programme (UNDP) to run a capacity-building programme aimed at SMEs.

Hindustan Lever

A dairy factory of Hindustan Lever, an Indian subsidiary of the Unilever Group, was operating at 50% of capacity and incurring losses because of inadequate milk supplies. A capacity-building programme for local farmers in some 400 villages led to security of supply and profitability. (For information on another project run by Hindustan Lever, addressing the environmental problems created by the washing of clothes in water courses, see Step 2, page 92.) In the mid-1970s Hindustan Lever established an Integrated Rural Development programme, which set out to assist farmers in building milk supplies by taking account of a range of their practices that needed improvement. The programme addresses education and training in animal husbandry, provision of local healthcare programmes, development of basic infrastructure, and the establishment of village development committees. Research has shown that living conditions in the area have improved significantly since the programme started. The project area has expanded from six to over 400 villages. Milk supplies to the Hindustan factory increased significantly to meet its capacity and increase its market reach. The dairy is now one of the company's most profitable units.

Source: Peter Brew and Frances House, 'Indian food company helps dairy farmers to improve milk supplies', Business Linkages for Sustainable Enterprise Development, International Business Leaders Forum, 2001

ChevronTexaco, Citibank and the United Nations Development Programme

In Kazakhstan, ChevronTexaco and Citibank, in partnership with the United Nations Development Programme (UNDP), initiated a programme targeted at developing local small and medium-sized enterprises (SMEs), with the dual aim of improving quality and reliability of local suppliers for the oil field operations, and also helping to strengthen the local economy. As a result, the need to bring goods into the area from outside reduced and the quantity of local goods supplied rose from zero to over 38%, leading to reduced costs for the large corporate partners, increased employment and a rise in the local tax base. The trigger for ChevronTexaco's involvement was a contractual stipulation from the government to pay a mandatory social tax, direct funds into local development, or both. Citibank, through its subsidiary Citibank Kazakhstan, wanted to find a way to build goodwill with local authorities.

Source: Jennifer Barsky, 'UNDP and the Business Sector: Working Together to Fight Poverty' (undated)

Processes have a significant impact on the other strategic marketing considerations, as summarised in Table 8.

Impacts of processes	
Area of impact	**Nature of impact**
Market segment	Can allow greater penetration of existing market: e.g. as the changes in supply processes allowed Hindustan Lever (above) to achieve greater reach in its market
Product	Can increase availability and improve quality
Price	Can build volume of supply, allowing greater price flexibility (less unit cost) through economies of scale
Promotion	Provides opportunity for 'good' messages: e.g. support for local community, such as the Citibank Kazakhstan example (above)
Place	Can help improve distribution channels
People	Different processes which enable positive involvement of workers and suppliers can improve motivation, and, hence, efficiency

Table 8 **The impact of processes on the other strategic marketing considerations**

Place

Sample business-case questions

- Does the strategy call for the product to be sold or the service presented through new distribution channels, and, if so, does this require capacity-building?

- Do existing distribution channels need to be phased out or contracts renegotiated?

'Place' considerations encompasses a number of elements, each of which are variable. Think of the 'place' distribution channel stretching lengthways from the source of the product's raw materials, up to the point of consumption by the consumer. The channel's width is made up of four flows:

- The flow of the product

- The flow of funds associated with the product

- Legal ownership of the product — which will often not coincide with physical possession

- The flow of information about the product

The marketer will consider which people or organisations are touched along the channel's length and across its width. For example, the decision of Interface to lease rather than sell carpets was a change in the flow of legal ownership (see page 97) P&G providing cheap loans to help suppliers in emerging markets buy equipment necessary to produce the standard of goods they require is an example of innovation in the flow of funds. And in the Coca-Cola example below the provision of training is an example of innovation in the flow of information.

Coca-Cola

As part of a strategy to increase market penetration in southern Africa, Coca-Cola South Africa invested in a Entrepreneurs Development Programme, designed to encourage small, micro-business start-ups and build a network of local community retailers of Coca-Cola products. Nearly 13,000 jobs have been created, and, of 5,000 new outlets created in 2000, 3,500 were participants in the programme. In order to then service these retailers, the bottling companies, responsible for distribution, developed a range of innovative equipment such as delivery bicycles, mobile kiosks and coolers for street vendors.

Source: WBCSD, 'Doing Business with the Poor: A Field Guide' (2004)

People

Sample business-case questions

- Does the success of the strategy depend on the demographic or ethnic profile of the workforce?

- Does the strategy call for the introduction of programmes that will produce a more stable workforce with lower rates of absenteeism?

- Is it critical to the strategy to attract those able and willing to work flexible hours (e.g. unsociable or irregular hours) by providing child- or eldercare?

- Will the strategy include different patterns of sourcing and therefore changes to supplier relationships?

Examples

Dara Mayers, in a Summer 2003 report for the Ford Foundation, titled 'Out of Balance', describes the cases of ConAgara, Wawa and the Marriott Corporation, which illustrate the benefits of caring for the workforce.

ConAgara

In 1992, in Arkansas, ConAgara, a US-based international food company, introduced at one of its plants a prenatal healthcare programme for its low-wage workers. Four years later it had saved US$4 million in terms of maternal benefits.

Wawa

Wawa, a chain of 500 convenience stores in the USA, reported a 10.4% drop in employee turnover in the first year of providing healthcare services to its low-wage workforce. For each employee retained, the result has been a saving of US$1,000 (i.e. it costs US$1,000 in the recruitment and training of each employee).

Marriott Corporation

According to 'Corporate Voices for Working Families', an NGO promoting work–life balance, 'for every US dollar the Marriott Corporation spends helping employees with work–life issues, it saves four US dollars due to lower turnover and absenteeism'. The hotel group established a range of programmes to help workers deal with personal problems, offering advice and counselling on issues such as managing household budgets through a 'Associate Resource Line'. The company also ensured good provision of childcare services. An additional saving was in managers' time, which prior to the initiative had been spent on 'social work' rather than business management.

▶ Business drivers and business goals matter

Different companies will have different definitions of what are key business drivers as well as different ways of expressing corporate business objectives or goals. Proposed strategies must be considered in the light of such drivers and goals, resulting either in one or in both being modified accordingly. Does a strategy add or detract from those drivers or goals? If a strategy runs counter to normal drivers or is out of line with business goals it may not be accepted or acceptable within the business or may require special dispensation before it is allowed to go ahead.

A number of research projects have asked business leaders to identify the link between CSR and business drivers. The results of two substantive surveys are shown in Figure 6.

In the following sub-sections we explore factors that should be considered within a common set of business drivers, as listed below, when strategies are being formulated. For each we ask: Does the proposed strategy contribute to, pose a danger to, or take advantage of, that driver?

Corporate views on the business case

(a) Results of 2003 SAM survey in which respondents were asked to indicate 'the five most important options where you perceive the most value is added from your sustainability strategy in terms of value generation/competitiveness enhancement'

(b) Results of 2003 survey by the World Economic Forum in which respondents were asked to indicate which three of the eight listed factors 'you consider the most important in making the business case for your corporate citizenship activities'

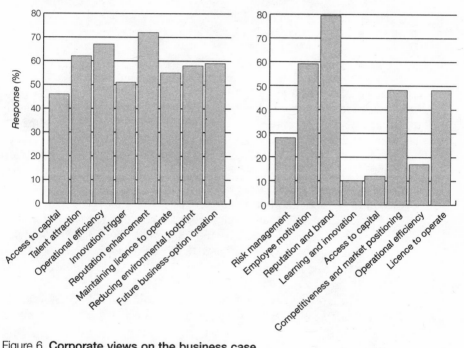

Figure 6 **Corporate views on the business case**

Source: World Economic Forum, and International Business Leaders Forum, *Values and Value: Communicating the Strategic Importance of Corporate Citizenship Initiatives* (2004), p. 15

OF WALES, NEWPORT
UNIVERSITY
LIBRARY
AND
INFORMATION
SERVICES
ALLT-YR-YN

- Reputation

- Innovation

- Cost cutting

- Market growth

- Relationships, alliances and the licence to operate

- Access to financial capital

- Development of human capital

Reputation

It has been reported that the average person recognises 1,000 corporate logos.[2] This highlights the importance of 'intangibles' such as brand, knowledge and reputation to business success and value. According to Interbrand 2000, 96% of the market capitalisation value of Coca-Cola, 97% of that of Kellogg and 84% of that of American Express is 'intangible'.[3] Figures such as these highlight that companies are vulnerable as reputation is highly perishable, and companies need to protect themselves along their extended supply chains.

A survey by Hill and Knowlton and by Korn Ferry found that 60% of the world's CEOs think that reputation is much more important now than it was five years ago, and a further 28% believe it is somewhat more important now that it was five years ago. Consequently, 65% have taken direct charge of corporate reputation. Customers were reported as having the most influence (78%), followed by the media (48%).[4]

There is also growing evidence to show that a commitment to CSR can add significantly to reputation, levels of general trust and consequently to gaining or retaining business:

- UK telecommunications firm BT estimates that a third of its corporate reputation is driven by its socially responsible business endeavours.[5]

- The Co-operative Bank in the UK reports that it owes 31% of its business directly to its good reputation in corporate responsibility.[6]

Kevin Beeston, executive chairman of Serco, agrees. CSR can be a competitive advantage in helping to create the right corporate ethos:[7]

2 *Adbusters Magazine*, quoted in D. Grayson and A. Hodges, *Everybody's Business* (London: Dorling Kindersley, 2001), page 31.
3 Quoted in *The Business Case for Corporate Responsibility*, published in 2003 by Arthur D. Little and Business in the Community.
4 Reported in *Financial Times*, 'Creative Business: Reputation is Top Executive Concern', 14 October 2003.
5 Reported in *Fortune*, 'Corporate America's Social Conscience', 8 December 2003.
6 CFS *Sustainability Report*, 2003.
7 Interview with authors, August 2003.

I see CSR as a real competitive differentiator, I really do, and I say this all the time. One of the things that is changing in our world of contracting for government services is the ability to deliver an entrepreneurial public service ethos. In turn, diversity and other aspects of CSR are becoming factors that the public sector is taking into account. We've got good evidence of the way that we run the business and integrate into the community, and this is a real differentiator for us.

As general levels of trust in business are low, strategies that support and build trust may carry a premium. As John Sunderland, CEO Cadbury Schweppes plc, says:[8]

Corporate reputations are fragile animals if internal behaviours and values are not explicit, recognised and lived.

The reputation quotient (RQ), developed by Charles Fombrun of New York University, encapsulates the idea that corporate reputation can be distilled into five simple principles:[9]

- Distinctiveness (i.e. among stakeholders, for products and services)
- Focus (e.g. the promotion of a single core theme)
- Consistency (i.e. in actions and communications)
- Identity (i.e. basing identity on espoused principles rather than on advertising or 'spin')
- Transparency (i.e. by disclosing more information and by engaging in dialogue with stakeholders)

There is a strong correlation between Fombrun's principles and key elements of CSR, such as the ability to respond to stakeholder interests; consistency between claim and action; and the need for transparency in business practices.

Innovation

Innovation in products, services and processes has been seen to be the key to long-term growth and competitive success. However, despite increasing investments in research and development (R&D), many firms are not achieving the benefits they seek from innovation. Evidence from research in five broad industry sectors by the Accenture Institute for Strategic Change (Accenture) suggests that companies are increasing their reliance on external sourcing for innovation.[10] However, most companies lack an innovation-sourcing strategy to help them determine what

8   Quoted in *The Business Case for Corporate Responsibility*, published in 2003 by Arthur D. Little and Business in the Community.
9   Reported in *Financial Times*, 20 November 2003.
10 Jane C. Linder, Sirkka Jarvenpaa and Thomas H. Davenport, 'Innovation: A Little Help from their Friends', Accenture Institute for Strategic Change (www.accenture.com/xdoc/en/ideas/outlook/2.2003/pdf/summary_innovation.pdf).

combination of internal and external sources they should use and how to deploy them throughout the innovation chain. The approach we are advocating — one of being open to new business models — would be a practical implementation of this Accenture model.

Avid innovators, according to Accenture, create and manage a diverse set of innovation 'channels' that incorporate not only sets of sources of innovation but also well-established approaches to managing at the interfaces. According to Accenture, 'they cultivate multiple external sources and master a range of boundary-spanning approaches in support of a clear innovation sourcing strategy'. Accenture go on to say that:[11]

> Leading companies also manage the entire innovation-sourcing network holistically — including both internal and external sources. In addition to accepted project- and risk-management techniques, they use big ideas to define agendas and drive new sources of value.

We believe CSR can be one such 'big idea'. A 2002 survey, carried out by Business in the Community, found that over 80% of of European business leaders saw the inculcation of more creativity and innovation inside their organisations as one of their top management challenges. In the same survey, over 75% of respondents agreed that the integration of responsible business practices into the way the business is run would help to stimulate more creativity and innovation.[12] How might this be so? We suggest the following are important:

- Identification of employees with the company

- Diversity in the organisation

- Commitment to performance

- Engagement with stakeholders

- Fresh perspectives on the world and opportunities

- Business transformation

Identification

Employees will feel greater affinity and show greater commitment to the business if business and employees have shared values. In such a business, employees will be more willing 'to go the extra mile' that leads to a breakthrough in thinking. In the words of Jim Loehr and Tony Schwartz, 'in the old paradigm, reward fuels performance; in the new paradigm, purpose fuels performance'.[13] A range of other recent

---

11   *Ibid.*

12   Business in the Community, 'Responsibility: Driving Innovation, Inspiring Employees (Fast-forward Research, 2003).

13   J. Loehr and T. Schwartz, *The Power of Full Engagement* (New York: Simon & Schuster, 2003).

books have argued the case for using much more diverse sources of insight and innovation.[14]

A company where the benefits of identification have been reaped is KPMG.

KPMG

KPMG's values are:

Clients: 'We are passionate about working with our clients to deliver exceptional value.'

People: 'Our people flourish and realise their potential.'

Knowledge: 'We continuously extend the frontiers of our shared knowledge.'

To support these, one of their community partnerships has led to some interesting innovation. With Earthwatch they created the Environmental Innovation Scheme, which has developed to be open to staff and suppliers. It encourages people to engage and contribute to their environment practices but, importantly, through a competition, asks people to respond to 'how KPMG can improve their environmental and community performance'. Employees submit ideas and the winners are rewarded with a place on one of the Earthwatch projects. One employee designed a KPMG foldable paper bin/box which employees could take with them to client sites; they would then use the box for waste confidential papers which they would then bring back to the office and recycle, folding up the box for the next day.

Source: KPMG presentation

Diversity

Diversity of employees — whether of ethnicity, gender, age and so on — can provide varied insights into potential business strategies as well as improved operational procedures. Pharmaceutical company GlaxoSmithKline describes diversity as a 'business imperative' — and claims that its human resource diversity policies have led to learning and innovation in how it has related to its customers.

Commitment

Commitment to higher standards of performance stimulates a search for new and better ways of doing things, as seen in BP in a challenge to address the threat of global warming.[15]

---

14 See e.g. Richard Florida, *The Rise of the Creative Class* (New York: Basic Books, 2002), who argues that the most creative cities and organisations are those that value and engage people outside the traditional mainstream; T. Homer Dixon, *The Ingenuity Gap: How Can We Solve the Problems of the Future?* (New York: Alfred A. Knopf, 2000), who argues that there is a gulf between the rate of new problems opening up and new solutions being created; Lawrence Lessig, *The Future of Ideas: The Fate of the Commons in the Connected World* (New York: Random House, 2001), who argues against closed, proprietary innovation systems making a powerful argument for openness and a 'creative commons'; and Ilkka Tuomi, *Networks of Innovation: Change and Meaning in the Age of the Internet* (Oxford, UK: Oxford University Press, 2003), who argues that technological innovation is socially situated and that drawing on diverse social networks is vital for economic success.

15 For more detail on global warming, see the example of the reinsurance firm Swiss Re in Step 2, page 59.

GlaxoSmithKline (GSK)

As part of its commitment to equality of opportunity and treatment for employees, GSK aspires to 'have a workforce and working environment that reflects the diversity of background, culture, beliefs and characteristics of the communities' in which the company operates. The company has a number of practices designed to embed the values of diversity into business processes. It was this commitment to diversity that has provided an impetus and knowledge for the firm's US General Pharma sales operations. In 2001 this unit made it a key objective to improve access to GSK medicines to patients from ethnic-minority communities. In Southern California, part of its marketing territory, there are high numbers of Vietnamese, Koreans, Armenians, Central Americans and Mexicans. Cultural awareness training, based on human resource experience, improved understanding of the needs of these communities, which was then passed on to doctors, who were able to better understand how GSK products met the needs of their patients. The success of this approach led to a similar training across the US, to increase multi-cultural awareness and understanding relating to GSK brands.

Source: GSK, 'The Impact of Medicines: Corporate and Social Responsibility' (2002) and correspondence with authors

BP

John Browne, CEO of BP, has challenged his company to respond to the threat of global warming, requiring every new investment decision to factor in a notional cost of emissions of the greenhouse gas carbon dioxide (CO_2). This challenge has speeded up the development of a range of new technologies and processes at BP.

Engagement

Engagement with different stakeholders can produce new insights from fresh minds, as found by UK rail operators in consultation with a committee of disabled passengers. Further examples of innovation through stakeholder engagement are described in Step 6, page 237.

GNER and the UK Disabled Passengers Transport Advisory Committee (DPTAC)

In a private interview with Ann Bates of the UK Disabled Passengers Transport Advisory Committee, we learned how disabled rail passengers who use wheelchairs have helped rail companies and rolling-stock manufacturers to redesign their rail carriages. In a case involving GNER, instead of having to lose six conventional seats to accommodate a second wheelchair place in a to-be refurbished carriage, Ann was able to show how to accommodate the second wheelchair place and *gain* two other seats!

Fresh perspectives

Companies that foster an inquisitive culture among their staff about the world around them, and encourage employees to be sensitive to the needs of the communities in which they operate, are exposed to fresh perspectives which can lead to corporate social opportunities for business operations or product or market development.

British Gas

UK energy company BG solved the problem of a shortage of fork-lift truck drivers in its warehouses by recruiting ex-offenders from hostels for young offenders. It also solved staff shortages in its customer call-centres by recruiting and training disabled people. The scheme has been so successful it has provided good-practice guidance and training to other companies.

Vodafone

In 2002 telecommunications firm Vodafone made a commitment as a central part of its CSR strategy to assess market needs and opportunities, and to identify commercially viable wireless applications that deliver specific social, environmental benefits. This entailed working with product development managers to look beyond a traditional simple economic case for product development, and led to the establishment of a tool that helped to identify additional sources of value. Criteria to assess and rank social and/or environmental benefits were established and a number of pilot product development projects activated — one to assist blind or partially sighted customers (in partnership with the Royal National Institute for the Blind and Nokia), one in the 'telemedicine' area (tested with the Spanish Red Cross), and one a missing-persons alert application.

Source: Vodafone CSR Report, 2002–2003

B&Q

DIY homeware retail chain B&Q has found ways to improve services to disabled customers and those who shop with them through a network of some 300 partnerships between staff and local disability groups across the UK. Staff competence for this market group has improved as a result, attracting disabled customers as well as increasing employee satisfaction, retention and productivity (see Simon Zadek, *Doing Good and Doing Well: Making the Business Case for Corporate Citizenship* [The Conference Board, 2000]).

Business transformation

CSR can help at critical points in programmes of organisational change. For instance, adherence to principles of responsible business can help a company to achieve much more significant breakthroughs and greater clarity regarding strategic intent and the direction the business is to take. This was the experience of Shell (see the example in Step 1, page 19). Further examples are provided by Pfizer and The Co-operative Bank.

Pfizer

Pfizer, led by chairman Dr Henry A. McKinnell, achieved the goal it stated in 1997 of becoming the world's premier pharmaceutical company by 2001 in terms of revenue, some two years ahead of schedule. Looking to the future, McKinnell went on to articulate a vision of Pfizer playing a key role in advancing sustainable health that builds on prevention, disease management and discovering new medicines. As we shall read in Step 4 (page 145), he spearheaded the articulation of a new corporate mission in support of this vision. As part of that process, he set the goal to 'go beyond number one' and stressed the role of leadership required for that transformation:

> We all know companies that made it to the top and then declined. We must learn what it takes to go beyond number one. The journey includes a self-imposed transformation. Companies that endure in leadership work to build on their best qualities. However, they also lead in internal revolution to instill behaviours that foster change.

On 4 October 2002, McKinnell announced Pfizer had signed up to the UN Global Compact, believing that his vision for the company fitted with the vision of UN Secretary-General Kofi Annan for stability and prosperity and the sharing of the benefits of globalisation of all peoples (as stated at the World Economic Forum in January 1999). Signing up to the Compact (Pfizer was one of few US companies to do so) sent a strong signal internally and externally that leadership through corporate citizenship was part of that 'revolution' — a key plank of the future for Pfizer, and critical to its ability to fulfil an ambitious vision. As McKinnell underlined:

> Some companies may fear that if they sign up to the Global Compact, they'll be held to higher standard of corporate citizenship. That's a challenge we frankly welcome.

Sources: authors' interviews with McKinnell and Nancy Nielsen, Senior Director of Corporate Citizenship; M. McIntosh, S. Waddock and G. Kell (eds.), *Learning to Talk: Corporate Citizenship and the Development of the UN Global Compact* (Sheffield, UK: Greenleaf Publishing, 2004).

Cost cutting

That conservation and good management of environmental factors can save money is now a well-established fact. In 2003 one of the authors were told how Hewlett-Packard had built state-of-the-art recycling plants for its printed circuit boards, in association with Miranda Mines of Canada. It found that, whereas traditional copper mines produce 6 oz of copper per ton, the recycling plants are producing 12 oz per ton of waste — making these Hewlett-Packard recycling centres excellent 'copper mines'! New Zealand retailer The Warehouse has designed a software

The Co-operative Bank

Starting in the early 1990s, under a new CEO, Terry (now Lord) Thomas, The Co-operative Bank was transformed from an old-fashioned organisation with a rather dated image into a successful institution with a high profile and international reputation. Terry and his colleagues put business ethics and a commitment to sustainability at the heart of their vision of how the bank would be run.* The Co-operative Bank (now part of CFS [Cooperative Financial Services]) has developed a number of innovative approaches based on its ethical and sustainability principles. This has included turning away business inconsistent with those principles (see page 143).[†] In 2004, Echo Research released the findings of their third international CSR report, consisting of opinion research and analysis of over 5,000 CSR-related media mentions across the globe. In terms of positive coverage, the bank was ranked first in the UK and third in the world.[‡]

* Authors' interview with Lord Thomas, June 2003
† CFS Sustainability Report, June 2004
‡ Echo Research, *CSR and the Financial Community: Friends or Foes?* (2004). Based on analysis (January–July 2003) of over 5,400 media items from Australia, China, France, Germany, Japan, South Africa, the UK and the US

program that controls its energy use so effectively that its power consumption has been halved. Beacon Press provides a further example in cost saving through environmental excellence.

Beacon Press

The commitment of Beacon Press to the environment and to innovation has made it one of the leading UK printing companies. It was one of the first companies to convert to waterless printing, having introduced waterless presses when existing machines were due for replacement. The extra capital expenditure incurred to purchase the waterless technology has been offset by reductions in operating costs. The company's leadership in environmental performance has made it a preferred supplier to other companies looking to green their supply chain. Beacon Press now has 1 in 10 of the FTSE 350 companies as customers and was winner of the 2002 Environment Award for Excellence, given by Business in the Community (see BITC 2003, *The Business Case for Corporate Responsibility*, published by Arthur D. Little).

Experience is now showing that social factors can also be managed in ways to reduce costs. Texas Instruments implemented a local procurement policy in Dallas, TX, achieving savings of US$100 million over five years.[16] The Caribbean-based manufacturer of clothing, the Argus Group, has reduced absenteeism rates to 4%, compared with an average of 10%, by offering free access to full-time medical staff on-site. Research had shown that some 80% of absences were due to employees

16 For more detail, see Roger Cowe, *Investing in Social Responsibility* (Association of British Insurers, 2001).

missing a day's work while visiting state-provided medical services.[17] Similarly, Volkswagen Brazil implemented a HIV/AIDS education and treatment programme in 1996, which by 1999 had resulted in a 90% reduction of hospitalisations and a 40% drop in costs for treatment and care under its health plan. In addition, 90% of the patients were active and without symptoms.

On the issue of HIV and AIDS, Anglo American reports that 97% of its HIV-infected workers in South Africa who are receiving treatment provided by the company are back in full-time work, including heavy physical labour. This figure can be contrasted with the findings of Sanlam, a life insurer, in a 2003 survey of South African firms, suggesting that infected workers who get no treatment typically take 55 days of sick leave in their final two years at work — a big loss in areas where skilled labour is scarce.[18]

Market growth

In a competitive marketplace firms are, of course, looking for ways to attract new customers, to increase the loyalty or spending of existing customers or to find ways to serve unserved markets. In the chapters on Steps 1 and 2 we described some consumer trends that are linked to CSR factors (pages 39-42, 74-76). When determining how a business strategy will contribute to market growth, managers will need to consider whether the proposals will appeal to the consumer niches emerging as a result of these trends.

Recent research in the USA has highlighted a category of the population said to be worth US$227 billion per year — those who demonstrate 'lifestyles of health and sustainability' ('lohas'). A typical 'lohas' will buy fair-trade coffee and organic produce, save through socially responsible investment (SRI) funds, use complimentary medicine and go on eco-friendly holidays.[19] Similar markets are being identified in the United Kingdom, as evidenced by the 2003 Ethical Consumer Report. Since 1999 The Co-operative Bank in the UK has produced the Ethical Purchasing Index (EPI) to record and report on UK sales of goods and services marketed as 'ethical'. The latest report, published in December 2003, reported that the total value of ethical consumption in the UK was £19.9 billion, and the recorded sales of ethically marketed goods and services was £6.9 billion — a 13% increase from 2001.[20]

In addition to the growth in the 'ethical consumer' market, companies may see opportunities in meeting the needs of under-served consumers — as illustrated by the broadcaster BSkyB in seeking to provide 'disability-friendly' programming — and in promoting their environmental credentials to business-to-business (B2B) customers — as illustrated by the construction services company Carillion in its designing of environmentally friendly halls of residence for students. (On the

---

17   For more details, see SustainAbility, and the International Finance Corporation, *Developing Value: The Business Case for Sustainability in Emerging Markets* (London: SustainAbility, 2002).
18   See *The Economist*, 11 October 2003.
19   Reported in *Financial Times*, 'Guilt is no solution', 16 October 2003.
20   The Co-operative Bank, *Ethical Performance*, January 2003.

benefits of good environmental practice in attracting B2B contracts, see also the example of UPS given earlier in this chapter, page 108.)

BSkyB

Like other broadcasters, BSkyB has a number of regulatory obligations concerning disabled viewers — such as the amount of programming that has subtitles for deaf viewers and audio-description for blind users (audio-description is a voice-over commentary explaining what is happening on-screen when there is no dialogue). Sky has a strategy for meeting and exceeding these regulatory requirements.

Sky's Disability Manager, Kay Allen (a veteran pioneer, who played a similar role at retailer B&Q [see the example on page 119]), has persuaded senior management to invest in becoming disability-friendly. This has included disability awareness training for, among others, senior programmers and editors and has already led to more disability-aware descriptions of forthcoming programmes. It has also led to skills being taught to operatives at its customer call-centre to enable them to respond better to disabled customers. For example, call-centre staff are trained to use Texbox communications with deaf customers.

Sky's investment in subtitling, audio-description and in remote controls that can be used easily by older and disabled viewers totals approximately £12 million. However, as part of the Rupert Murdoch business empire, Sky is focused on the financial bottom line — how, therefore, did Kay Allen convince the company to make this investment? The answer, she told us, was through a mix of arguments concerning licence to operate and hard business-case numbers concerning the potential revenue to be gained by attracting disabled customers to the broadcasting service.

Carillion

In B2B markets, tenders that reference good CSR practice can help win contracts. For example, the business and construction services company Carillion won the 2003 *Building Magazine* award for sustainability. One project cited by the magazine was a contract to build new halls of residence for Hertfordshire University. These halls use 60% less energy than typical halls of residence, at no extra construction cost. The building design will thus generate less carbon dioxide (CO_2) emissions and will generate £3 million of energy savings over a 25 year period).

A spokesperson for Hertfordshire University noted that 'this was an important factor in Carillion's selection as our private partner in the development' (see also the case studies on awards for excellence, on the Business in the Community website, at www.bitc.org.uk).

Relationships, alliances and the licence to operate

The trend from manufacturing-based to service-based economies makes relationships — based on the quality of 'soft' transactions between people in networks — more important. Therefore, investment in those relationships that are key for associated business strategies and CSR-related policies and programmes provide a vehicle.

Mark Goyder of Tomorrow's Company, writing in *Redefining CSR*, notes that:[21]

> Every company needs to create economic value to distribute to its
> shareholders. But the creation of that value happens through the
> relationships the company develops with customers, employees,
> suppliers, communities and shareholders. Companies are only as
> successful as the quality of these relationships. The relationships
> overlap, and much of the value that is created is at the interface
> between relationships — for example in the impact that loyal
> employees have on the customers they meet, or the impact that
> excellent community activities have on the motivation and skill levels
> of employees. You cannot have successful relationships unless you
> have clear purpose and clear values.

Relationships are often key to securing the 'licence to operate' — whether at the
level of formal permission to carry out business that is given by governmental
authorities or the more intangible level of acceptance and support for aspects of
business operations by local communities and other key stakeholders. The importance of CSR to business relationships is recognised by Placer Dome Inc.:[22]

> It is our belief that this commitment to environmental protection,
> social progress and shared economic benefit will give us preferred
> access to gold projects around the world, thus ensuring our con-
> tinued success and growth.

One way in which new relationships are forged is through partnership arrangements
between businesses, communities, government organisations, non-governmental
organisations (NGOs) and so on, as illustrated by the case of the construction and
materials company RMC.

RMC and BirdLife International

RMC, the UK-headquartered construction and materials company, has worked with NGOs to
develop new forms of partnering in order to move forward biodiversity issues. For example,
RMC is working with international bird organisations and has signed a global memorandum
of understanding with BirdLife International (the Royal Society for the Protection of Birds
[RSPB] is the UK partner) to promote biodiversity on its aggregate sites worldwide. It
believes that this not only has a positive impact on the company's reputation but also has
facilitated getting planning permission as a 'neighbour of choice'. RMC also reports that this
approach has resulted in a decrease in management time spent on non-core issues,
increased speed of goods to market and less confrontation with local stakeholders (reported
in the Business in the Community Corporate Responsibility Index, 15 March 2004).

Source: interview with author, March 2004

21   Mark Goyder, *Redefining CSR* (London: Tomorrow's Company).
22   Quoted in Simon Zadek, *Doing Good and Doing Well: Making the Business Case for Corporate Citizenship* (Report R-1282-00-RR; The Conference Board, 2000).

Access to financial capital

As described in Step 2 (see pages 70-74), there is growing interest from a range of investors and their agents in social, ethical and environmental factors.

Some 50% of fund managers, investor relations officers and analysts across Europe are of the belief that social and environmental considerations will become a significant aspect of mainstream investment decisions over the next two years. CSR and governance practices in emerging markets are seen as a particularly 'hot' area of non-financial risk for which increased scrutiny by the investment community is prudent.[23] This view is reinforced by a number of examples:

- Changes made to governance practices by the Bank of Shanghai in China contributed to it attracting an 8% equity investment from HSBC in 2001.[24]

- In the USA there were US$2.34 trillion of SRI funds under management in 2001,[25] representing approximately one in every eight dollars under professional investment.

- In Europe, £12.2 billion has been invested in the SRI retail market and £336 billion in the SRI institutional market.[26]

These issues are not limited to the SRI community: at time of writing 33% of mainstream analysts say environmental factors are important in their evaluation of companies, compared with only 20% in 1994. The figures for social issues have increased by an even wider margin, from 12% to 34%.[27]

In the UK, only 1% of total assets (£3.3 billion) were in socially responsible investments in 1999. Socially responsible investments, however, were estimated to reach £10 billion by 2003.

In a related development, we are seeing the integration of social and environmental considerations and criteria into lending and credit risk-assessment processes, thereby influencing terms under which credit or capital is accessed. The Brazilian operation of ABN AMRO has successfully achieved this and branch managers have gone through training on how to integrate such criteria into their credit operations.[28]

Finally, multilateral funding institutions such as the World Bank — including the International Finance Corporation and the Inter-American Development Bank — are making investments and loans based partly on adherence to particular CSR-

23   Reported in Deloitte, CSR Europe and Euronext, 'Investing in Responsible Business: The 2003 Survey of European Fund Managers, Financial Analysts and Investor Relations Officers'.
24   SustainAbility, and the International Finance Corporation, *Developing Value: The Business Case for Sustainability in Emerging Markets* (London: SustainAbility, 2002).
25   Quoted at www.sustainability-index.com.
26   Quoted by Deloitte, CSR Europe and Euronext, *op. cit.*
27   Source: BITC, www.bitc.org.uk.
28   Source: George Starcher, co-founder and Secretary-General of European Baha'i Business Forum, a network of 350 members in 50 countries.

related standards and behaviour, such as the Equator Principles (see the section on the Equator Principles in Box 19, page 72).

Development of human capital

Clive Mather, oil giant Shell's Global Head of Learning, told us that being recognised as a responsible business was a prerequisite nowadays to attracting and retaining top talent. For those large companies who aren't recognised as such, even paying a significant price premium may not be enough to recruit the resources they need. Specific business strategies can contribute to or detract from that recognition.[29]

At the most basic level, when companies treat their employees 'well' — a 'state' that inevitably has different interpretations — then this is good for business. A survey by PwC looked at more than 1,000 companies in 47 countries and provides some evidence that treating people well is good for business as well as being the right thing to do. It measured employee morale by looking at absenteeism; this is not a perfect measure, but a company with lower absenteeism is generally a happier company than one where large numbers of people are habitually off sick — and companies with lower absenteeism have markedly higher profit margins.[30]

However, companies can go further than meeting basic legal requirements to protect the health and safety of their employees. Some examples where a broader view of investment in employees has had a positive impact include the following:

- The US Labor Department reports that 88% of employers with childcare assistance programmes have an increased ability to attract and retain employees.[31]

- The Nationwide Building Society in the UK introduced flexible working options in 1995. Over the following seven years, employee satisfaction levels rose by 14% and employee turnover was at 9.8%, despite an industry average of 24%. The Nationwide estimates that for every 3% increase in employee satisfaction, there is a 1% increase in member (customer) satisfaction.[32]

- The British train-operating company GNER applies what it calls the Service–Profit Chain, believing that from employee commitment comes customer satisfaction, which leads to customer loyalty and ultimately to better profits.[33]

- International healthcare business BUPA achieved improved employee satisfaction, with increases measuring 20%, and contributed to a business turnover increase of 32% through a programme that integrated ethical

29   Interview with author.
30   Reported in PwC, 'Global Human Capital Report', December 2002; reported in the *Financial Times*, 11 December 2002.
31   Reported in R. Cowe, *Investing in Social Responsibility* (Association of British Insurers, 2001).
32   Reported in *The Guardian*, 'Investing in Diversity: Equality at Work', 10 September 2003.
33   Source: author's visit to GNER HQ, York, UK, 18 September 2003.

values into the business, helping to engage, motivate and inspire employees.[34]

In relation to fundamental issues of health and safety, there are a number of physical and mental impairments that are linked specifically to modern work practices and the workplace. Research in Australia found that, of people of working age with a disability, 23% of their main impairments were caused through accident or injury or were due to working conditions or overwork (15%).[35] Of those attributable to accidents, 36% of the accidents occurred at work. This trend is likely to be reflected worldwide. In countries where workplace standards are lower, the incidence of disability caused by workplace accidents and other work-related factors is likely to be higher. Some 6% of all adults who have worked in the United Kingdom (about 2.2 million people) report a health condition that they believe was caused or aggravated by work. The most commonly reported problems are musculo-skeletal disorders, followed by mental health difficulties such as depression.[36]

Thus business strategies that can be implemented by integrating good practice in relation to human resources, embracing CSR, and that are tuned in to the values of employees can pay dividends, as illustrated by Adnams. Such practice is being described by some as harnessing 'organisational energy', as exemplified by Stanton Marris's 'energy business'.

Adnams

Adnams is a brewer that runs its own pubs, hotels and wine shops from Southwold on the UK Suffolk coast. Adnams management believe its Southwold connections are of fundamental importance to its authenticity as a niche brand. They ensure that the brand is associated with the traditional values, tranquil landscape and sense of community that the town offers. Indeed, its stated values — presented under headings such as community, pride, quality and integrity — reflect this, and the performance of all staff is measured against value-related objectives to ensure that the company's vision is embedded in every part of the organisation.

An employee survey in 2003, which had an 80% response rate, revealed that nearly 90% of respondents were motivated or extremely motivated to work for Adnams. A similar proportion was proud or extremely proud to be part of the company. Increased sales and profits have been driven by the strength of the brand, staff motivation and the company's determination to express its values in everything it does. Adnams was the first small company to win top honours in Business in the Community's annual Awards for Excellence — the 2003 Impact on Society Award (UK Small Business Consortium to Promote CSR to Small Businesses 2004).*

* The Small Business Consortium brings together a range of organisations representing small firms with those championing CSR to develop the arguments, examples, language and tools for responsible business practice by small and medium-sized enterprises. These can be accessed at www.smallbusinessjourney.com.

---

34   Reported in *The Business Case for Corporate Responsibility*, published in 2003 by Arthur D. Little and Business in the Community.

35   *Ibid.*

36   Reported at Disability Online for CSR Practitioners, www.employers-forum.co.uk.

Stanton Marris: the energy business

UK management consultancy Stanton Marris, which describes itself as an 'organisational energy consultancy', has been working with blue-chip clients in the commercial and public sectors on the crucial issue of organisational energy, which it defines as 'the extent to which an organisation has mobilised the full available effort of its people in pursuit of its goals'. In its 2003 publication titled *Energising the Organisation: The Sources of Energy*, it observes that:

> Collins and Porras's famous study of the stock market performance of 36 paired companies over 60 years showed that when what excites and drives people is also what delivers business results, sustainable success is designed into the DNA of the organisation. Gary Hamel's analysis of revolutionary companies demonstrated how they had harnessed the passion of their employees in order to succeed. Ghoshal and Bartlett's six-year research programme in dozens of global firms concluded that 'companies cannot renew their business unless they first revitalise their people'. Gallup having interviewed a million employees worldwide proved a strong correlation between employee engagement and customer satisfaction, productivity and profit. The factors determining organisational energy have also been shown to be leading indicators of employee retention and business and product innovation.

As more businesses move from closed to open organisations (i.e. to more networked organisations, such as those seen in Hollywood studios, where teams are assembled and re-assembled amoeba-like to work on different films) then the need for unifying cultures and behaviour and values becomes all the greater.

▶ Making a business case in emerging markets

How might business-case issues vary for business strategies and operations that involve either trading with or investing or selling in markets such as Brazil, China, India and South Africa? As would be expected, aspects of the business case (e.g. market growth opportunities through niche consumer groups interested in ethical issues, or licence-to-operate issues) will be determined by local customs and conditions.

One study by consultancy SustainAbility, the International Finance Corporation (IFC) and Brazil's Instituto Ethos identified a range of business-case categories relevant to emerging markets, including:

● The reduction of costs by decreasing environmental impacts and treating employees well

● The increasing of revenues by improving the environment and benefiting the local economy

● The reduction of risks through engagement with stakeholders

● The building of a good reputation by increasing environmental efficiency

- The development of human capital through better management of human resources

- Improvements to the ability to access capital through better governance

- The creation of other opportunities through community development and through the creation of environmentally friendly products

Notwithstanding the specifics of local conditions, the process of globalisation and increasing trade liberalisation is resulting in the spreading of expectations regarding standards and behaviour, impacting local and international firms alike. Rafael Wong, Executive Vice President of the banana producer Reybancorp, in Ecuador, noted that: [37]

> When we first obtained financing from the IFC, the environmental standards seemed like an obstacle, but now we realise that they have helped us to build a strong business. In five years, there will be no access to international markets for companies which do not show respect for the environment. It is becoming fundamental to international trade.

For some business leaders of companies based in emerging markets, a commitment to elements of CSR helps to achieve a competitive edge in an increasingly competitive environment, as explained by K.N. Agarwal, Managing Director of Alexandria Carbon Black, in Egypt:

> [You] cannot increase production this rapidly unless your workforce is behind you and you have the trust of the community you are operating in and the partners you are working with . . . To attract the best talent available in the country, you have to create a clean, green and healthy environment and an atmosphere where the people like to work to grow, which is extremely important for improving the bottom line.

Emerging and developing markets are — by definition — 'undeveloped' and contain some of the most interesting business opportunities, and this applies to CSOs too. Many of the examples of companies quoted in Step 2 that have found CSOs are operating in less-developed countries. A particular set of CSOs are those that meet the needs of the poorest of the world's population, as explained by the concept of the bottom of the pyramid.

---

37   Quoted in SustainAbility and the International Finance Corporation, *Developing Value: The Business Case for Sustainability in Emerging Markets* (London: SustainAbility, 2002).

The bottom of the pyramid

The model

Seminal work by professors C.K. Prahalad and Stuart L. Hart, described in their article 'The Fortune at the Bottom of the Pyramid', published in the *Harvard Business Review* in 2002, has helped to draw attention to the business opportunities provided by what they call a 'tier 4' category of four billion people around the world whose purchasing power parity in US dollars is less than the US$1,500 per annum level acknowledged as needed to sustain a decent life. They argue that it is a lack of imagination that is preventing Western-based international companies thinking of these people as potential consumers.

Speaking at a Conference Board event in New York, Professor Hart said:

> Unspoken assumptions [are that] the corporate sector serves the rich, and the government and NGOs protect the environment and the poor. The real opportunity lies in breaking this code, linking the poor and the rich across the world in a seamless market organised around the concept of sustainable development.

If companies were to embrace the idea of moving from the mind-set of CSR to CSO this would, in our view, make a substantial contribution to making this vision a reality.

In their article, Prahalad and Hart argued that although individually the four billion poorest people have few resources, their collective purchasing power can be substantial (see Figure 7) — but that business needs new approaches if it is to tap this purchasing power. The poor in Rio de Janeiro, for instance, have a total purchasing power of US$1.2 billion (US$600 per person). Shanty towns in Johannesburg and Mumbai are no different. It can also be surprisingly cheap to market and deliver products and services to the world's poor, because many of them live in cities that are densely populated and will be even more so in years to come. Figures from the UN and the World Resources Institute indicate that by 2015, in Africa, 225 cities will each have populations of more than a million; in Latin America, there will be another 225 such cities; and in Asia, a further 903.[38] The population of at least 27 cities will reach or exceed eight million. Collectively, the 1,300 largest cities will account for some 1.5 billion to 2 billion people, roughly half of whom will be consumers at the bottom of the pyramid who are currently served primarily by informal economies. Companies that operate in these areas will have access to millions of potential new customers, who together have billions of dollars to spend.

Examples

Typically, bottom-of-the-pyramid strategies involve all forms of CSO. First, they are aimed at serving new markets; second, they usually involve a new (or substantially

---

38   C.K. Prahalad and A. Hammond, 'What Works: Serving the World's Poor Profitably' (World Resources Institute, 2003; www.wri.org).

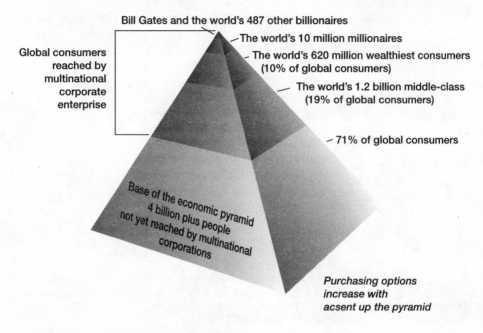

Figure 7 **The global economic pyramid**

Source: Medard Gabel, www.bigpictureconsulting.com

reformulated) product or service; and, third, they involve new business models such as using new delivery channels and new financing methods.[39]

- New products:
  - Unilever has developed dietary products enriched to improve the nutrition of, for example, pregnant women in Ghana (see page 91).
  - Hindustan Lever has developed a detergent that is more suited for use in washing clothes in rivers, being more environmentally friendly than other formulations (see page 92).

- New delivery channels:
  - Procter & Gamble is marketing PuR® water-purifying sachets to people in the developing world, to provide safe drinking water (see page 95).

Further examples are the extension of banking services to those on a low-income provided by Standard Bank, in South Africa, and by Citibank, in India. These two examples also illustrate the fact that many bottom-of-the-pyramid CSOs are about

39 Prahalad and Hart have continued to develop their thinking on the bottom of the pyramid, working with different collaborators. For example see C.K. Prahalad and A. Hammond, 'What Works: Serving the World's Poor Profitably' (World Resources Institute, 2003, www.wri.org).

harnessing new information and communications technologies, such as e-banking and iris technology (see below), to bring new products and services to low-income, emerging markets. Another example of how new technology is being brought to 'the bottom of the pyramid' is that of Hewlett-Packard, which has provided 'digital town centres' to towns and villages in Costa Rica as well as photographic services in India (this latter example also illustrating the use of micro-lending in developing countries). Thus there is a two-way connection between technology and micro-lending here: technology is making banking to low-income people possible; micro-lending is enabling people to access new technology.

Standard Bank of South Africa Ltd

In South Africa, 73% of the population earns less than R5,000 ($460) per month, according to a 2001 World Bank study. Retail banking services for such low-income customers are becoming one of the most competitive and fast-growing mass markets. In 1994, Standard Bank of South Africa Ltd, Africa's leading consumer bank, launched a low-cost, volume-driven e-banking business, called AutoBank E (hereafter referred to AutoBank), to increase its revenue by providing banking services to the poor.

Standard Bank is considering a loan programme for low-income clients. Computerisation of micro-lending services not only makes the overall operation more efficient but also makes it possible for the bank to reach many more people — lending money to individuals with no collateral and no formal address. As overheads are lower and there is little paperwork, the costs of AutoBank are 30–40% lower than those at traditional branches.

Citibank

Citibank's Suvidha is a consumer-banking product with a low deposit limit (US$25). It was an unqualified success when launched in Bangalore, with over 150,000 new accounts opened in the first year. Latent demand for trusted financial services proved to be much stronger than Citibank imagined. Citibank is also experimenting with new iris recognition technology (for individual identification) and the use of iconic tools to overcome poor people's inability to read and write.

Pharaohs at the bottom of the pyramid

[The bottom of the pyramid] means reaching consumers we have never reached before in rural villages and urban slums of the developing world. It means developing totally new products specific to the needs, frustrations and aspirations of those new customers. It means exploring totally new business models, often built on volume instead

Hewlett-Packard

Costa Rica

In Costa Rica, a pilot programme by Hewlett-Packard brought the 21st century to remote towns and villages. The company converted old shipping containers into 'digital town centres', each container holding a satellite link, several computers with access to the Internet and e-mail, educational videos and a phone service. The project, known as Lincos, is sold to towns and villages through credit and also creates work.

Source: Medard Gabel, 'Global Links Initiatives', www.bigpictureconsulting.com

India

Hewlett-Packard discovered a strong latent demand for photographs in India, especially for wedding and identity cards. To tap into this demand, it developed two companion technologies to support low-cost picture-taking and image development. One was a retail concept called the HP Photoshop Store, where basic image development through its printing and PC technology could be bought or licensed by locals in small villages. The second innovation was a high-quality camera, powered through a solar backpack, for mobile street photography. The result was the launch of a mini cottage industry for aspiring local entrepreneurs who wanted to become village photographers. Financing models, through micro-lending, helped make this possible. The concept made financial sense to Hewlett-Packard because it makes most of its margins selling printing paper and replacement cartridges, not actual hardware — therefore fostering the demand for picture taking and development was an ideal way to boost supply sales.

Source: Reported by Nicole Boyer in 2003 in *Global Business Network* in an article titled 'The Base of the Pyramid: Re-perceiving Business from the Bottom Up', www.gbn.com

of margin, and with new supply and distribution systems to lower cost and reach where we have not gone before.

George Carpenter and Peter White, Procter & Gamble[40]

As readers will already be noticing, only a relatively small number of company names — such as Citibank, Dow, DuPont, Johnson & Johnson, Procter & Gamble and Unilever — regularly crop up in discussions about bottom-of-the-pyramid opportunities. We believe that many more companies will be added to this list over the next few years.

However, there are possible negative environmental consequences for this expansion into emerging and new markets if attention is not paid to CSR principles. Bottom-of-the-pyramid consumers increasingly have access to television, enabling them to see a different lifestyle from their own. They will become increasingly assertive in wanting a taste of this. Such demand will not be met without creating unsustainable pollution and resource depletion unless businesses create CSOs. The

40   G. Carpenter and P. White, 'Sustainable Development: Finding the Real Business Case', *Corporate Environmental Strategy: International Journal for Sustainable Business* 2.2 (February 2004).

doyen of the Silicon Valley venture capitalists, John Doerr, whose shrewd investments in new technology start-ups in the 1990s did so much to make the Silicon Valley phenomenon, observed: [41]

> I am interested in making things again: clean water, clean transportation, clean power — those are the big markets of the future.

How, then, are companies specifically applying CSO thinking for the bottom-of-the-pyramid market? Philips has established a Bottom of the Pyramid Council because of the interest displayed by its CEO. Unilever has opened research centres in India. Hewlett-Packard has developed partnerships with academic institutions and NGOs such as the MIT Media Lab and the Foundation for Sustainable Development for its Costa Rica projects. A number of organisations are now tracking bottom-of-the-pyramid developments and sharing expertise. Some of these are listed in the 'Signposts' at the end of this book (pages 372ff.).

Philips

More than half the world's population do not have electricity. Lack of electricity in many parts of the LDCs means no clean water and also means local populations cutting down more trees in order to get wood to burn to purify their water — a vicious circle of unsustainability. Hence the importance of light-emitting diodes (LEDs). These outlast conventional, incandescent light bulbs by a factor of 10; use 80% less electricity; and, when used with solar-generated power, have a particularly positive environmental impact. LEDs are already being used for growing food (your salad in two days not three weeks!) and for disinfecting food, water and air. The LED market is growing at almost 60% a year — and Philips believes it could be worth $3 billion by 2006 — 10% of the total light market. LEDs are one of a number of bottom-of-the-pyramid projects that Philips is currently working on. Others include a $1 radio for which the Indian market alone might be 200 million sets.

Source: Speech by Jan Oosterveld, Member, Group Management Board Royal Philips Electronics, to IESE Responsible Business Conference, Barcelona, 27 March 2004

If more companies are to serve these and other markets in a responsible way then the case must be made for a positive link between CSR and shareholder value and financial performance. We turn to this business case in the next section, but first let us look at the business case for catering for consumers at the bottom of the pyramid. Procter & Gamble, for example, wants to build leadership in fast-growing developing markets (*P&G Annual Report* 2003), and Unilever anticipates that by 2010 half its sales will come from the developing world, up 32% from current sales.[42] For Unilever, the poor are already a huge market.

---

41 Nicole Boyer, 'The Base of the Pyramid: Reperceiving Business from the Bottom Up', Global Business Network Working Paper, May 2003.
42 See www.sustainablebusiness.com.

Unilever

Unilever, the US$50 billion Anglo-Dutch consumer-goods giant, has made an art of selling its products in tiny packages costing the equivalent of a few cents each. The conglomerate's Indian subsidiary, Hindustan Lever Ltd, adopted the concept in 1987, when it began selling single-use sachets of Sunsilk shampoo for between 2 and 4 cents. Now, mini-packages account for half of Hindustan Lever's US$2.4 billion in sales in India, and the strategy has gone global (as reported in *Business Week*, 26 August 2002):

- Unilever's Rexona brand deodorant sticks sell for 16 cents and more. They are very popular in India, the Philippines, Bolivia and Peru, where Unilever has 60% of the deodorant market.
- In Nigeria, Unilever sells 3-inch-square packets of margarine that do not need to be kept in a refrigerator.

▶ Making a business case: the link between corporate social responsibility and shareholder value and financial performance

> Corporate social responsibility is a hard-edged business decision. Not because it is a nice to do or because people are forcing us to do it . . . because it is good for our business.
>
> *Niall Fitzgerald, retiring co-chair and CEO of Unilever*[43]

Those looking for watertight evidence to demonstrate that there is a link between CSR commitment and practice and shareholder value will be disappointed. The problem is the classic challenge of causality: of isolating cause and effect in a complex and dynamic environment. However, one does not have to look far to see that shareholder value has been damaged — in some cases irreversibly — by 'irresponsible' business behaviour.

Certainly, if you are CEO of a major corporation then research by PwC suggests that you believe the business case for seriously addressing CSR: 70% of respondents in PwC's fifth global survey of CEOs, drawn from 33 countries, said that CSR is critical to profitability.[44] There is a growing body of evidence to show that the market values of those companies that have appropriate measures in place to manage material CSR risks fare better than those companies that do not. We summarise some of the most pertinent research below:

43   Quoted in *The Guardian*, 7 July 2003.
44   Quoted in World Economic Forum and International Business Leaders Forum, *op. cit.*

- The Dow Jones Sustainability Index has outperformed the FTSE World Index by 17% since its launch in 1994.[45]

- Those sectors that are less likely to traditionally face CSR risks (e.g. telecommunications and the media) have higher price-to-earnings ratios, suggesting, according to the *Financial Times*, that investors are already pricing in social, environmental and ethical factors.[46]

- Innovest — strategic value advisors — estimate that in some exposed sectors 45% of earnings and 35% of market capitalisation are at risk from the consequences of climate change; for this reason, institutional investors are banding together through the Carbon Disclosure Project (see Box 19, page 72).[47]

- Innovest studies also point to a correlation between environmental sustainability ratings and corporate financial performance. A study into the performance of food companies states that 'sustainability leaders' outperform 'sustainability laggards' with reference to food companies' high agricultural impact. Leaders outperformed laggards by 20.2% over the last two-year period studied (2002–2003) and by 9.4% over the last single year (2003). (This study method is illustrative of attempts to quantify qualitative factors so that financial markets can access data in a format with which they are familiar and can then use in analysis.)

- A survey of the transparency and disclosure practices of over 1,500 companies found a direct correlation between disclosure and market risk and market valuation.[48]

- In its April 2003 report, 'Does Business Ethics Pay?', the Institute for Business Ethics in the United Kingdom found that in a sample of FTSE350 firms 'ethical' companies outperformed those which made no such claims on three out of four financial measures (market value added [MVA], economic value added [EVA] and price/earnings ratio) between 1997 and 2001. The Institute's study concludes that 'there is strong indicative evidence that large UK companies with codes of business ethics/conduct produced an above-average performance when measured against a similar group without codes'.[49]

The data provided in the examples quoted above refers to financial performance, but there is a move to broaden the nature of performance and value assessment to include non-financial measures. Credit Suisse, in *Trust Us: The Global Reporters 2002 Survey of Corporate Sustainability Reporting*, states that:

45   See J. Fuller, 'Banking on a Good Reputation', *Financial Times*, 23 July 2003.
46   Reported in Fuller, *op. cit.*
47   M. See Keirnan, 'Taking Control of Climate', *Financial Times*, 16 July 2003.
48   See S. Patel and G. Dallas, 'Transparency and Disclosure: Overview of Methodology and Study Results' (USA, Standard & Poor's, 2002).
49   Quoted in *Financial Times*, April 2003; see also www.ibe.org.uk.

> The market value of businesses is no longer determined solely by
> traditional financial data . . . but also by intangible factors such as
> brand reputation, intellectual capital, risk management, codes of
> conduct, the inclusion of stakeholders and customer loyalty.

Figures in support of this are provided by Rd Jürgen H. Daum, in his book *Intangible Assets and Value Creation*, in which he states:[50]

> The proportion of a company's total market value that exceeds its
> book value has increased from 40% in the early 1980s to over 80% at
> the end of the 1990s. This means that only 20% of a companies value
> is reflected in the accounting system . . . [thus the largest portion of
> a company's economic activities] can easily be overlooked.

The Rose Foundation in its Environmental Fiduciary Report (www.rosefdn.org) is thus correct in our view in concluding that 'trustees, directors and fund managers that do not respond to evidence that environmental performance is an economic value driver are failing to meet their fiduciary responsibilities'.

Further evidence comes from the Work and Enterprise Panel of Inquiry, an extensive study into high-performance working and productivity launched by The Work Foundation in 2002. The study included the participation of major companies Tesco, Microsoft, Lloyds TSB, Manpower, Eversheds and AstraZeneca as well as the trade union Unison. The Panel of Inquiry found that businesses that are regarded as high-performing do on average 42% better financially than do businesses that are regarded as low-performing. Further, the Panel found that such high performance appeared to be linked to the management of five key areas and, critically, the trade-offs between them.[51] The key areas concerned:

● Customers and markets

● Shareholders and governance systems (including finance and investment)

● Stakeholders (not only suppliers, customers and other people but also communities and CSR objectives)

● Human resources practices

● Creativity and innovation management

We would argue that a business might perform at even higher levels if rather than having separate CSR objectives these were woven into all aspects of running the business rather than being treated as stand-alone issues.

The results of the above surveys and studies appear to provide support for the business case for CSR, but how did the early movers in CSR convince the financial directors, investors and commentators that investments in the area of CSR would pay dividends or that decisions to favour CSR were based on evidence that this

50 J.H. Daum, *Intangible Assets and Value Creation* (New York: John Wiley, 2003).
51 Work and Enterprise Panel of Enquiry, 'The Missing Link: From Productivity to Performance' (2003); see The Work Foundation website, at www.theworkfoundation.com.

strategy would benefit the company? The business case is, by definition, based on a *lagging* indicator of the health of those first companies seeking competitive advantage through leadership and innovation. Such early-mover companies were acting *ahead* of the evidence. Indeed, without the pioneering role of such companies there would be no business case.

What insight prompted those companies to act before the business case could be proved? Perhaps the answer lies in how the first movers viewed the idea of a 'business case'. The words of David Varney, Chairman of mmO_2 and of Business in the Community, speaking to us in an interview in July 2003, may give a clue:

> People say the business case is post-hoc rationalisation — absolutely — like for penicillin! . . . I'm involved in creating sustained shareholder-value — I use all the panoply of corporate responsibility tools to help build a sustainable business — this is part of the core business. I don't know another way. I'd like to hear the case for sustainable irresponsible value-creation — but I haven't heard it! There's lots of value to learning faster — how quickly you respond to the weak signals — like Cadbury's with saturated fats — if you can see these weak signals . . .

▶ Synthesis of Step 3

Here we look at how Steps 1–3 might apply — in the view of the authors — to the example of drinks company Diageo operating in Africa, and responding to a high incidence of HIV/AIDS among its workforce and local community.

Making a business case in response to HIV/AIDS

Diageo is the world's leading premium business producing alcoholic drinks and employs 5,000 people in 25 different African countries. Step 1 triggers for Diageo might have been:

- Growing levels of employee absenteeism in its African operations because of the spread of the AIDS pandemic in Africa
- Projected possible reductions in market growth for its products in Africa because of AIDS
- Johannesburg Stock Exchange (JSE) listing requirements to publish an HIV/AIDS corporate policy, if it were listed on the JSE

Triggers from stakeholders might have included:

- Investor reports
- Missing orders from suppliers because of staff absenteeism
- Concerns raised by NGOs about binge drinking, especially among young males, leading to unsafe sex and therefore to high rates of infection with HIV

continued ➜

Standard Bank estimates that 10% of its staff in Africa are off sick at any one time as a result of HIV or AIDS. If Diageo were aware of this statistic then, applying this 1:10 ratio to its own business, it might have concluded that the pandemic would have a substantial impact on its costs and revenues.

Scoping of its options (Step 2) might have involved an evaluation and comparison of the implications of:

- Doing nothing
- Recruiting further employees to allow for staff attrition due to illness
- Implementing policies aimed at the prevention of infection with HIV, the prevention of the onset of AIDS and care for those with HIV and AIDS

This scoping process would have included a stakeholder analysis and a refinement of the options, including the relative costs and feasibility of implementation of the possible strategies.

In Step 3, the business case is tested against market and organisational considerations. This might include the need to:

- Develop personnel policies to ensure non-discrimination in the workplace
- Organise cover at short notice for sick workers
- Organise the distribution of retroviral drugs to employees and their dependants

There may also be knock-on issues of ensuring consistency of advertising and overall marketing messages so that Diageo products are associated with responsible drinking.

Step 3 might have thrown up issues of a short-term increase in expenditure in order to save money late, and to protect the value of the company's existing investment. Volkswagen Brazil, for example, has been able to reduce rates of new infections within its workforce through an intense programme of education (for a brief description, see page 122). This process might also raise issues of how Diageo might take its learning from its African operations into other parts of the business and issues related to setting a precedent in one part of the world.

And as we shall see further in Step 4, if Diageo had then put this decision through the 'sift' of fit between the business decision and its corporate values, it would fit squarely with Diageo's corporate citizenship commitment. In its corporate citizenship report (available at www.diageo.com) Diageo defines corporate citizenship as 'a natural part of doing business': It involves all the ways in which our business and products interact with society and the natural world, and encompasses the balance between acting responsibly and the right to trade freely. It includes ethics, governance relations with employees, customers, consumers and suppliers, communities, health and safety and the environment.

▶ Moving from Step 3 to Step 4

In Step 3 we looked at a range of material and perspectives which need to be considered when building business strategies based on CSR factors while taking advantage of corporate social opportunities. In Step 4 we discuss how to analyse and adapt the chosen strategy in light of the company's corporate culture, values, leadership styles and governance arrangements.

Step 4
Committing to action

Focus

In this chapter we look at the implications of and for proposed strategies in light of organisational values, leadership style and governance arrangements.

Applying Step 4

In Part II — the worked example of the seven steps — the completed process forms show how, by applying appropriate tools and techniques selected from Step 4, the following outputs are produced (pages 323ff.):

- An assessment of the implications of proposed actions on corporate values and leadership – and vice versa

- An assessment of the implications for governance and management arrangements

- An identification of appropriate public commitments to be made and communications signals to be given

IT IS NOW, AT STEP 4, THAT WE CONSIDER THE IMPLICATIONS OF A business or one of its business units committing to action. This involves weighing up proposed business strategies in the light of corporate values, culture, leadership style and governance arrangements.

Firms looking to exploit specific business strategies built around corporate social opportunities (CSOs) will need to consider the consequences of existing, implicit or explicit company-wide principles and values that guide decision-making. If a business does not have a clearly articulated set of values and business principles — or these are inconsistent with responsible business principles — then this needs to be addressed before new strategies can be validated. Failure to ensure alignment between proposed strategies informed by ethical and responsible business drivers with a current dominant values-set that is not informed by these principles can lead to divergent and disruptive behaviour across a company, threatening not only the specific new strategies but also the sustainability of the business.

Assuming that a proposed strategy is consistent with corporate values that are themselves consistent with corporate social responsibility (CSR), then committing to action involves identifying what will be required from leaders; the implications for governance; and what signals will help reinforce the proposed strategy. In practice, this is the stage where, even if up to now the focus has been on a particular business strategy or market opportunity, broader issues of corporate culture and values, leadership and governance will have to be addressed. We would argue that CSR is not an issue that can be handled in a piecemeal fashion but rather requires and benefits from a holistic commitment to aligning business values, purpose and strategy with responsible and ethical business practices. This then creates the business environment in which CSOs are achievable now and more likely to emerge in the future.

In Step 4 we demonstrate how to achieve a successful alignment of business strategies and CSR-based values, articulating these values clearly. This will create a 'North Star' to help managers and employees steer their way through decision-making dilemmas that they are bound to face where it will not always be possible to defer to senior management. We also explore the role of sound corporate governance arrangements in providing checks and balances and adequate oversight within a CSR context. We explain the importance of good practice in institutional and personal leadership, stressing the need for integrity and consistency, as sound practice and leadership will drive change and create the enabling environment for the alignment of values and for embedding responsible business practices throughout the firm. We look at the benefits of publicly stating commitments to CSR and suggest that those who 'go beyond CSR' to commit publicly to the discovery and pursuit of CSOs will gain the most competitive advantage.

Traditional command-and-control cultures operating with long and protracted decision-chains are not sustainable in today's competitive, fast-moving, highly connected business environment. A tight rein on decision-making from the corporate centre can strangle initiative and innovation. The paradox is that if too much slack is given to front-line managers in their executive powers then this too can be a threat if it leads to bad decisions that expose a firm to unintended consequences and damage to reputation. Nowhere is this risk more apparent than in decisions that have a social, ethical or environmental impact. Some years ago, a company's response to an accusation of employee discrimination in a remote operation may have been determined locally, based on local custom and practice, at the site manager's discretion. The impact of that decision would have been felt only locally. Now, because of improved communications and increased public scrutiny, the implications of an inappropriate local response are potentially visible on a global scale.

The dilemma of local autonomy having potentially global consequences is a significant driver, leading corporations committing publicly to statements of global values and business principles, such as the Universal Declaration of Human Rights or Conventions such as those promulgated by the International Labour Organisation (ILO), which form part of the commitment required by organisations supporting the UN's Global Compact. To a greater or lesser extent these provide a guiding framework while allowing local discretion.

▶ Making a start: 'Should we be doing this? Does it meet the values test?'

It is through the act of crafting, communicating, applying and refining corporate values and principles that business leaders ensure that disparate parts of a business are being steered in the right direction and operating within common, defined behaviour. In a world where reputation is so vulnerable, this is key to sustainable success.

Before looking at how a range of companies are articulating and promulgating company-wide corporate values and principles, it is worth considering cases where new strategies need to be rejected — despite promising spectacular growth or high returns — that is, where they are incompatible with the core values of the business. For example, a private-sector water company that has publicly espoused a commitment to promoting sustainable water supplies should reject a potentially commercially attractive invitation to tender when the water source in question is not sustainable. A company's rejection of a business opportunity because of its expressed CSR commitments is a good test of whether that company is living up to its values.

In fact, the case of a water company facing such a decision was the scenario RWE Thames Water found itself confronting when invited to tender for a contract in the Middle East. The company determined that the aquifer concerned would not naturally be replenished. This, together with other concerns, was a major factor in the decision not to bid.[1] Other examples of companies faced with similar decisions may be found:

1   Jeremy Pelczer, President and CEO of American Water, part of the RWE Group, in an interview with the authors, October 2003. At the time of interview he was COO of RWE Thames Water.

- Mining firm Norsk Hydro withdrew from a bauxite project in India in response to stakeholder concerns regarding land rights.

- The Co-operative Bank's 2003 annual 'partnership report' reveals that it turned away more than £6.9 million of business the previous year from companies that failed to meet its ethical standards.[2]

- Following company policy, a loan manager at Banco Real ABN AMRO in Brazil turned down business from the owners of a lumber mill whom he believed to be illegally extracting mahogany from an Indian reserve in Amazonia. This manager had also declined to take business from the owners of an asbestos plant and of a coal mine.[3]

These examples show that there is a potential price to pay for CSR-oriented values — but, we argue, they also provide the basis for differentiation and CSO. The reputation of RWE Thames Water for sound environmental conservation practices and community relations has, its managers are convinced, helped to build important goodwill that has been critical in helping to differentiate the company from competitors. The companies listed above cite similar experiences:

- Norsk Hydro said that withdrawing from the Indian project was a crucial moment in building internal commitment to addressing wider stakeholder concerns.

- The Co-operative Bank may have lost £6.9 million of business, but the same policy helped attract some £40 million of new business (i.e. 31% of its £130.1 million profit) thanks to a growing niche of consumers attracted to its ethical trading policies.

- Banco Real ABN AMRO's stated that its 'Bank of Value' policy has helped it to win the loyalty and motivation of its employees. With the help of Friends of the Earth, some 1,600 managers have been trained to analyse social and environmental risk. Furthermore, owners of companies that initially were refused loans are welcomed back as customers if they accept support to rectify their CSR risks.

▶ Values built to last

We described in the Introduction to this book how many of the chairmen and CEOs we interviewed for this book quickly and unprompted steered the conversation around to the link between their personal and corporate values (see page 13). They described how in practice this shaped their businesses' approach to CSR and provided the filter through which to pass all business decisions. David Varney,

2   *Financial Times*, 'Co-op stance pays off as ethical profits hit £40m', 6 May 2004.
3   'Respect is Good as Well as Profitable', *Você S/A*, April 2003.

Chairman of mmO_2, repeatedly referred to the mmO_2 values (bold, open, clear, trusted) to explain why the business had adopted a particular approach to specific issues of CSR that his business is facing. He pointed out to us that 'business is not a moral desert — your stakeholders have to feel comfortable that you will make the right choices — so you should not shy away from values'; this is no easy matter. As one top consultant observed to us, 'how do you avoid values statements becoming a meaningless interchanging of a few key words and phrases?' Certainly, which business does not want to be 'customer-focused', to be 'innovative' or to 'value its people?' Yet all of us know all too many businesses that do not live out those values in practice.

A business with a well-established and widely understood values statement may choose to relate new commitments to responsible business back to the existing company values. US pharmaceutical firm Johnson & Johnson's values statement, the 'Credo', was laid down in 1943 and has been the explicit basis for the way in which the company has been run ever since.[4] In other cases, a company may be 'refreshing' a statement of values or codifying values for the first time. In these cases, an explicit endorsement of responsible business principles can be incorporated. The internationally renowned performance troupe Cirque du Soleil believe that their values — including commitment to CSR — have been crucial in preserving the essence of the organisation as it has transformed itself in recent years from a group of Quebecois street performers into a publicly quoted international company.

Generally, achievement of 'buy-in' to a set of values will be easier across an organisation if the whole organisation has been involved in the co-creation of those values, as was the case at Akzo Nobel. These company values, after all, are the values that each employee is expected to work by each day; they are the reference point in decision-making, the 'North Star' by which to guide behaviour. By 'co-creation' we do not mean that the values should be created by achieving consensus around the 'lowest common denominator'; rather, we mean they should be created by harnessing the best of the knowledge, passion and creativity of an organisation's employees in combination with the strategic direction of management. We recognise, how-

---

Akzo Nobel

Rather than imposing a corporate code of conduct from the top, the Dutch-headquartered company Akzo Nobel, the world's largest paint-maker, has handed responsibility for the implementation of the code to the people who run its individual businesses, who in turn have picked high-potential middle managers to ensure that the group's 67,000 employees in 80 countries are familiar with its principles. Hans Wijers, Chairman of Akzo, notes:

[The code] has to be aligned with what's going on in the company. We've used cases from the daily life of our own people. We're creating champions deeper and deeper in the organisation.

---

4   See www.jnj.com/our_company/our_credo.
5   Interview with authors, June 2003.

ever, that such co-creation may be harder to achieve where the prevailing culture is rigidly hierarchical.

However a set of values is generated, it is not enough for them simply to be posted on a website; they have to be lived. And they can only be lived if everyone in the organisation knows them, understands them and believes in them. This requires intense communication. It also requires long-term commitment and consistency — that is, values built to last. Clive Mather, Chairman of Shell UK and Shell's Global Director for Learning, gives the following advice:

> There is always a temptation to think after one or two years that people must be bored, and to change — don't — keep with it.[5]

Pharmaceutical company Pfizer has brought together the concepts of **values** and **value**. The company's mission is, it states (referring to itself in the collective, as 'we'), 'to become the world's most valued company to patients, customers, colleagues, investors, business partners and the communities where we work and live'. The statement of purpose continues: 'We dedicate ourselves to humanity's quest for longer, healthier, happier lives through innovation in pharmaceutical, consumer and animal health products'. All this is underpinned, the company says, by values, stating that 'to achieve our purpose and mission, we affirm our values of integrity, leadership, innovation, quality, teamwork, customer focus, and respect for people and community'.[6] Hank McKinnell, Chairman and CEO of Pfizer, sees the CSO role of Pfizer in competitive, global terms, stating that 'we want to be the company that does more good, for more people than any other on the planet'. The mission statement and the concept of being measured in the future, not only in financial terms but also non-financial, resulted from internal consultation and focus groups.

As we have seen in Step 1, there are many triggers that may encourage a company to examine its values. Crispin Davis, CEO of the Anglo–Dutch publishing conglomerate Reed Elsevier, described what prompted his company to determine a set of common, corporate values:

> Morale was low. The business had gone through tough times. The business was assembled by acquisition so it was in silos. It screamed out for a set of core values and a consistent business philosophy that people could identify with and take pride in.

A company-wide survey of employees asked which of the firm's implicit values were a source of strength, which they did not like — and what values were missing. Crispin and his senior management team then refined the responses into a set of five core values (www.reedelsevier.com). As he told us, this was necessary as 'the values also have to reflect me and the senior management team because otherwise we could not walk the talk'. The results were then re-circulated to all employees for comment before final agreement. At this point, each employee was notified of the values by five different means of communication:

---

6   Interview with authors, June 2003. Pfizer's statement can be read at www.pfizer.com.

- Crispin sent a letter to all 38,000 employees
- A brochure about the values was then sent to every employee
- Every business location ran a 'values day'
- Every manager communicated the values through a team briefing
- The values were implemented through '360° appraisal'
- The values were incorporated into personal development plans
- Each business unit was charged with developing a plan to put the values into action

How does a business define its core values consistently with responsible business principles? We don't think it is as simple as having a commitment to corporate social responsibility as one of its stated values! The process of establishing such values is probably easier in a small firm where the owners and employees all know each other, and can discuss this informally, than it is in a multinational, where more formal processes, as described in the Reed Elsevier example, are needed. The stages involved are probably rather similar, however, irrespective of size:

- Do we already have an explicit values statement? If not, what are the implicit values of this organisation?
- Whether explicit or implicit, what do we like and want to keep from these values, going forward? What do we dislike, feel to be inconsistent with responsible business principles and want to discard?
- What new values do we want to add that are consistent with responsible business principles?
- This will probably then involve a process of iteration with stakeholders (for effective stakeholder dialogue techniques, see Step 6) — as in the case of Reed Elsevier — before a final statement is agreed and then regularly · communicated.
- This then has to be followed through with opportunities to examine what these values mean for me and for my part of the business, and how do we live these values in practice?
- The values and how they can be lived in practice then becomes an integral part of recruitment criteria, induction and regular training.

For international businesses that operate in many different cultures, there is the question of finding values that transcend cultures and faiths — such as the Golden Rule, common to all the world's great religions: 'do to others as you would like them to do to you'. There is an organisation called the Institute for Global Ethics. It has conducted focus groups around the world asking people to list the five values that they would like to see over the entrance to a new school in their community. The five values chosen have been found to be remarkably similar across continents and cultures: **honesty, fairness, respect, responsibility**, and **compassion**. We can apply those five core values to environmental and social responsibility:

- **Honesty**: operating with transparency and integrity in all business dealings

- **Fairness**: particularly in the treatment of staff — not just in terms of traditional health and safety but also in relation to work–life balance and opportunities for continuous learning and improvement

- **Respect**: not just tolerating but positively encouraging diversity — respecting individuals and the contribution they can make irrespective of gender, race, faith, disability, age or sexual orientation — and respecting the basic human rights of stakeholders

- **Responsibility**: recognising the need for sustainable development and that business does indeed need to take responsibility for the environmental impacts that it has

- **Compassion**: sharing success with those less fortunate in society through encouraging employees to volunteer and through community involvement

▶ Recruiting for values

In Steps 1 and 2 we saw how a company's stance on CSR-related issues was a driver in the quest to attract and retain top talent. It is vital, then, that corporate values be linked to the recruitment and personnel development processes, both at induction and during ongoing management training. Also, in those industries where staff are spending shorter periods with a particular company the synergy between the values of employees and those of the employer becomes even more important. This is also why we believe that it is so important that more business schools incorporate CSR into their research and teaching in their core modules such as business strategy, finance and international marketing (see EABIS below, page 170).

The importance of linking CSR values to the recruitment process is increasingly being recognised throughout business. Over half of the companies surveyed for the World Economic Forum (WEF) in 2003 stated that they integrate corporate citizenship issues into recruitment and/or induction of new managers.[7] In many cases this process is built around exposing young managers to the company's values and

---

7   Findings are published in the 2003 report from the World Economic Forum, *Responding to the Leadership Challenge: Findings of a CEO Survey on Global Corporate Citizenship.*

business principles, or encouraging operational managers and new recruits to become actively engaged in community involvement initiatives in their own locations. Companies that are making the link between CSR values and the recruitment process include Siemens, MBNA Europe and Shell. At these companies, the commitment to CSR at recruitment is expressed by their CEOs.

Siemens

Siemens CEO Heinrich v. Pierer comments:

As part of our *Spin the Globe!* branding campaign we started a recruitment drive emphasising corporate citizenship issues because we believe that people are attaching increasing importance to working for companies committed to responsible business (quoted in the 2003 WEF CEO survey report).

MBNA Europe

Former US General Charles C. Krulack, CEO of credit card company MBNA Europe, explains that every potential MBNA recruit is put through six interviews to check for the core MBNA value of 'integrity'. In 2003 in a speech to the North West England Business in the Community (BITC) Conference he noted that 'we are looking for men and women of character'.

▶ The values gap

Professor Susan Cox, head of Lancaster Business School and then chairman of the Association of British Business Schools, warned of the 'values gap',[8] that is, the gap between values espoused and values practised. Such a gap is exemplified by:

- A perceived lack of fairness in the sharing of fortunes, both of the hardship during difficult times or of the gains during times of success (e.g. shop-floor employees may feel they are the first to be laid off or to have their pay frozen in hard times, or that they are not included in profit-sharing during good times)

- How a business treats its customers, its suppliers and its competitors (e.g. is there a suspicion of 'sharp practice' with one or more stakeholders?)

- How a business handles commercially necessary restructuring and downsizing (e.g. in failure to consult unions and employee groups ahead of such restructuring and downsizing or to provide careers advice and retraining)

8   Private BITC consultation on business schools and CSR, 16 December 2002.

The 2003 Fast Forward research undertaken by BITC found that there is a significant gap between employees' expectations of a responsible organisation and their own employer experience, with leadership being seen as a key barrier. Of the employees surveyed, few (less than 40%) heard senior management speak on the issue and even fewer (16%) knew of senior managers speaking outside the company on the issue.

Of course, changes in existing business strategies or the adoption of new strategies might require shifts in values and leadership styles if they are to succeed. For example, a company that wishes to look for product development opportunities created by evolving, tougher environmental legislation is unlikely to have the appropriate operating culture to succeed if it does not itself look to managing its own waste methodically and creatively. Similarly, a firm run by an efficient, but autocratic, management that has identified service delivery through a non-governmental organisation (NGO) as a potentially profitable route to market is unlikely to form a sustainable cross-sectoral partnership if it cannot adapt to working alongside a consensus-style NGO management style.

▶ Governance arrangements

We are frequently asked about appropriate governance arrangements for CSR. This is the wrong starting point! Rather, the question should be: 'Does the company have effective governance generally?' This is a crucial aspect of being a responsible business — as the failures of corporate governance at Enron, WorldCom, Parmalat, Hollinger and so on have exposed and which subsequent reforms, such as the US Sarbanes–Oxley Act in the USA and the Higgs Review of Corporate Governance in the UK, have sought to address. In the following sub-sections we look at the prevailing trends in approaches to conversion to CSR governance and at a typology of current methods of governance.

Governance and corporate social responsibility

Within corporate governance arrangements overall there is a growing link with CSR — as described in Steps 1 and 2. A specific question to address is: 'How is a company's commitment to CSR being overseen?' Perhaps in future a question asked will be: 'Does CSO require any specific measures?'

In a review of governance arrangements for corporate responsibility,[9] international fund managers Henderson concluded:

---

9   'Governance for Corporate Responsibility: The Role of Non-executive Directors in Environmental, Social and Ethical Issues' (May 2003).

> Corporate governance and corporate responsibility are closely linked
> to each other and to business performance. Corporate governance
> plays a large part in determining the extent to which a company is
> accountable to shareholders and can fulfil its responsibilities to
> society at large, including those relating to environmental, social and
> ethical issues. Corporate responsibility cannot be exercised fully
> unless corporate governance arrangements work effectively. Hen-
> derson seeks high performance in these areas from the companies
> in which it invests. We expect companies to demonstrate that the
> skills and personal qualities of non-executive and executive directors
> alike, the board structures within which they work, and the way
> boards as a whole are managed are equal to the challenges they face.

Through our observations, we see companies evolving their governance approach
to CSR from several directions, such as:

- **Audit and risk management.** Auditing and risk management expertise,
  traditionally focused on financial and political risks, is now being applied
  to wider social, ethical and environmental considerations, largely as a
  result of regulatory pressures and the broadening understanding of those
  issues that are 'material' to business strategy and performance.

- **Environment, health and safety.** Corporate environment, health and
  safety departments are well established in today's multinationals, and it is
  often this function that has managerial oversight for companies that are
  embracing policies and practices compatible with the principles of sustainable development and the social dimensions of corporate citizenship.

- **Values, principles and codes of conduct.** Many companies choose to
  create value statements, sets of principles or codes of conduct 'in-house'
  and sign up to, or reference within in-house policies, externally created
  standards and guidelines such as the UN Global Compact or the OECD
  Guidelines for Multinational Enterprises. Internal codes are often accompanied by whistle-blowing systems through which violations of the code
  can be reported by staff.

- **Corporate reputation and market positioning.** Oversight of appropriate
  communications processes and outputs is key to CSR-related governance.
  Inappropriate advertising — for example, to children, or in overseas markets with different cultural norms, can damage reputation. Specially
  created internal committees or external advisory boards help to ensure
  activities stay within acceptable parameters.

- **Public policy.** Aspects of corporate activity that impinge on public policy
  issues — for example, education, health, energy policy — require particular
  oversight arrangements, as the interface with public authorities requires
  particular management expertise. The area between engaging in public
  policy dialogue and transparent lobbying for specific business interests can
  be grey, and therefore express governance arrangements can be an advantage.

Current approaches to governance

John Drummond of CSR consultancy Corporate Culture says that current practice seems to break down into four options:

- Option 1: 'Leave it with the board'

- Option 2: 'Set up a formal sub-committee to the board'

- Option 3: Aim for 'high-level executive co-ordination', which in practice means a combination of board-level directors and other executives

- Option 4: Aim for implementation

In Box 22 we have collated data from our interviews, information from the Henderson Global Investors Report (HGIR) and material supplied by CSR consultants such as Corporate Culture and The Corporate Citizenship Company to classify major companies according to the Drummond categorisation approach. Note: the categorisation is subjective; furthermore, we are not implying that any one approach is better than or inferior to another.

Whatever the precise governance arrangements, non-executive directors can play an important role: putting CSR on the agenda based on their experience elsewhere; intelligently challenging — as in any other aspect of the performance of the business; championing one or more aspects; sitting in on some key stakeholder dialogues; ensuring the company is comprehensively addressing its assessment of its significant environmental and social impacts and using this as a basis for seeking CSO; and, of course, potentially chairing or being a member of the CSR governance arrangements whatever these may be.

From the sample of leading companies described, the dominant mode of CSR governance appears to be through a sub-committee to the board; however, we are by no means certain that such a separate, dedicated board committee will be the long-term preferred approach (see the next section, on the functional responsibility for CSR). The more that CSR is integrated into 'the way we do business around here' and the more that it is, therefore, aligned with business purpose and strategy; and is then embedded throughout the organisation, then the less likely it will be that a company needs dedicated or separate governance arrangements specifically for CSR. The Barclays arrangements established in February 2004 and described in Box 22 suggest one possible way forward — namely, to link board oversight of CSR issues to governance in the case of key business drivers (in this example, reputation).

For firms that operate globally, at many different sites and in many different contexts, particular challenges must be faced in communicating values and operating principles to business units and employees and in achieving successful CSR governance. A firm that is attempting to address these difficulties is Anglo American.

Differences in culture may also be of a business nature, as when two firms merge or when one firm acquires another. The company HBOS illustrates such a case.

Letters of assurance and all the other processes are simply devices to help to inculcate and embed responsible business practice — until it has become part of the 'unconscious competence of the company'.

In this box we have categorised the companies based on our interpretation of the information

Option 1: leave it with the board

- Pfizer said its corporate affairs and corporate governance divisions make periodic presentations to the board on current and emerging CSR issues
- London Electricity (now EDF Energy) said that 'ultimate responsibility rests with the LE Group board of directors, a fact which is reflected in the board's corporate governance policy and related procedures'
- Reed Elsevier considered a dedicated CSR committee but, after a two-day board 'away day' to examine the Higgs Report and the Sarbanes–Oxley Act, concluded that CSR should stay with the whole board, subject to a formal review of the situation once a year
- Six Continents said that 'the board of the company is responsible for all aspects of CSR through the executive committees of the Group, Hotels, Retail and Britvic'
- AstraZeneca has decided not to establish a separate board CSR committee, but has allocated specific responsibility for CSR to a non-executive director on the board

Option 2: set up a formal sub-committee to the board

- GlaxoSmithKline has a CSR committee, with four non-executives. It meets formally at least twice a year and holds additional ad hoc meetings and consultations
- 3M has had a public-issues committee of the board for more than 20 years. It meets quarterly and is made up of five members, four of whom are independent directors. More traditional corporate governance issues are covered by a board organisation committee
- Cadbury Schweppes has a corporate and social responsibility committee chaired by a non-executive director. It includes the chairman, two other non-executive directors, the group chief executive, the chief strategy officer and the chief HR officer.
- Severn Trent has an environmental and CSR advisory committee chaired by a non-executive director (who is a former senior governmental environmental official) and comprising the chairman, the chief executive, two non-executive directors, executive directors and three senior executives
- SABMiller has a formal board sub-committee, with joint membership of executives and non-executive directors. The sub-committee supports the infrastructure of operational committees and working groups, and issues statements of business principles, policies and so on.

Option 3: aim for high-level executive co-ordination

- Diageo has a corporate citizenship committee chaired by group CEO Paul Walsh. It meets regularly to monitor implementation of the group's citizenship strategy.
- BT has a CSR steering group chaired by the chairman of the board and consisting of a non-executive director, senior executives who are not directors, and two external independent members. to 'oversee the implementation of all social and environmental programmes across the BT Group'. It also involves social responsibility 'champions' nominated by the BT lines of business and four support functions.
- United Utilities has a CSR steering group responsible for policy and performance management. It develops strategy and reviews progress and plans. It also signs off major expenditure.
- Barclays have created a brand and reputation committee comprising senior executives (including the CEO of Barclaycard and the heads of the other three main businesses) and reporting to the executive committee chaired by Barclays CEO Matt Barrett. Five of its 15 members are on the Barclays board.

Option 4: aim for implementation

- Tesco has a CSR Group that is cross-functional and works under the chairmanship of the group corporate affairs director. It has a strong KPI (key performance indicator) focus which is devolved to the businesses.
- Novo Nordisk have several executive committees responsible for different aspects of CSR, including committees for the environment and bioethics, health policy, and social and industrial relations.

Box 22 Drummond's typology of approaches to corporate social responsibility (CSR) governance, with suggested corporate examples

Sources: John Drummond, Corporate Culture; authors' interviews; CSR consultants (Corporate Culture; The Corporate Citizenship Company); *Financial Times*, 'Barclays Banks on a Good Name', 19 February 2004; the Henderson Global Investors Report

Anglo American

Mining firm Anglo American has a statement of business principles. Since 2003, heads of operating companies have been required to produce an annual letter of assurance that they have run their business in conformity with that statement. The expectation is that they in turn will require letters of assurance from those reporting directly to them. Running parallel to this is an annual requirement for letters of assurance regarding health, safety and the environment.

To help managers, there is a website and a guidance manual. Material for the manual was initially generated principally from sources with which Anglo American works, such as the Global Mining Initiative (an industry-wide project investigating how the mining and minerals sector can contribute to the transition to sustainable development; see www.globalmining.com).

Management consultancy KPMG, while undertaking a review of health, safety and environmental policy inside the Anglo American operating companies, extended its work to look at the application of the business principles at each company site. CSR issues are now being integrated into Anglo American's internal advanced management programme, which runs annually with the participation of 60 senior managers; it is anticipated that other training will follow. Details of the two sets of letters of assurance (on the business principles and on health, safety and the environment) provided much of the input for Anglo American's first sustainability report, published in 2003.

Some of the generic issues raised by the letters of assurance include those concerning diversity, human rights and, specifically, the rights of indigenous peoples in a number of countries in which Anglo American operates.

Edward Bickham, External Affairs Director at Anglo American, says that the entire reporting process has worked well to bring the issues to the surface, noting that 'once you have got people to report the issues, then it is much more likely that they will manage them'. One of the big challenges Edward sees from a risk-identification and risk-management perspective is to help managers who come from and are working in emerging markets to look at their businesses through the lens of the Western, industrialised world and to see issues that might become of interest to the media and/or NGOs.

For businesses such as Anglo American that operate in a number of very different markets around the world and that work through operating companies with a substantial degree of autonomy this wide spread of operations may be one of several barriers in the way of getting the complete picture of what is happening on the ground. Other barriers may include: genuine differences in business and social cultures (i.e. in determining what will be 'the way we do business around here'); the desire for autonomy from the global headquarters; and the concern 'not to bother' global headquarters unnecessarily, in the belief that emerging problems can be sorted locally. Different companies have sought to handle this in a number of ways (on the identification and use of resources to implement CSR values, see Step 5; for a further case of a diverse multinational corporation that is integrating CSR principles into its business, see the example of Serco, pages 155f.).

HBOS

HBOS's integration of corporate responsibility into strategic decision-making has been particularly impressive as it was created by the merger of two very different banking cultures — the Bank of Scotland and the Halifax. HBOS Chief Executive, James Crosby, is leading a campaign to integrate corporate responsibility among its staff. Corporate responsibility has now become a core business issue, affecting product design, pricing, distribution and brand values. For example, HBOS's Insight Investment applies its 'global business principles' to nearly £70 billion of funds under management (see Step 2, page 72) (source: Corporate Responsibility Index 2003).

▶ Functional responsibility for CSR

A number of 'benchmark' studies about the differing options for board-level governance and the wider question of where the central co-ordinating function for CSR sits within a company's structure (corporate communications, company secretary, human resources, direct to CEO, etc.) have revealed that no one single model emerges — it is very much 'horses for courses'.[10]

We do not believe that there is a single right answer as to the location of the CSR co-ordinating function. Some questions that a company might consider in determining the best location for CSR co-ordination in their particular circumstances might include:

- What is the credibility of the sponsoring department across the business?

- Is the sponsoring department 'where the action is' in the business?

- Are the senior people in the sponsoring department passionate and committed to CSR?

- Does the location within the business properly reflect where the most critical CSR issues facing the business are?

The above list of questions emphasise the importance of the authority and respect given to the co-ordinator and of leaders being seen to 'walk the talk'. These elements were recognised by Jeremy Pelczer, President and CEO of American Water, part of the RWE Group. In an interview with us in October 2003, when he was COO of RWE Thames Water, he told us:

> When I took on the new COO position at RWE Thames Water we decided to firstly appoint a respected heavyweight in the subject — CSR Director Richard Aylard — who would command authority and respect across the business. This was key. Secondly, I insisted that he report to me directly — at the heart of the operational core of business. In 2004 I will be doing the same at American Water in the US, making the senior executive responsible for CSR head one of the direct reports to me as President. Thirdly, all my reports must include CSR factors in their business plans. If they don't they get sent back. And, finally, my own performance measure includes CSR and specific measures around environment, health and safety and employee motivation.

Wherever the function resides, George Carpenter and Peter White of Procter & Gamble believe that it is not sufficient to see sustainability only in terms of responsibility — that it must be tied to a search for opportunity:

> It [the company's approach to sustainable development] can also cause problems with how sustainability is managed within compa-

10   Canadian BSR and The Conference Board.

Serco

Serco positions itself as 'the leading global outsourcing company'. Growth has come from trends towards privatisation and the contracting out of public services. The firm was established in the 1920s when it was the services arm of RCA, installing sound systems in cinemas when the 'talkies' began. Now it operates through eight main companies handling over 600 separate contracts — 85% of which are for governments or government agencies around the world. These include most of the road traffic information used by the emergency services in the UK and the BBC; maintaining the parking meters in San Francisco, running buses in Adelaide, bridges in Auckland, tunnels and hospitals in Hong Kong, leisure centres in Sweden, the Ottawa Driving Licence Centre, Docklands Light Railway in London, Mersey Rail, speed cameras throughout the UK, the ground operations in French Guyana for the launch site of the European Ariane rocket; and the management of schools, education authority services and prisons. It is one of the largest providers of air traffic control in the USA. Since 1959, Serco has been responsible for the first two minutes of the UK's four-minute warning system of possible nuclear attack. Since its flotation in 1988, the company has consistently delivered increases in turnover and profits. It aims to win one out of every two new contracts for which it bids. It is currently enjoying a 62% success rate, and is renewing over 90% of its existing contracts.

Serco is now operating in 39 countries, with 34,000 staff in total. Many of these employees transferred from the public sector when Serco won contracts for various public services. Some may not have wanted to be working in the private sector and may not have initially felt any natural affinity to such a diverse corporate organisation, yet the success of Serco depends on maintaining and extending its reputation for effective management of public services and in instilling an ethos of entrepreneurial public service.

For large and diverse organisations, especially, there may be lessons from the Serco experience that are worth analysis. Formally, Serco has a CSR steering group chaired by the Executive Chairman, Kevin Beeston. It is supported by a small central CSR team that is part of the Serco Corporate Assurance Group. CSR issues form an important element of the quarterly reports from the Corporate Assurance Group to the corporation's board. Robert Smith, who heads Serco's Corporate Assurance Group, has held a number of different posts in the 14 years he has been with the company and says that the fact that he knows his way around the company plus the fact that, 'as [head of] Corporate Assurance, I have teeth', has been important in keeping the attention of the business on CSR issues. In the quarterly board reports, all businesses or 'contracts' now include community and other CSR measures alongside the financial data. Serco sees CSR as an integral part of its vision and strategy to be 'employer of choice, partner of choice and investment of choice'. CSR is also integrated into the corporate values — which were first articulated in the 1980s when four senior managers led the management buy-out and asked themselves what kind of business they wanted to run and what sense of purpose would get people out of bed in the morning and with the more recently articulated corporate behaviours. According to Smith, CSR is not about putting Serco on a pedestal but is 'another ingredient which we can bottle to help express the values of Serco'. Additionally, CSR is one of Serco's six generic business goals.

There are designated CSR champions on the Global Management Board, the boards of the eight business divisions and each of the 37 operating company boards — and also on the individual contract boards that exist for each of the 600 and more contracts held by Serco. There is a further speeding-up of the spread of existing practice and knowledge-management (on CSR and on every other aspect of business performance) through the 'non-executive directors' from other parts of Serco who sit on each of the contract, operating company and business divisional boards. CSR is one of the specific issues that these non-executive directors are asked to pay attention to and seek out.

continued →

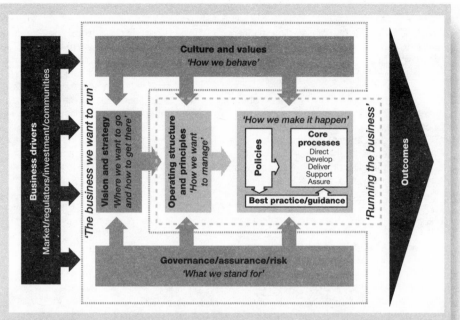

Serco describes itself as a highly decentralised federation of small businesses held together by a strong culture and common values and by a number of 'standards' that are mandatory throughout the business. One of these mandatory standards is the set of policy and standards (described as 'our values') that cover ethics and other CSR issues. CSR is incorporated into the regular letters of assurance through a process termed 'assuring the business'. Furthermore, each contract has its own 'area' on the Serco 'Our World' intranet, and one of the documents that has to be presented for each contract is a CSR plan and forward action plan for implementation of CSR.

Beeston says:

> We are saying to our managers, 'This is not fad. It won't go away. You can't just keep your head down and hope it will go away like previous initiatives.'

Serco is also investing heavily in training — incorporating CSR — to ensure a constant supply of people well versed in its management techniques.

North American Serco are now creating an 'opportunities register' as well as a 'risks register' on the basis that 'if you just look at the risks all the time you would price yourself out of the market'. One market that Serco withdrew from was a bid to run prisons in the USA because it did not want to be involved in prisons in states with the death penalty.

Source: based on several interviews of the authors in Summer 2003 with representatives from Serco and on annual results reported in *The Independent*, 3 March 2004

nies. If it is seen only as a responsibility, sustainable development will be treated as an issue to be managed rather than an opportunity to be pursued. Consequently, it will be managed by a corporate function, much as health, safety and environment has been managed in the past. Only if responsibility is linked with opportunity is sustainable development likely to get the attention of senior management and become built into businesses in a strategic way.[11]

▶ Leadership commitment to corporate social responsibility and corporate social opportunity

Much of the success of a commitment to responsible business depends on the leadership of the organisation — the tone the leaders set and whether they are perceived to 'walk the talk'. Leaders generally need to be able to explain 'where the company is going' (i.e. its vision); they need to demonstrate credibility by having a 'journey plan' (i.e. a strategy for achieving the vision); they need to be able to explain what the vision means for someone's immediate team, and what the vision means for an individual employee.

During a visit to Bangalore as part of a Leaders' Quest (www.leadersquest.org), the CEO of the Bangalore-headquartered multinational IT firm Infosys, Nandan Nilekani, told us that leadership is about aspirations — for things that are not yet there — and about inspiring people to reach for them — which means developing a vision of the future and getting people to buy into it. In the Infosys case this includes CSR.

CSO businesses need leaders who thrive in a multi-stakeholder and multi-values environment rather than being people who just make decisions. Leadership for CSO companies, we suggest, demands some new competences and qualities, such as:[12]

- The ability to lead and a desire to serve

- To have sensitivity and empathy, to show patience, serenity and humility

- An ability to learn and a *willingness* to learn

- An ability to inspire, engage and facilitate others, to be seen to be walking, talking, breathing symbols of corporate responsibility with strong ethical values

11 G. Carpenter and P. White, 'Sustainable Development: Finding the Real Business Case', *Corporate Environmental Strategy: International Journal for Sustainable Business* 2.2 (February 2004).

12 We are indebted to Professor Peter Pruzan of the Copenhagen Business School, to Professor Claudio Boechat of the Fundação don Cabral (FDC) business school in Brazil and to an FDC Leadership Summit in October 2003 for insights from which this composite list is built.

- To be tuned in to dialogue and to be good at listening rather than simply communicating

- To be an 'influencer'

- To be able to build on and add to ideas

- To be capable of showing trust and to be trustworthy

- To be reflective and accessible

- To be your employees' most valuable asset (rather than falling back on that ubiquitous statement in annual reports that 'our people are our greatest asset!')

- To be a multi-disciplinary team-worker, comfortable in 'different worlds', and a good networker

- To be entrepreneurial, with the assurance to take calculated risks

Personal leadership is not only to be found at the top of multinational corporations, as illustrated by Peri Drysdale's company.

Peri Drysdale and Untouched World

Peri Drysdale set up a home-based knitting business in Christchurch, New Zealand, in the early 1980s that has turned into an international success story. Peri's parent company, Snowy Peaks, now boasts a range of innovative products and has also launched new brands such as Untouched World, through which her fashion-designer daughter shows a range of natural, ecologically friendly clothing. Peri's vision is 'to provide a platform for growth of the human spirit based on a foundation of environmental sustainability and renewal'. She has a passion for brand values that promote sustainable lifestyles. Peri has established a voluntary sustainability task force within the company and has worked with a group of seven other pioneering organisations, including The Warehouse and Orion, to pioneer a path towards organisational sustainability: 'redesigning resources' (www.redesigningresources.org).

We first met Peri in Christchurch in 2002, at the 2002 Redesigning Resources report-back conference. In 2002, the company published its sustainable development report, which sets a blueprint for sustainable business practices. Untouched World's goal is that within ten years:

- Its rate of use of renewable resources should not exceed the rate of regeneration of those resources

- Its rate of use of non-renewable resources should not exceed the rate at which sustainable renewable substitutes are being developed

- Its emissions of pollutants do not exceed the assimilative capacity of the environment

---

In Box 23 we list some questions that a CEO may wish to consider in making his or her journey through CSR leadership to CSO.

Questions for a CEO to consider

The ongoing commitment of the CEO is obviously crucial in the journey towards the creation of a sustainable successful company. To aid the journey, CEOs may wish to consider the following questions:

- Are issues of respect, tolerance, fairness in business dealings and a commitment to sustainable development incorporated into the core values of the business?
- Are they explicitly included in the stated business principles of the organisation?
- Is the company regularly scoping how it can minimise its negative environmental and social impacts and maximise its positive impacts — and reviewing the risks and opportunities for the business in these?
- Is there a robust, coherent decision-making process where the totality of the environmental and social impacts of the business are treated holistically and where effective action can be taken?
- When mistakes occur on environmental and social issues, are these reviewed and lessons learnt and codified?
- Are different business functions and divisions regularly assessing and reporting their risks and opportunities on environmental and social issues?
- Is this process taken seriously, or is it seen as a 'tick-box' exercise?
- Is the business making a link between environmental and social impacts and prevailing business processes, such as total quality management or a culture of innovation?
- Are corporate values and environmental and social issues treated as a 'bolt-on' extra or are they in the weft and weave of induction processes and continuous professional development at all levels of the organisation?
- Are the risks and opportunities associated with environmental and social impacts regularly communicated to all stakeholders?
- Am I personally associated with these issues? Am I taking a leadership role inside and outside the organisation on a particular aspect?
- Where am I personally going for inspiration and new insights into corporate social opportunities? Where do I encourage my senior management team to look?
- In what frame of mind and with what outlook am I approaching these meetings and searches for inspiration and insight?
- As I look beyond my own tenure as CEO, do I really believe that these issues and attitudes of business responsibility are now embedded in the business (and, if not, what remedial action can I take)?

Box 23 **Questions for a CEO to consider**

▶ Public commitment

> We have to demonstrate that we can deliver reliability in the short term while also investing to secure the long term by renewing our asset stock and carrying out research to prevent unintended consequences and negative impacts of our operations. Public accountability is an essential element of our business success. It is very important to be joined up in terms of our vision, values, community responsibility and service delivery.
>
> *Bill Alexander, CEO of RWE Thames Water*[13]

At the opening of this chapter we mentioned how companies were publicly declaring CSR-related business principles and goals. For example, chemical giant DuPont has committed itself to making a 'zero' environmental footprint by 2005; US-based bankers Citigroup are among more than 40 multinationals subscribing to the World Economic Forum (WEF) Statement on Global Corporate Citizenship, issued in February 2002;[15] and well over a thousand, mainly multinational, companies have signed up to the Global Compact — launched by UN Secretary-General Kofi Annan in 1999.[14]

An alternative or complementary public commitment to action may involve joining a business organisation dedicated to the promotion of corporate responsibility such as our own organisations, Business in the Community based in London and the International Business Leaders Forum operating around the world, or to one of the similar organisations around the world such as Business for Social Responsibility, based in San Francisco, CA; CSR Europe, based in Brussels; Instituto Ethos in Brazil; or South Africa's National Business Initiative. But, to paraphrase a famous credit-card advertisement, 'membership has its responsibilities!' If a company makes such a public commitment and then these commitments are not taken seriously, this itself could become a trigger for action against the business by campaigning NGOs — because the business has signalled it is prepared to be judged by higher standards.

If the company takes its commitment to CSR seriously then such a commitment will almost certainly lead to some changes in how the business is run. For example:

- It could alter how it makes and markets its products; for example, it may:
    - Change the raw materials used
    - Reduce its consumption of water
    - Reduce its emission of noxious gases
    - Remove a particular ingredient or component from the product or processes

13   Quoted in World Economic Forum and International Business Leaders Forum, 'Values and Vision' (2002).
14   See unglobalcompact.org.
15   World Economic Forum, 'Responding to the Leadership Challenge: Findings of a CEO Survey on Global Corporate Citizenship' (2002).

- Alter the location at which its products are made so that there is no use of child labour
- Lease rather than sell its products

● It could alter how the business delivers and markets its services; for example, it may:
  - Proactively use ethnic-minority or disabled actors in advertisements
  - Join a minority suppliers' club

● It could alter how it recruits employees and how it approaches other human resource policies; for example:
  - It may offer flexi-time, homeworking and part-time contracts
  - At recruitment fairs, it may wish to choose a representative who will encourage all potential recruits (regardless of their social or cultural background and so on) to feel they will be welcome in the company

● It could alter how and where it purchases supplies; for example:
  - Companies using wood as a raw material (e.g. furniture-makers or pulp and paper manufacturers) or selling wood products to consumers (e.g. DIY stores) may wish to ensure any wood supplies are from sustainable sources
  - Companies may wish to look at electricity suppliers, to purchase from those suppliers that are expanding the proportion of electricity generated from renewable sources

● It could change the company's involvement in the community to focus on where the business has core competences; for example:
  - A small public relations business may help a local school to rethink and improve its communications with parents, local employers and prospective pupils

A recruitment process that favours people from one sector of society over those from others prevents a business benefiting from the entire pool of skills and knowledge available to it. Changes in recruitment practices may be quite simple and also fundamental. Although in many countries there is regulation against implied or overt discrimination (e.g. racial, sexual, religious) in recruitment adverts, the recruitment process itself may be inherently discriminatory.

Potential recruits may also be deterred from applying for or accepting a job where they perceive they may not 'fit in' with the rest of the workforce (e.g. a woman may be deterred from taking a job in an all-male department). Unilever noted that although decisions to purchase its products are made predominantly by women, women were under-represented in high-level jobs in the company; the company thus sought to recruit more women to top jobs.

By acting responsibly on a voluntary basis, companies may be able to demonstrate to government and regulators that there is no need for regulation. For example, the alcohol industry has so far escaped the type of regulation and litigation faced by the tobacco industry and now, in the case of litigation, by the food industry. This is partly due to the willingness shown by drinks companies to submit to responsible self-regulation as well as to achieve a clear differentiation between overall consumption and the need to curtail patterns of excessive drinking.

▶ The challenges of honouring public commitments: a case study

What happens when a company acts in good faith but events beyond its control negate its previous commitments? The privatised airport operator BAA (British Airports Authority) now faces this challenge. In 1995, in the middle of a long-running public planning inquiry into whether there should be a fifth terminal at London Heathrow Airport, the then leadership of BAA formally asked the UK government via the public inquiry to rule out any subsequent construction of a third runway at Heathrow. At the time, this was widely seen as a crucial factor in shifting local community attitudes to Terminal 5 (T5). The then BAA leadership positioned the request as an example of its commitment to turning BAA into a 'stakeholder corporation'. Writing several years later in the *Financial Times*, in an article titled 'Ethics are Good Business' (19 May 2003), the BAA Director of Corporate and Public Affairs at the time of the T5 Inquiry — the former environmental campaigner, Des Wilson — wrote:

> BAA . . . was told the company would never win permission for a fifth terminal at Heathrow. In fact, the local community has finally accepted the T5 go-ahead with equanimity, and construction is under way . . . likewise because [BAA] embraced the same approach, local authorities around Gatwick and Stansted approved expansion plans without even demanding a public inquiry. None of this happened by accident. The company won permission to grow from the community by acknowledging and addressing the community's concerns.[16]

In 2003, however, the UK government issued a White Paper on future runway capacity in London and the South-East of England. In its formal response, the new BAA leadership argued that the government had to choose three of four options — a 'short' additional runway for smaller aircraft at Heathrow, a second runway at Gatwick and up to two new runways at Stansted.[17]

As a result, BAA has been accused by anti-noise protesters of performing the 'mother of all U-turns' by publishing an expansion strategy that breaks earlier pledges to build no extra runways at Heathrow and Gatwick. John Stewart, chair-

---

16   For a fuller account of BAA's move to a stakeholder corporation see Sir John Egan and Des Wilson's book, *Private Business, Public Battleground* (London: Palgrave, 2002).

17   See 'Responsible Growth', BAA's response to the government consultation (2003).

man of Heathrow pressure group Hacan Clear Skies, said that 'local residents feel angry, betrayed and cynical; . . . the U-turn has significantly damaged relations between BAA and the community'.

In July 2003, in his first week in the job as CEO of BAA, we challenged Mike Clasper about the alleged breach of a very specific and public commitment; Mike was direct in his response:

> BAA asked the government to rule out a third runway during the T5 inquiry. The government didn't. The Airports Act puts an obligation on BAA to develop the infrastructure. In the real world, BAA could not refuse a government request to investigate options. BAA did not conceive the idea of a short runway — that option wasn't investigated by BAA at the time. We've not changed a jot — we have learnt what we can commit to and what we cannot. I came in and reviewed all our strategies — a number have changed — but one that has not changed at all is engaging stakeholders. The support and trust of our stakeholders is our mantra.

▶ Synthesis of Step 4

Here we see how Step 4 processes — committing to action — can be perceived in the case of Microsoft's mission 'to help individuals and businesses to realise their potential through technology'.

Committing to action at Microsoft

Microsoft reviewed its corporate mission in 2002 to read: 'to help individuals and businesses to realise their potential through technology'. This led to a redefinition of Microsoft values. Performance against these values is now included in the appraisals of all employees and in the general managers' scorecard, which is used for assessing executive compensation. The Microsoft CSR function reports to the Legal and Corporate Affairs Department, and the company's legal counsel who sits on the main board is the board 'owner'.

The company believes that it has exercised leadership and made a number of important external signals of intent. In 2003, Microsoft launched a code of conduct and a vendors' code of conduct. The CEO for Europe, the Middle East and Africa, Jean-Philippe Courtois, has co-chaired the World Economic Forum Digital Divide Initiative. In addition, at the 2004 Davos World Economic Forum, Bill Gates committed Microsoft to a 'spam-free Internet' and to a safe Internet.

▶ Moving from Step 4 to Step 5

Working through the stages outlined in Step 4 may result in the need to revise proposed strategies or equally may call into question existing governance, leadership and management styles and arrangements. It may also support the need for organisation-wide commitment to responsible business and principles of sustainable development. Once appropriate issues have been identified, the task is to consider implications for resources and how elements of the proposed strategies can be integrated into existing corporate polices and practices — as described in Step 5.

Integration and gathering resources

Focus

In this chapter, we look at how to integrate aspects of CSR and other operational requirements that emerge from reviewing business strategies. We also consider various resource implications.

Applying Step 5

In Part II — the worked example of the seven steps — the completed process forms show how, by applying appropriate tools and techniques selected from Step 5, the following outputs are produced (see pages 333ff.):

- An assessment of resources needed to implement proposed strategies and operational changes

- Identification of resource gaps and potential sources

IN THIS CHAPTER WE DESCRIBE THE PROCEDURES NECESSARY to help turn ideas and aspirations articulated in revised or new business strategies into operational reality. For each strategy there is a need to consider how it will be resourced, what specific actions are required by particular organisational functions and how those actions are to be co-ordinated.

By this stage a company may have come to the conclusion that individual strategies are more likely to succeed if policies and practices are put in place commensurate with an overall, top-level corporate commitment to corporate social responsibility (CSR) and the principles of sustainable development. If this is the case, then the resource-gap analysis and activity co-ordination we go on to describe in this chapter is equally applicable.

We use the word 'integration' in our title for this step to signify, first, the integration of the activities of individual functions with each other and, second, the integration of operational practices to manage CSR through adapting and 'stretching' existing company-wide business systems and approaches — such as total quality management (TQM).

In July 2001, in a New Statesman lecture on CSR, Vernon Ellis, global head of Accenture and Vice Chairman of the International Business Leaders Forum (IBLF), warned that a company will lose out on potential synergies and economies of scale and potentially experience clashes and inconsistencies if company functions operate in silos in their approach to CSR. Step 5 is critical to the joined-up approach.

The starting point is to consider resources required to fulfil the revised strategies captured in Step 4. Almost inevitably, the process of identifying needs demonstrated by a particular corporate social opportunity (CSO) will lead to broader questions about how a company hires, develops and promotes staff; how it markets its products and services, how it sources its materials and other supplies and so on (see the section on the implications of making a public commitment to CSR, Step 4, pages 160ff.). It is in integrating responsible business practices more broadly into marketing, purchasing and so on that the company opens itself to the possibilities of CSO on a larger scale.

The resources we are referring to here include not only cash and capital but also people and their capabilities, the necessary leadership style and corporate culture, the approach to knowledge-management and learning and the means used to secure an appropriate contribution to CSR practice from business 'facilitators' such as consultants and auditors. It also involves, depending on the nature of the business, access to sourcing and manufacturing processes and to marketing, personnel and distribution.

▶ Training and development

The skills required

Successful implementation of CSO-related strategies requires high levels of sensitivity towards environmental and social responsibility combined with commercial acumen on the part of a cross-section of managers. It may also require dedicated, specialist CSR staff, but — as we go on to illustrate — it would be a mistake to leave initiatives solely to such specialists. Think back to the Philips bottom-of-the-pyramid work described in Step 3. Commenting on the personnel implications, Jan Ooster-veld, Member, Group Management Board, Royal Philips Electronics, has said: 'our people have marketing training which is certainly not fit for these [bottom-of-the-pyramid] markets'.[1]

It is possible to identify a number of core CSR skills and competences for managers. A working party to identify such skills and competences was established by the UK government Department of Trade and Industry (DTI) and the Corporate Responsibility Group (consisting of the CSR directors of 60 major companies). It reported its findings in April 2003 in a publication titled 'Changing Managers' Mindsets'. It identified three discrete areas that need attention:

- Business skills
- Technical skills (or knowledge sets)
- People skills (including personal attributes or behaviour)

A fuller description of these CSR skills and competences can be found in the appendix of 'Changing Managers' Mindsets', but in Figure 8 we summarise the main skills that each of these areas represents.

Acquiring the necessary skills

As made clear in the publication 'Changing Managers' Mindsets', the appropriate skills will be acquired through a wide variety of means, including:

- Formal training, including:
  - In-house training of employees by company-based trainers or by external specialists
  - External training of employees by specialists
  - Business school courses

- Mentoring

- Secondments, such as:
  - Interdepartmental secondments (i.e. movement of employees within the business)
  - Secondments from external sources (i.e. with people coming in to the firm on secondment)
  - Secondments to external sources (e.g. employees may be seconded to work in the community, in other companies and so on)

- Partnering and networking with other companies to share best practice

1   Speech to IESE Responsible Business Conference, Barcelona, 27 March 2004 — author's notes.

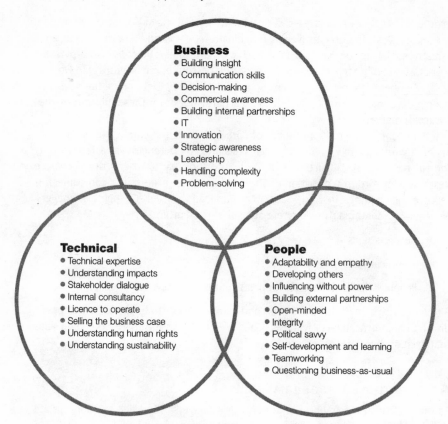

Business
- Building insight
- Communication skills
- Decision-making
- Commercial awareness
- Building internal partnerships
- IT
- Innovation
- Strategic awareness
- Leadership
- Handling complexity
- Problem-solving

Technical
- Technical expertise
- Understanding impacts
- Stakeholder dialogue
- Internal consultancy
- Licence to operate
- Selling the business case
- Understanding human rights
- Understanding sustainability

People
- Adaptability and empathy
- Developing others
- Influencing without power
- Building external partnerships
- Open-minded
- Integrity
- Political savvy
- Self-development and learning
- Teamworking
- Questioning business-as-usual

Figure 8 **A typology of business, technical and people skills**

Source: adapted from Department of Trade and Industry and the Corporate Responsibility Group, 'Changing Managers' Mindsets' (April 2003)

Formal training

In the the Corporate Responsibility Index (CRI) 2003 of Business in the Community (BITC), published 15 March 2004 (referred to briefly in Step 2, page 83), participating companies were asked about the degree to which training and development programmes had been implemented to support the integration of corporate responsibility issues throughout the company.[2] The results are shown in Table 9. From this table it can be seen that although all 139 companies provide some training and

2   BITC Corporate Responsibility Index 2003 (published 15 March 2004). As with the other CR Index data quoted here, there have to be several caveats about these figures: (1) the companies who completed the CRI are a self-defining group and are among the leaders in CSR; (2) the data covers UK-headquartered companies; and (3) although companies can show activities in the quoted areas, it may be variable in overall quality and comprehensiveness. Nevertheless, we believe it is worth including some of the key findings of the CR Index 2003 here. It represents what a universe of 139 leading companies are doing. As such, it provides useful benchmarks for others.

	Community	Environment	Marketplace	Workplace
No training	7%	1%	3%	1%
Ad hoc	68%	82%	73%	81%
Graduates and fast-track	54%	62%	65%	72%
Senior management	62%	81%	78%	90%
Board	75%	78%	72%	81%

BITC has developed a framework consisting of these four categories, which some of its corporate members use to help manage their social and environmental impact. Companies can consider aspects of their operations and ask what impact they have on communities where they operate, on the physical environment, to consumer or other markets, and on employees at work. In this instance, the framework is used to define the focus of CSR training.

Table 9 **The degree to which managerial training and development programmes address corporate responsibility issues at 139 companies, by focus: the percentage of companies providing training**

Source: Business in the Community (BITC) Corporate Responsibility Index 2003 (15 March 2004)

development in each of the four broad areas of CSR (community, environment, the marketplace and the workplace) it is aimed primarily at senior management and those on the board.

We would argue that CSR issues have to be an integral part of management training and should indeed be fully incorporated into *every* employee's induction and continual professional development and training. However, the reality today is far from this. For example, few companies are yet making the connection between the need to raise CSR knowledge and associated skills and the specifications for executive development programmes given to business schools by those responsible for management development in large companies.

Providers of training can look at ways of adapting existing programmes, either by adding specific modules or by 'stretching' current modules to incorporate appropriate CSR dimensions. For example, training on negotiating skills for use with employees, their representatives or suppliers can be extended to reflect the skills and techniques of 'stakeholder engagement'. Sessions within 'high-flyer' courses where participants meet the company CEO and other leaders can be broadened to encourage the CEO and other speakers to be more explicit about their personal values, about how they relate those values to corporate values, about how they try to 'live them' in their business lives and about cases where this has proved hard to do such that they have felt personally challenged or even compromised.

Just as senior managers have in the past been given media training so in future they might expect to receive training on engagement with non-governmental organisations (NGOs), perhaps including responses to a simulated situation.

For those who are considering whether to run specialist CSR courses, in-house or externally, the pros and cons to consider are listed in Table 10.

Type of course	Pros	Cons
Specialist	• More time can be devoted to the subject than if the issues are covered as part of general training • Outside specialists can be brought in to widen the knowledge promoted and to broaden perspectives	• For some managers CSR is still regarded as a 'soft' issue, and they therefore may not regard the course as important, or may not think it is designed for them
'Stretched'	• The courses are already well established and resourced • The courses have an allocated budget and a tried and tested structure • The courses have a proven track record in teaching what is required	• The 'owners' (teachers) of the existing courses may be unwilling to extend the subject matter and course material • Participants may be less willing to 'open up' and contribute their own opinions and feelings in this context • Time limitations may make it difficult to allocate sufficient 'space' to CSR within the existing curriculum

Table 10 **The pros and cons of running a specialist corporate social responsibility (CSR) course and of stretching existing management training to cover CSR issues**

A biannual survey, 'Beyond Grey Pinstripes', undertaken by the Aspen Institute for Business and Society and the World Resources Institute (WRI),[3] charts the teaching of CSR in MBA and executive management programmes, and suggests more schools are covering CSR than previously, although numbers are not great. The 2003 survey provides analysis on the teaching of social and environmental issues in MBAs in 100 business schools in 20 countries.

Another survey, by the European Academy for Business and Society (EABIS) in collaboration with the University of Nottingham and the European Foundation for Management Development, covers more than 600 European institutions.[4] This survey revealed that compulsory courses covering CSR are rare in European business schools: only 27% of business schools responded that the subject was mandatory and taught in a dedicated, stand-alone course.

Mentoring

An increasing number of organisations run mentoring programmes. One international expert on mentoring, Professor David Clutterbuck, claims that four out of

3   See www.beyondgreypinstripes.org.
4   For details of the survey, go to www.eabis.org.

five chief executives surveyed say that having a mentor was one of the keys to their success. Mentoring offers personalised learning through a developmental relationship with someone of substantially greater experience, who has taken a direct interest in the mentee. Clutterbuck argues that

> Powerful, often transformational, mentoring relationships have helped young graduates find their feet in an organisation, helped mothers of young children return to work, or enabled young offenders to turn their lives around. People coming up to retirement have been eased through this difficult time by tapping into the experience of others, who have been through it already. In short, mentoring can help anybody, who has a major transition to make in his or her life, whoever or wherever they are. Mentoring taps a basic instinct most people share: the desire to pass on their learning, to help other people develop and fulfil their potential.

A company that offers a mentoring programme is demonstrating a facet of responsible business: caring for the development of its people. But mentoring can also be one of the ways of transferring a feel for and skills in CSR. CSO companies will want to think about establishing mentoring programmes if they don't already have them — and, if they do, how mentors might be encouraged to incorporate their own experience of implementing responsible business practices more explicitly into their discussions with mentees.[5]

Some key questions relating to mentoring are:

- Do internal and external mentors share responsible business values?

- Are they encouraged to share some of the dilemmas and judgement calls that they have had to make in living those values in the real commercial world, with their mentee?

- Do the mentors know about any company CSR training and advisory services, so that, if it is appropriate, the mentor can refer the mentee to them?[6]

- As diversity is an important aspect of responsible business practice, are the mentors themselves role models of diversity?

- Are there opportunities to invite partner NGOs to join in mentoring training programmes that the company is already running anyway?

- Can existing mentoring programmes be stretched to include community goals — such as the new BITC programme of peer-mentoring between business leaders and staff in prisons in London?

5   David Clutterbuck, *How to be a Great Mentor* (Clutterbuck Associates, 2003).
6   The Advisory Committee for International Standards for Mentoring Programmes in Employers, chaired by Professor David Clutterbuck, is looking to incorporate CSR explicitly into the standards.

The BITC also runs mentoring programmes between business and other sectors:

- Partners in Leadership: matching business leaders and school head-teachers one to one to share experiences and issues with each other

- Partners in Leadership in the Community: a sister programme to Partners in Leadership which twins business leaders and social entrepreneurs from charities and NGOs

As well as these, BITC promotes 100 hour community assignments and team challenges to participating employees.

Secondments and development assignments

At the beginning of this section we mentioned the conclusion of a working party established by the DTI and the Corporate Responsibility Group, as published in its report 'Changing Managers' Mindsets' (see page 167). Many of the competences or qualities identified in the report as being required (summarised as business, technical and people skills) are core to those skills necessary for developing partnerships, engaging in stakeholder dialogue and respecting diversity, so it is not surprising that some of the most interesting experiential learning comes from training in, and secondments to, community-based organisations.

The notion of interaction and engagement in the community as a rich source of employee and management learning is spawning some creative initiatives:

- The NGO Common Purpose[7] is working in several countries to bring together business people with the public sector and with community organisations in town and cities to create powerful learning networks.

- A number of companies have instituted their own off-site community involvement programmes in order to create training or learning opportunities:
    - In collaboration with the Earthwatch Institute,[8] Mining firm Rio Tinto runs a Global Employee Fellowship Programme, enabling 24 employees each year to spend time with an international environmental NGO and then to share their experiences with their business units.
    - Pfizer has initiated a similar Global Health Fellows programme. Annah Sebolelo Amos, MD, a medical information physician at Pfizer South Africa, described the effect this has had on her: 'I've seen the faces of despair, hopelessness and palpable fear among those infected and affected by HIV/AIDS in South Africa. But I've also seen inspiration, determination and a measure of success in community-driven programmes to help those living with HIV/ AIDS. I am thrilled to have

---

7 Common Purpose currently works in Germany, South Africa, The Netherlands and Ireland (www.commonpurpose.org.uk).
8 www.earthwatch.org

an opportunity to share my experiences and gain new knowledge and insight through work in HIV/AIDS in Vietnam.'[9]

- Accenture has found that employees who take part in NGO assignments in less-developed countries through its Accenture Development Partnerships programme are more resourceful, conduct better client relationships and are more likely to be promoted on their return.[10]
- PricewaterhouseCoopers (PwC)'s Ulysses initiative combines the traditionally separate areas of employee community involvement and corporate leadership development.

Partnering and networking with other companies

The importance of relationships to business, identified as a business case driver in Step 3 (see the section on relationships, alliances and the licence to operate in Step 3, pages 123f.), is reflected in the popularity of an innovative post-graduate certificate in cross-sector partnerships that is delivered under the auspices of the Cambridge Programme for Industry in association with the IBLF and accredited to Cambridge University. The course attracts a mix of managers from business, government and civil society and is one of the first of its kind to formalise the learning required to build partnerships.[11]

Through establishing leadership teams and working parties on particular aspects of CSR, Business in the Community and IBLF encourage groups of businesses to capture existing learning, develop new solutions and share these with other firms.

In its 2003 Sustainability Report, 'Linking Opportunity with Responsibility', Procter & Gamble describe a partnership with the local food company Sada that also involved employees engaging with the local, low-income, community.

Procter & Gamble and Sada

Procter & Gamble in Brazil is developing new products and distributions systems as well as better ways of communicating with customers as a result of employee learning through the Living it! programme. Low-income households account for 76% of Brazil's population, and around half their income is spent on consumer goods. In order to understand the needs and concerns of low-income families, Procter & Gamble partnered with food company Sada in a programme where Procter & Gamble staff lived for two weeks in low-income homes. As a result of the experiences of those who participated in the programme, Procter & Gamble reports that it is developing new products, distribution systems and better ways of communicating with customers.

9   www.pfizer.com. An independent case study of the Global Health Fellows programme is posted on www.unglobalcompact.org.
10   Reported in International Business Leaders Forum, 'Developing People through Partnerships' (December 2003).
11   See www.cip.cam.ac.uk/pccp.

▶ Performance objectives, appraisal and compensation

It is widely accepted in traditional management areas that it is essential to set clear objectives and targets, to undertake regular reviews and to link compensation to reward. It is our view that if a company seriously wants to commit to CSR, this also has to be reflected in the appraisal and rewards of managers.

The whole issue of how to reward and promote managers who share the vision of responsible business is, we believe, one that should be considered by non-executive directors (e.g. on board remuneration committees). Candidates for the job would be non-executive directors who are committed to incorporating CSR in their own organisations. Through their influence they will be able to encourage better CSR performance from general managers by including CSR criteria in compensation packages. (For more on the role of governance structures, see Step 4, pages 149-53; for more on the role of leadership, see Step 4, pages 157-59.)

Evidence regarding whether companies are making a link between CSR performance and appraisals and rewards is conflicting, as highlighted below.

Evidence the link is being made

Some companies are adapting their reward and recognition schemes to ensure that every manager realises that the management of social, ethical and environmental issues is his or her business:

- The performance of Adidas country managers is measured against human rights policies and has an influence on annual bonuses.

- Texaco withheld a bonus from managers when diversity goals were not reached.

We have also been told privately of individual cases where very senior managers in some of the world's biggest countries have explicitly had their bonuses withheld because of their failure to perform on CSR objectives.

A survey of Standard & Poor's 500 found that some 75% of companies incorporated environmental criteria into executive compensation. Similarly, a survey of 139 leading CSR companies for the 2003 Business in the Community (BITC) Corporate Responsibility Index found that companies are making links between performance and remuneration. BITC asked these leading companies whether they make a link between corporate responsibility and performance management throughout the company. The vast majority of senior managers in the CRI companies reported having one or more specific objectives and targets for corporate responsibility in each of the broad CSR categories of community involvement, environmental performance, marketplace aspects of CSR and workplace aspects (Table 11a). Most companies also linked performance to compensation and bonus schemes (Table 11b).

In a worldwide survey of CEOs, executives and managers, The Conference Board found that 68% of managers cited the link between citizenship and performance

Link	Category			
	Community	*Environment*	*Market*	*Workplace*
(a) Percentage of companies making a link between CSR and performance management				
None	13	3	9	1
KPI for functional staff	83	95	85	96
KPI for senior management	64	79	79	90
Targets for board member(s)	54	65	63	73
(b) Percentage of companies with a remuneration or bonus system linked to CSR objectives and targets				
None	19	9	16	9
For functional staff	73	82	81	83
For senior management	47	65	69	79
For board members	35	42	50	55

Table 11 **The degree to which (a) links have been made between corporate responsibility and performance management (through use of key performance indicators [KPIs]) throughout the company and (b) remuneration and bonus systems have been linked to meeting CSR objectives and targets at 139 companies, by CSR category (community involvement; environmental, marketplace and workplace performance)**

Source: Business in the Community

appraisal as 'increasingly important', but, in contrast to the sample of 139 leading companies, 57% of managers said that their companies did not yet have appraisal systems built around their professed recognition of the significance of corporate citizenship. In the remaining 43% of instances where citizenship is used for appraisals, it does impact on compensation paid to management, particularly to business unit or line managers (in 18% of the sample) and to CEOs and senior management (in 16% of the sample).[12]

Remuneration linked to CSR alone may not be limited to managerial staff. In research conducted by SAM Sustainability Asset Management in 2002, about 1 in 10 of the companies surveyed said that more than 3% of their workforce received variable remuneration and compensation linked to environmental, corporate citizenship and corporate responsibility performance.[13]

One company that is making a link between CSR performance, assessment and remuneration is Danone.

12 Source: The Conference Board, 'Corporate Citizenship in the New Century: Accountability, Transparency and Global Stakeholder Engagement' (2002).
13 Data from 2002 yearly corporate sustainability assessment for Dow Jones Sustainability Indexes (DJSI), conducted by SAM Research Inc., the research arm of SAM Sustainable Asset Management, Zurich.

Danone

The Danone Way is a programme of processes, training and knowledge management that is designed to integrate CSR across operations worldwide. The company believes it has been a powerful ingredient in successfully integrating international acquisitions into the business. This is interesting given the mixed performance of many mergers and acquisitions in business generally.

Danone asks each company within its group to assess its own performance on the basis of 130 questions relating to issues such as food safety, human resources policies, environmental impacts and relationships with suppliers. At each operating company a management committee conducts this self-assessment with the assistance of working groups, bringing together managers and other employees.

Danone has also created a link between corporate citizenship performance and reward, with up to 40% of the bonuses paid to each company being based on the performance achieved as part of this 'Danone Way' exercise (see www.danone.com).

Evidence the link is not being made

Despite the results of the surveys cited above that companies are starting to link CSR performance to appraisal and remuneration, an international specialist advising organisations on executive compensation, told us in an interview that they are not yet seeing evidence of CSR being taken into consideration in executive compensation or bonuses — except perhaps where the company is working on a 'balanced-scorecard' basis. CSR may also be evident, they said, as an underpinning measure in long-term schemes (e.g. on issues of health and safety) but that in such cases it tends to be as a 'pre-qualifier' rather than as a driver of value. They suggested that the non-financial metrics of success are as yet very underdeveloped — noting that society has had 500 years since the time of the Medicis to develop such financial metrics.

It may be that some existing metrics, such as customer satisfaction, could be stretched to include stakeholder satisfaction and that in the exercise of discretionary bonuses, *how* a manager achieved his or her results as well as the results themselves could be taken into account (this is the case at Marks & Spencer, where 50% of managers' bonuses are awarded for what the manager has achieved — and the other 50% for how he or she did so). However, the management compensation experts we interviewed suggested that, generally, at this stage, the rewards for those managers who successfully follow responsible business practices tend not to be in the form of bonuses but rather in the form of promotion and advancement in the organisation because they are 'living the values and the culture of the business'.

▶ Company facilitators

Almost every business will have external 'facilitators'. For the small or medium-sized enterprise this may be the accountant, the bank manager, a business association of which they are a member or a small-business adviser. For larger companies, it will be an extensive network of lawyers, auditors, advertising and PR agencies, branding experts, management consultants and so on. Whatever the size of the business, if it is trying to align and embed corporate responsibility through its activities then these 'facilitators' also need to be fully briefed and involved along with employees and other stakeholders.

There are external developments among facilitators on which to build. For example, William McDonough, chairman of the US Public Company Accounting Oversight Board, believes that accountants should go back to basic principles in order to restore public trust. He argues that the quickest way for the profession to restore public trust shattered by US business failures such as Enron and Tyco would be for accountants to ensure their actions are consistent with moral principles.[14] In the United Kingdom, it has been proposed by the Auditing Practices Board that audit firms should create 'ethics partners', the role of whom would be to 'make sure the auditing firm implements new ethical standards, monitors them and acts as an arbitrator when there are difficult judgements to be made'.[15]

A number of international law firms and management consultants have told us privately that one of the drivers for their increased interest in corporate responsibility has been the fact that many of their key corporate clients have become committed to CSR.

Issues, therefore, that a company might consider in relation to its 'facilitators' include:

- Are we including environmental and social performance criteria in our selection criteria for professional advisers, creative agencies and other external facilitators?

- Are we regularly briefing these advisers on our own corporate responsibility commitments as well as encouraging them to work with us and to proactively suggest proposals for corporate social opportunities?

- Have we included the achievement of corporate social opportunity as one of the performance criteria in any incentives or bonus system we might have with professional advisers and creative agencies (finders' fees, share of intellectual property rights, etc.)?

Management consultants Marakon Associates used the BITC Corporate Responsibility Index as part of a wider programme of change to ensure that it met the corporate responsibility requirements that its clients (multinational corporations) now expect of business partners and suppliers.

14   Reported in the *Financial Times*, 19 December 2003.
15   Quoted in the *Daily Telegraph*, 'Audit groups act on ethics after Enron meltdown', 25 November 2003.

▶ In-house specialists in corporate social responsibility

> **WANTED:** multi-talented individual; simultaneously able to be salesperson, ambassador, compliance officer, internal risk assessor, social venture capitalist, strategist, broker, networker, translator, tactician, trainer, coach, philanthropist, urban guerrilla, animator, choreographer, conductor

The role of a CSR director or other specialist CSR staff is to act as a 'conductor', an 'animateur' and 'choreographer'. Their goal, in our view, should be to help all parts of the business incorporate CSR into their operations, working to ensure understanding and integration across the business as well as initiating their own new 'CSR' projects.

We are full of admiration for the job that CSR professionals do — they have an impossible job description!

CSR professionals must cajole, argue and seek to influence others who have direct control over tasks such as purchasing, marketing, personnel, corporate strategy and communications. It is the quintessential 21st-century job — namely, one that does not rely on command and control or on directing large armies of staff to go hither and thither. Instead, it relies much more on skills of networking and persuasion, of coaching, of spotting the eclectic and the unusual — but ultimately effective — connections.

They have to do all this and more, often with no settled view across their business of the necessity for their function, remit or even the nature of what they are meant to be doing! It is a profession largely without professional bodies, without standards, without a career structure and without much available formal training.[16]

The bit of the job that CSR directors and managers are most likely to have direct control over — corporate community investment — is only a small part of the CSR function. We have to wonder whether generally — and there are some excellent exceptions to the rule — corporate community investment managers have the credibility internally to take the CSR brief far within their own companies. That is why for us — even though some of the most effective CSR professionals recently have been 'refugees' from politics or campaigning NGOs — there are many advantages to moving someone into the CSR function from a successful line-manager career in the business, as such people will have a reservoir of contacts, a track record and influence to call on.

The CSR professional will play a crucial role in helping the business to integrate, align and embed CSR-related policies and practices, so, in our vision, the specialist CSR function becomes an internal consultancy for the business. To our knowledge, specialist CSR staff have:

16 Although, as we saw earlier in this step, in the United Kingdom a CSR academy to tackle some of these gaps was launched in July 2004.

- Blocked television commercials developed by the marketing department that could have offended ethnic minorities

- Worked to protect the interest of disabled savers, whose accounts were managed on their behalf, when financial business was de-mutualised

- Strengthened the purchasing department's processes for verifying labour conditions and human rights in suppliers' factories and farms and brokered deals with certifying bodies

- Advised on an 'exit package' when a company had to close a factory so that, in addition to redundancy and careers counselling services, the business also proactively worked with local public agencies to find a new use for the factory and its staff and supported the ongoing work of several local agencies involved in skills and business development

Is a separate CSR function likely long-term? At least one company, ABN AMRO, thinks not.

ABN AMRO Brazil

In 2002 ABN AMRO's Brazilian operation appointed a full-time director for CSR. She has the brief that within five years she should have made herself redundant — because, by then, CSR should have become absolutely mainstream in ABN AMRO Brazil and, therefore, there will be no need for a separate, specialist function.

This is certainly a novel approach! One might argue that even where responsible business practice has become an integral part of the way that a business works — and part of *every* manager's job description — there will still be a need for some specific, specialist expertise. Nevertheless, this example raises some interesting issues about how businesses that want to get serious about environmental, social and community responsibilities can best do so in terms of management and processes.

▶ Operational issues

Any new CSO-related strategy is likely to require changes in different company functions such as personnel, marketing and purchasing. Below, we explore some of the issues that need to be considered.

Personnel and recruitment

In a competitive operating environment, a company will want to be able to access the full range of knowledge and skills available from within the potential workforce. To do this, it must ensure its recruitment practices do not unintentionally lead to producing a homogeneous staff profile.

In order to achieve diversity targets a company may have to think more creatively about where it advertises job vacancies. For example, if it wants to attract more black and ethnic minority staff it will need to use media attracting large audiences from those groups.

An audit of existing company policies may reveal other gaps in representation, such as in the area of disability. For instance, many businesses are now seeking to market and to recruit new staff through use of websites, yet research in summer 2002 showed that only six of the FTSE 100 UK had disabled-accessible websites. The rest, therefore, were inadvertently discriminating against blind and partially sighted job applicants.

If companies move the recruitment function to the Internet, accessibility of the company website becomes important. McKinsey & Company have found that at least 1.3 million disabled people of working age in the United Kingdom face ongoing exclusion because companies maintain inaccessible e-recruitment websites, yet it is no more expensive to build an e-recruitment site that is accessible to disabled users than it is to build an inaccessible site. Where there is an existing inaccessible site, it will cost on average less than 5% of the total development expenditure to make it accessible. This investment can significantly increase the talent pool by improving the access and usability of a site for everyone. It also lowers maintenance costs, enhances reputation and reduces the possibility of discrimination.

In the USA, two-thirds of the websites of leading companies are inaccessible to disabled people. Other studies estimate that as much as 78–99% of online content is inaccessible to people whose impairments affect Internet use. Of the 50–100 most visited sites in the USA across six categories (including overall most visited, clothing sites, international sites, job sites and college sites) only 33% passed even basic accessibility tests.[17]

Similarly, if a company recruits from universities it needs to look at who the public face of the company on campus is going to be — who are the most appropriate people to speak to and to recruit graduates, and are they aware of the issues that are important to today's graduates?

17   Source: see the jointly owned website on global disability and CSR produced by AccountAbility, CSR Europe, Business for Social Responsibility (BSR) and the Employers' Forum on Disability. Sites can be tested for basic accessibility by using the online tool 'Bobby', provided by the website management company, Watchfire (bobby.watchfire.com). For further information on auditing websites and improving accessibility, see the Forum's publication 'Accessible Website Design: A Practical and Strategic Guide'. For more information on website accessibility go to www.employers-forum.co.uk/www/accessibility.htm.

To be able to attract and retain staff a company must be seen to be inclusive of all its workers. This includes non-discrimination on the basis of sexuality or gender (for an example of a company that sought to recruit more women to high-level jobs, see the case of Unilever in Step 2, page 62). For example, international banks are now setting up and promoting networks for gay and lesbian staff to emphasise their inclusive approach and to change their images as 'old-fashioned' places to work. In addition, in recruitment decisions a company may need to look more broadly for evidence of a candidate's capabilities and potential — such as in the case of women returning to work after raising families.

For workers who have family or other commitments outside the workplace it may be necessary to offer more flexibility in terms of part-time working, job-sharing and flexible working. In addition, employee compensation specialists report that advances in software make it easier for employers to offer much more flexibility for employees in terms of pensions, holiday entitlements, healthcare and so on, enabling them to choose and customise a package from a menu of employee benefits in order to suit their individual circumstances. For example, some people may prefer to receive greater family health insurance cover whereas others may prefer more holiday entitlement.

However well the company constructs its employee packages, and however inclusive it is, there will always be dilemmas. Some of these are explored later in this chapter.

The CSR questions that people in human resources might need to consider are as follows:

- Are you familiar with your organisation's CSR strategy and how human resources does or could fit in to this?

- Are you satisfied that the human resource aspects are sufficiently addressed in the CSR strategy?

- Is CSR included in internal management training programmes and in the executive management training and courses that you buy in from external business schools and other providers (see the section on training and development above, pages 166ff.)?

- Is CSR included in job descriptions, performance targets, management appraisals and compensation packages (see the section on performance and compensation above, pages 174ff.)?

- Does your organisation have an employee volunteering policy? Is employee volunteering linked to personal learning and organisational learning objectives?

- Has your organisation signed up for any external CSR codes and standards such as the Global Compact or the Global Reporting Initiative (see Step 7, pages 250f.)? If so, are you familiar with the human rights aspects of these commitments? Have you satisfied yourself that the organisation is compliant?

- Does your organisation have a diversity strategy? Is it using employer-led diversity campaigns (e.g. the Race for Opportunity,[18] the Employers' Forum on Disability in the United Kingdom,[19] the German Employers' Forum on Disability[20] or the Sri Lankan Employers' Network on Disability[21])? Are these handled separately or as part of a cohesive strategy?

- Does your organisation have operations abroad or significant overseas suppliers? If so, have you double-checked that your purchasing colleagues are checking sufficiently on issues such as child labour or basic human rights provisions? Are you familiar with the maps of Amnesty International and the IBLF showing human rights performance by country and sector?

- Is your organisation committed to lifelong learning and to a healthy work–life balance — and are your activities in these areas linked back into CSR strategies?

Marketing

Arguably, the marketplace aspects of responsible business practice are the least developed in most businesses championing CSR. This is ironic as this is the core of the business — and many of the risks to business reputation are to be found in the marketing area — and certainly where many CSOs exist. As one of the leading CSR intermediary organisations, Business for Social Responsibility (BSR), says in its publication *Corporate Social Responsibility: A Guide to Better Business Practices* (2002), 'the wide range of issues associated with the marketplace makes it difficult to provide comprehensive, detailed assistance with implementing socially responsible marketplace policies and practices'.

Marketers need to be conscious of the environmental and social impacts of the sourcing of raw materials used in their products and the health, safety and labour conditions under which branded products are manufactured in their own or in supplier factories (e.g. Nike; see page 19).

Advertising has become an increasingly fraught area — whether, for example, it reinforces stereotypes by the portrayal of particular ethnic, age or gender groups or reinforces, for example, the non-visibility of particular groups, such as through the non-portrayal of disabled consumers. A 2003 report from the Institute of Practitioners in Advertising concluded that advertisers are not reflecting Britain's ethnic minorities and that these communities do not believe that they see images of themselves that are balanced or truly representative.[22] There are also increasing

---

18 www.raceforopportunity.org.uk
19 www.employers-forum.co.uk
20 The German EFD was started in 2003.
21 The Sri Lankan network — part of the Sri Lankan Employers' Federation — has been written up as a case study by the ILO.
22 See www.ipa.co.uk.

questions about whether it is appropriate to target advertising at children. Already, businesses have been banned from advertising products such as cigarettes to children, and there is growing pressure on fast-food companies to do the same, as we discuss further in the worked example of the seven-step model in Part II of this book.

Marketers should certainly be thinking about the availability of their products and services to vulnerable groups such as children. When we interviewed mmO$_2$ chairman David Varney, one of the issues of most concern to him was the implications of advances in technology that would permit mobile telephone users to access the Internet, including pornography sites. Such content is clearly inappropriate for children — increasing numbers of whom now have their own mobile phones. Hence, the involvement of mmO$_2$ and other mobile telephony companies in the development of protocols to restrict the availability of such adult content, resulting in the launch of an industry agreement in January 2004, which calls for an independent body to determine whether content is suitable or not for those under the age of 18 (see Step 1, page 53).

At the other extreme, some companies face the challenge of the lack of accessibility of their products in some markets because of, for example, price (as in the case of pharmaceutical companies producing retroviral drugs for people with HIV and AIDS) and the consequent implications for pricing strategies in different markets (for examples of non-pharmaceutical companies that have responded to the issue of the availability of drugs and treatment for workers with HIV/AIDS, see the Diageo and Volkswagen Brazil case studies in Step 3, pages 138 and 122, respectively). Other marketplace issues include mis-selling, for example of financial services such as pensions or of utilities, and the environmental impacts of excess packaging and end use of products. Thus, in the future, we can envisage more debate about the role of responsible marketing in sustainable consumption, with questions asked about how much is enough and how the power of branding and marketing professionals can be harnessed to market sustainable goods and services — that is, about harnessing corporate social opportunities.

The CSR questions that people in marketing departments may need to consider include:

- Do we know the conditions under which raw materials for our products are sourced and how they are subsequently manufactured? Do these conditions match our public commitments on environmental and social responsibility?

- Are our marketing strategies and advertising campaigns to target diverse customer segments executed in ways consistent with responsible business practices?

- Are we regularly exploring the implications of potential misuses of our product(s) and are we taking active steps to protect ourselves legally and to protect our reputation?

- When did we last debate as a marketing team the potential for corporate social opportunities arising from the way in which corporate social responsibility issues are impacting our business?

Purchasing

The purchasing function is set to become one of the toughest battlegrounds in CSR. Companies face unrelenting competitive pressures, and a growing number find themselves compelled to consider outsourcing — whether of software development, call centres or the manufacture of sporting goods and branded clothes — to low-wage economies. As J.F. Rischard notes in his book *High Noon*, what this can mean in practice is that

> a Singapore manufacturer produces telephones in China for the US market with Taiwanese capital and an Israeli technology licence — five countries in the chain. Some clothes manufacturers based in Hong Kong supply US firms like DKNY from factories in Lesotho. Some 30,000 people are now employed in the Caribbean manning call centres on behalf of US businesses.[23]

Responsible businesses are trying to respond to these developments by introducing supplier guidelines, helping suppliers to meet environmental and social standards and instituting inspection and verification systems (see below; see also the section on business and supplier concerns in Step 1, pages 42ff.). Some of these systems are internal; some rely on external auditors and formal accreditation.

There are many examples of companies that have written CSR into their purchasing requirements and that have entered into closer relationships and partnerships with their suppliers. Only a few of these are listed below:

- B&Q is one of the most advanced in terms of helping its small and medium-sized suppliers to meet the environmental and social standards it sets.

- General Motors requires its suppliers to be certified to ISO 14001 or an equivalent environmental management system (see Step 1, page 44). Also, as we saw in Step 2, it no longer purchases chemicals but chemical services from its suppliers (page 97)

- SC Johnson has a 'green-list', consisting of criteria developed with its suppliers so that the suppliers have a better understanding of what they should be doing, why and how they should behave.

- Like many major companies operating in South Africa, Coca-Cola SA has a long-established programme to develop its small and medium-sized suppliers and customers as part of the post-apartheid Black Empowerment Programme.

23   J.F. Rischard, *High Noon: 20 Global Problems; 20 Years to Solve Them* (New York: Basic Books, 2002).

A company that has a long history of supplier care and partnerships is the super-market Waitrose.

Waitrose

The UK food retailer Waitrose has long-established principles of supplier care based on a spirit of partnership embedded in its constitution. This requires suppliers to be treated with honesty, fairness, courtesy and promptness. Suppliers must manage sub-suppliers in a similar way. Waitrose also operates a Responsible Sourcing Programme that takes account of the environment, health and safety, workers' rights and animal welfare throughout the supply chain. The results, say Waitrose, is that all parties benefit from being part of a socially sustainable relationship. Suppliers are paid a fair price that reflects the cost of production. Customer, employee and other stakeholder relations have been enhanced (see www.smallbusinessjourney.com).

▶ Community investment

Some business people and commentators continue to think that CSR is only about how a company helps the community. By now, we would hope that the reader does not share such views. Nevertheless, community relations should not be neglected or treated as an after-thought. The long-term experience of all three of the partners of this book — BITC, IBLF and The Conference Board — suggests that corporate community investments are most effective for both the company and the community when they:

- Are long-term
- Involve a range of corporate resources
- Incorporate the passion, energy and skills of employees
- Use the company's 'influence chains' to leverage other support and to lend credibility to the organisation or cause
- Address a business need that is understandable to employees, investors and society at large
- Have the potential to be adopted on a larger scale by others (e.g. in the public sector)
- Are not isolated programmes but are complimentary to and consistent with wider provision
- Are based on sound research and assessment of need
- Are evaluated and modified as necessary to maximise positive impact

- Are created with built-in opportunities to identify and disseminate learning

- Play to the core competences of the business

- Lead to learning that the company applies to its own core activities (e.g. hiring policies may change after a company has participated in a community programme on the employability of disabled or homeless people) or to other forms of corporate social opportunities

▶ Unifying processes

Even leading-edge companies continue to find it a challenge to integrate CSR into their business activities. For the 139 leading firms surveyed for the 2003 BITC Corporate Responsibility Index (CRI) a 16% gap was found between average scores achieved for strategy and average scores achieved for integration of CSR into the business. There is anecdotal evidence suggesting some of the participating companies have used the CRI itself as a management tool to aid integration, as illustrated by the case of Compass.

Compass

Compass is one the world's biggest food-service companies and is one of the world's top-ten private-sector employers (in terms of number of people employed). The company has recently committed itself to corporate responsibility and has used the CRI as an aid in assessing its corporate responsibility goals. The company's ethos of decentralised and entrepreneurial management has meant that the data it was required to submit in order to be included in the CRI involved assessments by 100 of its top managers — data that in the past had seldom been reported beyond a divisional level.

Most businesses nowadays have favoured and established business systems and processes (e.g. risk management or total quality management [TQM]). Management of CSR can be integrated into these systems. Some experts recommend the use of traditional health and safety functions as an additional convenient entry point for CSR into the company.[24] It is then possible to 'stretch' health and safety to a broader health and well-being approach, which incorporates a consideration of the work–life· balance and opportunities for employee learning, continuous improvement and help for employees to enjoy a healthier and more active life to a much later age.

24 See e.g. Paul Gilding, Rick Humphries and Murray Hogarth, 'Safe Companies: A Practical Path for Operationalising Sustainability' (Ecos Corporation discussion paper, March 2002; www.ecoscorporation.com).

Others may prefer to allow engagement with CSR to spread out from an area of CSR and sustainable development where they have a good track record and strong internal buy-in. Examples of companies that have taken this approach are listed in Table 12. For instance, Siemens has used its quality-control framework to provide an integrating strategy for CSR and has followed this up with a pilot programme, COSURE, for applying quality and CSR requirements to small and medium-sized suppliers.

Company	Approach or policy area
Cirque de Soleil	Creativity and innovation
Diageo	Community and corporate citizenship
DuPont	Environment
Novartis	Health and safety
Procter & Gamble	Environment; Diversity
Siemens	Quality
Unilever	Creativity and innovation

Table 12 **Examples of companies in which the integration of corporate social responsibility (CSR) has grown from a particular approach or policy**

We observe that 'quality' is a common springboard to integrating CSR policies and practices. Those who are responsible for ensuring quality within a company may want to ask themselves the following CSR-related questions:

- Does our company have a CSR strategy? Has it signed up to an international code of conduct or declaration, such as the UN Global Compact or the World Economic Forum's Corporate Citizenship statement? Is it a member of an organisation promoting responsible business practices, such as Business in the Community? Do we understand the significance of these commitments?

- Does our company have a director in charge of CSR? If so, who is that person and am I able to review with him or her, on a regular basis? How we can support each other's work?

- Does our company use the business excellence model (BEM)? Could I involve those responsible for CSR in reviewing the elements of the BEM that concern our impact on society?

- How does my work on quality affect the organisation's ability to continuously improve its positive impact on business and society?

- How can the expertise in our organisation in relation to quality be applied to help our suppliers meet faster, cheaper and more effectively the environmental and social impact standards that the company has or may impose on suppliers?

- How can the quality function assist our community partners and the causes that our company supports?

- How can I harness the company's track record as a responsible business in order to motivate employees to be more committed and engaged with quality circles and drives for continuous improvement?

- How might a commitment to minimising negative environmental and social impacts and maximising positive impacts become the basis for driving value up and cost down?

▶ Knowledge-management systems

One of the under-developed areas of CSR integration and resources is knowledge management. We have asked a number of consultants and other experts in the field to define the link between the two areas and the general reaction has been: 'That's an interesting question. We haven't seen very much of it — but do let us know what you find out!' One expert defines knowledge management as:[25]

> The discipline of enabling individuals, teams and the entire organi-
> sation to collectively and systematically create, share and apply
> knowledge to better achieve the objectives of the business . . . [It is]
> an emerging set of principles, processes, organisational structures,
> applications and technologies that help people to improve.

According to management guru Stefane Garelli of the IMD Business School in Lausanne, 'learning faster than competitors becomes the only source of competitive advantage'. This means that companies have to 'get smart' at identifying, capturing, codifying and disseminating knowledge — especially knowledge of good practice. However, it is a major challenge for most companies to persuade busy people to stop what other jobs they are doing in order to express what they know — as well as to create the climate where they *want* to share their knowledge and *believe* that it is in their own long-term interest to do so. This challenge is as much about sociology and psychology as it is about technology. Just as some companies have found that disability awareness training (as at B&Q and BSkyB; see Step 3, pages 119 and 123, respectively) or other CSR training is a good way of winning employee buy-in for wider customer service training, we wonder if CSR knowledge management could be a 'device' to persuade employees to participate actively in a broader corporate knowledge-management system.

A review in 2002 of CSR practice conducted by the Ashridge Management Centre on behalf of CSR Europe concluded:

---

25 Defined for a Unicom course on knowledge management for BLU, February 2004. See the BLU business plan on www.sbs.gov.uk.

The financial management of acquisition appears indeed to deliver longer lasting results when combined with a social approach relying on a culture of corporate responsibility.

● Danone includes knowledge management in its Danone Way programme (see the example on page 176).

● Serco makes a list of its cases of good CSR practice, submitted from the 600 different Serco projects around the world, available electronically to all parts of the business (for more details of how Serco integrates CSR into its diverse operations, see the example in Step 4, pages 155f.).

● Vodafone holds a fortnightly news briefing on telecommunications and CSR provided by The Corporate Citizenship Company. Details of the briefing are then given to CSR professionals. A monthly composite report — part news, part good practice and part an inspiration for the business to take CSR seriously — is sent to CSR champions around the business (for an example of how innovation is leading to CSOs at Vodafone, see Step 3, page 119).

Any CSR knowledge-management system needs the flexibility to collect and analyse a spectrum of material (see Figure 9). Such material may include:

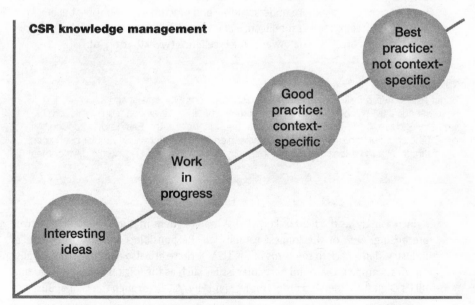

Figure 9 **Corporate social responsibility (CSR) knowledge management: the spectrum of ideas and practice**

- Interesting ideas, not yet tried

- Work in progress (presented enthusiastically by those responsible, but no hard data is yet available to show positive impact)

- Good practice (externally verified as showing positive impacts but it is context-specific, e.g. working only in a particular culture or corporate governance jurisdiction or under particular funding regimes)

- Best practice (externally verified as showing positive impacts and it is not context-specific)

There is a potential for a company to build up a team of committed CSR advocates and champions across the organisation to scope CSR issues, dividing responsibility for attending major CSR conferences and for reporting back on key lessons and insights for the company (see the 'Signposts' section on pages 372ff.) — all adding to the knowledge-management system (for the fundamentals of how to scope issues, see Step 2).

There are many other ways to gain and manage knowledge. Some companies, such as Tate & Lyle, are working with independent individuals or companies to access knowledge and gather it into an intelligible whole. Other companies (see BT in Step 6, pages 217f.) have established advisory panels or virtual advisory panels (e.g. through use of e-mail and video conferencing) of CSR specialists and thought-leaders to keep them sighted on major developments in the field. There are also companies that use internal and external corporate CSR awards in a strategic way not just to encourage more understanding and practice of responsible business but also as a source of market intelligence and as a contributor to knowledge development, such as BITC's annual Awards for Excellence (www.bitc.org.uk).

Tate & Lyle

Sugar refiner Tate & Lyle sponsors a distinguished community activist and social entrepreneur, David Robinson (founder of Community Links, www.community-links.org.uk), who works close to the Tate & Lyle corporate headquarters in the East End of London. As part of the sponsorship deal, David provides senior management with a regular briefing on significant local and national trends in community regeneration and economic development.

Increasingly, as the field of knowledge management matures, sectoral initiatives are arising. One of the longest established, Responsible Care, for the chemical industry, dates back to the 1970s in the USA.[26] There are also a number of specialist business campaigns around particular issues such as the 'digital divide',[27] including IBLF's Digital partnership programme[28] and HIV/AIDS, through the Global Business

---

26   www.americanchemistry.com
27   The divide between those who have access to new information and communications technology and those who do not.
28   www.iblf.org

Coalition on HIV/AIDS.[29] Various industry associations are now producing sectoral guidance for their members on implementing CSR policies and management systems. The British Bankers Association and The British Insurance Association, for example, have produced the FORGE Guidelines on CSR for financial service companies.[30] More examples are listed in the 'Signposts' section at the end of this book (pages 372ff.).

▶ Integration and the dangers of inconsistency

> [Long-term sustainable performance] is not about putting it down on paper, it is about living your values.
>
> *Sunil Misser, Head of Global Sustainability Practice, PwC, 2002*[31]

Frequently businesses who claim to behave responsibly are criticised for their actions on the ground failing to match the rhetoric of their words. NGOs in particular may accuse companies of 'greenwash': presenting a façade of responsibility while behaving irresponsibly. This may be true, but equally may be due to fundamental differences of what constitutes responsible business practice.[32] There are a number of areas where real challenges and dilemmas faced by management may lead to 'inconsistencies', as illustrated in the following scenarios:

- Managing a downturn

- Outsourcing

- Catching up and inconsistency, including breakdowns in communication within the company

- Inconsistency across the value chain

Managing in a downturn

One issue frequently raised as an example of companies being inconsistent is the treatment of their staff in difficult economic conditions. We would never argue that being a responsible business should mean avoiding tough decisions when necessary. Corporate responsibility should, however, effect *how* tough decisions are made — who should be consulted and how much the company should strive to find and

29   www.businessfightsaids.org
30   www.abi.org.uk/forge
31   Quoted in *Financial Times*, 'Risk management', 20 November 2002.
32   See e.g. Christian Aid's critique of Coca-Cola, Shell and BAT in 'Behind the Mask: The Real Face of Corporate Social Responsibility', published in January 2004; www.christian-aid.org.uk/indepth/0401csr/index.htm. For a critique of the Christian Aid Report see, for example, Mallen Baker in *Ethical Corporation*, 23 February 2004 (www.ethicalcorp.com).

implement creative solutions. In 2003 we visited Xilinx and heard the creative way in which it dealt with an industry slowdown.

Xilinx

We visited Xilinx (www.xilinx.com), a Silicon Valley company, early in 2003. Xilinx is a world leader in complete programmable logic solutions. Xilinx has gained market share and has successfully diversified its business, significantly extending its lead in the market for programmable chips throughout the high-technology industry downturn.

Xilinx has implemented a policy of using layoffs only as a last resort, protecting its employees by working closely with them to create innovative cost-cutting measures to avoid redundancies. The company reasoned that if it could avoid cutting its staff of 2,600 it would be better positioned once the industry recovered. In the words of chief executive Willem 'Wim' Roelandts, 'demotivated engineers do not create breakthrough projects!' With almost three-quarters of its staff working on future products, any layoffs of employees would delay recovery after difficult times.

Instead of sweeping reductions of staffing levels, Xilinx has relied on pay cuts and various creative means to reduce costs. Roelandts said that employees were allowed to go back into education on part of their salary, stating that Xilinx '[urges] people to take sabbaticals or part-time work, everything to reduce costs except layoffs'.

Salary cuts at Xilinx were also structured in a way that would breed loyalty among employees. Initially, cuts were on a sliding scale, where the highest-paid employees, including Roelandts, got cuts of 20% and the lowest paid saw no reductions. When this proved insufficient, and the situation continued to deteriorate, the human resources department took a leadership role and held focus groups with employees — soliciting their input regarding next steps and other viable options. Employees agreed to take an additional 7.5% pay cut, but they proposed a menu of choices to make that happen. Each employee had several choices of taking stock options in lieu of pay or taking time off without pay. In retrospect, it appears that providing choices to employees throughout 2001 was the key to success in these initiatives.

Under the sabbatical programme, if an employee agreed to take a year of leave from the company, Xilinx agreed to accelerate the vesting of stock options if the employee returned and remained with the company for the same amount of time that the leave encompassed. In addition, for any employee who went to work as a volunteer for a non-profit organisation or a school in the local community, Xilinx agreed to pay him or her a $10,000 bonus.

Xilinx's market share prior to the 1998 downturn in its core business was 30%. By the second quarter of 2003 it was 51%; in 2003 the company's revenues exceeded those of all three of its major competitors combined. During the period 2001–2003 Xilinx brought more products to market on time than at any other period in its 20 year corporate history (based on notes from the company visit in February 2003, various *Fortune* and *Business Week* magazine profiles and a 2003 case study by Wayne F. Cascio of the Business School, University of Colorado–Denver). In January 2004, Xilinx appeared again in Fortune's list of the top-100 companies to work for, for the fourth year in a row (*Fortune*, 12 January 2004).

Outsourcing

In the industrialised economies today there seems to be a widespread view that 'if you can make it, you can make it in China; if you can service it, you can service it in India'. In a 2003 survey, 43% of the members of the Confederation of British Industries (CBI) claimed that they felt pressured to move operations overseas to reduce costs, and 29% are already exporting jobs.[33] The outsourcing of jobs to low-wage economies is a hot topic in the 2004 US presidential election. Internationally, companies are being criticised for double-standards in espousing CSR domestically and then outsourcing jobs to the lowest-cost option available.

Our view? The global forces for change we outlined in Step 1 make a substantial amount of outsourcing inevitable. Fighting it is like to trying to stop the tide coming in. As with redundancies for other reasons, business has to be creative and evolve. It could be argued that, by creating jobs and economic activity in countries such as India these companies help to tackle global poverty; give more people a stake in the system and boost development all round. In his column in *The New York Times* (29 February 2004), Thomas Friedman wrote, during a trip to Bangalore:

> there is more to outsourcing than just economics. There's also geopolitics. It is inevitable in a networked world that our economy is going to shed certain low-wage, low-prestige jobs. To the extent that they go to places like India or Pakistan — where they are viewed as high-wage, high-prestige jobs — we make not only a more prosperous world, but a safer world for our own 20-year-olds.

For responsible businesses, however, there are some crucial issues about how such outsourcing is handled. Decision-makers and those implementing the changes need to:

● Consult the affected workers well ahead of any decisions being taken

● Undertake a genuine exploration of alternatives

● Help displaced workers to retrain and find alternative employment

● Ensure that health, safety and labour standards in the outsourced operations are to internationally agreed standards

● Ensure the move has a positive environmental and social impact in the outsourced location

Example of how companies may proceed with outsourcing are provided by Barclays Bank and British Telecommunications.

---

33   See *The Times* Business Section, 18 November 2003.

Barclays Bank and Unifi

Barclays Bank has an umbrella agreement with the union Unifi (the union for finance workers). The trade union has accepted that jobs will be lost in Britain because companies can access lower-paid labour overseas, but it has secured with Barclays Bank 'early consultation' with workers in cases where major decisions are being made that may affect employees and has negotiated extensive aid to help people find new jobs should they be laid off.

Barclays has already moved 500 jobs to India (lost to the UK but gained by India) and is in talks with UK consultants Accenture about outsourcing some IT jobs.

The agreement with Unifi 'applies to all projects that involve offshore outsourcing' and will also apply to some projects that 'restructure aspects of the business in the UK'. The bank has said that it will '[seek] wherever possible to re-deploy staff impacted by change within the group' and will form a special team to manage the redeployment of those 'impacted staff' that wish to stay with Barclays; it has agreed to fund external training 'if redeployment options are exhausted' (*Financial Times*, 6 January 2003).

British Telecommunications and Connect

British Telecommunications (BT) has transferred work from the United Kingdom to India and is also publicly committed to behaving responsibly. It has commissioned the consultancy SustainAbility to examine both its performance and the wider, often impassioned, debate about the migration of jobs from rich nations to poor.

Its report, which is published on the BT website,* concludes that moving work offshore to cut costs is a legitimate response to competitive pressure — that what matters is how companies do it. The authors of the report, Judy Kuszewski and Kavita Prakash-Mani, state:

> Although the trend overall may not be negative, individual companies' handling of their decisions has at times been irresponsible and unfair to those affected, particularly in relation to US software jobs. Companies seeking public support for offshoring must earn the public's trust.

In 2003, SustainAbility commended BT's deal with Connect (the union for professional and managerial staff). The deal ruled out forced redundancies and ensured that overseas suppliers treat workers well. BT is operating a policy of openness, is retraining affected staff and is setting high standards for Indian suppliers through its Sourcing with Human Dignity code. Staff turnover at the Delhi call centre is just 1%, far below the Indian industry average of 30–40%. BT also has a policy against changing the names of operators, a practice used in some call centres to conceal the location of the agent from Western customers.

However, in the same 2004 report, SustainAbility suggested that BT needs to take more responsibility for the consequences of its role in promoting 'offshoring' to business customers via BT Global Services.

* SustainAbility, 'Good Migrations: BT, Corporate Social Responsibility and the Geography of Jobs' (February 2004), www.btplc.com/Societyandenvironment/Hottopics/Geographyofjobs/Goodmigrations.pdf

Catching up and inconsistency

In some cases, businesses that espouse CSR values yet behave badly are simply being hypocritical. However, there are alternative explanations. In some instances there may be a time-lag between changes in stakeholder expectations of good corporate behaviour and the company's response to these changing expectations. In other cases, there may be inconsistencies in behaviour across a business due to a lack of coherence between different parts of the organisation.

How, then, can a distinction be made between real irresponsibility and cases of delayed response or 'teething problems' with integration of CSR into company operations? In our judgement, an irresponsible business will be indifferent to, negligent about or even positively culpable regarding its poor performance and behaviour.

So what is a company to do if a group of stakeholders does not feel the business is behaving in line with what those stakeholders believe should be the norms of responsible business? In such a case the company may be judged as inconsistent — or worse. One of our colleagues, Steve Hilton, from the consultancy Good Business and author of a book of the same name,[34] has the following advice:

> Consistency is the key to success in corporate social responsibility . . . Those of us who are keen to persuade sceptics that corporations can — and generally do — make the world a better place are often fighting with our hands tied behind our backs as companies splash gaily around in vast vats of corporate responsibility eyewash. Many corporate responsibility strategies lose credibility not through any inherent weakness or lack of careful, painstaking work, but through the language used to describe them — or the occasional step too far. Prattling on about sustainable development in your social report while parading the opposite in your annual report is spectacularly unhelpful. It's possible for excellent corporate responsibility initiatives to be devalued by a small step beyond the bounds of credibility.[35]

Steve goes on to describe the example of the Portman Group — an industry body established in 1989 by the major alcohol companies in the United Kingdom to promote aspects of responsible business for the sector, such as the introduction of a national proof-of-age card or the promotion of sensible drinking — noting that:

> While the Portman Group spends a pittance telling 18–24 year olds 'if you do drink, don't do drunk', their booze baron backers are busily and heavily promoting the opposite message — strictly within the Advertising Standards Authority guidelines, of course.[36]

34   S. Hilton and G. Gibbons, *Good Business: Your World Needs You* (London/New York: Texere, 2002).

35   S. Hilton, 'Consistency is the key to success in corporate social responsibility', *Ethical Corporation*, 23 September 2002; www.ethicalcorp.com

36   *Ibid.*

He goes on to say that if messages relating to, for example, sensible drinking are to be believed and effective then they must be delivered through mainstream marketing and advertising.

Today, we are seeing some progress in this area — for example in the case of Allied Domecq.

Allied Domecq

Allied Domecq has developed a global advertising and marketing code that provides guidance at the global and national levels. The purpose of the global marketing code is to ensure that commercial communications from any Allied Domecq brand do not show excessive or irresponsible consumption of alcohol since these may have personal, social or health consequences. In many countries where Allied Domecq operates there are already national advertising and marketing regulations, both mandatory and self-regulatory. The purpose of the Allied Domecq code is to set general principles that apply in addition to the local requirements. The code is also applied in countries where existing regulation is not yet developed and where the company is committed to promoting the responsible advertising of its brands and encouraging improved standards for the industry as a whole. Executives are required to abide by the spirit of the code as well as the letter. In conjunction with its Advertising Review Board, the codes help Allied Domecq marry its marketing agenda to its approach to corporate responsibility. On a day-to-day level, it is the responsibility of all Allied Domecq employees involved in advertising and marketing to safeguard compliance with the code. The company also now provides a staff training programme and a comprehensive manual to ensure that the code is fully understood within the company.

Communication breakdowns: the left hand doesn't know what the right hand is doing

For some large and multinational businesses the challenge may be that some employees or some parts of the business may not have understood the new commitment to 'responsible business' and what it means for them and their own roles or part of the business. Inconsistency between different parts of the same business is one possibility. Another possibility is that an individual business may have adopted a progressive position on, say, global warming but is failing in maintaining its membership in a trade association that promotes the opposite. On the one hand, the company may deliberately be trying to draw attention away from its trade association membership by diverting people's gaze to its policy on global warming. On the other hand, it could simply be that its actions (failure to withdraw its membership of the trade association) have not kept pace with its CSR intentions. Or it could be that it feels it could have influence on the association's policies and thus potentially have a positive effect on an entire sector, changing the industry from within.

Another specific action point, therefore, is to ensure that the business regularly briefs the trade associations and sectoral bodies of which it is a member about its overall CSR strategy and regularly reviews what changes to the policies, priorities and programmes of the trade bodies of which it is a member result from its commitment to being a responsible business. The resignation of Shell and BP from the Global Climate Coalition — a coalition of companies sceptical about the existence of global warming — was a powerful public signal of the kind we described in Step 4. BP and Shell recognised the inconsistency between their espoused policies and new commitments on specific CSR issues and sustainable development and their actions.

Related to this point on consistency of action is the case of lobbying activities. We fully expect issues concerning the way in which companies lobby governments and the content of their lobbying agenda to become a more significant issue in CSR in the future.

Another aspect of consistency is simply to ensure that all parts of the business can work through the consequences of their actions in tune with the core values of the business. Even deservedly well-respected corporate citizens may sometimes inadvertently find themselves in difficulties in this respect, as Cadbury Schweppes found out.

Cadbury Schweppes

In recent years Cadbury Schweppes has experienced several problems with marketing responsibly. It inadvertently caused offence over adverts in India for one of its chocolate bars, which appeared over a map of India with the advertising slogan 'Too good to share' — unfortunately superimposed over the hotly contested area of Kashmir! A few months later, Cadbury's again found itself in hot water over a cause-related marketing campaign in the United Kingdom offering sports equipment to schools in return for chocolate-bar wrappers. This campaign was criticised by some health campaigners for encouraging chocolate consumption while promoting a healthy lifestyle. The company vehemently disagreed with the critics, arguing it was part of the solution not the problem. The campaign was later criticised by UK government ministers even though it was originally endorsed by the Sports Minister.

Inconsistency across the value chain

A rapidly growing area in CSR is the need to ensure coherence and consistency of adherence to a company's CSR commitments not just across the company but also through its value chain. Good practice here is not just about arbitrarily imposing new environmental and social performance standards on suppliers — many of which will be small businesses, perhaps in emerging economies, with little internal capacity to meet the requirements of their big business customers. Rather, there is a need for engagement with and in many cases support for suppliers, typified by the approach of companies such as DIY retailer B&Q, which is offering guidance and training to help small business suppliers meet its standards.

B&Q

B&Q is the biggest home-improvement retailer in Europe, employing 36,000 people within the UK. B&Q's priority in supply chain management is the production of quality goods. Brand reputation is also an important driver for the company. The company has a well-established code of conduct that it applies to all the factories from which it sources. While this mitigates risk, B&Q is conscious that codes do not always succeed in communicating the sustainability message to its suppliers. The company is therefore looking to move beyond a compliance position and communicate not simply 'what' responsible measures they would like suppliers to adopt, but also 'why' they are asking them to adopt them. To achieve this, B&Q has developed a 'factory pack'. The measures in the self-help guide were designed to meet three core criteria: simplicity, low cost and sustainability. The pack includes B&Q's policy commitments. It also contains a CD with ideas on proactive measures that suppliers can take to improve production and quality, as well as reducing social and environmental impacts. B&Q is currently working on a factory management development model, which will be added to the resource pack. This training guide will include information on issues such as working conditions, safety standards, hygiene, contracts for employment, overpayment payments, environmental issues and dormitory conditions (www.diy.com/diy/jsp/aboutbandq/social_responsibility/BQ_OPERA.PDF).

▶ Increasing the prospects for finding and making corporate social opportunities

> Corporate social responsibility is not just about managing, reducing and avoiding risk, it is about creating opportunities, generating improved performance, making money and leaving the risks far behind.

> *Sunil Misser, Head of Global Sustainability Practice, PwC, 2002*[37]

We argue that where a company really embraces CSR and integrates it within the 'company DNA' then the business will become more open to and create possibilities for CSOs — for new products and services, in new and under-served markets and using different business models. The business will also be more able to achieve transformation into a company where such opportunities are systemic. This is because:

- A commitment to responsible business and sustainable development creates more pressure to find new solutions — it makes the business more receptive to 'out-of-the-box' thinking

- It makes the company more receptive to approaches from NGOs, governments and academia with ideas for collaboration

37   Quoted in *Financial Times*, 'Risk Management', 20 November 2002.

- A company genuinely practising CSR is more likely to have eclectic and effective stakeholder engagement processes in place — so stakeholders will have better understanding of the company's interests and areas of expertise and where it might be particularly open to new ideas

- Outsiders will be more likely to have the company on their radar screen as a potential collaborator and consider it more open to what at first might seem 'zany, crazy ideas'

- A company committed to stakeholder engagement will be more likely to have highly accessible and visible contact points that external stakeholders can approach and who in turn can link the external approaches to the most appropriate people inside the business

- The company is less likely to have a 'not invented here' mentality — rather, it will steal with pride approaches developed elsewhere and engage in what Tom Peters called 'creative swiping', being open to ideas not just from other businesses but also from other sectors[38]

- There will be a corporate culture that is not only willing to work with others but also widely known and respected so that outsiders *want* to work with it

- It is more likely to have the right mind-sets for fair and equitable collaboration with other sectors and partners

- By understanding sustainability it will be more alert to opportunities as an integral part of keeping costs down and value up

To take an example from business, we might interpret the work of Nestlé's Sustainable Agricultural Services, described in its *Sustainable Development Review 2002*, as an example of this approach. Figure 10 is our visual depiction of the positive spiral of benefits which Nestlé has achieved by applying good supply-chain development processes, as explained below stage by stage:

1. Nestlé buys its agricultural raw materials from farmers, and the quality of those materials are dependent on the quality of farming practices. In order to help meet its quality needs, Nestlé provides loans and technical assis-

---

38 An interesting recent development is the way in which social enterprises (businesses where profit is not distributed among shareholders and where the purpose is social benefit) are becoming more popular business vehicles around the world — and there are an increasing number of cases of learning being transferred between conventional enterprises and social enterprises. The business schools of both Harvard University and Stanford University, for example, have social enterprise programmes. In the United Kingdom, the business schools at the universities of Oxford and Cambridge are similarly developing social enterprise programmes. A 2003 study sponsored by the William and Flora Hewlett Foundation and the David and Lucile Packard Foundation explored this interconnection further; see J. Emerson, *The Blended Value Proposition: Integrating Social and Financial Returns* (Stanford, CA: Graduate School of Business, Stanford University, 2003).

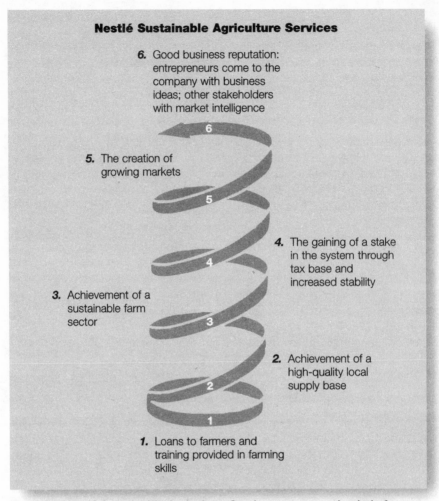

Nestlé Sustainable Agriculture Services

6. Good business reputation: entrepreneurs come to the company with business ideas; other stakeholders with market intelligence

5. The creation of growing markets

4. The gaining of a stake in the system through tax base and increased stability

3. Achievement of a sustainable farm sector

2. Achievement of a high-quality local supply base

1. Loans to farmers and training provided in farming skills

Figure 10 **Nestlé Sustainable Agriculture Services: an upward spiral of sustainable development and corporate social opportunity (CSO)**

tance to help raise production standards — for example, in Brazil some 300,000 farmers in the dairy industry have received this kind of support.

2. The quality levels of farmers who form the local supply base improve.

3. Farmers are not obliged to sell to Nestlé in order to receive the support, but many do. The knock-on effect is that farmers are able to market their higher-quality produce to other buyers in addition to Nestlé, creating a more diversified and sustainable farming sector.

4. Farmers — small businesses in their own right — increase their 'stake' in the local community and government system, with the local tax base increasing accordingly.

5. The local economy and local markets grow as they benefit from steady income and employment.

6. The relationship between farmers and Nestlé encourages dialogue and the transfer of ideas and exchange of information, which is all fed back into the capacity-building process and needs analysis.

▶ Synthesis of Step 5

In the synthesis for this section we briefly introduce a hypothetical company — The Exchange, a retailer. And we describe how Steps 1 through 5 of the seven-step process could apply to a company by suggesting issues, themes and operational challenges and opportunities that the process will throw up.

Steps 1–5 at The Exchange

Step 1
The trigger for this firm to act did not at first directly concern the company but involved a legal action against a major competitor. Ex-employees took legal action against it over allegations of racial harassment and discrimination. The ex-employees were successful, and the industry was threatened with a formal investigation by the Commission for Racial Equality.

Step 2
The Exchange, fearing the spotlight might fall on its own practices, scoped the potential issues it faced, discovering in the process that it had few female, black and other ethnic minority staff in supervisory or managerial positions (with those female, black and ethnic minority staff at the company being employed predominantly in cleaning, security and shop-floor posts). It also discovered that it did not know how many disabled staff it employed. Furthermore, it dawned on the board and senior management team that they were exclusively white, male and middle-aged or older.
   Scoping also showed that its female customers, black customers and customers from ethnic minorities saw it as being a very homogenous company with a salesforce that does not understand them. It learned also that female undergraduates, black undergraduates and undergraduates from ethnic minorities were not applying to The Exchange because they have a strong perception of the company as being unwelcoming to them. This perception was reinforced by language and visuals in the corporate literature and by the managers that the company sent to present the company at recruitment fairs on the university 'milk round'.

continued ➜

Step 3

The company made a business case for change in terms of a cost–benefit analysis of improving its policy for women returning to work — recognising that, in addition to immediate benefits in retaining 'institutional memory' and cost-savings in recruitment and training of replacement staff, there are intangible gains for the company in terms of the new policy signalling a broader change of approach towards diversity issues. Similarly, it made business cases for the costs of:

- Physical adaptations at specific company premises to accommodate new staff that use wheelchairs
- Providing childcare and eldercare facilities (this also bringing an early 'win' in terms of making the firm more attractive to mothers with young children)
- The company canteen providing a broader range of menus for staff from various communities
- Diversity training for the board and senior management team, to be cascaded through the business afterwards
- Establishing a company-wide 'diversity council'

Step 4

The Exchange then committed itself to taking action. The original commitment — to create a more diverse workforce at The Exchange — was rejected as being 'CSR for CSR's sake'. Instead, the commitment became to create a more diverse workforce at The Exchange in order to achieve a more sustainable and successful business. It realised that with the first formulation it would have been far harder to get buy-in within the business; investors might have questioned the scale of the commitment; and, at best, the business would have been constantly having to justify why it was expending so much energy on that commitment. The commitment to action involved setting annual targets for the percentage of women on the board and in senior management positions, targets for the number of women, black people and ethnic minority staff throughout the organisation, and initial targets to gather baseline data prior to setting targets for the number of disabled employees.

Step 5

The Exchange is now at the stage of identifying and developing resources and integrating CSR strategies into its operations. It is doing this by looking at the following areas:

- Human resources
- Purchasing
- Community involvement
- Innovation
- Strategy and operations

Human resources
The Exchange is:

- Improving existing data collection on job applicants and current employees (e.g. by postal district, by source and so on)
- Analysing surveys of employee satisfaction and information from exit interviews to check for attitudinal trends among women, black, ethnic minority and disabled staff

continued ➜

- Creating an accelerated development and promotion programme to bring on existing talent already inside the organisation
- Ensuring that its e-recruitment website is as far as possible accessible to all people
- Changing the imagery used in job adverts and corporate literature to ensure that it is more inclusive
- Extending domestic benefits to gay employees' partners rather than exclusively to partners in heterosexual relationships
- Revamping its benefits packages to reflect better the diverse lifestyles of its employees

Purchasing

The Exchange is:

- Analysing the existing supply chain
- Setting targets for the value of business placed with black and ethnic minority suppliers
- Working with trade associations and small business support organisations to help firms run by black and ethnic minorities to qualify for the tender lists of The Exchange

Community involvement

The Exchange is:

- Reviewing the community investment budgets, employee volunteering and the activities that The Exchange supports in the community with management time on school boards, etc. to ensure that it reflects the commitment to diversity (in comparison with its previous support for schools in predominantly white, middle-class communities)

Innovation

The Exchange is:

- Making changes to market research and R&D work to respond to more diverse markets

Strategy and operations

The Exchange is:

- Looking at all its professional advisers (i.e. facilitators) to ensure that they are attuned to and reinforcing the new diversity direction and are not undermining it (e.g. to ensure the external audit team is not exclusively white and male)
- Checking for inconsistencies (the 'reality check')

The 'reality check' has thrown up the information that one of the company's main suppliers is the subject of a boycott campaign from disgruntled ex-employees alleging racial and sexual harassment and that the company's main trade association in a key overseas market is rigorously lobbying against anti-discrimination employment legislation . . .

▶ Moving from Step 5 to Step 6

In this chapter we looked at integration and resource issues, both critical to achievement of individual CSOs and company-wide cultural shift to CSO. We suspect that the first businesses that truly break through to CSO will be small businesses, where change, integration, coherence and consistency may be easier to achieve than in multinational companies. However, regardless of the size of the company, if the full potential of CSO is to be realised it will be of critical importance to engage stakeholders, and it is to this that we turn in the next chapter, on Step 6.

Step 6
Engaging
stakeholders

Focus
In this chapter we look at how to engage stakeholders in the shaping and delivery of business strategies.

Output
In Part II — the worked example of the seven steps — the completed process forms show how, by applying appropriate tools and techniques selected from Step 6, the following outputs are produced (see pages 342ff.):

- An assessment of how proposed strategies impact stakeholders, and vice versa

- Identification of the roles required by stakeholders to enable implementation of the strategies

- Identification of the necessary actions needed to ensure the desired roles are undertaken

THAT STAKEHOLDERS CAN BE CRITICAL TO BUSINESS PERFORMANCE was established in Steps 1 and 2. That engagement with stakeholders is crucial for capitalising on specific business strategies designed to exploit possible corporate social opportunities (CSOs) was highlighted in Step 3. In this chapter, we go on to describe how stakeholder engagement can be managed, emphasising the types of engagement that will meet business strategy and operational needs.

We do not believe that it is sustainable in the long run to consider stakeholder engagement as a tactical process that should be used to respond to specific tactical requirements. Rather, it calls for an ongoing commitment made at the highest corporate level and a range of mechanisms to embed engagement throughout the company. For this reason, in this chapter we focus on how to introduce and maintain a company-wide engagement approach.

However, it is fair to say that few companies currently practise the level of systemic stakeholder engagement that we advocate. Many have ad hoc or piecemeal processes that are defence mechanisms activated in times of trouble (e.g. when a firm is under attack from a campaigning non-governmental organisation [NGO]). The majority of stakeholder engagement we witness is of the 'defensive' variety. It is designed to respond to corporate social responsibility (CSR) risks and problems. A defensive approach will not lead to the formation of long-term shared-destiny relationships with stakeholders based on mutual trust, made robust by open, honest and regular dialogue. This we believe should be the aim of such engagement.

We are wary, too, of companies that claim they are thorough yet principally engage with 'proxy' stakeholders — CSR experts, consultants and campaigners. Whereas the views of these people are relevant, this approach in itself will not lead to the benefits of direct engagement.

It is through a process of direct, managed stakeholder engagement that the cares, concerns, needs and motivations of stakeholders are revealed. This approach creates the conditions in which stakeholders move from being perceived primarily as potential obstacles to business progress to being a valued source of information and intelligence and, from time to time, as active partners with equity in the delivery of business strategies.

Having good stakeholder relations can help management to address unresolved social issues for the company. It can give a wider perspective of issues and reduce the risk of unexpected crises or problems. It can also help to build the 'license to operate' by building trust between different actors. Almost any course of action that a company is going to embark on will require co-operation from different stakeholders. Our argument is that this co-operation will be much more forthcoming and will be far more steadfast if stakeholders understand the context, feel they have had the opportunity of contributing to decisions and, therefore, feel a sense of ownership in those aspects of business operations that affect them.

There is growing evidence that proactive, non-defensive stakeholder engagement opens up possibilities for CSO. In a recent report from CSR Europe, the Ashridge

Centre for Business and Society and Enterprise and Personnel,[1] researchers looked at the practice of 12 companies and concluded that companies that have integrated stakeholder engagement into their business operations tend to be more able to identify future trends, exploit new market opportunities and gain competitive advantage.

For stakeholder engagement to go beyond a risk-minimisation CSR approach to a process that contributes to CSO, it is critical for the company to have an open attitude to considering different perspectives and opinions from its own. In Table 13 we compare risk-mitigation stakeholder engagement for CSR with stakeholder engagement for CSO.

▶ From confrontation to collaboration

We have seen in Step 5 the problems that can arise when a business does not achieve buy-in from internal stakeholders (such as employees) — a lack of an integrated approach within the company, or inconsistency between professed values and actual behaviour, can result in the CSR intentions of a company being thwarted or undermined (see page 191).

> The capacity of business to do things in the first decades of the 21st Century will have far less to do with technological constraints and more to do with how far business can win popular support for the use of new technologies — from both consumers and society in general.[2]

There are many ways in which companies can relate to stakeholders. Stakeholder dialogue occurs all the time, as managers communicate with staff, suppliers and consumers during the normal course of business. That dialogue continues in an organic fashion, after hours in the communities, clubs and families of company managers and employees. 'Stakeholder management' or 'stakeholder engagement' is the act of structuring that dialogue and its associated mechanisms into a formal process.

The nature of stakeholder relationships can range from the extreme of confrontation, such as physical attacks by some animal activists against staff and supplier staff at the research firm Huntingdon Life Sciences (see Step 1, pages 45f.) to collaboration and joint ventures, such as the public–private partnerships and alliances formed by US-based company Manpower, which provides workforce management services and solutions. Manpower offers staffing services through over

---

1   CSR Europe, Ashridge Centre for Business and Society and Enterprise and Personnel, 'Exploring Business Dynamics: Mainstreaming Corporate Social Responsibility in a Company's Strategy, Management and Systems' (2003).

2   D. Grayson and A. Hodges, *Everybody's Business* (London: Dorling Kindersley, 2001).

Stakeholder engagement for CSR and CSO

Benefit or focus	Stakeholder engagement	
	For CSR	For CSO
Information or knowledge?	Stakeholders provide information that helps the firm to deal with sensitive issues such as religion, ethnicity and disability	Stakeholders share with the firm knowledge about the needs of a particular community
Early warning or early mover?	Stakeholders represent an 'early warning' mechanism	Stakeholders introduce the firm to opportunities in new or under-served markets
Confrontation or collaboration?	Stakeholders act as 'honest brokers' to help introduce executives to hostile communities	Stakeholders readily enter into or seek partnerships with the company to develop commercial products or services to meet their needs
Defence or advocates	Stakeholders may be willing to speak up in defence of a company if it is criticised	Company reputation will be increased as stakeholders recognise it as a good and responsible partner
Capacity-building	Stakeholders have no direct input in capacity-building in the company	Stakeholders provide opportunities for corporate staff to develop interpersonal skills through volunteering and managed development assignments, transferring skills back to the company and increasing capacity

Table 13 **Stakeholder engagement for corporate social responsibility (CSR) and for corporate social opportunity (CSO)**

4,000 offices in nearly 67 countries. The company has a long track record of creating programmes to increase the skills of workers to meet business needs. It also has a long track record of philanthropic good works, engaging with local community groups. The combined knowledge and relationships gained from Manpower's commercial and non-commercial experiences provided the springboard for the launch of the 'TechReach' initiative. The company describes 'TechReach' as 'a strategic national workforce development programme to address long-term IT employment

Manpower

TechReach is an initiative designed to prepare economically disadvantaged individuals for, and provide them with opportunities to take up, well-paid careers. It brings together the expertise of a number of Manpower's stakeholders: employers, community-based organisations, educational institutions, government agencies and business associations.

The initiative developed from a philanthropic programme, growing out of relationships established as a result of that programme, and was a response to a call by the governor of Wisconsin to place welfare recipients in jobs. It has evolved into a primary domestic workforce initiative that focuses on increasing the technical and digital literacy in manufacturing jobs, call centres and office work. Since 1999, some 45 TechReach programmes have become operational across the USA, with development support from the Ford Foundation.

For example, in Chicago, Manpower has partnered with two community-based organisations — Instituto del Progresso Latino (serving the Latino community) and Shorebank Neighbourhood Institute (serving the African-American community) — that conduct outreach and the initial screening of programme candidates and provide ongoing social service support. Project management support is provided by a committee of the Commercial Club of Chicago. Funding comes from the Chicago Mayor's Office of Workforce Development. West Side Technical Institute provides training facilities and instructors for some of the training modules. The University of Chicago designed tracking systems to monitor results.

TechReach is an intensive, customised three-month programme. On completion, graduates are placed at employer sites. Manpower continues to be the legal employer and oversees a six-month mentoring programme, providing access to the company's extensive technical and business training resources. The mentoring programme helps overcome employers' concerns about the suitability of individuals for work. On completion, graduates either move into full-time employment or are placed at another employer site.

Director of Workforce Development for Manpower, Branka Minic, says she is clear that each stakeholder group brings specific sets of skills and experiences and is central to the success of the scheme. Branka and her team are working to replicate the model in other markets and to meet the needs of particular industrial sectors, with the goal of integrating the programme into the firm's field-office network as one of a menu of workforce solutions offered to clients and the public workforce system. Jeff Joerres, CEO of Manpower, believes that scale-up and replication will rely on the programme being a key element in Manpower's business strategy.

> When [an initiative] fits within the business strategy, it creates and gives you a higher probability of sustainability. If it doesn't fit the strategy, it has to be forced and it has to be pushed, always.

Sources: 'At the Speed of Work' (2002 Manpower Annual Report), and the company's *Employment and Training Reporter*, 14 July 2003; Center for Corporate Citizenship at Boston College, *In Practice: A Series About Integrating Business and Community Development*, Issue 3 (February 2003)

sector needs'. It uses a tri-sectorial — business, government, civil society — partnership model.

In a profile of the scheme published by The Centre for Corporate Citizenship at Boston College,[3] the authors said this was an example of how 'companies are

3   Center for Corporate Citizenship at Boston College, *In Practice: A Series about Integrating Business and Community Development*, Issue 3 (February 2003).

coming to find that developing the economic assets and social and human capital of low-income communities pays dividends to the bottom line. In the short and long term this kind of strategy develops untapped markets, new labour pools, effective suppliers and new operating sites.' We would say that Manpower had found corporate social opportunity.

▶ Types of stakeholder dialogue and engagement

The International Business Leaders Forum (IBLF) has identified four broad types of stakeholder dialogue and engagement:

- The avoidance of confrontation
- The sharing of information through communication
- The receipt of advice through consultation
- The creation of partnerships through collaboration

The avoidance of confrontation

When clashes occur between companies and a sub-group of stakeholders, companies can choose to take evasive action, as in the case of Sony in the 1990s.

Sony

In the late 1990s, electronics company Sony found itself under pressure regarding the alleged negative impact of the company's operations on the environment in the late 1990s. The company devised a strategy, revealed in a leaked memo, to respond to criticisms from Greenpeace, Friends of the Earth and others through 'detailed monitoring and network contact' as well as by 'pre-funding intervention' (e.g. by co-sponsoring research and thereby seeking to gain an influence on the conclusions of that research). (For details of the leaked memo, see Environmental Protection Agency, *Inside EPA*, 'Industry Goes on Global Offensive against Environmentalists', Weekly Report 21.37 [15 September 2000]); quoted by J. Bendell in 'Talking for Change: Reflections of Effective Stakeholder Dialogue', *New Academy of Business* [October 2000].)

The sharing of information through communication

Early social and environmental reports were typically about the information the company wanted to share with key stakeholders. This then evolved to include companies responding directly to information requests about CSR policies and practices received in the form of questionnaires and surveys. Both these examples are, however, rather static. The current move is towards a more dynamic two-way communications process which is more than simply an exercise in 'telling'.

Monsanto

Following resistance to Monsanto's efforts to persuade others as to the benefits of the development and use of GMOs (genetically modified organisms), CEO of Monsanto, Bob Shapiro, came to the realisation that one-way communication is insufficient:

> Too often we thought it was our job to persuade, too often we forgot to listen . . . We're now publicly committed to dialogue with people and groups who have a stake in the issue (quoted in J. Bendell, *Terms for Endearment: Business, NGOs and Sustainable Development* [Sheffield, UK: Greenleaf Publishing, 2000]).

Farmers in Canada and the US, and European consumers and public opinion have continued to be resistant to arguments for GMOs. In May 2004, Monsanto announced that it was abandoning its herbicide-resistant wheat (Roundup Ready spring wheat). This is part of a wider strategy shift by the new Monsanto CEO Hugh Grant, who has also admitted that the company needs to do more to live down its arrogant image. (see *Financial Times*, 'Modified stance will not dent Monsanto', 12 May 2004).

The receipt of advice through consultation

In this approach, in summary, a company accesses stakeholders' general opinions or specific views on a proposed course of action or dilemma before it makes a decision on how to proceed. If necessary, plans are amended to take the offered opinions and views into account. This approach is particularly relevant to companies in the extractive and utility industries, such as RWE Thames Water. Such an approach may also involve the creation of stakeholder advisory groups and committees.

RWE Thames Water

In its 2002 publication 'Water Partner to the World', Thames Water states that:

> We listen to the views of clients, customers, local communities, workers and neighbours. Before we make recommendations, we keep our eyes, ears — and minds — open.

The creation of partnerships through collaboration

Collaborative stakeholder engagement can drive innovation, mobilise additional skills and resources to address shared challenges and influence wider policy positions, such as in the Manpower TechReach programme described in the previous section ('From Confrontation to Collaboration'). Collaboration has also been key to the partnership between oil company ChevronTexaco, Citibank, the United Nations Development Programme and a local authority in Kazakhstan (see Step 3, page 109).

▶ Choosing the best method of engagement

A business has to decide on its overall approach to stakeholders and then make an assessment of the possibilities of engaging with each stakeholder group (perhaps even taking a different approach to different categories of stakeholders). Some NGOs, for example, will be interested in working with the business whereas others will on principle not talk to businesses.

To find the appropriate level of engagement with its stakeholders, a company may wish to map the potential threat or opportunity posed by particular groups of stakeholders against the potential for communication or consultation. The resulting position of the stakeholder on this map will suggest the nature of the appropriate level of engagement.

Nevertheless, even when a company has attempted to identify the most appropriate form of engagement it is not unusual for relations with stakeholders to fail or not to start up at all — and for any number of reasons. In Box 24 we list some of the main factors that may pose barriers to successful stakeholder engagement.

Barriers to stakeholder engagement

The following factors — singly or in combination — are commonly encountered barriers to constructive engagement with stakeholders:

1. There is a history of conflict among key interests.
2. One partner manipulates or dominates the others.
3. The engagement process lacks a clear purpose.
4. Participants have unrealistic goals and are inflexible and unwilling to compromise .
5. There are differences in philosophies and ways of working.
6. There is a lack of communication both between stakeholders engaged and about the stakeholder discussions to outsiders.
7. Discussion or consideration of key interests is missing from the dialogue or the partnership.
8. Participants have hidden agendas.
9. The financial costs and time commitments outweigh the potential benefits.
10. There is an overall lack of 'know-how' and 'know-who'.

Box 24 **Ten critical factors in the failure of stakeholder engagement**

However, there are some tips to keep in mind which, if followed, will make engagement more likely to succeed. In Box 25 we provide a synthesis of critical success factors identified by a number of experts on stakeholder engagement and dialogue as well as some questions to be asked and answered. According to a report from the IMD Business School of Lausanne and the World Wide Fund for Nature (WWF), titled 'The Business Case for Sustainability':

> If you cannot answer the questions confidently and meet the criteria — better abstain from stakeholder dialogue for the time being. Save yourself from the frustration and wasted time you are otherwise going to face. Rather, invest in getting ready and then move on — life is full of second opportunities. And never start with a dialogue when the battle is already in process.

An illustration of the dangers to be faced if the critical success factors are not observed is provided by the tobacco firm, BAT.

BAT

In 2001 tobacco firm BAT tried to engage a number of stakeholders — including NGOs critical of smoking — in a 'multi-stakeholder dialogue', brokered through a number of church leaders, including the former Bishop of Durham, David Jenkins. In September 2001, anti-smoking organisation ASH sent a letter to the former Bishop outlining its concerns with the process:

> The agenda was very vague; the participation from BAT was not specified; the objectives and expectations of the dialogue were not stated; the subjects to be addressed during the dialogue were not specified; the subsequent process was not articulated; the 'rules of engagement' (who would put forward what points and how they would be handled) were not established; the leaflet by Durham Ethics was shockingly simplistic about the conflict between health and tobacco; the independence and capacity of the review to publish analysis that is embarrassing to BAT is not clear; and the route by which views, facts and evidence presented by BAT's critics would be incorporated in an assessment of BAT's corporate social responsibility is opaque.

(The full response can be read at www.ash.org.uk/html/conduct/html/dialogueresponse.html.)

Ten critical success factors for stakeholder engagement

1. Engage the key stakeholders

Engage those with the most power, influence and interest in your business and its activities. Select the participants carefully but, suggests John Elkington of SustainAbility, don't be afraid to 'invite at least some difficult voices'. Be prepared to undertake periodic re-evaluations of who the key stakeholders are.

Questions to be asked and answered

- Does each participant bring a specific competence to the table?
- What is the reputation of each participant?
- Do external stakeholders have experience in dealing with companies?
- Can participants be trusted (e.g. to keep sensitive business information confidential)?

2. Build trust

Take the time to build up trust among the participating stakeholders — and be prepared for this to be a long time.

Questions to be asked and answered

- Do all participants understand and respect the perspectives of the other participants and why they are present, so that there is mutual understanding (if not agreement!)?
- Do we understand where different stakeholders are coming from — what is the legacy of past dealings with the company and/or the industry? Do we know if there has been a history of broken promises, and stop–go dialogue in the past which has to be overcome?

3. Be flexible

Be prepared to change the way in which stakeholder dialogue is conducted with different stakeholders. Not all stakeholders — even within the same category — will have the same attitudes or perceptions and they will not all desire the same intensity of dialogue.

Questions to be asked and answered

- Are different forms of engagement appropriate to different stakeholders?
- Is there a need to alter the form of engagement with any one stakeholder as time progresses and the relationship evolves?

Box 25 **Ten critical success factors for stakeholder engagement**
(continued opposite)

Sources: authors' distillation of lists from J. Elkington, of SustainAbility, *The Chrysalis Economy* (New York: John Wiley, 2001); IMD Business School of Lausanne, and WWF, 'The Business Case for Sustainability' (itself adapted and extended from H. Leitschuh-Fecht, *Societal Expectations for Corporate Stakeholder Dialogue* [2002]); J. Bendell, *Terms for Endearment: Business, NGOs and Sustainable Development* (Sheffield, UK: Greenleaf Publishing, 2000); Institute of Social and Ethical Accountability (ISEA)

4. Allow time

Devote adequate time to the process.

Questions to be asked and answered
As an ongoing assessment, ask:

- Are participants willing and able to learn how to communicate with people from different backgrounds and with different experiences of life?
- Will the participants show patience to others, including the patience to listen (often hard for business people more used to doing)?

5. Be open

Be open about information and be prepared to appreciate that stakeholders will tend to withdraw from the process if they perceive that dialogue is being misused for PR purposes.

Questions to be asked and answered

- Will external stakeholders be suspicious (rightly or wrongly) that the company wishes to use them as a 'green fig leaf'?

6. Be realistic

Have realistic expectations about what the process of engagement is to achieve.

Questions to be asked and answered

- Are all participants clear about their objectives and hopes for the dialogue? (e.g. if your purpose is to consult, make sure that the other stakeholders do not think they are co-decision-makers)

7. Share the agenda

Don't be afraid to ask stakeholders to play a role in co-evolving the agenda. But the company itself must have clarity about its own strategy and direction — otherwise the dialogue will be very ineffectual.

Questions to be asked and answered

- Is the atmosphere conducive to different stakeholders proactively raising issues for discussion?
- What techniques are we using to ensure different stakeholders feel 'ownership' of the issues?

8. Create a common understanding

Seek a common understanding of the purpose of and the process to be followed in the dialogue. Determine the 'rules of engagement' — perhaps through a process of co-creation with the other participants — and embrace the standards that are to govern the process.

Questions to be asked and answered
According to the IMD Business School of Lausanne, and the WWF: 'Negotiate the rules and document them transparently, because nothing is as obvious, self-evident or legally-framed as business-to-business relations'. Thus, they advise you ask:

Box 25 (from previous page; continued over)

- Are you ready to embark on new rules and act according to a different script from that with which you are familiar?
- If you engage a neutral, professional moderator to serve as an 'interpreter' and to 'calm the waters' if needed, are you ready to relinquish control of the meeting and obey the moderator in implementing the negotiated rules?

9. Field your very best people
Participants should be those best suited to the job rather than those you can best spare from other duties.

Questions to be asked and answered

- Do participants have the patience to listen very carefully?
- Will participants ask additional questions instead of simply responding to questions asked of them?
- Will participants be open to new perspectives rather than simply looking for confirmation of their own prejudices?
- Do participants truly appreciate diversity and different forms of logic as sources of learning?
- Are participants ready to put themselves, for the purposes of understanding, 'into the other person's shoes'?

10. Be prepared for change
Be prepared to make real changes to your project, company or business model as a result of stakeholder dialogue — if you are not prepared for that, then even dialogue established at the 'communication' or 'consultation' (as opposed to the collaboration) levels will be a sham and, from the business perspective, the business will not be alert and alive to possibilities for corporate social opportunity.

Questions to be asked and answered

- Have we set objectives for the number of CSOs being suggested by or developed with stakeholders?
- Do we have measurement and reporting systems permitting the company to track business changes attributable to stakeholder dialogue and to feed this back to stakeholders (see Step 7)?
- Does the company have a process to allocate rewards fairly to stakeholders who have contributed to CSOs (see Step 6, page 240)?

Box 25 (continued)

▶ Tools to aid stakeholder engagement

There are a number of initiatives available to a company to join or sign up to that provide frameworks for managing stakeholder engagement and access to expertise, including the AccountAbility 1000 (AA1000) Framework and Social Accountability

8000 standard (SA8000), described in Box 26. Many companies have their own stated principles or guidelines on how they relate to key stakeholder groups, such as the UK telecommunications firm BT and the brewer SAB Miller.

AccountAbility 1000 Framework

AA1000 requires that a management system should include documentation of ways in which stakeholders are identified and classified and their relationship to the company. The AA1000 Framework stresses the principle of inclusiveness, so that an organisation should seek to include as wide a collection of stakeholder groups as possible. For more details, visit www.AccountAbility.org.

Social Accountability 8000 standard

Social Accountability International (SAI) operates the labour practice auditing standard SA8000, which requires accredited auditors to conduct a stakeholder mapping exercise. This is a simple process, involving a pictorial representation of primary and secondary stakeholders, with relations drawn between them to depict which group influences or is influenced by the other, or which has an interest in the other. This map is intended to help in the identification of key stakeholders in order to speed the process of consultation undertaken during an audit. For more details, visit www.cepaa.org.

Box 26 **Standards for managing stakeholder engagement: the AccountAbility 1000 Framework and Social Accountability 8000 standard**

British Telecommunications

British Telecommunications (BT) has a statement of business practice — *The Way We Work* — that sets out the aspirations and commitments that apply in each of its stakeholder relationships. BT states:

> We believe that effective dialogue with each stakeholder group is essential to BT. Quite simply, the more positive and mutually beneficial these relationships are, the more successful our business will be.

BT seeks the input of specialists in social and environmental policy through a Stakeholder Advisory Panel and a Social and Environment Report Independent Advisory Panel.

The BT website is itself part of the company's dialogue process, where the company hosts a number of e-mail and live, online debates on issues of interest and concern to stakeholders. Readers can also provide feedback, directly by e-mail, on BT's social and environmental performance.

Engagement mechanisms, by stakeholder, are as follows (for more details visit www.bt.co.uk):

- Customers:
  - Consumer liaison panels
  - Surveys of customers on the quality of service and on future expectations
  - Telecommunications advisory committees

- Employees:
  - Annual employee survey
  - Relationships with trade unions
  - European Consultative Works Council

continued ➜

- Suppliers
  - Supplier relationship management programme
  - Ethical trading forums with key suppliers and industry colleagues
- Shareholders:
  - The Investors section of the Better World website (this was developed following close consultation with analysts specifically interested in the social and environmental performance of companies)
- Community
  - Surveys (recent surveys of stakeholders found that education should be a top priority for BT's social investment)

SAB Miller

International brewer and bottler SAB Miller has articulated a series of guiding principles for each of its key stakeholder groups to help steer its relationships and act as a basis for reporting. In its Corporate Accountability Report for 2003, it says that the majority of engagement is undertaken at the operating level. Examples of those principles, by stakeholder, include:

- Shareholders:
  - Shareholder value: SAB Miller is committed to increasing long-term shareholder value, exceeding that achieved on comparable investments.
  - Return on investment: SAB Miller seeks to maximise total shareholder return.
  - Communications with investors, lenders and analysts: SAB Miller values the support of all its providers of capital and seeks to communicate with them regularly and openly, providing reliable and timely information about the company.
- Partners:
  - Long-term relationships: guided by its values, SAB Miller seeks to build long-term relationships with its partners to achieve sustainable success.
  - Franchisers and partners: SAB Miller seeks to do business with those joint-venture partners and franchisers that share its values.
- Other providers of capital:
  - Meeting obligations: SAB Miller will meet its obligations towards other providers of capital.
- Customers and consumers:
  - Quality and value: SAB Miller provides brands and services of consistently high quality and value to meet the needs and standards of its consumers and industry customers worldwide.
  - Product safety: SAB Miller is committed to providing products that are safe for their intended use.
  - Advertising and promotions: SAB Miller seeks to advertise and promote its products in an honest and ethical manner, respecting the values of its consumers' societies.
  - Innovation: SAB Miller aims for continuous improvement at all levels in the group by encouraging employees to be creative, innovative and open to new ideas.

▶ Getting started: some difficulties

Making connections

For most companies, a significant issue is how to make the connection between individual aspects of formal and informal stakeholder engagement, such as between:

- Employee satisfaction surveys
- Customer complaints
- Reports from focus groups and other consumer research
- Feedback from suppliers' councils
- Rating within a corporate communications reputation index
- Information the CEO is picking up in conversations with peers at places such as the Davos World Economic Forum

Typically, today, all these insights are coming into different parts of the business but need to be looked at as part of a whole. Co-ordination of these sources of information and feedback can be set as a function for a specialist CSR team, described in Step 5 (see pages 178f.).

Making the right choice

In the section above on types of stakeholder engagement we highlighted four forms of engagement — avoidance of confrontation, information-sharing through communication, receipt of advice through consultation and partnering through collaboration. The last of these, collaboration, is intensive and time-consuming for all involved and this form of engagement will not be appropriate in all cases of stakeholder engagement. Even where it is appropriate, it is unlikely to be possible simply to move straight from having no contact or dialogue to collaboration. As noted in Box 29, it will take time and patience to build the necessary degree of mutual understanding and trust and to agree on a common agenda.

Handing over control?

Some critics allege that the adoption of responsible business practice means handing over the running of the business to an NGO. For example, the economist David Henderson has criticised CSR as damaging business and government, quoting the comments of one un-named CEO to another (paraphrased here): 'Greenpeace is running my business and my job is to make sure that tomorrow it is running yours'![4] CSR should not mean anything of the sort — but it does mean being prepared to have ongoing dialogue with internal and external stakeholders — and that may well include some critical NGOs.

4   Martin Wolf, 'Sleepwalking with the Enemy', *Financial Times*, 16 May 2001.

This realisation has grown out of the broadening view taken of the intellectual and other resources that a company must harness — reflecting that the boundaries within which a company operates are becoming much more fluid. We have already seen this with the growth in long-term attachments to consultancies, the greater use of temporary workers and greater interaction between company employees and the staff of key customers and suppliers.

In some cases it is possible to chart the progress and influence of stakeholder engagement. According to Gill Samuels, Executive Director for Science Policy and Scientific Affairs for Pfizer's European operations, stakeholder engagement played a part in shifting understanding of and attitudes towards the use of animals in the discovery and development of new medicines. Gill describes how the company was triggered into taking a more proactive approach to managing the issue in 1997 following a rise in aggressive anti-vivisection lobbying towards members of parliament in a newly elected UK government. Pfizer initiated a strategy of 'informing and influencing', both internally, to reassure staff and to keep managers up to date, and externally, based on a more thorough scoping of animal issues as they were developing. Five years later, Gill is able to point to a marked shift in how the issue is now perceived among key stakeholder groups (see Table 14).

Stakeholder	Year	
	1997	2002
Government	Government of the day is mistrustful and hostile to those putting the case for animal testing	Government of the day is supportive of arguments for why animal testing is necessary
Anti-vivisectionists	Anti-vivisectionists have high expectations that their demands will be met	Anti-vivisectionist organisations are relatively 'quiet'
Media	Media is cynical in its reporting of industry's case for animal testing	Media reporting of anti-vivisectionist views and activities is less adverse
Police	Police are having to deal with a continuing rise in extremist attacks by some groups of anti-vivisectionists	There is better control of extremism through the Criminal Justice and Police Act 2002 and through the creation of the National Crime Squad in 1998 and a high-level government committee to address the issue

Table 14 **An assessment of changes in stakeholders' attitudes towards the use of animals in the discovery and development of new medicines**

Source: Gill Samuels, Executive Director for Science Policy and Scientific Affairs for Pfizer's European operations

▶ Engaging different stakeholders

We predict that in the future successful companies will need more than grudging acquiescence from their stakeholders. They will need to work hard to be an employer of choice, supplier of choice, investment of choice, partner of choice and neighbour of choice. In today's connected, global information society few, if any, businesses will survive for long on the old paradigm of 'command and control'.

Attitudes are changing — in October 2003, in an interview in the *Financial Times* (6 October 2003), Jeff Schwartz, CEO of Timberland, spoke of employees as 'paid volunteers'. In addition, with the rise of mail-order and Internet shopping, companies no longer have a 'captive consumer base', as many people are no longer constrained to buy from local retailers. In July 2002, in a speech to the Inspired Leaders Network in London, management guru Kjell Nordstrom, co-author of the book *Funky Business*,[5] talked of the bewildering degree of choice now confronting consumers. Furthermore, with the deregulation of utility firms and the use of subcontractors in the public sector (e.g. for cleaning, catering, running prisons and schools and so on), companies are in competition for contracts from governments and regulators. Thus, to be successful in the future we predict that businesses will need enthusiastic commitment and engagement from employees, customers, suppliers, investors and wider society.

Engaging stakeholders is not something that can or should be left 'to happen' — it is a crucial process of management to be handled with thought and care. Indeed, we believe that training in stakeholder engagement will become a core management competence. Those involved in stakeholder engagement will need to be able to analyse the characteristics of effective — and not so effective — engagement (as highlighted in Boxes 25 and 26).

The foundation for stakeholder engagement within a CSR context for most firms will tend to be through relationships with employees (including with trade unions), owners (shareholders) and civil society (often in the form of relationships with NGOs). In the following sub-sections we explore some of the relevant issues for these three key groups, and in Box 27 we summarise some of the mechanisms that may be appropriate for engagement with other stakeholders — consumers; business partners and suppliers; government and regulators; and communities. Before we leave this section on individual stakeholders we also take a brief look at some of the difficulties that may be faced with regard to supplier engagement.

Employees

Changes in business practices and/or the adoption of new strategies will inevitably impact employees and, if those strategies are to succeed, they will require the support of the employees. They may require changes to the jobs performed, in working conditions, to the knowledge required and so on. These are classic opera-

5 Kjell Nordstram and Jonas Ridderstrale, *Funky Business: Talent Makes Capital Dance* (London: Financial Times Prentice Hall, 2000).

Mechanisms for stakeholder engagement

Consumers

- Establish consumer clubs
- Use interactive marketing (e.g. online)
- Set up help-lines
- Make customer charity appeals
- Possibly, in future, smart barcodes on product packaging will permit in-store communication of CSR information

Business partners and suppliers

- Inspect factories (to be undertaken by an in-house customer staff team, independent consultants or hired specialist NGOs)
- Start 'enterprise development' programmes that build the capacity of suppliers to fulfil customer requirements, including social and environmental standards
- Take a proactive due-diligence stance regarding potential suppliers, providing support if necessary to bring them up to the required standards

Government and regulators

- Participate in government task forces or working groups
- Second staff to government departments or projects
- Offer *pro bono* advice and support

Communities

- Form and invite community leaders onto community advisory panels
- Form employee community outreach groups

Box 27 **Mechanisms for stakeholder engagement**

tional needs that are more likely to succeed if there are good employee relations and a culture of employee engagement. In Step 5, we discussed some aspects of good practice in involving employees in difficult decisions, such as in responding to a bad economic situation (pages 191f.) or in handling plans for outsourcing (pages 193f.). When there is not such engagement, this leads to costs for the employer — a Gallup survey of 2002 found that 17% of the US workforce was 'actively disengaged' from their jobs, taking more sick leave and costing employers around $300 billion a year.[6]

A company that is aware of the growing importance of CSR issues to business activities and that is awake to the possibilities from CSO will be faced with some very specific issues. Not least of these issues will be the need for management to tap into the social and environmental concerns and interests of employees as a way to

6 *Gallup Management Journal*, 10 October 2002, http://gmj.gallup.com/content/default.asp?ci= 829.

motivate and energise them (on employee concerns as triggers, see Step 1, page 36; on scoping of employees by attitude and behaviour, see Step 2, pages 69f.).

For example, companies may wish to make it clear — in words and in deeds — that the people who will be successful, who will get on in the organisation, are those that understand how to combine commercial 'savvy' and effective commitment with responsible business practices. As discussed in Step 4, an increasing number of companies are recognising that by engaging employees with brands and their values they can gain potential value added for selling those brands to the public (e.g. see the section on 'values built to last', describing how employees should be involved in the co-creation of company values, pages 144f.). Firms such as cosmetics company The Body Shop International or clothing retailer Patagonia are well known for making a virtue of their social and environmental credentials as a way of motivating sales staff.

Encouragement of all employees to be passionate about improving the company's environmental and social performance is one way in which a company can motivate and inspire its employees generally. If employees feel their company has living values, and identifies with those values, then — as we saw in Step 3 (page 116) — employees are more likely to be energised 'to go the extra mile' for the business. Here, too, though, there are dangers with the appearance of any inconsistencies in corporate behaviour — in any hint of 'do as we say' not 'do as we do' (on the need for leaders to 'walk the talk' see the sections on CSR focus and leadership commitment in Step 4, pages 157ff.).

Employees, of course, are in pole position to see any 'values gaps' — any chasm between values espoused and values lived (on the values gap, see Step 4, page 148f.). This is particularly the case precisely because many of the core aspects of being a responsible business are about how a company treats its employees: pay, conditions, opportunities for continuous learning and to grow in the job, health and safety, provision of care for dependants, help in achieving a healthy work–life balance and encouragement of involvement in the community and in public life. It is therefore worth considering whether existing 'whistle-blowing' procedures in the company, if it has any, can be stretched to incorporate 'values gaps'.

There are a range of CSR-related employee engagement techniques used by companies to ensure open communication channels to encourage the sharing of ideas and insights. For example:

- Supporting employee volunteering (whether in company time or with matched giving schemes for employee fundraising efforts) or support for the mentoring of young people

- Setting up internal employee councils (e.g. Cisco has a number of voluntary 'civic councils') that determine the company's local social investment priorities and identify philanthropic beneficiaries

- Setting managed assignments in the community as part of structured employee or management development

- Nominating staff as champions of a social issue or cause in the workplace (such as diversity)

Few companies, however, have yet taken what we would call the CSO approach, which would entail:

- Encouraging employees to feed insights from their voluntary activities into the business

- Encouraging employees to share perspectives that have arisen from personal membership in a community of interest (such as citizens' groups concerned about, say, global warming or GMOs) or from a community of identity (e.g. as a single parent, as a gay person, as a disabled person or as a member of an ethnic minority)

Some first steps can be taken within the immediate confines of more traditional business processes. Managers should be aware about what a commitment to CSR practices means for an individual's job and how practically those individuals can contribute. Key issues can be regularly included in team briefings and other internal company communications; for example:

- Telecommunications firm mmO$_2$ launched an internal information campaign in July 2003 in conjunction with the launch of its first CSR report in order to 'raise awareness among employees throughout mmO$_2$, that corporate responsibility is fundamental to our success as a company'.[7]

- The Brazilian subsidiary of paper producer Meadwestvaco requires each salaried employee to review and sign up to adherence to a global code of conduct; and employees worldwide of the US-based company are invited to report violations of the code or company policies anonymously online.[8]

- Electronics giant Sony engages employees through a 'green management' programme

- In 2002 the drug firm AstraZeneca stretched its existing survey of employee attitudes to include questions and parallel focus groups on CSR issues; it then published the results on its public website as part of its communications with its stakeholders.[9]

In an interview with us in 2003, Sir Mark Moody-Stuart, former Chairman of Shell and current Chairman of Anglo American, noted:

> The trick is to put something into the corporate processes which forces employees to think about CSR in the normal course of their work — once it is in the back of people's minds, you get people thinking.

7   Author's interview with mmO$_2$ chairman, July 2003.
8   The Code of Conduct can be viewed at www.meadwestvaco.com.
9   www.astrazeneca.com

In Moody-Stuart's previous firm, Shell, this was the decision that all major investment decisions should include the shadow cost of carbon. Once engineers are routinely doing comparative calculations, many easy gains are identified. Sir Mark further explains:

> Then you need a mechanism for identifying good ideas and recognising them — get some competition going — for example, Shell's internal idea generation process has a rapid screening of bright ideas from employees and funds for checking them out further.[10]

There are a number of indicators to show whether a business is being successful in embedding thinking about social, ethical and environmental considerations through engagement with employees:

- Are there positive responses to questions in (regular) employee surveys and focus-group discussions about how the company is doing on its commitments to responsible business?

- Are employees coming forward with proposals to help the company improve its implementation of responsible business practice, and are those proposals being acted on?

- Are new recruits to the business quoting positively the company's reputation on CSR as a factor in their decision to work for the company?

- Are exit interviews throwing up any contrary data on a perceived 'values gap' between values espoused and values practised?

Trade unions

In some companies, sectors and national markets, organised labour will be an important channel for engaging with stakeholders. Is CSR a regular part of business–union dialogues? Such CSR dialogue will obviously be easier if the trade unions concerned have embraced the concept of responsible business and internalised it as part of their negotiating agenda. Unions may also have trained their representatives who serve as trustees of pensions funds to ask fund managers questions about their attitude to CSR and make it clear that they believe that CSR businesses offer better long-term investments for their members, all other issues being equal.

In an ideal world, trade unions will be proactively promoting good CSR practices across their negotiations with organisations where they have members. Although this seems to be an area where little good practice has been reported and evaluated, the following examples have been noted in the UK:

- The British Trades Union Congress (TUC) has established Union learning representatives to help small firms increase workforce skills and encourage staff to develop new competences that improve the business. There are currently 7,000 learning reps working across the UK.

10   Interview with authors.

- The British trade union Amicus/MSF (Manufacturing, Science, Finance Union) is partnering with the disability charity Scope to recruit 'diversity champions' from among union members who can be trained to promote diversity issues during the course of their work and regular trade union activity.

Investors

Another critical stakeholder group with which to engage are investors. This group ranges from family members in a small firm to pension fund managers for a large firm, and so investors cannot be treated as a monolithic grouping, all with the same world-view, objectives or attitudes. Currently, it is a minority, albeit a growing minority, that is proactively concerned with how a company handles its social and environmental impacts. In Step 2 (page 71) we mentioned how definitions of 'materiality' are expanding to embrace CSR risk and opportunities (see also the section on investor concerns in, Step 1, page 39).

In his interview with us, Sir Mark Moody-Stuart noted that companies should be taking the initiative and not waiting for investors to ask about these issues. Shell, where Sir Mark was chairman, started briefing investors on non-financial issues in 1997/98. Anglo American, which Sir Mark now chairs, commenced briefing of investors in 2002. Leading the briefing in 2003, he was struck by how much more sophisticated investors' attitudes to CSR had become in the interim.

In talking to friends in the world of finance, and from ideas discussed at a meeting, hosted by BITC, on engaging investors we identified a number of key stakeholder dialogue issues and noted related observations, as follows:

- The financial community will listen if information is presented specifically about risks and avoiding losses.

- Participation in voluntary indices, such as the BITC Corporate Responsibility Index,[11] is one way to communicate performance, as such indices are often used in investor analysis, correlating performance against a range of measures.

- The finance director should take the opportunity to talk about responsible business practice at his or her regular presentations of results.

- Tailor-made briefing sessions can be organised. For example:
  - Drinks firm Diageo hosted a meeting at banker HSBC to discuss its corporate citizenship work with a group of 35 investors from the mainstream and socially responsible investment (SRI) communities.

11 On the basis of the BITC Index, see Step 2, page 168.

- Swiss group Nestlé worked with JP Morgan and the IBLF to host an investor discussion on the topic of obesity and how this could influence the food industry.

● Relevant issues should be addressed in the annual report and included in related presentations:
  - David Varney, Chairman of mmO_2 and of BITC, led off the presentation of his company's 2003 results with details of the company's CSR strategy.
  - 95% of the companies surveyed in the 2003 report from the World Economic Forum (WEF) and the IBLF, titled 'Values and Value: Communicating the Strategic Importance of Corporate Citizenship to Investors', had some kind of mention of their corporate citizenship performance in their annual report, although the level and detail to which these issues were addressed varied greatly.

● CSR issues and values can be mentioned in speeches or presentations to investors. For example:
  - 83% of the companies surveyed in the report by the WEF and IBLF claimed to be speaking to a targeted group of investors about these issues, whether it through meetings or conference calls with SRI investors or at annual shareholder meetings.
  - Statoil includes corporate citizenship in its presentations on its 'Capital Markets Day' (an annual conference where company management present updates on corporate performance, targets and strategy to analysts, investors and the press).
  - The ING bank, in co-operation with Shell, organises 'investor days' on the issue of sustainability.

● CSR issues can be addressed on the investor section of the company website. For example:
  - 64% of the companies in the report by the WEF and IBLF address corporate citizenship issues on their investor relations web page and some, such as drugs company Abbott Laboratories and apparel firm Phillips Van Heusen, include links between relevant CSR web pages.

Nevertheless, we are also very mindful that several CSR-friendly chairmen and CEOs of FTSE 100 companies, whom we interviewed for this book, told us in the summer of 2003 that they are not interrogated about CSR issues when they meet institutional investors and analysts and that most of the very limited discussions they have had have been largely at their own instigation. This being the case, it is even more important that businesses trying to engage investors focus on how CSR impacts the bottom line — on the risks of inaction and the opportunities that are accruing from taking the issue seriously.

We believe that over the next few years there will be an increasing number of funds, including venture capital funds, where mainstream investors proactively seek investments based on CSO.

Non-governmental organisations

Some NGOs proactively solicit sponsorships and look for collaboration and partner-ship with companies; others choose to put forth demands through vocal criticism and/or media and boycott campaigns. In a report titled 'It Simply Works Better: Campaign Report on European CSR Excellence; Making Stakeholder Engagement Work' (December 2003), The Copenhagen Centre and CSR Europe noted that:

> In recent years . . . the global agenda has matured, creating a more coherent political framework, with increasing focus on the inter-relatedness of environmental, social and economic goals. As a result, a number of NGOs have now entered into active dialogue with com-panies in an effort to ensure that they can have their say in the further development of this agenda.

There are fears from some businesses, however, that proactive engagement with NGOs is somehow akin to handing over control of the business (see the comments of Henderson above, and quote from Martin Wolf, in the section on 'Handing over control?', page 219), that the NGO will keep on demanding more,[12] that NGOs cannot be trusted and that they may be in the pocket of commercial competitors. A further question that may be asked is: 'To whom are these NGOs accountable anyway?' Some companies, and their trade associations, are trying to undermine NGOs by accusing them of illegitimacy because of a lack of democratic account-ability. Larger NGOs are responding to these pressures, but the vast majority will not. NGOs thrive on freedom, flexibility and non-conformism. If you tie one (respon-sible) NGO down too much, the non-conformists will in all probability simply set up a splinter organisation.

Many educational, environmental, health or humanitarian needs might not be met if it were not for NGOs. These institutions can be crucial contributors to the stable and sustainable operating environment that many business leaders say they require if business is to prosper. Travis Engen, President and CEO of Canadian-based global aluminium and packaging firm Alcan Inc., puts it like this:

> We know that the profitable growth of our company depends on the economic, environmental, and social sustainability of our communi-ties across the world. And we know it is in our best interests to contribute to the sustainability of those communities.[13]

And Alcan believes that NGOs are critical players in achieving and promoting sus-tainable development. The company's whole corporate citizenship programme is geared towards supporting civil society and not-for-profits who advance the goals of sustainability. The programme includes a substantial annual US$1 million cash prize launched in 2003 and committed to run for nine years.[14]

12   See e.g. Don Tapscott and David Ticoll, *The Naked Corporation: How the Age of Transparency Will Revolutionize Business* (New York: The Free Press, 2003).
13   www.alcanprizeforsustainability.com
14   *Ibid.*

Engagement between business and NGOs can take many forms: meetings to debate contentious issues, alliances to bring different skills and resources to a project with shared goals, or the engagement of an NGO to undertake some research or to deliver a social investment activity.

Moving beyond dialogue to joint action through partnership is where some of the exciting possibilities lie for companies interested in pursuing CSOs. Many of the initiatives we described in Steps 2 and 3 as examples of innovation in products and services, identifying unserved markets and creating new business models (see pages 78-81, 130-35) involved partnerships between business and NGOs.

So, how does a business choose potential NGO partners with which to engage? The answer is: 'By asking the same questions the NGO might want to pose to the business'. Some common issues that are raised are given in Box 28.

Potential partner assessment

Does the prospective partner have:

- A good track record?
- Reasonable standing and respect from within its own sector?
- Reasonable standing and respect within other sectors and key players?
- Wide-ranging and useful contacts it is willing to share?
- Access to relevant information, resources and experience?
- Skills and competences that complement those of your own organisation and/or other parties?
- Sound management and governance structures?
- A record of financial stability and reliability?
- A stable group of staff (i.e. low turnover of staff)?
- Sticking power when things get tough?

Box 28 **Potential partner assessment: questions to consider**

Source: International Business Leaders Forum, and the Global Alliance for Improved Nutrition, *The Partnering Toolbook*, 2003

US business group the Global Environmental Management Initiative (GEMI, www.gemi.org) surveyed its 40 blue-chip corporate members about partnerships with NGOs focused on CSR and sustainability issues. In answer to the question 'What are the most important considerations in determining which organisations you belong to or partner with?', the response was as follows:

- 50% stated that value for resources is an important consideration, including:
  - Networking
  - Best practices
  - Knowledge
  - Public policy development

- Regulatory impact
- Marque value

- 19% mentioned the need for a balanced viewpoint

- 17% valued personal experience with the partner

- 14% saw credibility as being a major criteria

We spoke with Chris Marsden, who has been on both sides of the stakeholder dialogue fence, now as Chairman of Amnesty UK's Business Group and previously as CSR specialist at BP. He offered the following advice to businesses, drawing on his own experience:

> Most NGOs, even the reasonable ones, will be staffed (paid and volunteered) by idealists who often need help in learning about the art of the possible; the real added value of second best solutions. Business people tend to be good at finding doable solutions but sometimes are weak on social ideals. Companies entering dialogue with NGOs would do well to allow time for exploring these differences in order to reach common understanding . . . [and] companies would do well to remember they need (reasonable and responsible) NGOs as a sort of countervailing power in order to police bad practice and promote development of good practice. NGOs should not be seen as 'the enemy' but as necessary voices of civil society on specific issues.

Chris further counselled that, even assuming that a particular NGO is prepared to engage in dialogue, a business has to understand whether the NGO is essentially geared to whistle-blowing and campaigning or whether it is open to solution-seeking and partnering:

> If it is mainly a campaigner then this needs to be respected. It is very unhelpful challenging such an NGO with 'OK, we, *XYZ*, company accept that we are part of the problem, now help us to be part of the solution', because such NGOs are simply not set up nor resourced to be solution partners.

He further cautions that:

> Membership NGOs like Amnesty can be very useful round the table as commentators on policy and practice and may be persuaded from time to time to give advice on policy statements, reports, etc., but they cannot become active consultants and most certainly can never be used publicly to endorse a particular company action.

We asked Henk Campher, Policy Adviser, from international development NGO Oxfam, what tips he would give companies who were considering stakeholder engagement with NGOs. In Box 29 we display a summary of his response, which provides some illumination on NGO sensitivities and frustrations.

Tips for engagement with NGOs

- Do your homework and find out about the mandate of the NGO and what it regards as its 'bottom line' — it is unlikely to be financial!

- Respect differences between NGOs by not lumping them all together in the same room for a consultation exercise — NGOs are proud and competitive too.

- International NGOs may have shared common goals between their national counterparts, but national chapters are not necessarily clones of one another, unlike national offices of some multinational companies, so be prepared for different approaches and attitudes.

- Don't make the mistake of thinking that you are the only company that is the target of the NGO's campaigning efforts, or that the NGO hasn't other programmes and projects that may have nothing to do with business.

- Respect the NGO's ways of working and its cultural norms (e.g. some may take decisions through consensus) — but don't stereotype those norms.

- Appreciate that NGOs have severe financial constraints compared with business, and so don't judge NGOs by the same standards (e.g. in terms of presentation) as you do other businesses.

- Start by talking, learning about each other and building trust rather than starting by expecting ground-breaking strategic partnerships.

- Remember that cash does not necessarily have the same currency as it does when buying products or services from other companies.

Box 29 Tips for companies wishing to enter stakeholder engagement with non-governmental organisations (NGOs)

Source: interview with Henk Campher, Policy Adviser, Private Sector, Oxfam UK, March 2003

Some companies with well-developed CSR programmes tell us privately of their frustration that they always seem to be picked on by NGOs and not given the credit they deserve for the progress they have made, while other companies, less advanced in CSR practices, get away with far worse. This is a problem that some NGOs are aware of and will privately give companies credit, but even the fairest NGOs will be cautious about publicly praising a particular company, because even the best company is vulnerable to a bad CSR failure in some part of its operation, which could damage the NGO's reputation with its constituents should it be seen apparently to endorse the company. High-profile companies will just have to put up with this 'unfairness' — even make a virtue out of necessity and view the criticisms as a useful part of their reputation risk management. One sophisticated example of this is in the RMC–Birdlife memorandum of understanding described in Step 3 (page 124). This includes an explicit right of either party to criticise the other.

Suppliers

Big business can help to introduce social and environmental issues to their small-business customers, but this needs to be handled sensitively if it is not to be seen by small suppliers as more bureaucracy. Good practice suggests that if big businesses are going to introduce CSR issues through their supply chains they need to explain carefully to their small and medium-sized suppliers why they are doing so and to offer training and advice on how to comply to the new standards and in ways that will benefit the small firm as well.

In an interview with us in 2003, Edward Bickham, Executive Vice President, External Affairs at mining company Anglo American, and responsible for CSR, highlighted the dilemma that, although the company is actively trying to develop its own purchasing requirements and supply-chain expertise through the small and medium-sized enterprise (SME) sector, in countries such as South Africa the rigorous enforcement of some CSR requirements needs to be managed flexibly to ensure it does not slow down implementation of the Black Economic Empowerment Programme.

▶ Smart government

The nature and the quality of engagement need to change for all stakeholders if a business is to achieve CSO. This includes engagement with government (local, regional and national) and with international agencies. In Step 5 we stated that, in our view, CSR will increasingly require companies to consider the transparency, accountability and appropriateness of their various lobbying efforts with governments (see page 197). This extends both to the subject of the lobbying as well as to how it is undertaken. It is also about ensuring coherence and consistency between stated CSR commitments and what is done in the company's name by trade associations and other groups of which the company is a member.

Many of the tough issues facing business, governments and society — such as obesity and healthy living — cannot be tackled by any one sector in isolation. They require an understanding of the respective roles, responsibilities and potential contributions of different players — and the platforms for dialogue — where these kinds of understandings can be thrashed out. Furthermore, for CSOs to be achieved we think there is more to be done. Many CSOs, by their very nature, will involve government. The Tesco regeneration partnership described in Step 2 (see page 98) or the Manpower partnership described earlier in this chapter (page 209) are commercially viable only because of the involvement of public agencies and funds on the training side. It may, therefore, be appropriate for the business community to work with governments to ensure that governments appreciate the potential of partnering with business — for government and society. There may also be scope to help equip governments with the capacity to participate creatively in these deals in ways that are simultaneously entrepreneurial and respect the norms of transparency, public accountability and value for money for taxpayers.[15]

15   See BLU, 'Redesigning Public Service: Towards a More Entrepreneurial Public Service Culture (July 2004).

We recognise that it would be easy to caricature this as a back-door way of reversing the privatisation process or of reintroducing failed state industrial policies by trying to 'pick winners'. What we are suggesting is more sophisticated and nuanced. It is about governments giving 'smart specifications' as to what they want the private or voluntary sector to deliver. It is about governments being willing to think creatively about how public resources might support those CSOs that fulfil government needs. And it is about looking at regulations to see if they are enabling or hindering social opportunity. For instance, consider the case of Procter & Gamble and its failed introduction to the Philippines of its micro-nutrient drink Nutridelight® (see Step 2, page 91). This product launch failed partly because local regulation on 'fair and true' advertising was lax, allowing competitors to make comparable assertions for their products to those made for Nutridelight® (that the products would make the consumer 'taller, stronger, smarter'), without being held to account to provide proof. Similarly, in relation to the enabling environment for bottom-of-the-pyramid commercial activities, Philips's Jan Oosterveld (quoted in Step 3, page 134) makes the point that in India, there are currently at least 100 different business-led health projects and that there is a need for some government role to standardise and if necessary, legislate, so that confusion is avoided.[16]

▶ Alignment of goals

It could be argued that the act of serving societal need is the essence of all business. Of course, the argument over how to define societal need is a fraught one, but, as our examples of CSO have shown, there is a case to be made for all businesses to look for the potential 'win–win' situation where alignment of business purpose and public interest can be achieved. For instance, Pfizer's response to changes in the operating environment is to recognise that, if it is to continue to help to shape the future healthcare environment, it will need to 'partner differently, operate differently and communicate differently' (see Figure 11).

Pfizer recognises that in order to achieve alignment between business and societal interests it needs to shift its approach to stakeholder engagement away from one that too often has been reactive to one based on an appreciation of developing agendas and issues. The aim, the company believes, is to be recognised as a 'partner' in society (see Figure 12).

In our view, Pfizer has recognised that a continued 'licence to operate' for the pharmaceutical sector — which has been the subject of considerable demonisation in recent years — will be influenced by the ability of the industry to partner for what it calls 'a healthy future' (see Figure 13).

16   Speech to IESE Responsible Business Conference, Barcelona, 27 March 2004.

Alignment of business and societal interests

- Align with society's health needs and a desire for healthy ageing
- Converge public and industry interests towards improved health
- Engage in dialogue with stakeholders
- Align actions and business practices to support objectives

Figure 11 **Alignment of business and societal interests at Pfizer**
Source: Pfizer

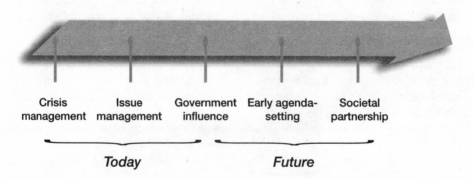

| Crisis management | Issue management | Government influence | Early agenda-setting | Societal partnership |

Today   *Future*

Figure 12 **Pfizer's path to societal partnership**
Source: Pfizer

Operating differently; thinking differently

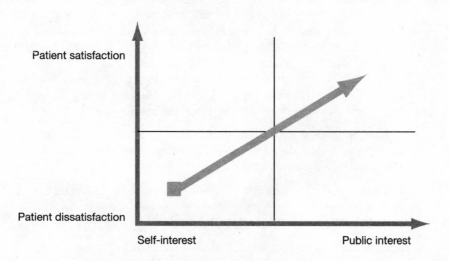

Figure 13 **Acting differently and thinking differently at Pfizer: acting differently requires a different way of thinking about industry's role in society**

Source: Pfizer

▶ Partnership-building

Partnerships between institutions from other sectors (e.g. NGO sector, public sector and so on) and business are important means by which firms engage with stakeholders — and they are particularly important for companies that want to progress from CSR to CSO, as they can provide the intensity of relationships that can lead to the sharing of problems and of the generation of ideas for solutions to those problems.

We are not fans of businesses creating or joining partnerships — even for worthwhile social causes — when there is no connection between the subject of the partnership to the purpose or the competence of the business. This is because such company commitments:

- Are hard for staff to understand

- Create suspicions in the minds of consumers and the public because no clear motive can be seen (and the assumption in a cynical world that if it can't be seen it must be bad . . .)

- The company's contribution is unlikely to be cost-effective

- It will be very hard to sustain in difficult trading times

By contrast, where there is some obvious fit with the company's interests and competence, community partnerships are much more sustainable — because it is easier for staff to feel proud about what is being done, and it is more likely to produce spin-off benefits to the company in terms of insights and extra expertise — even though that genuinely may not be the company's motivation.

Partnerships can be a means for addressing a range of challenges and tasks. Companies in many sectors have public policy issues that they are helping to address through partnerships and alliances with NGOs and the public sector; for example:

- In the information and communication technology (ICT) sector, initiatives are being started to address the 'digital divide', specifically addressing the lack of access to the Internet for the poor.

- In the pharmaceutical industry, initiatives are starting up to address the issue of HIV and AIDS, specifically addressing the availability to and price of drugs for the poor.

- In the alcoholic beverages sector, initiatives are being set up to promote responsible drinking, focusing specifically on addressing the problem of binge drinking and underage drinking.

Other initiatives address specific operational or strategic needs, such as:

- To safeguard the supply of products, as in the case of the Marine Stewardship Council

- To fulfil and surpass regulatory requirements, as in the 'Here to Help' initiative

- To secure a committed and skilled workforce for the future, as at Grupo Vips, Spain

- To strengthen the financial security of key customers, as at Grupo Bimbo and FinComún, Mexico

- To give back to the community and to promote organisational cohesion, as in the case of Cirque du Monde

Each of these partnerships is described below.

The Marine Stewardship Council

The Marine Stewardship Council (MSC, www.msc.org) was initiated by Unilever and the international conservation NGO, the WWF, to, first, develop good practice in sustainable fishing practices and, subsequently, to provide an external certification scheme for fish caught in a sustainable way. The MSC aims to help Unilever and other participating companies to address potential challenges in sourcing fish in the future and has had wider sustainable development benefits. Unilever has been frank about its continuing challenges — notwithstanding the efforts of the MSC and other initiatives — to change consumers' preferences for the type of fish they want to buy. Consumer recognition and buy-in to sustainable fishing certification does not yet appear as widespread as that carried out by, for example, the Forest Stewardship Council (FSC, www.fscoax.org) and the consumer-driven demand for the use of renewable wood in the furniture and construction industries.

Here to Help

Centrica, the British energy utility firm, was created following the demerger of British Gas in 1997. It participates in a partnership aimed at achieving energy savings in low-income households and giving people access to a range of charitable services. Some 5.5 million households in Britain live in poverty and face a daily struggle to survive on low incomes and in poor-quality homes. British Gas's Here to Help initiative is making a real difference in combating household poverty. Some 329 communities across the United Kingdom are signed up to the initiative, potentially impacting 168,000 households.

Launched in November 2002, the £150 million scheme brings together the private, public and voluntary sector to provide aid and advice in deprived communities. The target is to improve the quality of life for half a million households within three years and, to date, £1.5 million in unclaimed benefit has been identified. British Gas has teamed up with seven major charities — Help the Aged, the Royal National Institute for the Blind (RNIB), Scope/Capability Scotland, the Family Welfare Association, Save the Children, the National Debtline, and Gingerbread (for single parents) and is working with local authorities and housing associations to offer residents a package of free measures. The initiative is an attempt to turn regulatory requirements for British Gas to address fuel poverty into something much more creative.

▶ Creating sustainable partnerships

The word 'partnership' is used by different people to mean different things. We define it as an undertaking in which responsibilities, risks and resources are shared to achieve outcomes that are best secured by working together rather than alone. Of course, the number of variables involved — which organisations, addressing what issues, in which places and at what times — are rarely the same; nor should they be. What works for an education–business partnership helping to raise school standards may not work for getting local companies to take charge of the revitalisation of their industrial estate. The details of each partnership will need to

Grupo Vips

In Madrid, restaurant and retail company Grupo Vips has, since 1999, worked to offer employment opportunities to members of minority and/or marginalised communities, including migrants, the disabled and criminal offenders. Rather than taking on this task alone, Grupo Vips decided to work together with public authorities and NGOs. Its programme now offers jobs to 2,440 immigrants, representing some 40% of its entire staff. Miguel Angel Garcia, Human Resources Manager at Grupo Vips, recognises the importance of the input of other stakeholders:

> The public authorities have helped us with administrative procedures and ensured that our objectives were in line with societal objectives. And the NGOs have helped us understand the distinctiveness of each one of the marginalised groups that we have worked with; they have helped us with identifying potential beneficiaries and also with vocational training for them. This kind of training is often crucial for later integration into the labour market (quoted by The Copenhagen Centre and CSR Europe, in 'It Simply Works Better: Campaign Report on European CSR Excellence; Making Stakeholder Engagement Work', December 2003).

Grupo Vips recommends other companies and partners to follow its example. Garcia goes on to note that:

> Once objectives have been defined, it is much easier to achieve them with the help of different social actors . . . Moreover, it opens up companies to new ways of thinking and acting, bringing us closer to the realities of society.

Grupo Bimbo and FinComún

Grupo Bimbo is Mexico's largest baking company and the third largest baking company in the world, with sales of US$3 billion and profits of US$210.5 million. It has succeeded by paying great attention to the smallest retailers in nearly every part of Mexico for the past 55 years. In Mexico City, with a population of more than 18 million people, there are twice as many Bimbo delivery trucks as city police cars. It now controls nearly 95% of Mexico's market for packaged bread.

In a entrepreneurial move, Bimbo has formed a partnership with community bank FinComún. On the one hand, Grupo Bimbo is taking advantage of FinComún's expertise in providing micro-loans; on the other hand, FinComún is tapping into Bimbo's distribution network and product delivery systems. Under this partnership, FinComún loan advisors accompany Bimbo delivery drivers on their daily rounds. At each stop, the driver briefly introduces the loan officer to the retailer; the loan officer will then have approximately four minutes to make a presentation to the retailer while the driver unloads the products. Follow-up visits are then made if requested.

Bimbo derives 80% of its income from small 'mom and pop' stores; 20% of these clients regularly ask for credit.

Previously, Bimbo had an informal programme to provide credit services to these stores. As a result of the partnership with FinComún, Bimbo expects to reduce bad debt, reduce the amount of time in which loans are repaid and achieve its goal of providing credit to 22–30% of its clients.

Cirque du Monde

In an interview with one of the authors in July 2003 the performance company Cirque du Soleil told us how the group has created Cirque du Monde, a partnership to teach circus skills to young people in deprived communities. We are both great fans of the professionalism, artistry, stylishness and boldness of Cirque du Soleil and of its philosophy that 'if you can imagine it, you can try it!' It provides a fascinating story of artistic and commercial success in its own right — from its origins as a small group of Montreal street performers to a global brand. As we explained in Step 4 (page 144), strong articulation of its core values has been an important element holding the organisation together. This was especially pertinent after the substantial restructuring provoked by the departure of one of its two co-founders.

One important value within the company is to give back to the community from which it has grown — in a practical and added-value way. Hence it began a partnership, with several international aid agencies, under the social brand of Cirque du Monde, through which 'disaffected' young people are trained in circus skills, giving them something positive to do and increasing the sense of self-worth of the participants.

Cirque du Monde is now operating in disadvantaged areas in 18 countries on five continents in cities such as Rio de Janeiro, Amsterdam, Kabul and Ulan Bator. The main partner in Brazil now has 16 sites, and the Chilean partner is creating a Circus School with a social mission. The aim is to empower local partners to grow in ways that meet opportunities and local circumstances — a good example of a flexible 'social franchise'.

be tailored to individual circumstances. Nevertheless, there are some generic guiding principles for creating and sustaining sustainable partnerships. Observation suggests that winning partnerships are like winning companies:

- They have a shared **clear vision** of what they are there for and **strong leadership** to make the vision a reality, with bold audacious **goals** and the ability to **communicate** the vision to all stakeholders.

- They have a stated and agreed **strategy**.

- There is genuine engagement and clear **accountability** between the partners and each partner knows where its own activities and work programme fit into the broader strategy.

- There is a vehicle for **action**.

- Partners have spent the **time** to develop **mutual trust** so that they feel able to articulate what they are bringing to the party — and what they need to take away — and, importantly, what they can't do or conceive of. There is also enough **trust** so that non-performers or underachievers can be taken to task by their peers.

- Successful partnerships are **entrepreneurial**: together, participants know how to mobilise resources from many different places and take a holistic approach rather than tackling problems in isolation.

- They have a **passion for excellence** and **continuous improvement**. They are built around people: **social entrepreneurs** with the enthusiasm and commitment to make things happen.

- Particularly for partnerships either specifically established for corporate social opportunity or that migrate to this purpose, they have a system and process to agree the **sharing of benefits** of any intellectual property or physical assets earned, created or otherwise generated.

In August 2003 we interviewed Harry Fitzgibbons, a successful technology venture capitalist of more than 20 years' standing (www.toptechnology.co.uk). He has been a good friend both to us and to our organisations and has been involved in a number of initiatives to help 'spin-out technology businesses from universities. On the final point listed above, he offered the following advice:

> Agree up front what percentages the different people will get. It is infinitely easier, the further away you are from commercial value, and from the crystallisation of cash value, to divide up the spoils. This is a fundamental premise of the investment business. If I were an NGO, I would want it to be part of any agreement with a company upfront — 'What is the royalty on any revenues that might come to the company as a result of our collaboration?' The problem is likely to be if there is some rip-roaring success and, in retrospect, it looks as if the NGO's share is too big and out of all proportion to their contribution. It happens all the time when royalties are seen to get out of whack. The problem might be that if the NGO 'plays hardball' that the company would decide to replicate the original product and promote that instead. That would be the threat for the NGO if it was being unreasonable about renegotiating — and the corresponding threat for the company would be media exposure if it was being greedy. But the important thing is to get an agreement up front.

▶ Stakeholder communications matters

The OECD Principles of Corporate Governance encourage active co-operation between corporations and stakeholders and, importantly, require companies to provide access to relevant information to stakeholders. There is an important statement in the commentary to the Principles (see www.oecd.org), noting that 'concern over corporate reputation and corporate performance often [requires] the recognition of broader interests'.

In an interview with us in December 2003, John Drummond, Chief Executive of Corporate Culture at consultancy Corporate Culture, pointed out that 'even the best don't invest in communications, and when they do, they make key mistakes'. He noted that:

- They sometimes forget that people are interested in people.

- They sometimes forget that good communications are about a dialogue not about an annual report.

- They sometimes forget that people are as interested in future plans as past performance.

- One of the main audiences for CSR reporting is employees and yet the majority of current CSR communications are not aimed at those groups at all.

- Communications implies a dialogue and the majority of current CSR reporting is just about telling.

- People frequently forget that a balanced case makes their communications more credible: i.e. acknowledge the issues still to be tackled.

- The heart of communications should be around the purpose of the business and its core products and services.

John suggests a number of options for communicating CSR. He suggests companies report:

- On their CSR activities

- On their impacts on society

- On social issues most pressing on the company

- To key audiences

- On social, environmental and economic performance

- On their principles and values

A survey of company websites of FTSE 100 and FTSE 250 companies by communications agency CTN and corporate responsibility consultancy Futerra reveals that most companies do not offer opportunities for online stakeholder dialogue. According to the research, which ranked sites according to criteria from the Association of Chartered Certified Accountants (ACCA):

- Only 36 sites among the FTSE 100 and a further 17 in the FTSE 250 offer a platform for interaction.

- Only 14 FTSE 100 websites use Flash animation.

- Only Shell, BP and British Telecommunications (BT) have a forum or bulletin board.

- Only Royal Bank of Scotland and BAT use stakeholder-focused webcasts, whereas nearly 90% use webcasts for their financial reporting.

- Effective CSR requires stakeholder engagement, yet 28 of the FTSE 100 sites offer no CSR contact details.

In an article in the online *Financial Times*, on 23 May 2003, Solitaire Townsend, director of Futerra, said that, for some companies, CSR remains a peripheral activity, adding that 'if they are not giving it public profile you have to question how far it's part of the fabric of the company'.[17]

▶ Synthesis of Step 6

In the view of the authors, the themes and issues described in Step 6 reflect how product development was organised in this example from IBM.

IBM: a case of CSO through stakeholder engagement

The US-based IT corporation IBM provides products and services in over 140 markets. The company has a business strategy to move from being a hardware producer to become a services and solutions based company. As part of this strategy, the company identified that the relationships formed through its community relations activities contained the potential for informing product innovation.

IBM encourages internal partnerships between its Research Laboratories and the Corporate Community Relations Unit (CRU), and then externally between these operations and stakeholders such as community groups and public agencies. For example, the Research Laboratories were looking at ways to tackle accessibility issues on the Internet for elderly users and users with disabilities. Managers in the Research Laboratories approached colleagues in the CRU and explained their needs. The CRU already had strong links with SeniorNet — a not-for-profit organisation bringing technology to senior citizens — and felt that the organisation would be open to developing this relationship further, and so helped broker engagement with the Research Laboratories.

After initial discussions a partnership arrangement was created and, through high levels of responsiveness displayed by each stakeholder, particular skills and know-how were shared that enabled IBM to create new technology for transforming web pages to make them easier to read, understand and interact with. The technology can also be incorporated into other IBM products and services, such as web-based services and support for Internet service providers (ISPs). It has also had the benefit of strengthening the firm's position before US regulatory changes regarding media accessibility. (For more details, see AccountAbility, 'Community-enabled Innovation: Companies, Communities and Innovation', 2003.)

---

17   At http://search.ft.com/search/article.html?id=030523000897.

▶ Moving from Step 6 to Step 7

Stakeholder engagement that informs the development of business strategy and supports strategy implementation relies on relevant and timely information. This — like other elements and processes in Steps 1–5 — requires companies to effectively track, monitor and analyse appropriate data, and to effectively measure and report on environmental and social impacts. This is the theme of Step 7. Intelligence and learning gleaned from undertaking Step 7 can then be fed back into the whole seven-step process afresh as 'trigger' information for Step 1.

Step 7
Measuring and reporting

Focus

In this chapter we look at how to measure and report on issues identified in the previous steps. We also examine the implications of measuring and reporting for corporate social opportunity. Finally, we show how to track the progress of actions identified and agreed to be necessary during progression through the seven steps.

Applying Step 7

In the worked example of the seven steps in Part II, the completed process forms illustrate how, by applying appropriate tools and techniques selected from Step 7, these specific outputs are produced (see pages 353ff.):

- Identification of what data to measure and report

- A summary of actions agreed

- A framework for tracking progress on agreed actions

STEP 7 SERVES A NUMBER OF PURPOSES. FIRST, IT IS THE PLACE where a number of issues identified in Steps 1–6, such as regulatory pressures for social, ethical and environmental risk assessment, growing requirements to demonstrate transparency and accountability and the need to track stakeholder relationships, can be addressed through a common response of data collection, measurement and reporting. Second, it is where the differences between measuring for corporate social opportunity (CSO) rather than just for corporate social responsibility (CSR) can be considered. Last, it is where actions identified in Steps 1–6, and now Step 7, can be assigned, where targets and deadlines can be agreed and where methods to assess and report on progress can be determined.

There is no doubt that more companies today are reporting on social, ethical and environmental issues. According to the Global Reporting Initiative (GRI)[1] there are now over 2,000 businesses globally that voluntarily report on their environmental and social impacts, and in 2002, nearly half the global FTSE 250 companies published a report, up from 35% in 1999.[2] In addition, as would be expected, sophistication is also growing. In 2002, nearly 80% of those reporting on their sustainability performance mentioned the use of international reporting guidelines, such as the Global Reporting Initiative, 40% mentioned the inclusion of stakeholder statements and 30% were independently verified.

However, KPMG, in its survey on sustainability reporting,[3] found that companies in some sectors are more likely to report than those in others. For instance, extractive industries and utilities scored highly in terms of measuring and reporting, which, we suspect, is because of the high level of scrutiny they receive from non-governmental organisations (NGOs) and the intrinsic impact they have on the communities in which they operate.

Despite this trend, there is much contention about the value of the data included and the reports themselves — either to the companies or to their stakeholders. We encounter considerable angst from managers within companies regarding the amount of resources used on putting reports together compared with the use they are put to. What and how a company measures and reports should flow from *why* it is measuring and reporting those items. On the face of it, this seems a straightforward principle.

Our view is that too many firms are trying to please too many audiences rather than focusing on what should be the most important purpose of all: the measurement of data and reporting of information that can be used to help improve the performance of the business. In the context of the seven steps, that means focusing on those things for which measurement and reporting will influence the firm's ability to achieve proposed business strategies and continuously improve its business practices.

---

1   Global Reporting Initiative, 2001 (www.globalreporting.org).
2   KPMG, 'International Survey of Corporate Sustainability Reporting', 2002.
3   *Ibid.*

▶ Why measure and report?

The reasons why measuring and reporting have taken off in recent years are many and varied, including:

- Compulsory ('have to do') reporting. For example:
  - Public legislation in some countries makes CSR reporting mandatory again, e.g. the 2002 Financial Services Reform Act of Australia and, potentially in practice, in part at least, the OFR for publicly quoted companies in the UK for their future performance.
  - Some stock exchanges will not list a company unless it has met CSR reporting requirements (e.g. the Johannesburg Stock Exchange requires firms to publish their policies on AIDS and HIV).
  - There may be specific legal requirements, relating to, for example, the composition of the workforce (e.g. in terms of number of disabled employees, women, people from ethnic minorities and so on) or levels of emissions to air, water and soil and so on (e.g. as in the US Toxics Release Inventory).
  - In some countries larger companies are required to report on the materiality of social and environmental issues (e.g. as stipulated under the UK operating and financial review).

- Increasingly expected ('need to do') reporting. For example:
  - Fund managers, analysts and rating agencies may request CSR data (such as Morley Fund Managers).
  - There may be peer pressure to join up to and endorse global initiatives, standards and principles such as the Global Compact, Publish What You Pay and the Extractive Industries Transparency Initiative.
  - Potential recruits may ask questions on CSR performance and company values.
  - The company may wish to participate in the Business in the Community (BITC) Corporate Responsibility Index (CRI).
  - Business-to-business (B2B) customers or government contractors may require CSR data.
  - 'Brand editors' and journalists may ask for information.

- Self-interest ('want to do') reporting. For example, the company may wish to:
  - Track the impact of initiatives on business performance
  - Collect external data for analysis of impacts on the company
  - Provide data to support staff and management incentive schemes
  - Measure the state of stakeholder relationships
  - Demonstrate social and environmental impacts to stakeholders
  - Show values in action

This final list of 'want to do' reporting mirrors that of the President of the World Business Council for Sustainable Development (WBCSD), Björn Stigson, who succinctly summarised the reasons why measuring and reporting on CSR helps a company (see www.wbcsd.org). According to Stigson, it helps to:

- Assess progress

- Evaluate the relative effectiveness of different approaches

- Brief stakeholders

- Provide incentives to and reward managers and other employees for achieving improvements in performance

- Send clear signals that the business is serious about CSR — if it measures and reports other major aspects of the business and not CSR then it could imply the company is paying lip-service only

- Build and maintain trust with stakeholders

- Effectively defend against criticism

Such reporting is part of a greater need for companies to show transparency in the midst of a 'revolution of values' (see Step 1, page 25). Recognising this revolution, Don Tapscott, co-author of *The Naked Corporation*,[4] argues that:[5]

> Greater transparency is an unstoppable force. It is the product of growing demand from everybody with an interest in any corporation — its 'stakeholder web' — and of rapid technological change, above all the spread of the Internet, that makes it far easier for firms to supply information, and harder for them to keep secrets. Firms now know that their internal e-mails may one day become public knowledge, for instance, and many big companies must co-exist with independent websites where employees can meet anonymously to air their grievances. With greater transparency will come greater accountability and better corporate behaviour. Rather than engage in futile resistance to it, firms should actively embrace transparency and rethink their values and generally get in better shape.

Small and medium-sized enterprises

A very few small businesses may have some very specific and controversial business issues that require a very high degree of transparency and accountability (e.g. the animal testing firm Huntingdon Life Sciences, caught up in attacks and protests from animal rights activists [see Step 1, pages 45f.]). Otherwise, the main motivation for small firms to measure and report will either be to communicate with employ-

---

4   Don Tapscott and David Ticoll, *The Naked Corporation: How the Age of Transparency Will Revolutionize Business* (New York: The Free Press, 2003).

5   Quoted in *The Economist*, in an article on *The Naked Corporation*, 18 October 2003.

ees — which in most cases, may be very informal — or to demonstrate adherence to particular standards to larger business customers. This may be achieved through a letter of assurance or, for some customers, through meeting an internationally recognised standard such as ISO 14001 (see www.iso.org) or the Social Accountability 8000 (SA8000) standard (on this standard, see Box 26, page 217).

Unless it is making its CSR performance a significant part of its 'unique selling proposition' for customers, employees or funders it is unlikely that a small business will need a specific CSR report — or even to make it a significant part of the business website. However, for small and medium-sized enterprises (SMEs) that do wish to produce a CSR report, CSR Europe has developed an SME Key — an online support tool aiming to promote socially responsible business practices among SMEs and, in particular, to assist them in producing their first social report. The key is available as an online database at www.smekey.org.

Non-governmental organisations and governments

The arguments for and principles of measuring and reporting CSR are relevant to NGOs and to public bodies too. There is growing pressure on campaigning NGOs trying to change business behaviour to demonstrate their own transparency and accountability through measurement and reporting.[6]

Although not predominantly a campaigning NGO (it is more about service delivery), one of the best social impact reports we have seen is the 2002–2003 social report from the Royal National Institute for the Deaf (RNID) because it clearly sets out organisational targets; performance against those targets; and future targets. It signposts to more detailed information on each activity described, on a specific part of the RNID website; and highlights a series of externally assessed quality measures achieved during the year.[7]

▶ What should be measured and reported?

At various stages during the seven steps there is a need for information and data to be gathered to aid decision-making. The information and data required may be directly related to what is going on within the business or may be about market conditions and trends outside, for example about the behaviour of competitors.

Box 30 lists some of the issues and topics that may require research, tracking, measuring, monitoring and reporting, as suggested by each of the seven steps. Inevitably, the precise areas will vary for each company, depending, among other things, on sector and geography. By establishing systems to record the sort of data described in Box 30, managers debating the pros and cons of changes to business strategy will have evidence at hand to aid their deliberations.

6   See SustainAbility, *The 21st Century NGO: In the Market for Change* (London: SustainAbility, 2003).
7   www.rnid.org.uk/ImpactReport

- At Step 1 (identifying the triggers) the company will need to:
  - Keep track of trends and developments in broad categories of political, social, economic and technological issues to help analyse emerging and shifting CSR factors

- At Step 2 (scoping what matters) the company will need to:
  - Track trends in specific corporate social responsibility (CSR) issues such as ecology and environment, health and well-being, human rights and diversity, and community relations
  - Track general trends in stakeholder interests, concerns, expectations and behaviour and, in particular, those trends specific to the company and its sector
  - Track competitors' responses in relation to particular issues

- At Step 3 (making the business case) the company will need to:
  - Commission and track data that will help to identify the cost–benefit impacts of risks and opportunities (e.g. market trends, patent applications and pricing movements)
  - Monitor issues relating to access to capital issues (e.g. to understand shifts in popular stocks, trends in venture capital investments and the loans policies of multilateral agencies)
  - Monitor indexes relating to reputation, commissioning specific reputation-tracking surveys for its brands or for the company itself
  - Develop key performance indicators (KPIs) relating to sources of innovation
  - Develop mechanisms to track cost-cutting innovations in the market

- At Step 4 (committing to action) the company will need to:
  - Develop indicators to survey the awareness and understanding of values among its employees
  - Develop KPIs to report on adherence to values across business units
  - Track breaches of behaviour that are counter to the agreed business principles
  - Produce regular reports on CSR progress and performance to the board or other appropriate committees
  - Make a public commitment to CSR

- At Step 5 (integration and gathering resources) the company will need to:
  - Develop functional and cross-organisational KPIs to track compliance with internal policies or external commitments in areas such as diversity and human rights — where necessary, taking into account cultural sensitivities
  - Track resource allocation and usage through business planning and budgetary processes
  - Monitor skill levels and mix
  - Develop KPIs to support appraisal, performance and pay systems

Box 30 **Issues and topics that may require research, tracking, measuring, monitoring and reporting — from internal and external sources, and for internal and external audiences** (continued opposite)

- At Step 6 (engaging stakeholders) the company will need to:
  - Monitor and report on shifts in stakeholder perceptions
  - Report to stakeholders on its social and environmental impacts
  - Analyse the effectiveness of different stakeholder communication campaigns, channels and vehicles in relation to stakeholder perceptions
  - Track social investments and their impacts
  - Examine the effectiveness of partnerships and alliances against objectives

- At Step 7 (measuring and reporting) the company will need to:
  - Produce organisation-wide or country-level reports based on data gathered in Steps 1 to 6, for internal and/or external use
  - Track progress on actions agreed in the seven-step process
  - Track the performance of business strategies built around corporate social opportunity (e.g. innovation in products and services, serving unserved or under-served markets, use of different business models)

Box 30 (continued)

There is much debate in the world of CSR as to what companies should or need to measure and report on. As a guide, we would point readers to two different frameworks:

- The Global Reporting Initiative

- The framework of indicators selected by business leaders under the auspices of the Business in the Community Impact Reporting Group

The first is an ambitious attempt to achieve a common reporting framework through a process of multi-stakeholder consultation, having the advantage of including non-business perspectives and being very comprehensive but having the disadvantage of being potentially unwieldy for some companies. The second has the advantage of being designed by business for business but has the disadvantage of receiving no direct input from other stakeholder interests.

The Global Reporting Initiative

The Global Reporting Initiative (GRI, www.globalreporting.org) describes a number of indicators under 'triple-bottom-line' (economic, environmental and social) headings. The GRI guidelines explain how the process works, and adapted guidelines are available for small and medium-sized businesses and for first-time reporters. Companies can also choose to report 'in accordance' with the guidelines, to distinguish between informal and formal use.

GRI has had, and is likely to continue to have, a significant impact on reporting areas and processes. Many believe that the GRI will emerge as the universal global sustainability reporting framework. Ernst Ligteringen, CEO of the GRI, has also now indicated a preference towards industry-based guidelines, a prototype of which are the recent GRI Telecommunications guidelines. Working groups have also been set up by the GRI for the automobile and mining industries.

The GRI has acknowledged practitioner concerns about the number of current indicators it contains, and envisages reducing these in the future to those that are the most material. Ligteringen has also stressed that the GRI will be attempting to develop better output metrics in the future. There also seems to be an appetite for an assurance methodology to complement the GRI — something that the GRI is currently discussing with AccountAbility.[8]

In 2002 the Johannesburg Stock Exchange (JSE) became the first in the world to recommend that publicly listed companies report to the standards developed by the GRI. The recommendation took effect by virtue of the JSE's adoption of the code proposed in the King Report on Corporate Governance.[9] The GRI may be used in conjunction with other initiatives, such as the Global Compact.

Business in the Community Impact Reporting Group

A set of indicators for companies wanting to measure and report on their social and environmental impact has been developed by Business in the Community (BITC).

The *Indicators that Count* report highlights four impact areas: workplace, marketplace, environment and community, and separates the indicators into two groups. These are 'core' indicators: 27 basic indicators on which all companies are encouraged to report — or know why they have not done so; and a further six advanced indicators judged more difficult to measure. The other group is made up of 17 'specific' indicators not relevant to all companies. The indicators were produced by BITC's business impact review group, which tested a set of social and environmental indicators previously identified in BITC's *Winning with Integrity* report published in November 2000.

Phil Hodkinson, Chief Executive Insurance and Investment, HBOS, and chair of the group, said, 'Reporting on social and environmental performance as part of the Operating and Financial Review is likely to become a requirement for all large UK companies. The reporting framework tested by the Group offers valuable learning in anticipation of these proposals. The framework has been road-tested by companies of different sizes and from different industries.' BITC is recommending the use of the indicators for its 700 members.[10]

The indicators chosen by the business leaders are listed in Box 31.

8 The description of the views of Ernst Ligteringen are based on his presentation to the Business for Social Responsibility Conference, November 2003 (based on personal notes of authors' colleagues attending conference). For the GRI metrics, see www.globalreporting.org.

9 See the 2003 Lifeworth Annual Review of Corporate Responsibility, supported by the New Academy of Business and *The Journal of Corporate Citizenship* (Greenleaf Publishing), at www.lifeworth.net.

10 *Indicators that Count* is available free of charge from reporting@bitc.org.uk.

Marketplace

- Number of customer complaints about products and services
- Number of advertising complaints upheld
- Number of complaints about late payment of bills
- Number of cases of anti-competitive behaviour upheld
- Customer satisfaction levels
- Customer retention
- Provision for customers with special needs
- Average time to pay bills to suppliers
- Customer loyalty measures
- Recognition of and catering for diversity in advertising and product labelling
- The social impacts, costs or benefits of the company's core products and services

Environment

- Overall energy consumption
- Water usage
- Quantity of waste produced, by weight
- Number of cases of prosecution for environmental offences upheld
- Emissions of carbon dioxide (CO_2) and other greenhouse gases
- Other emissions (e.g. ozone, radiation, sulphur oxides [SO_x], nitrogen oxides [NO_x])
- Use of recycled material
- Percentage of waste recycled
- Net contribution made to CO_2 emissions
- Environmental impact over the supply chain
- Environmental impacts, benefits or costs of the company's core products and services

Workplace

- Workforce profile, by
  - Gender
  - Race
  - Disability
  - Age
- Rate of staff absenteeism
- Number of legal non-compliances on health and safety and equal opportunities legislation
- Number of staff grievances
- Number of cases of corrupt or unprofessional behaviour upheld
- Number of recordable incidents (fatal and non-fatal), including at subcontractors
- Staff turnover

Box 31 **Indicators chosen by the Business in the Community Impact Reporting Group, by business area** (continued opposite)

- Value of training and development provided to staff
- Pay and conditions compared with local equivalent averages
- Workforce profile compared with the community profile for travel to work area, by
  - Gender
  - Race
  - Disability
  - Age
- Impact evaluations of the effects of downsizing, restructuring, etc.
- Measures of employee perception of the company

Community

- Cash value of company support to the community as a percentage of pre-tax profit
- Estimated combined value of staff company time, gifts in kind and management costs given to community
- Individual value of staff time, gifts in kind and management costs given to community
- Project progress and measures of achievement
- Leverage of other resources
- Details of impact evaluations carried out on community programmes
- Measures of the community's perception of the company in terms of being a good neighbour (or not)

Human rights

- Number of cases of non-compliances with domestic human rights legislation upheld
- Existence of confidential grievance procedures for workers
- Wage rates
- Measures of progress in adherence to stated business principles on human rights as stated by UK law and international standards on human rights
- Proportion of suppliers and partners screened for compliance with human rights standards
- Proportion of suppliers and partners meeting the company's expected standards on human rights
- Proportion of company's managers meeting the company's standards on human rights within their area of operation
- Perception of the company's performance on human rights by employees, the local community and other stakeholders

Box 31   (continued)

Measuring and reporting particular aspects of corporate social responsibility

In addition to the comprehensive approach to measurement and reporting of CSR issues that the GRI and other initiatives provide, there are also specific projects for the measurement and reporting of particular aspects of responsible business. Here we highlight just two aspects:

- Human capital
- Disability

We have chosen human capital management and disability as two elements that will have growing importance in CSR reporting. They are also illustrative of the way individual aspects of environmental and social responsibility reporting are being developed by different players and through varying mechanisms.

Management of human capital

> Accounting for people provides organisations with the framework to demonstrate the effectiveness of their people strategies and their impact on business performance.
>
> *Fred Goodwin, CEO, Royal Bank of Scotland*[11]

In the United Kingdom the Accounting for People Taskforce has proposed a reporting framework for human capital management (HCM). The Taskforce was appointed by the UK government, chaired by Denise Kingsmill and involved a number of business leaders such as John Sunderland (Executive Chairman of Cadbury Schweppes) and Fred Goodwin (CEO of the Royal Bank of Scotland). The report of the Taskforce makes the point that people typically account for up to 65% of a company's costs yet there has been very little strategic reporting of how companies develop their people.[12]

The Taskforce suggests there should be a close link to any operating and financial review (OFR; see Step 2, pages 56-57). There are close analogies between the tensions that the Taskforce highlights over compulsory reporting of HCM and the wider debates over compulsory reporting of CSR. The Taskforce's endorsement of a discretionary approach based on what it calls 'broad but firm guidelines which can be developed further as consensus grows' matches our view on CSR reporting, as does the Taskforce recommendation for strategic focus and the need to articulate the link between 'people strategy' and business strategy, how such a people strategy is to be delivered and its impact on the firm.

The Taskforce report suggests five items relating to HCM on which to measure and report, as summarised in Table 15.

---

11   Quoted at www.accountingforpeople.gov.uk.
12   Accounting for People Taskforce, 2002 (www.accountingforpeople.gov.uk).

Issue	Reason for inclusion	Examples
Size and composition of workforce	These form the foundations for understanding key issues in relation to the workforce	• Is the workforce increasing or decreasing? • Does the workforce profile fit the strategy? • How reliant is the organisation on external workforces?
Retention and motivation	This provides an indicator of management quality and corporate buy-in	• Is staff turnover running at the optimum level for the business? • Are there differences in staff turnover between different parts of the workforce? • Is everyone working to the same goals?
Skills, competence and training	These show how well-placed the organisation is to meet its goals	• What is the level of fit between skills and business needs? • Is this level of fit set to improve? • What contribution is being made by formal training?
Remuneration and fair employment	This allows an assessment to be made of the fit between people and jobs	• Does remuneration practice support business strategy? • How should non-financial performance be rewarded? • What assurance is given regarding unfair discrimination?
Leadership and succession planning	Such planning demonstrates the sustainability of performance	• What leadership skills are needed? • Do existing managers fit the bill? • How reliant is the company on externally recruited leaders? • Can more leaders be developed internally? • How effective is succession planning?

Table 15 **The Accounting for People Taskforce recommendations on items to measure and report**

Source: www.accountingforpeople.gov.uk

Disability

> Truly inclusive organisation[s] will publicly demonstrate that they
> address disability as a business and societal priority.
>
> *Employers' Forum on Disability and AccountAbility*[13]

The Employers' Forum on Disability (EFD) — a coalition of more than 400 organisations sharing experience and good practice on disability issues — has worked with
AccountAbility to analyse a cross-section of the best CSR reports internationally. The
findings have been published in 'The Global Inclusion Benchmark'.[13] Piloted in 2002,
and released again in 2003, the Benchmark reveals the extent to which some of the
world's leading companies in the area of CSR report on the interests of their disabled
stakeholders. The aim was to identify the extent to which disability issues featured
in such reports and to suggest where the issue might have been included. As a result,
the EFD and AccountAbility have developed a series of recommendations for what
a company needs to do to address the needs of the disabled and for what should be
measured and reported on in relation to disability. The company should:

- Have an equal opportunities or diversity statement or general statement
  of corporate values that explicitly includes disability

- Have a CSR strategy that explicitly commits to addressing disability

- Show a commitment to engaging with disabled stakeholders

- Name a board director responsible for corporate governance in relation to
  disability (working with disability either as a single issue or as a specific
  component of policy on equal opportunities and diversity)

- Determine and report indicators and targets to measure performance in
  relation to the disability dimension of CSR and in relation to disabled
  stakeholders — employees, customers, partners, shareholders, suppliers
  and community members

- Report its performance on recruitment, retention and career development
  for disabled employees and for employees who become disabled

- Determine the impact on disabled people of employment practices that
  affect every employee (e.g. work–life balance, health and safety, and so
  on)

- Work to make company products, services and the built environment
  more accessible to disabled consumers

- Become involved in partnerships with government or NGOs — particularly
  organisations run by disabled people — to build the capacity of the company to become 'disability-confident'

13   Quoted in Employers' Forum on Disability, and AccountAbility, 'The Global Inclusion Benchmark', www.employers-forum.co.uk/www/csr/index.htm (2002).

- Provide details of the disability dimension of any corporate investment that encourages social inclusion and community economic development

- Provide evidence that social reports, annual reports and accounts are written in straightforward language and are available in accessible formats (e.g. Braille, large print or in electronic format on an accessible website)

▶ The challenges of reporting well

The stakeholder view

A word of caution: a badly conceived report can do damage. That is the message from one survey of NGOs and their views of CSR reports. According to the authors of Burson-Marsteller's 2003 survey, titled 'Building CEO Capital' (see www.bm.com), 'major corporations are at best wasting time and at worst damaging their reputations if they fail to develop active and open dialogue with NGOs and [if they] produce less than transparent CSR reports'. The most important approach a company can take, according the survey, is to acknowledge non-compliance, poor performance or significant challenges.

However, some would argue that caution is also required, as the action of putting information in the public domain may have unintended consequences. According to Margery Krauss, CEO of public relations firm Apco, speaking in February 2004 at the Corporate Citizenship Conference of The Conference Board, New York, a Russian oil company discovered the drawbacks to honest reporting. In a spirit of transparency, Russian oil giant Yukos placed on its website information it had discovered about some inappropriate business practices within the group. This information was then quoted by the Russian government when prosecuting the company.

There is, nevertheless, still a good argument for honesty in reports. Ultimately, poor practice will be discovered, and the sooner a company is forced to confront such poor performance the sooner it can transform itself into a company that embraces not only CSR but also CSOs. In addition, the 'fallout' from non-compliance and poor practice will be less severe in most countries if the company is seen to be honest about its failings and to be genuinely concerned about them rather than appearing to try to hide them so that it can continue, unworried, with 'business as usual'.

The most common major criticisms of CSR reports are as follows:

- The reports often lack hard data.

- The form in which data is provided is often peculiar to the reporting company or branch rather than to recognised external norms, making it hard to make comparisons between different companies in the same sector (or even sometimes between different operations across the same multinational corporation).

- The type and way in which data is reported may vary from one year to the next — making it difficult for readers to evaluate progress.

- Data on 'everything but the kitchen sink' (or even including the kitchen sink, if water use and release of cleaning chemicals to the environment are reported) may be included and so it is difficult for stakeholders (and possibly even for the company producing the report) to 'see the wood for the trees'.[14] Thus the drive for comprehensiveness militates against accessibility and materiality.

- Like traditional financial reports from companies, reports are good for looking back and less useful for looking forward.

- Reports are 'dated' by the time they are published. Even material on the company website is often simply a downloadable pdf version of a hard-copy report rather than being updated on a regular basis.

- Reports tend not to refer to corporate objectives and strategy — or to stakeholder concerns — either because the company has not attempted to gather such information or because it has chosen not to include it.

- Few companies fully link reporting methods and results to other management and decision-making processes.

Although this paints a depressing picture of company reporting, there are more positive signs that companies are getting their reporting right. A study of self-selecting stakeholders in 80 countries, by Fishburn Hedges and ECC Kohtes Klewes, seeking stakeholder views of company reports, noted there was general satisfaction with such reports. The findings were generally positive, with some 90% saying companies met expectations when reporting on environmental issues, 52% on economic issues and 64% on social issues. There was also a strong majority in favour of making reporting compulsory, particularly for companies over a certain size.[15]

The business perspective

Businesses themselves complain of 'survey fatigue' — with too many overlapping requests from different, external groups demanding similar data but in different forms, which, of course, is one of the arguments for an international standard and format for reported data. Supporters hope that this is what GRI will eventually become, if a critical mass of businesses and other organisations can be convinced to

---

14 SustainAbility found that the average length of the reports it reviewed had grown by 45% over the period 2000–2002 (as described in 'Global Reporters', 2002).

15 Fishburn Hedges and ECC Kohtes Klewes, 'Global Survey of Stakeholder Expectations of Environmental and Social Reports: Autumn 2003'.

coalesce around it or — more likely — a next-generation version of it that is more user-friendly. A survey by the Investor Relations Society (IRS) of its members in 2003 found that 68% were suffering from 'survey fatigue', eroding goodwill among businesses toward corporate social responsibility issues. Andrew Hawkins, Chief Executive of IRS, said that businesses were being bombarded by a plethora of 'ill-conceived' time-consuming inquiries from lobby groups, adding that the problem for business was deciding which groups to deal with.[16]

As we stated at the start of this chapter, managers embarking on CSR measurement and reporting need to define clearly what is required by law, what is useful to aid their own decision-making and performance and what may also be required to satisfy particular stakeholder needs. The courier firm UPS makes some suggestions on what to measure and how to construct the report from the data and information gathered, recommending the use of a six-stage process (see over).

Constructing the report: questions to consider

The task of finding one's way through the measuring and reporting maze might seem a bit daunting, but there are some key questions to keep in mind when negotiating the problem. Hence, those constructing the report or determining the contents should ask themselves the following questions:

- What is the purpose of the report? For instance:
  - Is the objective to comply with legal requirements?
  - Is the objective to respond to criticism?
  - Is the objective to provide internal data for continuous improvement?

- Who is the target audience?
  - Who is it for — which primary stakeholders, which secondary stakeholders?
  - Are their needs and expectations understood?
  - Are their preferences regarding information format and style known?
  - How will the report reach the audience — through the post, online, at the AGM during open-days?
  - How will we know it has reached that audience?
  - How will we ensure feedback and thereby generate useful information that can become a trigger to fire further action?

- What sort of measurement framework should we use?[17]
  - Shall we adopt a formal framework such as the Global Reporting Initiative (see above, pages 250-51) or follow the process outlined in

---

16   Quoted in the *Financial Times*, 16 April 2003.
17   For details of the main frameworks available, see D. Leipziger, *The Corporate Responsibility Code Book* (Sheffield, UK: Greenleaf Publishing, 2003).

UPS

US logistics and courier firm UPS published its first sustainability report, titled 'Operating in Unison', in 2002. In February 2004, at the Corporate Citizenship Conference in New York, organised by The Conference Board, the company presented the stages that it went through in producing its report, which it broke down into six stages (see www.sustainability.ups.com). The company recommended that any reporting process consist of six stages.

Stage 1: determine the key performance indicators to be measured and reported

First, it developed accepted economic, social and environmental measures and key performance indicators (KPIs), such as the following:

- Economic KPI:
  - Return on equity
- Social KPIs:
  - Percentage full-time workers retained in the workforce
  - Performance on an index representing extent to which the company is an 'employer of choice'
  - Time lost to injuries
  - Frequency of automotive accidents
  - Amount given as charitable donations
- Environmental KPIs:
  - Gallons of fuel per package (carried by the company)
  - Compliance with noise regulations
  - Emissions from aircraft (e.g. pollutants and carbon dioxide [CO_2]) per payload capacity
  - Energy consumption per package and per revenue dollar
  - Emissions of CO_2 to air
  - Water consumption
  - Fines as a percentage of total inspections

Stage 2: benchmark performance against other companies

Second, companies should use these KPIs to benchmark their performance against that of other organisations.

Stage 3: establish a theme

Third, UPS recommends companies establish a theme to work to. For example, UPS uses the theme 'Operating in Unison' to reflect its belief in the need to achieve a 'healthy balance . . . between economic success, social responsibility and environmental stewardship'. This will give the report coherence.

Stage 4: ensure an external perspective

Fourth, companies should aim to gain an external perspective on their performance and seek third-party verification of reported data, as provided by, for example, the World Resources Institute or Business for Social Responsibility.

Stage 5: order the contents

Fifth, UPS suggests the contents reflect the recommendations of the Global Reporting Initiative, with sections on economic, social and environmental performance and a separate section that looks to the future, including a description and quantification of targets and objectives.

Stage 6: create the report in a suitable medium

Last, a suitable print medium needs to be chosen. Perhaps a limited number of printed copies, of a manageable size (i.e. not too long), may be created, with a web-based version being made available.

the Social Accountability 8000 standard (SA8000) or in the AccountAbility 1000 (AA1000) standard?[18]

- Shall we create our own framework, or a hybrid?[19]
- How do we ensure we achieve synergies with other requirements such as the Turnbull risk register?[20]

● What medium or format are we to use?
- Should there be a separate report or should it be an integral part of existing company reports?
- If it is to be an integral part of existing company reports, how can the CSR data and information be integrated into the report as a whole (rather than confining it to a section on its own, as an 'add-on')?
- Is it going to be published annually?
- Is there going to be a web-based version?
- Will any web-based version be the same as another published version or will it have greater detail and be interactive?
- If it is to be web-based, with what frequency can the data be updated?
- How can a variety of other reporting channels be used to supplement the written report?[21]

● What assurance and verification procedures are required?
- Do we need external input for full or partial external verification?
- Do we need external input to provide some kind of external commentary?
- What are the pros and cons of external verification?
- Where and how should we recruit external verifiers?
- Are there issues of privacy?

● How do we assure readers of the report of impartiality if the external verifiers are in our payment?

▶ Likely trends in measurement and reporting

In this section we would like to share with you an amalgam of thoughts from our survey of CSR experts, from a survey undertaken by Coro Strandberg on behalf of

---

18 For details of SA8000 and AA1000, see Step 6, Box 26, page 217.
19 The Canadian CSR organisation Imagine has developed a website to help companies wishing to report against different codes; visit www.imagine.ca.
20 On the 1999 Turnbull Code, see Step 2, page 57.
21 These might include meetings with institutional shareholders, analysts' meetings, AGMs, staff meetings, team briefings, extranet sites, websites (with opportunities for feedback), open days at company sites and so on.

Vancouver City Credit Union (VanCity, *The Future of Corporate Social Responsibility*, 2002) as well as adding our own deliberations.

The following observations can be made:

- The trend towards greater transparency will continue.

- Demand for greater consistency, comparability and verification will grow.

- Reporting will increasingly serve as a predictive management tool, rather than merely as a 'rear-view mirror' so that, increasingly, measurement and reporting will be forward-looking rather than simply backward-looking.

- Reporting will become more concerned with specifying what an organisation is trying to do, where it needs help and what it is interested in learning about and thus will become as much 'invitations to collaborate' as progress reports.

Other trends can also be discerned. For example, John Drummond argues that companies will increasingly hire CSR journalists to write their CSR reports — not only to make them more readable but also to provide some third-party verification, authentication and endorsement without having to go to the trouble of independent auditing. We would also expect to see a growth in the number of CSR and sustainable development reporting portals on the Internet, such as that of the World Business Council for Sustainable Development (WBCSD; www.sdportal.org).

In addition, we see trends towards site-specific reporting, as already required under EMAS (EU Eco-management and Audit Scheme) and for stakeholder-specific reporting: for example, Deloitte Touche Denmark and the Danish Consumer Information Centre are piloting a consumer portal about 'companies behind the brands' and their CSR track record.

We would expect reporting requirements to be further integrated into market instruments, such as the Johannesburg Stock Exchange (JSE) requirements for listed companies to report on their policies on HIV and AIDS following the King Report. Thus, we would also expect integration of CSR reporting with financial reporting to accelerate.

There have been calls in the European Parliament for compulsory reporting on CSR,[22] and in the United Kingdom there have been unsuccessful attempts to introduce compulsory reporting of CSR through private members' bills organised by the CORE campaign.[23] We would therefore expect some reporting requirements to become enshrined in legislation. However, we are yet to be persuaded by those calling for mandatory reporting of CSR. There is, we believe, a danger that compulsory reporting might freeze CSR at a particular point in time — when both CSR itself and certainly environmental and social reporting are in their infancy. Furthermore, there are dangers that compulsion might perpetuate the idea that this is a bolt-on

22 In May 2002 the European parliament voted on corporate social responsibility reporting. Although the resolution still treats CSR as a voluntary concept, it also states that companies should be required to supply information on the social and environmental impact of their operations.

23 www.amnesty.org.uk/business/campaigns/core/index.shtml

activity. The counter-arguments are that compulsion would encourage it to be developed further and to become an integral part of accounting degrees and research, integrating it into the mind-sets of accounting professionals and allowing it to mature and become an accepted part of business practice.

In the UK, the new requirement to produce an operating and financial review (OFR; see Step 2, page 56) may, however, 'do the job' anyway. Under the OFR requirement, boards of directors will be required to report on their most materially significant environmental and social impacts — and it is inconceivable that companies would want to do so without explaining what steps they are taking to tackle these impacts because, otherwise, they would be laying themselves open to scrutiny from the media, investors and pressure group. Companies that recognise the value of capitalising on CSOs will be seeking ways to measure how different elements of corporate behaviour contribute to CSO-based business strategies. Compulsory reporting is already a fact in Australia and France and may follow in some other countries. We would prefer to see more experience from these different jurisdictions and to compare the results of different approaches; while, simultaneously, expecting further evolution of CSR reports anyway.

For those readers who want to delve deeper into reporting trends, some of the increasing number of studies available are listed in the 'Signposts' section, pages 372ff.

▶ Synthesis of Step 7

In the view of the authors, the themes and issues described in Step 7 reflect how banana producer Chiquita Brands International Inc. has adopted and benefited from social and environmental reporting.[24]

---

24 The information is drawn from our own work with the company, from the company's corporate responsibility reports and from Don Tapscott and David Ticoll's book, *The Naked Corporation* (New York: The Free Press, 2003).

Measuring and reporting at Chiquita Brands International Inc.

Chiquita Brands International Inc. has published three corporate responsibility reports since 2001. The pages tell a remarkable story of how, over a short space of time, the company has turned its CSR performance and its reputation around from being 'bad' to being a leader in the field. The process of producing the reports — the research, the benchmarking, the internal management debates and the new management procedures and measures that producing the reports has necessitated — has been a catalyst for significant change in the company.

The first report was produced under the leadership of then CEO Steve Warsaw, who was determined to find a way of making people in the business accountable for the firm's social and environmental performance and for overall adherence to company values. Along with the then CSR manager (now Director), Jeff Zalla, he wanted to use social responsibility as a means to set expectations for standards of behaviour throughout the business. The company chose the SA8000 code of conduct as a base standard and worked with a long-term partner, the Rainforest Alliance of the Better Banana Project, to establish procedures for independent verification of labour and environmental practices in its banana plantations (on the Better Banana Project, see Step 1, page 44).

Since 2000 the company has achieved 100% certification in its Latin American farms, and, in 2001, this was followed by a groundbreaking agreement over workers' rights between the company, the International Union of Foodworkers and COLISBA, a coalition of banana workers in Latin America. In 2003 the firm won the prestigious Award for Sustainability Reporting, presented by the Coalition for Environmentally Responsible Economies (CERES) and the Association of Chartered Certified Accountants (ACCA). The reports were acutely transparent — openly discussing the company's failings and the problems it was experiencing. This level of honesty represented a significant transformation for the company previously known as the 'United Fruit Company' and notorious for its role in establishing Central America's 'banana republics' and with a reputation for treating workers badly.

The information that Jeff Zalla and his team diligently collect each year provides valuable data that is fed back into the company's policies and processes, acting as positive triggers for continuous management improvement and innovation.

▶ Moving from Step 7 to Step 1

The techniques of measuring and reporting described in this chapter fulfil three separate but connected functions: they provide the means to monitor and track CSR-related issues and company impacts; they capture information that is invaluable in aiding decisions as a company moves from CSR to CSO; and they allow managers to know performance levels against targets agreed within the seven-step process. With all three elements combined, they enable integrated management for continuous improvement of business performance and of societal impacts. For the facts and data recorded in Step 7 provide fresh inputs for Step 1, Identifying the triggers. It is these inputs that can be used by management to stimulate new thinking about the impact of CSR on business strategy, and what CSO-inspired business strategies might be developed.

Part II
Putting the seven steps into action: a worked example

Part II: Introduction

In Part I we described the complete seven-step process and introduced associated concepts and analytical techniques for each step. Here in Part II we focus on explaining how to apply the seven steps to an individual company, showing how they can be used by managers to assess the implications of corporate social responsibility (CSR) on their own business and how they can identify their own corporate social opportunities (CSOs) with supporting business strategies.

To do this we have broken down key elements of the seven steps into a number of individual and sequential processes, as shown in Figure 14, which we have converted into the format of a series of tabulated forms. The forms can be used to capture information and data that result from working through tools and techniques selected from Part I, chosen on the basis of whether they are appropriate to that company's sector and general operating situation.

Rather than showing this treatment of the seven steps in the abstract, we have elected to provide a worked example and demonstrate its application to Advent Foods plc, a fictitious company operating in this case within the context of real trends and issues in the food industry.[1] The process forms can be used as a practical yet stimulating planning tool, and to illustrate this our worked example is set in a facilitated one-day management retreat built around the seven steps and attended by the executive directors who are members of Advent's fictitious board and other members of the senior management team. The retreat is chaired by the Advent chairman. We have attempted to mimic real life. Consistent with a real-life brainstorming session, not all the process forms are fully completed in the limited time that the group have, so gaps are inevitable and they can be revisited after the meeting.

In the remainder of this section we provide an introduction to Advent Foods plc and give a contextual briefing on some of the issues the company is facing. And we go on to describe a number of events that subsequently informed the agenda of the management retreat.

This is followed chapter by chapter with the seven steps in action. Each chapter contains a mixture of narrative and extracts of hypothetical dialogue from the retreat, along with copies of the completed process forms filled with inputs and outputs captured at the meeting. The process forms are supported with explanatory notes, helping to clarify exactly what sort of information is required at any particular stage.

1 Disclaimer: the characters and company depicted here are fictitious. Any similarity to real persons, living or dead, or actual companies, is unintentional.

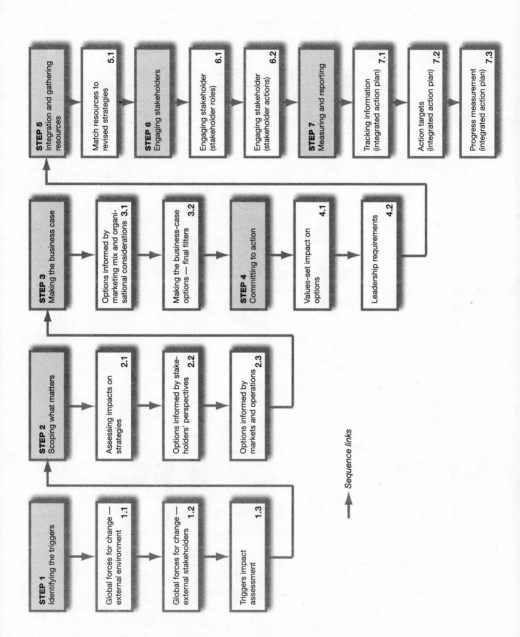

Figure 14 **The seven steps and related processes**

The end result of the exercise is the identification of a number of CSR-informed and CSO-inspired business opportunities for Advent, along with analysis of their implication for the business.

In fact, the seven-step process lends itself to a number of different practical applications in addition to the structure of a one-day retreat illustrated here. A top-line version can be completed in half a day, or a more detailed version completed over a protracted period with inputs from colleagues in different teams and time allowed for testing assumptions and researching data. It is designed to be iterative, as data from Step 7, 'Measuring and reporting', can provide the trigger (Step 1) for further scoping (Step 2). Blank process forms are available for download at www.greenleaf-publishing.com/catalogue/csoforms.htm or via links at www.bitc.org and www.iblf.org; and for examples of these different application options, see the 'Signposts' section on pages 372ff.

▶ The Advent story

Advent Foods is a niche supplier in the food industry. It provides a range of savoury snacks and savoury ingredients, based on processing a wide selection of fruits, nuts and vegetables. It supplies own-label products to business and retail stores, such as supermarkets, and consumer products under its brand name Snackotreat to convenience stores, tea and coffee shops, and catering outlets.

Advent Foods began in the second half of the 20th century as a family-owned company. It grew rapidly during the 1980s and 1990s and became a listed company. It still has original family members on the main board, but the chief executive and main directors are career managers in the food-supply business. See Box 32 for a profile of Advent Foods plc.

Half of Advent's $250 million revenue is derived from business-to-business (B2B) customers that buy its own-label products and branded products for use in their own catering services. One such example is Superfly Air which uses Superfly-branded Advent snacks both in-flight and in its executive lounges. Advent also supplies Snackotreat-branded products to consumers, though not directly. It reaches consumers through a range of small, medium and large distributors, including national supermarket chains in Advent's domestic market.

Advent Foods prospered initially on the strength of its production capability of turning basic savoury raw materials into tasty snacks. Its original recipes provided a range of innovative flavours, adding value to the basic commodities, and allowed a significant margin on top of the base prices of the raw materials. The company benefited greatly from the upsurge in the snacking and 'grazing' culture of the 1980s and 1990s. It has come to see the needs of the consumer largely through the input of its B2B customers and its big distributors, rather than from its own direct tracking of customer needs. Its recipes and product range have increasingly been driven by shopping patterns revealed through the mining of barcode data provided by its big distributors. It has always prided itself that its strength is in processing and production to meet growing demand.

Advent Foods at a glance

Established: 1955

Headquarters: Cherchend, Hampshire, UK

Stock Exchange listing: 1984

Major markets: Australia, Brazil, Canada, Mexico, Middle East, Europe, USA

Own manufacturing and processing sites: Port Talbot, South Wales; Peterlee, County Durham

Licensed manufacturers: Brazil, USA, Australia

Sales regions: Europe Middle East Africa (EMEA), based London, UK; Americas (North and South), based Miami, USA; Rest of World, based Canberra, Australia

Raw materials: nuts, fruits, vegetables and salt, sugar, flour — sourced from around the world

Financials: 2003/04 revenue (turnover) $250 million

Product lines: savoury snacks

Major branded product line: Snackotreat

Box 32 **A profile of Advent Foods plc: a fictitious company**

▶ Context and issues of concern

One source of Advent's strength is in its ability to achieve high output with relatively low capital and labour costs. The average employee in an Advent warehouse or production job tends to be low-skilled and, in many cases, a person in his or her first job. This has enabled the company to keep its labour costs low, with the inevitable flipside that it has experienced relatively high rates of staff turnover. The average rate is 20%, but has been known to peak at 40% in the worst years when the economy was at its strongest and rates of employment high. Partly for this reason, Advent relocated its production facilities from its Hampshire base to areas of the United Kingdom suffering from high unemployment as a result of the closure of industrial manufacturing plants; however, it has kept its headquarters within Hampshire, in new premises.

The board members and senior management of Advent Foods plc are all too aware how much of a challenge it is to run a company like Advent in an increasingly competitive marketplace and to adequately plan for and respond to what appear like constant changes in the operating environment. Some senior executives put the changes down to 'so-called technological progress', which is affecting manufacturing and logistics operations. Others blame the impacts of globalisation, which have led to massive consolidation in the food sector. Some managers were anxious about the impact of demographic trends in the communities from which they draw their young workforce. And, being not only business executives but also parents of inquisitive children — as well as consumers in their own right — all are conscious of apparent shifts in consumer attitudes towards the social and environmental behaviour of companies.

The impact of all these trends are naturally manifesting themselves in different ways for different executives; and there have certainly been few opportunities to get the team together to sit back and look at the 'big picture'.

In fact there are a number of seemingly unconnected social, ethical and environmental issues bubbling away and affecting the sector that the company has not, to date, really focused on, but the impact of which will soon have to be taken into account. These include:

- Because of higher degrees of interconnectivity and greater scrutiny by international non-governmental organisations (NGOs), governments, food manufacturers and processors are having to respond to pressures from activists, the media and customers who now have access to information about working conditions on plantations and farms around the world. Issues such as the alleged use of child labour on farms in developing countries have been highlighted and raised.

- There is a growing and significant niche group of consumers who are looking for food companies to provide 'fair-trade' products, and some are interested in a combination of more 'natural' products (i.e. grown with less use of chemicals or organic) and fair trade.

- There is a broader population concerned with foods that contain genetically modified (GM) ingredients and with a rise in international food-safety scares, such as those surrounding BSE (bovine spongiform encephalopathy) and Asian bird flu.

- There has been a dramatic increase in public, media and governmental concerns with nutrition and rising rates of obesity. More science has produced more data to fuel concerns. In 1996 there were 120 papers on nutrition science in peer-reviewed journals and, by 2002, 1,000 papers.[2]

- Some sections of the food and beverage industry have been demonised as the cause of increasing poor health and obesity — particularly in the young — and the damaging knock-on effects on the economy and healthcare costs.

- High-profile corporate scandals undermining trust in business have led to questions about the food sector's ability to respond to accusations and criticisms.

The obesity 'scare' stories, as they are perceived within the company, which seem to be increasing in frequency in the press, have become the subject of some banter among managers and production staff. Initially they were not given any real importance. It was not until a series of events came together to raise the profile of

---

2   Julian Mellentin of the New Nutrition Business consultancy, quoted in *The Economist*, 12 December 2003.

the issue that it has become apparent that these stories had been early warning signs of potential future challenges for the business. The principal trigger arrived during the course of conversations at the Annual General Meeting (AGM), when an analyst, representing a pension fund with a considerable amount of stock in the company, was overheard querying whether Advent had a strategy to address growing concerns on the impact of 'unhealthy' snack foods on consumers.

Analyst: I've heard some ethical investment funds are reconsidering their investment policies and threatening to move stock from companies who are not taking the issues seriously. I'm going to keep an eye on this issue to see if it should affect our clients' equity stake in Advent.

At the post-AGM dinner for board members and the senior management team, prompted by the analyst's remark, the Chairman asked colleagues for their views on the obesity debate. Discussions around the table elicited a fairly heated exchange of views:

Sales Director: It doesn't really matter. It won't affect Advent.

CEO: It's a passing story in the press . . .

Personnel Director: I've read some of our press cuttings on the subject.

Chairman: Where were they then?

Personnel Director: Here, tucked at the end of the cuttings pack — behind the pieces about financial performance and new product launches . . .

Corporate Affairs Director: Look, I've got cuttings from *The Economist*, the *FT*, *The Daily Mail* and *Mirror*, *The Wall Street Journal* — and look at this *Newsweek* cover story and its headline: 'Fat for Life: six million kids are seriously overweight'. Here take a look at them. This issue could come up and bite us, you know, and really damage our reputation.

CEO: Have you got any analysis to back this up?

Corporate Affairs Director: No . . . Not as yet . . .

Personnel Director: Do you have any thoughts on what sort of action we should take?

Corporate Affairs Director: Not as yet . . . I just think this is something we need to start thinking about . . . I don't think these stories are going to go away that quickly . . .

Chairman: I don't know about reputation; we seem to be a long way from it affecting this business, but then again I am concerned about what the investors are saying . . . I'll tell you what: let's mull it over during the next few days — and perhaps the corporate affairs team can co-ordinate some background research for the rest of us? We've got one of our strategy away-days — a management retreat — in the diary in a month's time. Perhaps we should look at that research then and consider its implications for the business?

Step 1 in action
Identifying the triggers

▶ Setting the scene

It is a rainy Sunday in November. It is one month since the AGM and the chairman and the senior management team are gathering at a hotel in Buckinghamshire for their management retreat. After some consultation following their post-AGM conversation, the Chairman and CEO agreed that the focus of the meeting should be the implications of rising concerns about obesity and nutrition. As they are preparing to take their seats, the CEO is quite clear that, in his view, it is a straightforward PR issue:

> *CEO:* All we need to do is get the PR department to develop a good campaign . . . you know the sort of thing — responsible consumers, responsible eating, all that kind of thing. We just have to get the message out . . .
>
> *[This comment elicits nods of agreement as everyone takes their seats.]*

Those present include: Chairman, CEO, Corporate Affairs Director, Finance Director, Marketing Director, Personnel Director, Production Director and Sales Director.

The Chairman, who was also a non-executive director in another company, had suggested that on this occasion they use the services of a particular facilitator. He had seen this facilitator steer a group of fellow company directors through a seven-step process which was designed especially to help managers consider the implications of social, environmental and ethical-type issues for corporate strategy and business operations. The facilitator did not have any direct experience of the food sector, but this was deemed as potentially an advantage because he would not be so easily drawn into parochial interests and attitudes of food industry experts.

The Chairman opened proceedings by welcoming his colleagues and handed over the meeting to the facilitator and his assistant.

> *Facilitator [handing round agenda]:* Hello everyone. Here's the timetable for today's workshop. We should have enough time to get through each of the seven steps today if we stick to this itinerary. It will be hard work but, from my experience, we can do it.
>
> Keep in mind that each step is equally important. We may find, though, that some steps will take more time to consider. In my experience, Step 2 on 'Scoping the issues' and Step 3 on 'Making the business case' need the most time — perhaps 25% each of the total time allocated for this meeting — as you

Advent Foods Board and Management Retreat

AGENDA

8am	Start. Greetings and introduction
	Step 1: Identifying the triggers
	Processes 1.1, 1.2 and 1.3
9am	Step 2: Scoping the issues
	Processes 2.1, 2.2 and 2.3
11.15am	Step 3: Making the business case
	Processes 3.1 and 3.2
1.30pm	Lunch
2.15pm	Step 4: Committing to action
	Processes 4.1 and 4.2
3.15pm	Step 5: Integration and gathering resources
	Process 5.1
4.15pm	Tea break
4.30pm	Step 6: Engaging stakeholders
	Processes 6.1 and 6.2
5.30pm	Step 7: Measuring and reporting
	Processes 7.1, 7.2 and 7.3
7pm	Dinner

are going to need to review in detail the marketing and organisational information linked to your current strategy.

I should point out that this seven-step model isn't a one-off process — it's an ongoing process that needs to be given attention and updated as regularly as your accounts are updated. Today, we are going to create a snapshot of the current status of Advent Foods.

November 30th, 8:00 am . . .

▶ Step 1, Process 1.1: identifying global forces for change in the external environment

The facilitator invites everyone at the meeting to describe their expectations for the day, and an initial consensus is reached that obesity is essentially a PR issue.

The facilitator is supported by an assistant able to capture in real time on his PC the key points made by individual speakers. The facilitator 'drives' a printing whiteboard, steering also the flow of the conversation and keeping to the timetable. His assistant tidies up the debate and enters the key points as they emerge into 'process forms'. The first of these forms is labelled 'Process 1.1 Global forces for change: external environment'.

The facilitator takes them through a process examining the context of the obesity issue and the operating environment for all of Advent's business, using the heading 'global forces for change'. He uses key headings based on the PEST (political–economic–social–technological) analysis, which is familiar to the company.

The facilitator is looking for the board members to brainstorm the key CSR factors under the headings provided in the form. (Revisit Part I, Step 1, pages 24-34 for an illustration of relevant CSR factors and potential triggers in the food industry.)

> *CEO:* I have heard it said that there is a possible threat to us of legal or class action, as in the tobacco industry. It's already happening in America . . . [*He hands around a press cutting about a legal conference in the USA that focused delegate lawyers on ways of suing the food industry for promoting a surge in obesity and related diseases in recent years.*][1]
>
> *Corporate Affairs Director:* Yes. I've been monitoring the press and other sources and have noticed an increase in activist campaigns about the origins of food and about fair trade . . .
>
> *Production Director:* That's right. I've noticed that too, and it's not just about the sources of our ingredients, either; it's about the ingredients themselves. We're increasingly having to screen out chemical additives. We've an issue with the impending new legislation on food labelling as well . . .

The facilitator is not simply looking for identification of the CSR factors, though. He is explicitly looking for the group to identify the resulting potential triggers flowing from these factors. The Corporate Affairs Director notes she is especially worried by demonstrations on the streets and media campaigns inspired by NGOs and consumer associations against other well-known global food brands. Another senior management team member brings a recent trigger event to the attention of the group.

---

1   There was such a conference in Boston, MA, reported in the *Financial Times*, 19 June 2003.

Sales Director: You were talking about fair trade [*looks at Corporate Affairs Director*]. This brings us back to what we were discussing at our last senior management team meeting, doesn't it?

Production Director: You're talking about Superfly Air threatening to withdraw its contract with us?

Sales Director: Its CEO explicitly said she was looking for a supplier that could provide products that reflect the growing trends and interests of consumers.

Corporate Affairs Director: This is exactly what I'm talking about. I'm seeing a trend towards a demand for organic foods, with ingredients grown using environmentally friendly farming.

Sales Director: Do we have any figures on the size of the potential consumer market for those types of products?

Finance Director: Not as yet . . . though it should allow us to maintain our contract with Superfly Air, which gives us a good sales base to start with.

Corporate Affairs Director: We need to look at fair trade and labour practices at our suppliers — as well as what sort of farming methods are used. Do we have any organic producers as suppliers? Superfly Air is aiming to appeal to environmental and socially conscious travellers to whom working practices, community development issues and sustainable farming are key concerns.

Sales Director: They're linking it to a new push to encourage travel to eco-tourism destinations, aren't they?

Production Director: That's right. It's already changed the supplier of its in-flight wash-bag products to a well-known socially conscious brand!

Process 1.1 Global forces for change: external environment

Processes 1.1 and 1.2 are designed to help prompt thinking about a wide range of developments outside the immediate business and to list resulting 'CSR factors' — themes, issues or topics of a social, ethical or environmental nature — which may have a bearing on the company's strategies or operational practices. They use the classic business strategy and marketing terminology of external environment and external forces. Potential 'trigger' events or incidents which may arise from CSR factors, and subsequently affect the company adversely or provide an opportunity, are then also listed.

Process 1.1 **Global forces for change: external environment**

External environment	CSR factors	Resulting potential triggers[a] (C/F)
Political and legal	Legal/class actions spreading to food and drink industry – some say these are analogous to the experience of the tobacco industry.	– Specific lawsuits for Advent – Fat taxes – Profusion of new and potentially critical public research
	Increased anti-ageist legislation	Pension trustees raised value of deferring pensions
	Increased government and NGO focus on fair trade issues and sustainable farming issues	Questionnaires about Advent's sourcing practices received by Company Secretary and Corporate Affairs Director
Social and cultural	Activist campaigns on food origin and sourcing (labour, environmental) conditions, and on the content of processed foods	Demonstrations on streets against global food brands and specific companies targeted in boycotts
	All social classes talking about diets etc, 'dinner party' conversations re the Atkins diet	– Stories appear daily in media critical of the content of snacks and fast-food products – Shoppers query shop assistants whether particular products 'are good for you' and what certain food products contain.
	Greater expectation of 'well old age'	Press reports that pensions need to stretch over longer life
	Loss of trust in authorities over food scandals such as BSE, foot-and-mouth disease, Asian bird flu, etc.	Public and media look to non-governmental and non-business sources for information they can trust
	– Growing awareness of the dangers for the next generation – children/diabetes and obesity – Parents querying school meal ingredients and quantities – Studies show that the occurrence of high levels of sugars, fats and salt are more prevalent in the diet of the less well-off	– Pressure on food companies to reduce portion size – Pressure on marketing to children. – Parent and teaching associations demand changes to school menus – Pressure groups demand greater information be made available re food content/impact for those who can't afford higher-priced 'healthy eating options'

External environment	CSR factors	Resulting potential triggers (C/F)
	With increasingly long work patterns, there are less 'family meals', apart from breakfast	- Increased cost of breakfast advertising spend as breakfast is one of the few times to reach target market - Reduced return on advertising budget at other times
	Breakdown of family structure (single parents, working mothers, both parents working)	Higher demand for convenience foods that provide good source of nutrition
	Increase of proportion of older people in population - Active 'grey groovers' - Less active 'grey dribblers'	Enquiry received about availability of high-nutrition food with limited preparation time for use in sheltered accommodation – for both self-prepare and staff prepare
	More need for assisted shopping for the elderly, from the store experience to the after-sale experience	Increase in complaints logged by retailers about Advent packaging (size and form), which is perceived as difficult to handle and difficult to open
	General growth of concerns about healthy eating is reflected in Advent's own staff	Annual staff survey shows increased concern about the ethics of Advent's major marketing drives, especially to young people, by linking with sports celebrities
Economic	Mass production is cheaper but badly viewed by a significant group of consumers, influenced by best-selling books such as 'Fast Food Nation'	- Specific legal cases around portion size - Consumers look for non-mass-produced alternatives such as fair trade and organic
	The economics of mass production allow portion sizes to be increased for the same or marginally increased investment	Food spend as proportion of family income drops
	Larger portion sizes may have detrimental effect on consumers	Food advertising in schools is restricted, with the prospect of more restrictions to come
	Age composition of the workforce shifts, as more older staff are employed	Less job applications for factory-floor positions from the traditional pool of school leavers
	Grants available for companies signing up to fair trade initiatives	Advent's Finance Director heard of the availability of finance at a 'Finance in Foods' conference
Technological	Online management information systems help push up the productivity of food giants who can consequently target better	Advent, as mid-sized producer, has margins squeezed by giants

Process 1.1 **Global forces for change: external environment**

External environment	CSR factors	Resulting potential triggers (C/F)
	Sophisticated 'small batch' technology challenges mass production	Micro producers can gain advantage, squeezing Advent as mid-sized supplier
Raw materials	Increased percentage of foods with GM ingredients	Consumer resistance to GM foods, and a competitor declares a 'GM-free' policy
	Unknown sources and unknown additives	Consumers lose trust in food companies and ask questions about products from 'farm to fork'
	Publicity on greater use of locally sourced, organic and fair trade ingredients	Questions raised on Advent policy by shareholders at the AGM
International	Food travelling vast distances, out of season	Questions are asked in the media and by NGOs on quality and safety, and combine with specific food scares, such as Asian bird flu
	Overseas labour exploitation	Unions call a strike at one of Advent's overseas suppliers
	Economic migration/immigration leads to exploitation on farms for unregistered workers	Increases the difficulty of maintaining hygiene and safety standards as a result of language barriers and 'informal' nature of employment contracts
Other		

a The triggers we are noting at this time are 'potential'; the actual triggers will be refined later.

C/F = carried forward

▶ Step 1, Process 1.2: identifying global forces for change in external constituencies

The first session, short though it is, immediately reveals a much more complex set of issues than could be addressed simply through good PR. The executive directors on the board and the rest of the senior management team move on to the second set of global forces for change, in this case looking at stakeholders concerns and expectations. The facilitator has done his homework and had talked with the Corporate Affairs Director the week before and so has produced a checklist of Advent's stakeholders. After a brief discussion, the board members agree to use the facilitator's checklist, which is already included on the blank process form, titled 'Process 1.2 Global forces for change: external constituencies'.

This part of the discussion immediately seems more real to the board and senior management team, who can relate to what people around them are doing and saying at work.

> *Finance Director:* Our staff — particularly our older staff — are concerned about their pension provision. I've been hearing murmurings since the auditors mentioned their concerns at the AGM.
>
> *Personnel Director:* Yes, I'm aware of that: many of them have been reading about the challenges that companies are having with their pension schemes, and we do need to look at our own situation seriously. One of the interesting factors, of course, is that with life expectancy increasing we may actually be able to employ people until they are older.
>
> *Chairman:* We've discussed that some of the problem will be solved by employing people for longer, haven't we?
>
> *Sales Director:* Yes, we're all living much longer now. It might be possible to extend the working age to 70 years.
>
> *Production Director:* That's right. I think that could be an answer to more than one problem. The high turnover of staff is worse among our young warehouse staff — that was the main cause of our missed and late shipments. Last year, my desk was covered in complaints from customers. For several weeks I dreaded the phone ringing . . . We certainly need to address that problem . . . Is this something we could do? [*He turns to Personnel Director*]
>
> *Personnel Director:* It's something that has been mentioned, but we haven't given it serious thought before . . .
>
> *Production Director:* Well, perhaps the personnel department could switch its attention to recruiting people from older age-groups . . .
>
> *Personnel Director:* It's definitely a possibility, but we'd need to look at whether we'd need to make changes to our employment practices. There could be implications for the type of equipment we use too, and other facilities.

Process 1.2 **Global forces for change: stakeholders**

Bodies of individuals whose attitudes, interests, concerns, expectations and behaviour impact the company, creating CSR factors. Potential 'trigger' events or incidents that may arise from CSR factors, and subsequently affect the company adversely or provide an opportunity, are then also listed.

Stakeholder	CSR factors	Resulting potential triggers (C/F)
Customers[a]	(B2C) Increasing concerns of parents on the issue of childhood obesity	Parent-Teacher Association pressure causing contractual problems on Advent's B2B school contracts
	(B2C) Increased perception and concerns about the spread of GMOs in food	Advent's head of customer service needs more staff to handle more calls and letters about the issue
	(B2B) Purchasers of pre-processed food seeking ethically sourced organic/natural solutions	Advent's largest airline customer, Superfly Air, threatens withdrawal of contract unless new specifications are met
	Ageing customer base	Complaints about packaging inaccessibility increase
Employees	Current employees in older age bracket asking for greater pension reassurances	Auditors report balance sheet problem with forecast pension requirements
	More people: – Able to work longer – Wanting to work longer – Allowed to work longer – Needing to work longer	Production Director reports inability to meet orders caused by inability to recruit staff.[b] (He fails to see that staff shortages are because he continues to expect to recruit from their traditional pool of young, unskilled and cheap labour).
Investors	Share price volatility increases due to 'food scare' stories	Pointed comments overheard at AGM from both analysts and individual investors
Local communities	Leaders of local youth groups concerned about poor fitness levels of children	– Advent's usual donations of wholesale party packs of snacks for raffles at local community events less welcome – Corporate Affairs asked to sponsor schools' healthy eating project
Business partners	Some partners investigating fair trade sources	Production Director invited on fair trade study tour
Suppliers	Worried about shifting specifications and ability to meet demands from clients	Suppliers' factories are getting more distributor queries re ingredients, product formulations

Stakeholder	CSR factors	Resulting potential triggers (C/F)
Competitors	Conference debates and gossip suggest world phenomena of doubts about food safety and how healthy content is	Trial products launched in smallest TV region
	Increase in specialist 'natural' food stores, products, distributors, suppliers	– Tentative inquiries from possible new outlets – Competitors launching new fair trade/healthy products and gaining first-mover advantages
Distributors and dealers	Retailers spending more time on customer queries re product formulations	Factories are getting more distributor queries re ingredients, product formulations
		Other companies' trucks and depots from other industry sectors being picketed by protestors
		Head of customer service needs staff to handle more calls and letters
	Increased purchasing power of sheltered accommodation companies	Enquiry received about possible supply contract
Distribution channels		Increased enquiries about Advent's position on food scares
Opinion-forming groups	Consumer Associations becoming vocal on food safety	Advent asked to submit food formulations for evaluation trials about fat content
Government	Government consultation exercise about eating habits of the young	CEO asked to join cross-party working party
Inter-government agencies	Increased consultation between health, education and agriculture policy bodies	CEO asked to give evidence to committee of inquiry
NGOs	NGOs underwriting fair trade tours	Production Director invited on fair trade study tour
Influencers (media, etc.)	Increased prominence of food stories and obesity	– Advent's name included in a list of suppliers to schools – CEO called by journalists for interview

Stakeholder	CSR factors	Resulting potential triggers (C/F)
Facilitators[c]	Marketing trade press report showed an increased number of PR firms offering 'reputation management' services for food and drinks industry	Marketing and Corporate Affairs departments receive PR agency sales pitches
	Law firms developing food specialist practices	Retained law firm queries Company Secretary re company preparedness on current public affairs issues. Company Secretary raises at Board meeting potential need to recruit specialist lawyer.
	Auditors challenged book value of food companies	– Advent's valuation of an acquired company challenged by auditors – Doubts on Advent's book value for same reason
Other		

a 'Customers' are considered here generically, including but not specifically as customers of Advent.

b Operations Director sees the need to invest in better equipment for handling products by older but better qualified employees as barrier to hiring such staff.

c These are individuals or organisations who help Advent run its business, but who do not supply products for our onward distribution. This group will include lawyers, auditors and all professionals ranging from PR and advertising companies to specialist consultants. Cleaning companies operating in Advent factories are also facilitators.

C/F = carried forward

▶ Coffee break

The meeting breaks briefly to refill coffee cups, while the facilitator's assistant cuts and pastes the list of potential triggers out of the two forms comprising Processes 1.1 and 1.2. He copies these into a third form, titled 'Process 1.3 Trigger impact assessment', under a column headed 'Potential triggers (B/F)'.

▶ Step 1, Process 1.3: assessing and ranking triggers, by impact and time-scale

The immediate discussion after the coffee break is about the business impacts of the triggers identified and the time-scale of these impacts. It is clear that each individual trigger has a different business impact. It is also clear that some triggers are affecting the business right now, whereas others may have an impact in the future. It is also beginning to become clearer in the discussion that not all triggers are in effect risks. Some triggers could be managed into business *opportunities*. The facilitator guides the senior management team to prioritise the triggers in order of importance.

The ranking activity causes some of the meeting participants to want to go back to add new CSR factors. The facilitator resists, but ensures that the points thrown out are noted down by his assistant. The facilitator promises they will be added to the completed document to be provided by the end of dinner later in the day.

Process 1.3 **Trigger impact assessment**

It is important to capture actual or potential triggers in an open-minded way, preventing conscious or unconscious editing during this 'exploratory' phase. The trigger list should become a 'live', valuable asset, to be updated from time to time.

Process 1.3 **Trigger impact assessment**

Potential triggers (B/F)[a]	Impacts				Trigger priority ranking[b]
	Business impact[c]	R/O[d]	Timescale impact[e]	R/O	
External forces					
Specific lawsuit for Advent	If case won, as probable, legal fees $100K	R	Within 12 months	R	7
PTA demanding changes to menus, causes education authorities to change order specifications	Schools form 20% of B2B (i.e. $25m p.a.)	R	Within 12 months	R	6
Reduced return on advertising budget	20% of $20m ad spend wasted	R	Now and ongoing	R	5
Increase in complaints about packaging logged by the retailers	Possible business loss, low initially	R	Major impact some way off, gives time for change ahead of competition.	O	
whom Advent supply (size and form are difficult to handle and difficult to open for elder customers)	Remedial action of package redesign, new packaging equipment and transport spend, plus costs during transition phase	R	– Revenue impact not for 24 months, but progressively hits all markets – 24 month lead time for packaging redesign and re-equipping	R	
	Opportunity to steal march on competition if quick off the mark	O	Opportunity to add 5% of market share, say $25m p.a.	O	

Potential triggers (B/F)	Impacts				Trigger priority ranking
	Business impact	R/O	Time-scale impact	R/O	
Stakeholders					
(B2C) Head of customer service needs more staff	3 staff costing say $90K, but improved customer relations	O	Now and ongoing	O	3
(B2B) Superfly Air will withdraw contract if specifics not met?	33% of total $125K million B2B revenues = $42 million	R	Within current budget year	R	1
Our valuation of acquired company challenged by auditors	Share price dropped by 10c - company value down by $20m	R	Immediate (but will recover if appropriate action taken)	R	4
Not able to fulfil orders because of staff shortages - because company continues to expect to recruit from traditional pool of young, unskilled and cheap labour	10% of current-year budget at risk, $25m	R	Within current 12 month budget year	R	2

a In normal usage, all the previously identified triggers would be analysed further here to end up with those most material, according to their business and time-scale impacts. For this example, only a few selected triggers are being shown, carried over from the previous two analyses (Processes 1.1 and 1.2).

b In this column, it is required that a strict ranking is enforced in terms of 1, 2, 3, etc. The facilitator should encourage hard decisions to avoid many items being given the same priority. Ranking is informed by an initial assessment in financial terms and time-scale.

c This column outlines trigger impact in financial terms, and at least in terms of 'high', 'medium' or 'low'. Thus an example might be "loss of revenue, medium', or 'increase in costs of materials, high'. It is more powerful if actual figures can be estimated.

d 'R' identifies risks; 'O' identifies opportunities. In both cases, these arise from triggers from the external environment or from stakeholders. There are two R/O columns. A factor of business opportunity might be an opportunity, but the time-scale might constitute a risk. One organisation's risk if it is unable to respond can be another organisation's opportunity if it knows how to respond.

e 'Time-scale' indicates when the effect of the trigger might happen. It allows differentiation between short-term impacts of, say, low business impact, and long-term impacts of high business impact.

B/F = brought forward

By now, the apparently easy PR solution has turned into an appreciation of a more complex set of causes and effects and, specifically, of triggers and impacts. The most pressing trigger identified is the threat by the head of Superfly Air to withdraw its contract for Advent to provide its savoury snacks, known to the rest of the market as Snackotreat, but branded by Superfly Air for use in its flights and in its executive lounges.

If Superfly Air goes ahead with its threat, the business impact at worst would wipe out 33% of Advent's $125 million B2B revenues, which is significant. Such a loss could happen within the current budget year, as the contracts are up for renewal.

The second most important trigger is agreed to be staff shortages in a workforce dominated by younger unskilled labour. The problems this is causing for fulfilling orders is threatening some 10% of the whole $250 million turnover — again within the budget for the next 12 months.

It is mid-morning, and the Advent board and managers have completed Step 1, 'Identifying the triggers'. It has taken longer than the target time, but the participants are now getting into the whole process. The real difficulty facing the facilitator is how to keep within the timetable so that the board completes all seven steps, albeit in overview, in the time available. This, the facilitator believes, is essential if everyone is to go away with a complete analysis of how CSR pressures might present manageable opportunities — a deliverable output to share with their colleagues. This will allow them to involve many more people constructively in managing their new insight into corporate social opportunity.

However, the facilitator also recognises that each step, and each individual process, is providing the Advent team with much more understanding than can be assimilated in a single day. Information will need to be gathered and co-ordinated for subsequent analysis. At the end of Step 1 it has become clear to the board members and managers alike that they face a huge challenge — namely, to discipline the thoughts that are tumbling out of them, through and into this structured process, while not losing the momentum of the day. Most present sense their personal tendency to need to see their own ideas recognised while not giving quite the same relevance to or placing the same importance on the input of their colleagues. Fortunately, good humour and teamwork are keeping the day on track.

Step 2 in action
Scoping what matters

▶ Setting the scene

It is 9.35 am and the Advent team is working on Step 2, scoping the issues identified during the Step 1 sessions. This next step consists of three principal processes. The overall task is to understand and to begin to list actual or potential risks and opportunities that CSR factors and their corresponding triggers are posing to Advent's business strategies. In practice, this will require some collection of data and information through a number of feeder exercises. This might have been done before the workshop — or, as here in the case of the Advent meeting, this work will be identified as necessary follow-up action in Process 7.1. to be done after the meeting.

9:35 am . . .

▶ Step 2, Process 2.1: assessing impacts of triggers on strategies

Facilitator: Right! We're now going to take the top-ranked triggers that we've just identified and refine how they've affected your current business strategies. You may find each trigger has a single business impact but leads to a number of options. The loss of the contract with Superfly Air is obviously a risk, but our colleagues from production have shown some creative thinking by suggesting you could turn this risk into an opportunity — a corporate social opportunity. There is an opportunity here to create a new product line to meet the requirements of Superfly Air *and* to market it to a wider consumer base with similar interests.

CEO: I'm concerned to address the risks facing us. How do we minimise them?

Marketing Director: Why don't we see if we can turn Superfly Air's threat to withdraw business on its head — couldn't this be an opportunity for a new product line . . . that could be very exciting . . . why don't we explore that further? Let's make it the number 1 option!

Production Director: I am happy with that — to explore it at least — but only if we can spend some time thinking about this idea to recruit more older workers. Let's make that the second option.

Process 2.1 Assessing impacts on strategies

This is the stage where the important triggers are mapped to the organisation's existing strategies and possible responses brainstormed. It prepares the way for reviewing impacts at the individual market segment level.

Trigger priority ranking[a]	Current business strategies impacted[b]	Resulting options[c]	R/O	Option rank[d]
1. (B2B) Superfly Air	B2B is 50% total revenue. Superfly Air 33% of this, and influences the rest of Advent's market	1. No action. Lose Superfly business	R	
		2. No action. Lose all airlines	O	
		3. Create new product line to keep Superfly	O	1
		4. Modify existing product line	O	
2. Not able to fulfil orders because of staff shortages because company continues to expect to recruit from traditional pool of young, unskilled and cheap labour	10% of current year budget at risk, $2.5m	1. Stick with current labour recruitment	R	
		2. Reduce labour force, increase skill levels and equipment support to maintain output	O	
		3. Move to new labour pool of older staff supported with some new equipment, and use the potential of higher skills	O	2
		4. Move factories and warehouses to places of young unemployed	R	
			O	
3. Customer service needs more staff	B2C is 50% of business, i.e. $12.5m p.a.	1. Ignore	R	
		2. Informed dialogue with consumers to protect and rebuild current sales	O	3
		3. Modify current products; might put at risk majority of customers	R	
		4. Develop new niche business with 'natural' formulations	O	

a Derived from previous analysis stage.

b This describes the impact of each trigger on any current strategy noted in Process 1.3. A strategy in these terms is likely to be defined in terms of a market, its revenue streams, and maybe how the market is being serviced by the organisation. An example might be 'the strategy of deriving 30% of revenues from ongoing sales of core products to existing public-sector customers is at risk'. One trigger may impact more than one current strategy.

c This takes the possible impacts of the trigger on the current strategy from the previous column, and derives one or more new or changed strategy options. Thus the current strategy of 'deriving revenues of core products' might suggest strategy options of: (a) introducing new core products; (b) reducing the percentage of revenues from the current products; or (c) withdrawing from the market.

d Having listed the possible resulting strategy options, these are then ranked in order of importance as understood at this stage of the analysis. Again, ranking must avoid strategy options being given the same rankings.

▶ Step 2, Process 2.2: options informed by stakeholder perspectives

Facilitator: OK. [*Name of Assistant*] is going to paste these options into the next form so that we can start to evaluate how your top-ranked triggers are seen from the perspective of your stakeholders.

Before this workshop [*Name of Corporate Affairs Director*] kindly agreed to co-ordinate pulling together some background material in the form of an information pack for the meeting [*passes them round*] and which contains a mix of information on consumers' attitudes and general developments in health issues as well as specific information on the obesity issue, as well as associated data on demographic trends on age and longevity. If you'd like to take a few minutes to glance over it.

Corporate Affairs Director: You'll notice the material comes from various sources. I'm afraid I haven't had time to gather it together in a very coherent way.

Production Director: So, what are the sources . . . ?

Corporate Affairs Director: Some are from existing industry-wide market research, by Morgan Stanley . . . And there's feedback from our customer focus groups . . .

Sales Director: They've only been going a few months, haven't they?

Corporate Affairs Director: That's right — they are giving us some really good feedback, though. I've also drawn together some reports from our key accounts.

Facilitator: The marketing department has provided the data on demographics and ageing trends.

Marketing Director: The other week I was in the USA at a marketing conference. I met a friend who works in the leisure sector . . . He's been doing some research for his leisure sector chain on the theme of healthy ageing and he came across an interesting report from a pharmaceutical company. He immediately thought the information was very relevant to us. His team have been working with this seven-step model [*nods at facilitator*] and he reckoned that we should be looking at this issue to see if it presents a risk or opportunity to us. He was really enthusiastic about this way of working; he said it's really changed things for them . . . in a good way. He showed me some of their new brochures for the sports facilities and membership options and they are offering some really unusual packages, but they seem to be what people want. Their membership is beginning to increase quite rapidly.

Finance Director: This report into obesity from Morgan Stanley is an eye-opener, isn't it? I know it is becoming an increasing problem, but look what this report says: it's 'a growth opportunity for companies that have the best-positioned portfolios and the best ability to bring the right innovation'. Do we know what our competitors are doing on this issue? Are we keeping up with the rest of the field, do you think?

Chairman: That's what we're here for, isn't it? To keep ahead of the field . . .

Corporate Affairs Director: I think it is interesting that the Morgan Stanley research shows that although consumers don't blame us food companies for the problem, they are critical — especially here in Europe — about food and fast-food attitudes. And it is interesting what you ask about other companies . . . we got back yesterday some preliminary research from a benchmarking exercise we commissioned — I didn't have time to include it in the packs. Listen to these examples of how some companies are responding:

- Kraft has announced it is reducing its portion sizes and is reducing sugar, fat and calories in most of its products.[1]

- Sainsbury is committing itself to reducing the amount of salt in its ready meals.[2]

- Coca-Cola is going to stop aiming its advertising at children under 12 years old.[3]

- Unilever is going to produce some 20% of its brands as diet products.[4]

- Kellogg recently spent $30 million for 'Kashi', a firm whose organic cereal lines contain no highly refined sugars or preservatives.[5]

Finance Director: Well, that is quite an impressive list — perhaps we should be seriously considering our own product line!

Corporate Affairs Director: Yes, but I also found in my research that many of those same companies are not just changing product formulation, product size and marketing — they are also making a concerted effort to demonstrate that consumers have individual responsibility for taking appropriate exercise, too. In fact I came across an interesting initiative organised by International Business Leaders Forum called 'Healthy Eating Active Living',[6] which is campaigning to show that the issue needs a holistic solutions approach involving not only food and soft drinks companies but government education and health departments, local authorities and even non-food companies like insurers, auto firms and computer manufacturers. We should look more into this.

Sales Director: This benchmarking exercise . . . do we need to be looking at the soft-drinks industry?

Corporate Affairs Director: I think we do. You'd be surprised at the influence of campaigning groups on the soft-drinks industry . . . that could be us in a few months . . . a few days, even . . .

Production Director: Is there any way we can see that kind of trouble coming?

---

1 *USA Today*, 1 July 2003.
2 Food Standards Agency press release, 10 November 2003.
3 'Coca-Cola withdraws all adverts aimed at under-12s', *The Evening Standard*, London, November 2003.
4 'Unilever plans diet ice cream', *Sunday Times* Business News, December 2003.
5 USATODAY.com, 'Under fire, food giants switch to healthier fare', 1 July 2003.
6 Healthy Eating Active Living (HEAL) at www.iblf.org.

Corporate Affairs Director: There's a radar technique they taught on my MBA course to track how issues are emerging over time and what the NGOs are doing . . .

Sales Director: Causing trouble for us . . .

Corporate Affairs Director: They may be campaigning or working in collaboration with companies, helping to find solutions to problems. Here's a radar-tracking exercise I've done for NGOs and the obesity issue . . . [*the Corporate Affairs Director hands round copies of a table to illustrate her point*].

NGO campaign issues on the radar screen: obesity

Emerging

↓

Obesity: Fast Food Nation published.

Food content: Studies identify 'trans fat' issue.

Campaigning

Obesity: Studies published revealing growing endemic; first lawsuits.

Food content: Diabetes/sugar content. Portion size.

Labelling: Lawsuit on mis-labelling.

Marketing to children: Studies claim link between obesity, unhealthy food intake and children's marketing. Vending in schools. Marketing through schools.

↓

Codifying

Food content: GMOs.

Labelling: New voluntary labelling accord.

Marketing to children: New voluntary marketing to children code.

↓

Monitoring

Marketing to children: NGOs monitor advertising and promotions.

↓

Consulting

Food content: Collaboration on new nutritionals.

Demographics and ageing

The next 50 years will see significant divergence in population growth between countries around the world, with the number of people in many Western European countries reducing, whilst 'big markets' such as China, India and the U.S. would continue to grow.[7]

Germany, Spain and Italy could have more citizens over 80 than under 20 by 2050.[8]

As the world gets older, so its willingness to spend money on staying healthy grows.[9]

Projections to the year 2010 suggest that the percentage of the global population aged 65 and over will grow by 847,000 people every month. In Europe, by 2030 12% of all Europeans are projected to be over the age of 74, and 7% over the age of 79. The fastest growing portion of the elderly population in many nations around the world is 80 and over.[10]

The age of retirement from employment is traditionally regarded as the beginning of old age, although this age varies between countries. As a consequence of the ageing population these definitions are likely to be under constant review.[11]

Globalisation and changing social attitudes have meant migrating populations, a rising divorce rate, and alternative lifestyles resulting in different family dynamics. It has been shown that families, spouses excepted, are increasingly less willing to look after their elderly relatives.[12]

World Life Expectancy is Rising

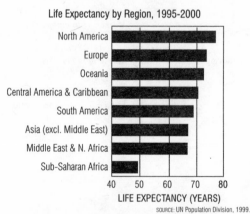

Life Expectancy by Region, 1995-2000

LIFE EXPECTANCY (YEARS)

SOURCE: UN Population Division, 1999.

---

7 This is taken from an article in *The Economist*, titled 'Half a Billion Americans?', 24 August 2003.

8 Also from the special report in *The Economist*, 24 August 2003.

9 From *The Economist*, 'Spoilt for Choice: Food Survey', 12 December 2003.

10 Quote taken from the US Department of Health and Human Services and the US Department of Commerce, 'An Aging World: 2001', published in 2001.

11 This is a quote from a Pfizer briefing, titled 'Ageing Population', 2003.

12 Taken from Malby A. Walker, *Ageing Europe* (Buckingham, UK: Open University Press, 1997); also quoted in the Pfizer briefing, 'Ageing Population', 2003.

Obesity

Obesity is a global phenomenon – not only a compelling problem in developed nations but also a growing concern in developing countries – particularly among children . . .

The World Health Organisation (WHO) estimates that over one billion people are overweight worldwide, with 300 million being obese.[13]

Globally, obesity puts more pressure on healthcare systems already under massive pressure from pandemics like HIV/AIDS and the increased demands of a large number of older people. The ill-effects of obesity already cost the UK National Health Service £500m.[16]

In the USA, 120 million are overweight or obese.[14]

The growth of overweight and obesity . . . is a health time-bomb with the potential to explode over the next three decades. Unless this time-bomb is defused the consequences for the population's health, the costs to the NHS and the losses to the economy will be disastrous.[15]

Obesity Prevalence Rates Reveal Global Phenomenon

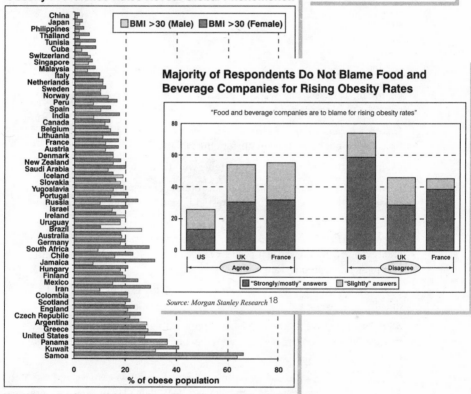

Majority of Respondents Do Not Blame Food and Beverage Companies for Rising Obesity Rates

Source: Morgan Stanley Research [18]

Note: Most recent data available: surveys conducted between 1988 and 1994

Source: International Obesity Task Force [17]

13   Quoted from Morgan Stanley report, 'Obesity: A Big and Complex Issue', Appendix II in *Consumer Staples: Global Insights*, 31 October 2003, p. 43.

14   Quote from *The New Statesman*, 25 August 2003.

15   These are the words of Sir Liam Donaldson, British Chief Medical Officer, quoted in *The Times*, 4 July 2003.

16   Data from National Audit Office.

17   From Morgan Stanley report, *Consumer Staples: Global Insights*, 31 October 2003, p. 43.

18   *Ibid.*, p. 7.

Later

Finance Director: So we think that Superfly Air's interest in repositioning its brand could be to our advantage?

Personnel Director: Yes. The CEO could take the credit for encouraging us to create a new product line, yes?

Corporate Affairs Director: Absolutely! It might be a very good move in the marketplace to get her endorsement of our new product brand.

Finance Director: And Superfly Air could share in the cost of launching the new brand . . .

Facilitator: [*Name of Assistant*], can you include that as a revised option on the form?

. . .

Later still

Chairman: Do we really want to redirect the whole B2B division towards natural and fair-trade products? What about our existing lines?

Finance Director: We could create a new department in the B2B division, and have it report at board level to nurture the initiative.

Chairman: I think I'd be more comfortable with that.

Finance Director: We could look at the option of using any new product department to attract investors interested in natural, healthy and fair-trade formulations.

Corporate Affairs Director: I like that idea — it would help to protect the image and revenue from our current product ranges while we're making the transition to any new product range.

Sales Director: Do we really need to be abandoning the existing range? That's a dreadful risk. We've got a good customer base for those products . . .

Marketing Director: I still think the best option is to acquire a business already in the natural foods market — we'd be buying into its know-how and marketing capabilities, and we'd benefit from its brand name and reputation . . .

Sales Director [*looks at completed form on screen*]: We didn't know what we were letting ourselves into at the beginning of today, did we?

Chairman: Well, I have to admit, this exercise has made me rethink the importance of stakeholders and getting them on board.

Process 2.2 Options informed by stakeholders' perspectives

This activity matches strategy options derived in the previous forms against the impact on current or future stakeholders. It prepares the way to put into context the following review of the strategy options which focus on current or potential market segments.

Resulting options[a]	Stakeholders and how impacted[b]	Revised options[c]
1. Create new natural, healthy, fair-trade product line to retain the Superfly Air contract in B2B market	**Customers (also in markets and operations)[d]**	
	Superfly Air take some credit for the change and promotes to rest of world	– Superfly endorsement in product branding – Superfly share launch costs for own publicity – Anti-obesity strategy matches Superfly's market positioning, especially for business customers
	B2B and B2C world recognises and supports new initiative	– Opens up possible product range transfer to B2C market – Lower salt and fat formulations match growing market expectations – Shared development costs between B2B and B2C market
	Employees	
	– See new business good for job security – Expressions of concern over health impact of free access to Snackotreat products	– Superfly Air could offer incentives to Advent staff – Revised product formulations could ease concern
	Investors	
	Recognise added long-term value of company	Get investors to see alliance potential and fund expansion.
	Local communities	
	Local church groups recognise responsible behaviour and commitment to fair trade	Potential new target group for communications messages
	Business partners	
	Want to learn about and support initiative (and thereby benefit their wider business)	

Resulting options	Stakeholders and how impacted	Revised options
	Suppliers	
	Want to learn about and support initiative (and thereby benefit their wider business). Perhaps however also worried that they will have to foot the bill in changing processes to be able to meet new specifications, or may lose business	Possibly have to institute capacity-building programmes for suppliers/offer to help finance necessary plant/machinery, crops, etc. Alternatively, find new suppliers able to meet the spec.
	Distribution channels	
	Want to learn and support initiative (and thereby benefit their wider business)	
	Opinion-forming groups	
	B2B and B2C opinion formers recognise and support new initiative	
	Government	
	Applaud initiative and encourage others	Seek openings for sales into health, education and other services/sectors
	Inter-government agencies	
	NGOs	
	Applaud initiative but concerned about conditions of farm labourers in emerging markets	Need to consider system of verification of workplace practices of suppliers
	Influencers (media, etc.)	

Resulting options	Stakeholders and how impacted	Revised options
2. 'New workforce'. Move to new labour pool of older staff supported with some new equipment, and utilise the potential of higher skills	**Customers**	
	B2B will see greater reliability of delivery	
	Employees	
	Current employees may be unsettled by new recruitment and work practices (e.g. part time, flexitime and new equipment skills needed)	Access to pool of workers wanting part-time and flexitime working allows longer hours' usage of capital (e.g. 24 hour warehouse and production line usage rather than 8 or 12 hour only)
		Opportunity to extend more flexible working to whole workforce, improving staff quality, performance and company reputation.
	Investors	
	Risk of profit dilution or need for increased capital. Revenue risk arising from management change risks	
3. B2C market – informed dialogue with consumers through retail chains to protect and rebuild current sales	**Customers (also in segment attractiveness)**	
	Word-of-mouth spread of good news	
	Feedback generates on-going innovation and quality improvements	Create 'Customer Club' brand for new products
	Employees	
	Word-of-mouth spread of good news	Staff purchase incentives for 'Customer Club' to increase early volume and feedback

Process 2.2 **Options informed by stakeholders' perspectives**

Resulting options	Stakeholders and how impacted	Revised options
	Feedback generates ongoing innovation and quality improvements	
	Like and support responsible management	
	Take greater responsibility themselves for improved dialogue	
	Investors	
	Recognise added long-term value of company	See expansion potential and approve funding
	Community	
	Recognises responsible behaviour	Public space displays and roadshows to introduce new products
	Improved recruitment opportunities	
	Better relations with local councils/bodies	
	Business partners	
	Want to learn about and support initiative (and thereby benefit their wider business)	New more vigorous R&D pursued on shared basis
	Suppliers	
	Want to learn about and support initiative (and thereby benefit their wider business)	New more vigorous R&D pursued on shared basis
	Fair trade implications	Increased role for fair trade suppliers
	Distribution chain	
	Will see initiative as supportive of their own repositioning into natural formulations	Get separate shelf space for 'Customer Club' product range

Resulting options	Stakeholders and how impacted	Revised options
	Opinion-forming groups	
	– B2C opinion formers recognise and support new initiative – Snack foods are seen as contributing to obesity by fitness and health bodies	– Reduced dependence on advertising budget through increased editorial support – Saving diverted to product development – Possible link-ups with fitness chains, weight-loss clubs promoting the new product formulations as healthy alternatives
	Government	
	Applaud initiative and encourage others	Seek openings for sales into health, education and other services/sectors

a These are the strategy options derived from the previous form. This analysis starts with the highest-ranked strategy option. It may well not be a good use of time to continue through the steps with all possible strategy options. By this stage, it is likely the more important ones only are worthy of continued analysis.

b The impact of the highly ranked strategy options are reviewed from the perspective of each type of stakeholder. Their possible impact on each stakeholder is listed under each of the identified stakeholders.

c The strategy options coming into this stage are reassessed by their impact on current and new stakeholders. The result of this review may produce further refinement producing the 'revised options'.

d Customers are here treated 'generically' as stakeholders but not as consumers of the organisation's products or services. The way customers behave as consumers is part of the following analysis of overall segment attractiveness.

▶ Step 2, Process 2.3: options informed by markets and operations

Facilitator: We're making very good progress. What you need to do now is consider the various organisational responses you can make to bring this new product line into being. What options have we got, [*Name of Assistant*]?

Facilitator's assistant: I've got them formulated like this [*sends details to screen*].

- Redirect the whole B2B division towards the new product range

- Create a new department in the B2B division, reporting to the Board

- Use the new product department to attract investment and to protect the image and revenues of the current products during the transition period

- Acquire a business already in the natural formulation market

---

The Advent team members start to discuss the options. Debate is heated. How long will the transition period last? Will the market for the current product range continue well into the future? It becomes apparent to the CEO listening to the comments that, although the obesity issue had up to now been the main topic discussed, in fact they were branching out into a much broader array of issues related to responsible business behaviour.

Sales Director: I keep saying . . . can we really see our core market collapsing? I don't see why we need to nanny our customers by giving them only the no-salt no-fat no-sugar organic fair-trade option. People want our products and if we stop producing those products then our customers will go to our competitors . . .

Corporate Affairs Director: Superfly Air is already thinking of going to our competitors . . . And, anyway, don't we want to produce more wholesome products in any case?

Chairman: I'm losing my way here. Are we talking about the obesity issue or about fair trade and organic ingredients?

Production Director: Yes, let's get back to the point. Let's suppose we do go into this new market — and I'm talking about the change in the sourcing of our ingredients — how long is the transition period going to be?

Finance Director: And how much is it going to cost . . . ?

CEO: If we acquired a company already in that market we wouldn't have any problem with acquiring know-how and suppliers . . .

Facilitator: OK, let's just stand back a minute and see if we can prioritise these options now we've had a chance to consider the consequences of each option.

Later

Facilitator: Right, so we're in broad agreement that option 1 is to create a spin-off department for the new product, with the aim of attracting new investment and protecting the existing range.

OK. We're doing well. Let's keep the momentum going. We've still another five steps to go. Let's revisit some of the other options we've discussed. I'd like to carry forward some of the other options you've been discussing as they are worth further analysis. This is a complex situation, so in my experience we don't want to focus exclusively on what might seem the most obvious answer — some of the other options may lead to a different but better solution.

Production Director: I'm glad you've mentioned that. We've been focusing so much on the media coverage and what-not of the obesity issue you're forgetting that I've got . . . we've got a problem with missed deliveries. These are my immediate concern — they are not something that may happen to us at some unknown point in the future, they are happening now . . .

Facilitator: [*Name of Personnel Director*], you mentioned earlier this morning that you've been looking into this already . . .

Personnel Director: Only that it's been mentioned . . . I can't claim I've looked into it in any detail. I feel a bit guilty. [*Name of Corporate Affairs Director*] and [*Name of Marketing Director*] have got all this material together [*holds up information pack*] but I don't seem to have contributed much background.

Facilitator: Not at all . . . You've made some valuable contributions.

Production Director: So what about this option of recruiting older, better-skilled staff?

Personnel Director: I'll look into what would be involved in modifying any specialist equipment that might be necessary given different physical abilities of an elder workforce. We could think about subcontracting the packaging tasks and some equipment operation. I'll get some figures and time-scales together. We could subcontract the packaging tasks and operation of equipment to a third party.

Production Director: No, I don't think that is feasible, or at least I wouldn't support that idea.

[*All agree.*]

Personnel Director: Could we use this as an opportunity to introduce some more flexible and part-time working options? I've heard staff talking about that possibility, with the media coverage of new laws on entitlement to flexible working for families and so on . . .

Production Director: I agree that is something we need to look at. I'm in favour of the idea, but it will have repercussions, especially for our current human resources practices.

Facilitator: Good. We've got plenty to work with. May I suggest we also carry forward a third option — to develop new product formulations in your business-to-consumer market through the retail chains?

Sales Director: Do we need to treat that as a separate option? We could consider that alongside the option of having a spin-off department, couldn't we?

Marketing Director: We could roll the two options together, yes, but we would need to bear in mind that that approach would pose a risk to our customer retention — the new product range will be so different from the current range in packaging, branding and market positioning.

Facilitator: Let's recap, then. This is the ranking we've got so far [*sends options to the screen*].

Facilitator: Right! Shall we have a quick break for coffee?

- Top priority: set up a new product department

- Second priority: employ older workers on a part-time and/or flexible basis

- Third priority: piggyback the new product formulations on the B2C market

Process 2.3 Options informed by markets and operations

This activity identifies the consequences of revised options when analysed against current markets and current operational practices.

Process 2.3 **Options informed by markets and operations**

Revised options	Revised options informed by current markets and operations[a]	Consequences[b]	Attractiveness: new ranking[c]
B2B market private airline segment	A. Redirect the whole B2B division towards the newly formulated products and new segments they will attract	Lose some market share by massive disruption to the current business	
	B. Separate new department from sponsoring division, reporting at board level to nurture the initiative	Retain Superfly Air business but resource allocation is a challenge	
	C. Spin-off the new product department for natural and fair trade formulations to attract investment and protect image and revenues of current products	– Retain Superfly Air business and grow – No 'halo effect' on current segments	1
	D. Acquire existing business in this field	If acquisition available, protect innocent business but have different integration challenges	
New workforce	Part-time and flexitime working allows longer hours' usage of capital More flexible working improving staff quality, performance and company reputation	– Opportunity to increase productivity increases profit margins, for increased competitiveness and sales, and improved bottom line – Need for a whole new set of human resource practices – Change of conditions may cause short-term disruption to current staff	2
	Subcontract packaging and shipment to third party	– Lower profit margins – Less control over service quality	

Revised options	Revised options informed by current markets and operations	Consequences	Attractiveness: new ranking
B2C market through large retail chains	A. Ignore short-term pressures because of perception that only B2B affected	Begin to lose market share as the importance of natural foods grows, indicated by B2B current interest	
	B. Piggyback on the redirection of the whole B2C division towards the newly formulated products and new segments they will attract	– Lower risk of losing current customers by using B2B department knowledge across whole B2C division. – Learn from B2B – Share resources (money and people) – Double 'halo effect' with opinion formers and investors	
	C. Piggyback on the separation of new department from overall division, reporting at board level to nurture the initiative	Higher risk to customer retention by separating from core division of the company	
	D. Piggyback on the spin-off of the new product department for natural formulations to attract investment and protect image and revenues of current products	Higher risk to customer retention by separating from core division of the company	3
	E. Piggyback on the acquisition of existing business in this field	Higher risk to current customers until integration provides products and 'halo effect' to existing company	

a Current segments are referred to in this column by some recognised term within the organisation. Such a term may be 'consumer market for heavy-duty cleaning materials' or 'B2B market for office cleaning contracts'. It is logical to start with the segments that are important to the organisation, if not the very highest ranking, then high-ranking segments most affected by the new strategy options.

b Current market segments are likely to be affected by strategy options derived from the analysis to date. In this column, the impacts of the strategy option on key market segments are defined. Also, the marketing activity and internal organisation may be affected.

c This ranking is a combination of feasibility and market potential, resulting in an expression of 'attractiveness'. The result might be the higher ranking of segments most likely to be important for the organisation's future given the changed environments indicated by the triggers.

Step 3 in action
Making the business case

▶ Setting the scene

The board returns to the conference room with hastily acquired cups of coffee in their hands.

> *Facilitator:* We're going well, but we've still got a lot of ground to cover today. If you're all in agreement I think we need to pick up the pace a little.

> [*Others murmur agreement.*]

> *Facilitator:* I think we need to set ourselves the target of getting to the end of Step 3 by lunchtime. I suggest we look only at the first two, top-priority options.

> *Finance Director:* I'm not happy with the idea of rushing this step. If we don't get the business case right then anything we discuss afterwards may be a waste of time.

> *Chairman:* I'm surprised, [*Name of Finance Director*]. I thought you were in favour of this . . .

> *Finance Director:* I know, but during the coffee break the implications of some of the things we've been talking about have suddenly hit me. I'm afraid we're getting carried away. If what we are suggesting is worth doing then it is worth doing properly, in a considered way. I don't see why we need to rush it through in one day. The company has taken years to reach this point — we shouldn't decide on a major change to our business strategy in one day. At meetings like this anything can sound like a good idea. I'd like my in-house experts to take a closer look at what we've got so far.

> *Sales Director:* I agree. It wouldn't hurt us — or the company — if we were to go away and think quietly about the options we've discussed so far — there's a lot to think about.

> *CEO:* It's not often we get this chance for a whole day together to concentrate on the bigger issues facing the company. Our regular meetings are usually about operational matters. Which is why these retreats are so important.

11:55 am . . .

▶ **Step 3, Process 3.1: options informed by marketing mix and organisational considerations**

Facilitator's assistant: OK, I've cut and pasted the two revised options from the previous forms and discussions [*sends summary to the screen*].

- Form a new product department

- Introduce part-time and flexible working as part of a strategy of attracting more mature employees to warehousing and distribution

Chairman: This idea of corporate social opportunity that [*Name of Facilitator*] has introduced is new to me, but I'm finding it very insightful. It's certainly a new perspective. Thank you [*nods at Facilitator*].

Facilitator: Let's keep it going then . . . Let's look at the implications of your revised options. If you'd just like to take a look at the form for Process 3.1 . . . I want you to consider the options with regard to their implications for product range, pricing strategy, place (distribution channels), promotional strategy, sales, administration and production, process and people and organisational issues. This form allows you to estimate one or more of the financial inputs in terms of revenue or cost of the combined effect on the bottom-line — that is, the overall P&L account.

Corporate Affairs Director: Well, the new product range obviously will create new market segments . . .

Marketing Director: . . . and we can use the new range as the basis for educating current market segments about the new products.

Production Director: I think that providing we can get the suppliers we should look to making the new range from fairly traded ingredients.

Marketing Director: I can see possibilities . . . opportunities . . . if we can take that forward . . .

Finance Director: I've seen some figures on how that market is growing. It still seems to me to be a small market, but it is definitely growing, and we could benefit from joining that market . . .

Sales Director: Perhaps you could rustle up some figures for our next board meeting?

Marketing Director: I'll get my team to schedule in a meeting so that we can have a brainstorming session on a new promotional strategy — we're going to need to change our current marketing strategies.

Production Director: I think we ought to start with a new distribution channel to build the new brand.

Personnel Director: Yes, that would avoid confusion with the current channels and products.

Sales Director: What kind of pricing strategy are we going to adopt?

Finance Director: I think it's too early to say until we've got more information available. I really do draw the line at trying to decide that . . .

Facilitator: Let's stop a minute and redirect our attention towards how Advent can grasp the corporate social opportunity that is beginning to emerge from these discussions — and it *is* starting to take shape and become clearer, I think you'll agree, despite any differences of opinion of the exact details of how to move forward. A lot of progress has been made since we convened this morning at 8 o'clock, but we've still a lot to do.

Corporate Affairs Director: I think our opportunity lies in the new consumer concerns we are detecting on our radar screens.

Sales Director: Yes, but we are going to need to set up some sort of process to monitor these developments in a more scientific and systematic way.

Marketing Director: My colleague from [*Name of leisure-sector company*] mentioned the importance of people and organisation. This is true for us with the fair-trade aspects, I think.

Production Director: Yes, we are going to need to find new suppliers, and I imagine the new relationships are going to have to be managed in a different way from how we do things with our large suppliers at the moment.

Facilitator: We will come to that in Step 5.

Personnel Director: We haven't talked yet about the workforce option.

Corporate Affairs Director: That's more an internal organisational issue, isn't it?

Sales Director: If we could improve our logistics, and if we had the human resources, we could get our products on the shelves of some additional supermarket chains — some of their stores are starting to open 24/7. I've several contacts who have shown an interest, but their stores are open 24 hours a day, seven days a week, and our logistics just don't match up to their all-day anyday delivery requirements. We don't have the internal capacity.

CEO: I've always felt that was a direction we could move in. The workforce could sweat a bit harder.

Production Director: We do have a problem with staff motivation . . .

Marketing Director: Listen, [*Name of leisure-sector company*] has several membership options for older customers — [*Name*] says that that age-group is now a major part of the centre's customer base, and it's growing all the time. We're thinking about employing older workers, but what about the market potential of older customers?

CEO: What? Appeal to the 'grey groovers'?

Production Director: Our Snackotreat bars are popular with the younger staff. Perhaps with a new formulation . . .

Marketing Director: . . . and new packaging and marketing . . .

Production Director: We'd definitely need new packaging for older customers.

Marketing Director: We'd need a design that will be attractive to that agegroup . . .

Production Director: I'm not thinking so much of pretty pictures as about how difficult they are to get into . . .

Production Director: But we need good packaging because of the long shelflife . . .

Sales Director: We could probably factor in easier packaging into the price.

Marketing Director: I don't think we should even be think about adding price premiums . . .

Production Director: I think we can add a price premium for it being natural and organic and fair trade, but easy to open . . . ?

Personnel Director: Can we get back to the issue of recruiting older employees? During the coffee break I gave some thought to the need for new handling equipment. I think perhaps we need to invest in new equipment anyway . . .

Production Director: Yes, what we've got at the moment requires more in the line of brute strength and ignorance . . .

Personnel Director: If we had more up-to-date equipment we might find we lose less stock from damage caused by careless handling?

Finance Director: I'd welcome any chance to reduce losses from mishandling of stock. The figures are too high at the moment. We'd have to look at capital investment for the new equipment, and the costs of training the workforce to use the new equipment . . .

Production Director: Yes, it would require more skill . . .

Finance Director: . . . and we can set those costs against savings on lost stock . . .

Marketing Director: Yes, my 'back-of-the-envelope' calculation is that the new product formulation will have the potential to provide 10% of total current revenue within two years — a $25 million addition.

Sale Director: Are sure you've got your figures right?

Marketing Director: I think it's a good estimate. Regardless, I think the second source of revenue will at least protect our current revenues . . .

Corporate Affairs Director: Yes, if not in the short term then certainly in the medium and the long term.

[*All murmur agreement.*]

Finance Director: Where did you get your figures from? You've just plucked them from the air . . .

Production Director: I can see the new product range costing $25 million to establish, but if we implement it properly and combine it with taking on more mature and more stable staff then I think we could prevent the $25 million delivery risk.

Personnel Director: I'd need to look at the accounts to check this figure, but I think we could save $2 million in hiring temporary staff to cover unforeseen absences.

Facilitator: I think these figures give us an approximate idea of the financial impact of the two options on Advent. I don't think we need to get bogged down at the moment in refining the numbers.

Chairman: Especially when we haven't agreed on the options yet.

Finance Director: We can carry out a more detailed analysis in-house later.

Facilitator: I think we can move on to the next part of Step 3 now.

Process 3.1 Options informed by marketing mix and organisational considerations

The strategic impact of revised options on segments, the marketing mix and organisational considerations helps identify whether current needs are changing or new needs are emerging, and also whether there are gaps in what is offered by current suppliers to that segment. Essential to making the business case is quantifying new segment opportunities and marketing strategies, against which new investments driven by this CSO analysis are to be judged. (Both to illustrate the necessary prioritisation of options, and reflect practical realities in a facilitated workshop such as at Advent's Management Retreat, the third priority option in the B2C division is not being taken forward.)

Revised option	6 Ps filter	Implications[a]	Revenue impact[b]	Cost impact	P&L impact
Spin off the new product department to focus on natural, healthy and fair-traded formulations, to attract both investment in the new products and protect the image and revenues of current products	Segments[c]	1. Create new market segment for new formulation 2. Educate current segment customers about the new formulations 3. Emphasise more healthy qualities of the new formulations	Potential to generate 10% of all revenue in two years ($25m), and keep growing		

Process 3.1 **Options informed by marketing mix and organisational considerations**

Revised option	6 Ps filter	Implications	Revenue impact	Cost impact	P&L impact
	Product	1. New product range of healthy snacks 2. Fair trade opportunities cause higher costs in the short term, but should lead to higher or more sustainable revenues in the middle-term	Short-, low-, medium- or long-term high. Protects $250m revenues in long term.	$5m estimate	
	Price				
	Place	1. New market needs new distribution channels, to begin to build new brand		$2.5m initially	
	Promotion	1. Current value of Advent brand threatened by emerging consumer trends 2. Need to develop trusted image with consumers 3. Healthy diet and anti-obesity messages protect/build brand reputation 4. Ongoing campaign to effect incremental change in attitudes of consumers 5. Build reputation for investors, etc 6. Protect core asset of Advent's brand reputation in a changing world	ultimately should protect the majority of Advent revenues. Protects value of Advent brand as balance sheet item	Targeted $5m PR spend, gradually replacing all PR spend	

Process 3.1 **Options informed by marketing mix and organisational considerations**

Revised option	6 Ps filter	Implications	Revenue impact	Cost impact	P&L impact
	Process	1. Need new marketing processes to give better intelligence on new consumer concerns 2. Need new product development processes for more responsive product formulations		$1m on process development, with follow-on costs	
	People (organisation)	Needs new supplier relationships and ability to manage and monitor fair trade relationships		Some increase in staff costs. Increase in travel spend	
- Part-time and flexitime working allows longer hours and more effective usage of capital - More flexible working improving staff quality, performance and company reputation	Segments	1. Basis for influencing Advent's distribution channels' access to new market for use of 'grey groovers' 2. Gives Advent access to 24/7 retailers by providing 24/7 delivery capability	Low impact		

Process 3.1 **Options informed by marketing mix and organisational considerations**

Revised option	6 Ps filter	Implications	Revenue impact	Cost impact	P&L impact
	Products	New packaging for older customers		$5m	
	Price	Price premium or price discount?			
	Promotion	Promote Advent as a good employer of a more age diverse workforce	Some but low impact		
	Process	- Training required in new working patterns - Training required in new handling equipment			Potential for improved margins
	Organisation	- Employing older staff - Policies, terms and conditions supportive of older workforce - New supervisor methods and standards	Protects $25m revenues at risk because of staff shortages	Reduced cost of staff shortages, saving $2m in staff	

a These are the main impacts of the revised options on segments and the 6 Ps. This allows consideration of whether and how these main marketing factors are changed by the CSR issues analysed to date.

b This should be completed in terms of the type of financial impact and an estimate of the size of the impact. Main financial factors will include revenue and costs, with values shown as increasing or decreasing. The size of impact should be estimated in round terms.

c The segments here are those analysed in overall segment attractiveness. All that is required here is a reasonably acceptable label for each segment. The challenge is not to fall back into only thinking about the 'current' status of market, marketing mix, organisation.

▶ Step 3, Process 3.2: final filters on options

Facilitator: Right, let's move straight on to Process 3.2.

Facilitator [to Assistant]: Transfer the options across . . . thanks.

Facilitator: We now need to map the two options against business drivers and current business goals. You need to consider the following questions [*displays the questions on the screen*].

- Do the options being considered align with the drivers that are dominant in your business - or do they potentially cut across them?

- Will they help Advent to meet its business goals?

- Will Advent's business goals need refining?

Facilitator: You'll see on the empty form that, as before, we've got a checklist to work to [*sends list to screen*].

- Market growth

- Cutting costs

- Innovation

- Human resource development

- Reputation

- Relationships and alliances

- Risks

Marketing Director: I've been listening to talk about adding a price premium for different packaging and because it's more 'natural' and fair-trade produce and so on, but what you've got to understand is that the household spend on food is putting pressure on us to reduce costs to maintain our margins.

Corporate Affairs Director: That doesn't seem to agree with what we're seeing in the growing markets for organic and fair-trade food. For the most part, they are carrying a price premium and there's a significant market segment that is willing to pay extra . . .

Finance Director: I think we're going to have to look at premium pricing, certainly in the short term.

Corporate Affairs Director: On the plus side, we're going to strengthen our reputation.

Marketing Director: Yes, I think we need to align ourselves with the consumer trends we're seeing — towards environmentally friendly, ethical, healthy and fair-trade products.

Personnel Director: I'm concerned about the possibility mentioned earlier that we might move to part-time working, at least in the short term. I'm not sure whether we've got a sufficient pool of labour.

Finance Director: We don't know yet what kind of support we can expect from our partners and suppliers — they may not be willing to share the investment.

Sales Director: We're talking about an entirely new way of working. Just what are our business objectives?

Corporate Affairs Manager: Yes, if we go ahead with either of these options we may need to revise our existing business objectives.

Production Director: Can we get on to the 'how' of the options now?

Sales Director: Yes . . .

Facilitator: I don't know about anyone else, but I'm ready for lunch. Shall we . . . ?

Process 3.2 **Making the business-case options: final filters**

Outline financials for the optional business strategies alone do not make a business case. These options need also to be assessed by considering the impact of and on the firm's typical business drivers and goals, and whether they are in line with current stated business objectives.

Revised options (C/F)	Filter by business drivers, business goals[a]	Revised business objectives	New CSO ranking[b]	Explanation
Spin off the new product department for natural, healthy and fair trade formulations to attract investment in the new products and protect the image and revenues of current products			1	The case is stronger and the relative priority remains the same because of the potential long-term benefits for Advent
	Market growth			
	– A growing number of customers looking for healthier snacks – The market for fair trade products is growing among consumers in developed countries	– Increase planned revenues to B2C market by 5% for each year after the new product line launches – Increase B2C planned revenues by 10% at the end of the 3 year business plan		
	Cutting costs			
	Reduction of household spend on food puts pressure on producers to reduce costs to maintain margins. The move to higher-cost food components runs against this trend.	Look to create a premium price brand to offset (short-term) higher input costs		

Process 3.2 **Making the business-case options: final filters**

Revised options (C/F)	Filter by business drivers, business goals	Revised business objectives	New CSO ranking	Explanation
	Innovation			
	HR development			
	Reputation	Supports then enhances Advent brand		
	Relationships/alliances			
	Risks			
	What were thought to be CSOs turn out not to be commercially viable	– Link new department's performance to explicit tracks of CSR rate of impact – Allow for six-monthly variation of budgets, up or down		– Need to motivate new team by achievable targets – Need to match investment in line with progress achieved
Part-time and flexitime working allows longer hours and more effective usage of capital. More flexible working improving staff quality, performance and company reputation			2	The internal benefits and cost and revenue arguments strengthened, but this option still does not rate higher than the option of developing new products
	Market growth Growth of 24/7 markets requires 24/7 operations to support the supply chain	Identify new B2B customers in 24/7 markets		

Process 3.2 **Making the business-case options: final filters**

Revised options (C/F)	Filter by business drivers, business goals	Revised business objectives	New CSO ranking	Explanation
	Cutting costs			
	Reduction of household spend on food puts pressure on reducing costs to maintain margins. Working capital plant harder by moving to a 24/7 schedule can reduce unit costs			
	Innovation			
	Innovation in employment practices			
	HR development			
	Improving staff skill levels, providing more support for flexitime working in line with a CSR agenda			
	Reputation			
	Utilising older workforce, good for local reputation			
	Relationships/alliances			

Revised options (C/F)	Filter by business drivers, business goals	Revised business objectives	New CSO ranking	Explanation
	Risks			
	New type of staff not available	Research job market before committing to large investments		
	Business partners and suppliers refuse to share investments	Increase dependency on investors		

a   The organisation should decide what are the relevant drivers and business goals in their circumstance — some examples are given in Part I, Step 3. The following list might be useful as a prompt: Market growth; Cutting costs; Innovation; HR development; Reputation; Relationship/alliances.

b   This calls for the updating of any earlier ranking of segments, resulting from this review of the revenue and cost factors. The ranking should not just be on the basis of revenues or even profits. It may be that a small segment in the short term is highly ranked because it has a long-term impact on the organisation's larger segments, or indeed on its whole sphere of activities.

C/F = carried forward

1:55 pm . . .

▶ Lunch break

Chairman: Shall we agree on a 20 minute break?

[*All agree.*]

Facilitator [*aside to Assistant*]: [*Name of Assistant*], while they're taking a break, shall we get the information up to date?

Facilitator's Assistant: I was worried they'd want to work through the break.

Facilitator: It will do them more good to have something to eat and to take a rest. They were just moving on naturally to the next step, but I didn't want to mention it to them — it may have distracted them from their need for a break.

Facilitator's Assistant: If they keep to a 20 minute lunch break we may only just have time to tidy up the forms filled in so far.

Facilitator: Have you ever known a lunch break to take much less than an hour?

Step 4 in action
Committing to action

▶ **Setting the scene**

The team drifts back into the conference room some 45 minutes later; everyone is ready for the afternoon session.

2:40 pm . . .

▶ **Step 4, Process 4.1: evaluation of the impact of current value sets against new options**

Facilitator: I hope you've all had a good break. Before the break one or two of you were ready to move on to the 'how' of corporate social opportunity. This is where it starts! Step 4 is about committing to action! First, we need to match the new options against the values set of Advent Foods.

Production Director: I'm wondering how we are going to build relationships with fair-trade suppliers who also grow produce using up-to-date 'natural' farming methods, bearing in mind these are perhaps going to be farming collectives rather than commercial farms.

Sales Director: Advent is known for being a very tough negotiator with suppliers — it has stood the company in good stead for many years. Are we supposed to change that?

Production Director: if we're going to pursue the idea of this new natural and fair-trade formulation of Snackotreat the new product department is going to require a new team, working in a new market.

Personnel Director: Yes, it's going to ask for a more entrepreneurial management style.

Corporate Affairs Director: We're going to be dealing with low volumes and low income in the start-up phase.

Chairman: We'll need some expertise in forging relationships with new types of suppliers in the fair-trade world, not to mention suppliers who know something about organic farming or progressive 'natural' farming methods.

Production Director: And what about the other option we're considering?

Sales Director: I think we're looking for a 24/7 working regime.

Personnel Director: Is that going to fit in with the idea of recruiting an older and more skilled workforce?

Facilitator: We seem to have a lot to work with there. How do you think these are going to impact the set of values for Advent, not only for the company as a whole but also for you as members of the board?.

Production Director: Like [*Name of Sales Director*] says, I pride myself on my reputation for being a tough negotiator with suppliers. I've tried to keep a tight rein on cost as well.

Chairman: I think we've a potential conflict between new fair-trade relationships and previous tough negotiating practices; does everyone agree?

[*All agree.*]

Chairman: We're going to have to learn how to work with nascent supplier organisations in parts of the world where we've no experience at all — but how?

Sales Director: How is this new spin-off department going to be received in the company? We're saying it is of utmost importance to our future strategy . . .

CEO: That's pretty important . . .

Sales Director: Yes, but that's going to go against the grain with the way our staff rate importance. They think 'Big budgets mean big clout', but this new department just isn't going to have that kind of financial clout at the beginning.

Personnel Director: We're going to have to find ways to overcome those kinds of preconceptions.

Corporate Affairs Director: Everyone is going to have to realise that budget size is no longer going to be related directly to strategic importance . . .

CEO: What about all the effort we have put into being seen as a young-minded company? This idea of employing older staff could make us a laughing stock . . .

Corporate Affairs Director: It needn't work that way, and part-time and flexible working are actually seen as being family-friendly and the future . . .

Production Director: I'm not sure how the staff will react to being expected to work anti-social hours. Our staff, especially our current older staff, see us as being very much a 'nine to five' sort of organisation.

Personnel Director: I'm not so sure about that. Some of our older staff mentioned they'd like to 'wind down' nearer their retirement so that they can start adapting to their new retired lifestyle and spend more time with their grandchildren — many of them are providing childcare for their children's children . . .

Production Director: A common reason I'm given for absenteeism is because of family commitments . . . I suppose these changes would give employees more flexibility over their social lives and time with their families . . .

Personnel Director: We're going to need a lot of time to work this through, especially sorting out balanced flexitime for round-the-clock operations. If we don't get it right it has the potential to wreck some of our employees' social lives.

Corporate Affairs Director: I think we all recognise the need for us as a group to walk the talk and show a respect for a healthy work–life balance.

[*There are signs of grudging agreement.*]

Marketing Director: I remember [*Name of a non-executive director, not present*] telling me about the time he worked for a sports goods company, and they had some big trouble over working conditions in their overseas markets.

Finance Director: Didn't they come under attack from the media, NGOs, politicians . . . the lot? And all because of some of their supplier's dodgy employment practices?

Marketing Director: That's the one. [*Name of a non-executive director, not present*] said the real tipping point was when employees' children started getting ragged at school because their mum or dad worked for [*Name of company*] — He said it lit a fire under the board of directors as they hadn't thought they were running a 'bad company'. As far as they were concerned, they had always prided themselves on their ethical dealings in everything they did. It offended their sense of the unspoken values of the company.

Sales Director: And the moral of the story is . . . ?

Marketing Director: That we don't want to end up in a similar situation.

Corporate Affairs Manager: Well, we certainly don't want our employees demoralised because they are pilloried for working for us . . .

CEO: Why on earth would that happen?

Corporate Affairs Director: If we were seen as an immoral food company that doesn't care about what customers eat or about the health consequences. [*She quotes some recent polling data about consumer attitudes to food manufacturers.*][1]

Facilitator: I think we've some genuine contributions and observations there, but I want to keep the momentum going as we are doing so well. Remember that any process that involves upheaval is going to be uncomfortable, but we don't need to dwell on that right now.

The facilitator realises that this first step after lunch is making the group uncomfortable. It is not going as smoothly as previous processes. Senior and experienced managers are being asked how they *feel* about issues that they would be tempted to label 'soft' — namely, Advent's values set. He is happy to leave this part of the analysis as some insights have been gained and noted.

Facilitator: Right, the options are still as they were before: the creation of a new product line and a move to more flexible working. [*Name of Facilitator's Assistant*], can you note the comments for our next step?

---

1   A Guardian/ICM poll revealed that 82% of Britons want food advertisements aimed at children to be banned, and 79% think that food manufacturers are irresponsible. The telephone survey of 1,006 adults, which marked the launch of a major investigation by *The Guardian* into the food Britons eat, found that 45% of respondents were worried or very worried about how healthy their food is (*The Guardian*, 11 May 2003).

Process 4.1 Values-set impact on options

Do any of the proposed options clash or undermine value sets or leadership styles to such extent that they should be dismissed or at least revised accordingly? Or, equally, do those values and leadership styles themselves require revision in light of changed circumstances? It might take so long to be able to change value sets that this changes the ranking of options.

Process 4.1 **Values-set impact on options**

Revised options	Our value set	How we feel about this	New corporate social opportunity ranking[a]
Spin off the new product department for natural, healthy and fair trade formulations to attract investment in the new products and protect the image and revenues of current products	Strong cost controls typified by tough negotiations with suppliers	Need to find a way of reconciling new international fair trade values with local efficiency drives	Remains 1, but needs new leadership to manage new values
	Stability of the organisation preferred over reorganisation	Worried about destabilising the organisation	
	Senior executive views that size of the organisation indicates power and importance may stifle spin-off initiative	Board need to recognise commitment to the spin-off as important to Advent's strategy	
	The increase in snacking was previously seen as a lifestyle choice	Need to avoid the new product line damaging the current business	
– Part-time and flexitime working allows longer hours and more effective usage of capital	Young-minded company	Don't want to be surrounded by older workers	Remains 2, but needs careful line management; attitude changes will be needed
– More flexible working improving staff quality, performance and company reputation	9 to 5 mind-set, allowing time for social life and families, especially for younger staff	Will need time to build recognition that balanced flexitime can give value at work and preserve family life. Biggest problem will be among remaining full-time staff.	

a This calls for the updating of any earlier ranking of revised options, in this case based on an assessment of the impact on the value sets of the organisation.

▶ Step 4, Process 4.2: leadership requirements

The group look at the blank forms with which they were provided before they started the workshop.

Facilitator: You have already been raising points that show you are aware that these options need new types of leadership and some careful changes to the attitudes of line management, as well as new skills in different parts of the organisation, from purchasing, to marketing to production. There are three main items to consider now [*sends list to screen*].

- Implied leadership roles and values

- Implied governance and structures

- Required signals

Personnel Director: If we are going to employ an older and more skilled work-force, then management must recognise the experience of those members of staff despite the fact they may be doing routine and perhaps mundane jobs.

Production Director: Is there going to be a problem with younger managers feeling subordinate to their more experienced and older staff?

Sales Director: We can't have a blurring of roles and accountabilities — we've got factories and warehouses to run.

Marketing Director: We won't have to be so hierarchical. We will have to find ways of involving the experiences of the older workers more widely across the business, not just for their immediate jobs.

Personnel Director: We've got the union active at the moment on the pensions problem. That is something we need to look at urgently at our next regular board meeting. In terms of the options we're talking about here, I think an older workforce is almost certainly going to require even stronger representation on pensions.

Production Director: If [*Name of Sales Director*]'s contacts lead us to supplying our products on a round-the-clock basis then I can see we'll have to provide some sort of in-house support for our business customers within our current governance and structures . . .

Corporate Affairs Director: We may need to look at providing other support as well — what about a 24 hour customer help-line?

Chairman: It seems to me that if we do this properly — if we can do this properly — then flexible working practices may actually deliver higher productivity.

Marketing Director: Yes, but we must deliver — and be *seen* to deliver — a good work–life balance to our employees. And we have to value — and be *seen* to value — the comments and advice of the more mature staff we employ.

Corporate Affairs Director: We aren't the first company to recognise the potential of recruiting older employees . . .

Marketing Director: Or to design and market products to that age-group . . .

Corporate Affairs Director: Has anyone any links with companies that have gone down that road? Would they be willing to share some of their insights with us?

Marketing Director: [*Name of former colleague*] at [*Name of leisure-sector company*] would be happy to come into a conference with us . . .

Facilitator: Are you managing to get all this down? [*Looks at Assistant.*]

Facilitator's Assistant: Yes, I'm just putting the finishing touches to the form.

Process 4.2 **Leadership requirements**

It is dangerous to assume that the response to new business opportunities should naturally be driven by the leadership of current businesses, or in the same leadership style. Leaders and leadership style should be derived from the nature of the new business opportunity itself. Sometimes different leadership styles may need to run alongside existing styles.

Process 4.2 **Leadership requirements**

Attributes of new business opportunity[a]	Implied leadership role and values[b]	Implied governance and structures[c]	Required signals[d]
Spin off the new product department for natural, healthy and fair trade formulations to attract investment in the new products and protect the image and revenues of current products			
Attributes			
New team in new market for Advent	– Main board needs to show support to fledgling business – Board to provide mentoring for new team members	Pay and status schemes need to be de-coupled from current revenues, to attract high fliers to potential new opportunities	– Equal air-time for the spin-off business in in-house publications would show the importance of the new product lines – 'In-house tours' for established staff to the new spin-off showing the markets of the future – Healthy eating in-house by management
Entrepreneurial management style	Main board needs to be able to show different management styles – tight control for established markets, loose control for start-up	Delegated decision-making power to spin-off team.	Budget review styles must differentiate between stable and mature businesses and the new business

Process 4.2 **Leadership requirements**

Attributes of new business opportunity	Implied leadership role and values	Implied governance and structures	Required signals
Low volumes and income in start-up phase	- Board need to value the future potential more than initial volumes - Board need to share the risk with spin-off team	Financial controls need to be light, allowing fast decision-making in line with financial scale	Budget review styles must differentiate between stable and mature businesses and the new venture
New types of suppliers in fair trade world	- Greater international and ethnic sensitivity	Fair trade suppliers might request representation on the main board to validate the transparency of Advent's motives and practice	The value of fair trade needs to be communicated to stakeholders as a business opportunity not just as a cost
- Part-time and flexitime working allows longer hours and more effective usage of capital - More flexible working improving staff quality, performance and company reputation			
Attributes			
24/7 working		Supervisory and stakeholder support functions become 24/7 and networked, including to the home	- Flexitime is 'productive' - Advent supports good work–life balance
Older, more skilled workforce	Recognition should be given for experience irrespective of current job	Stronger employee representation on pensions' governance	Experienced staff given opportunities to contribute advice to the wider Advent community

Process 4.2 **Leadership requirements**

a Each of the most highly ranked business opportunities from above should be assessed. As with earlier stages in this analysis, a number of opportunities may well be put on hold for possible later consideration. Each opportunity will have core attributes of direct importance in CSO leadership terms. If the resulting business opportunities are very new to the organisation, it will require a leadership used to innovation. It may be that the business is initially small, and may have to fight for resources to be diverted from the established mainstream activities. Other attributes include the usage of new technologies; entering markets new to the organisation; meeting new or higher levels of competition; requiring different partnerships, supply chains or distribution; being more or less regulated. Each of these attributes implies leadership roles and values.

b The leadership roles and values should be thought through in the new context of the CSO-derived business opportunities. Leadership roles may include the extent to which the leader works with different communities, internal or external, new or established, market-facing or supply-chain-facing. The values to be considered are in the context both of the business opportunity and the new impacts on stakeholders. Values such as respect for new types of contacts with perhaps new types of knowledge and behaviours; the ability to tolerate uncertainly in new markets.

c The new business opportunity may bring with it new regimes of external governance or require new internal regimes and structures. Increased regulation brings new governance. Changing the behaviour of the organisation may require new supporting and validation processes, at least during a transition period. Supporting a fledgling business that holds little short-term organisational power, but which may be crucial to the future, may require organisational protection and structural support at the highest level.

d To effect changes in strategy, leaders must communicate with their internal and external constituencies. This item summarises the content of core signals necessary to communicate and maintain support for the new CSO-derived strategy, among customers in markets and among stakeholders. The analysis in Step 2, 'Scoping the issues', will inform this analysis.

Facilitator: Right. Before we move on to Step 5, let's pause for a while and reflect on where we are. First, I noticed that when we were discussing the values fit of the two new strategies not everyone seemed to be fully engaged. Is it possible that this might be because it has been a long time since you — or the company as a whole for that matter — have spent any time considering what the company values were, are or should be?

Personnel Director: Job applicants increasingly are asking questions about our company values . . .

Chairman: I think there's a tendency for us who've been in the company a long time to take the company values for granted. Perhaps we need to dust them off and raise their profile somewhat . . .

Facilitator: [*Name of Assistant*], flag this up as a priority for a future action, yes?

Facilitator's Assistant: I'll add it to the list.

Facilitator: Let's just look at the title page for Step 4 [*sends title page to screen*].

Step 4: Committing to Action

Facilitator: At some later time it will be worth your while looking at the accumulation of values, leadership and governance issues discussed. About a year ago I worked through the seven steps with another company. That company decided it should make a public commitment to being a responsible business, amend its values statement accordingly and add regular reporting on CSR issues to its audit committee. Is this something you would feel ready for?

Chairman: No, I don't think that's a route we want to go down at the moment. We'll revisit the idea . . .

Corporate Affairs Director: We *could* benefit from addressing CSR issues at the corporate level. It will be more efficient than expecting individual parts of the business to grapple with them. But let's pick it up at another time.

Facilitator: Let's press on then to Step 5.

Step 5 in action
Integration and gathering resources

▶ Setting the scene

Facilitator: Step 5 is about integrating strategies.

Production Director: Strategy — that's when I don't have to do something today because there's no deadline.

Facilitator: The strategies we're going to be looking at are about shifting resources around in order to enable you to seize the opportunities that you now see before you. This morning you probably felt that today was a bit of an infringement on your Sunday free time. Equally, at 9 o'clock this morning you probably knew that 'corporate' and 'social' went with the word 'risk'. But, now, on this Sunday afternoon you have replaced the R of 'risk' with the O of 'opportunity'. You are now well on your way to working out how you can secure Advent's future in response to the forces of global change and in a way that is emerging as demonstrably more sustainable to your wider stakeholders — not the least of which are your shareholders and investors, who I am sure, if they could be here, would be very pleased to have privileged access to the discussions on the promise of new revenues.

3:55 pm . . .

▶ Step 5, Process 5.1: matching resources to revised strategies

Facilitator: As you are familiar with them by now, we're going to be concentrating on the two potential corporate social opportunities that you identified earlier today. You are no longer searching for what your opportunities might be — you are now at the stage of gaining an understanding of how to resource them.

Chairman: The new product range requires a new 'spin-off' CEO, yes?

Finance Director: Yes. They'll need to be someone with expertise in international procurement and finance . . .

Production Director: Preferably with experience of fair-trade products, marketing, branding and the establishment of new distribution channels.

Personnel Director: That's quite a tall order, isn't it?

Production Director : I don't think it will be impossible . . .

Finance Director: We haven't really touched on the issue of labelling, yet . . .

Marketing Director: We were talking at our July meeting about the implications of the new labelling laws. It's being tightened up — not just in the UK but in the US, Canada and Europe.

Personnel Director: That was the business of food allergies, wasn't it?

Marketing Director: That's the one. Apparently, in the US there are over seven million people who suffer from food allergies, including two million children.[1]

Production Director: What can we say about resources for the second option . . . opportunity . . . for recruiting older staff?

Personnel Director: We'll need management capable of managing and sensitive to older and more experienced staff.

Production Director: We need to be able to get specifications for the new equipment; then there's procurement and training to be considered.

Finance Director: And new finance.

Facilitator: So can any of these resources be matched to current sources? Once those have been matched up you are left with the resource gaps. For those you need to consider potential sources to close those gaps.

Sales Director: The problem is, although we've plenty of expertise here and among our absent board members in our day-to-day operations — we've got experience in marketing, sales, production, administration — we just don't have anyone with experience in entrepreneurial start-ups. We haven't needed that expertise . . .

Personnel Director: There are some people in junior management who are keen to move up the company and who have the potential. We could look at fast-track promotion within our own ranks?

Sales Director: Alternatively, we could recruit someone outside the company. We'd have to be sure they would fit in with Advent, though.

Production Director: Whether junior management can fill the gap for experience in entrepreneurship I have my doubts. As for the junior factory managers, I'm even less convinced they will cope with managing older and more experienced staff.

Personnel Director: No, our warehouse and factory management team are experienced in logistics management but not in the management of people.

---

1   For more information on allergies, see *Financial Times*, 'A Matter of Life and Death', 10 September 2003.

Corporate Affairs Director: Perhaps the solution to our problem lies in the problem itself. There's surely the possibility of recruiting mature personnel to fit the key management roles?

Later

Chairman: If we are really seriously considering investing in the natural, healthy and fair-trade formulation, then perhaps we should look in our own back yard at how our own practices encourage or discourage a healthy lifestyle among employees. Take the staff canteen — do we offer enough healthy options to go with the more traditional fare?

Corporate Affairs Director: How about encouraging employees to come to work by bike rather than by car — perhaps we could discuss with the local authorities the possibility of opening up cycle lanes near our plants?

Marketing Director: I've been playing golf with the CEO of a friend of mine. Anyway, he mentioned that his company is campaigning with several other companies to improve the health of their workers. It costs employers in the US$12 billion a year in medical bills, reduced productivity, increased absenteeism and higher health and disability insurance premiums.[2]

Corporate Affairs Director: Perhaps we could get our people in the US to look into this?

Facilitator: This is a good time to take the *Private Eye* test: if you saw something about the company in the satirical magazine *Private Eye*, would you feel embarrassed? The point I'm making is that one of the biggest problems in practice, for businesses that are trying to align their purpose and strategy with the principles of responsible business, and then embed these through the organisation, is inconsistency. Let's put it like this: You work hard to get all your ducks in a row — and then, wham, bang! Something is going on, somewhere in the business that is demonstrably inconsistent with these principles. At best, people inside the company are disillusioned and don't think the commitment is for real. At worst, the company gets accused of hypocrisy by NGOs, the media or regulators — sometimes all of the above!

Chairman: So it's 'heads I win, tails you lose' to the media . . .

Facilitator: You can't ever insure against inconsistency 100%; but by being alert to the dangers it is possible to minimise the risk. First, you can try to identify ahead of time where there might be the biggest dangers of failing the *Private Eye* test. Second, you can build up trust and goodwill with different stakeholders, so that they will be more inclined to give you the benefit of the doubt — and the crucial time and space to rectify inconsistencies when they occur. And, third, you can react fast and decisively to tackle inconsistencies when they do surface.

2   Data from The Institute on the Costs and Health Effects of Obesity, Washington Health Group, USA.

Corporate Affairs Director: I can think of several areas where we need to pay more attention: we've taken no action to review the formulations of current products, despite my having raised the issue at one meeting after another; we give the impression of being indifferent to the conditions under which raw materials for our existing products are produced; and we have done nothing to change the advertising of our current products to reflect the need for a balanced diet and exercise.

Facilitator: Let's take a quick break here for a cup of tea.

Finance Director: I can recognise the value of what we are doing today, but I'm very concerned by the number of issues and problems we are glossing over or ignoring.

Facilitator: This is always a problem with one-day sessions like these, but the important thing today is to get the ideas out in the open.

Finance Director: Yes, but some of these 'wonderful ideas' are superficial and are not going to stand up to rigorous analysis. This is low-quality work — we're trying to cover too much ground in too short a time.

Facilitator: I agree we have glossed over many issues, but we have captured important insights in your industry. The purpose of today is to steer the company in a new, more profitable and sustainable direction. You will be able to use some of the new insights and ideas as a basis for potential immediate action. Later, after your specialist teams in the company have refined the analyses you will have yet more options for action. The work you are doing today will set the basis for you to involve your stakeholders to build the complete strategy.

Finance Director: We'll see . . .

▶ Tea break

Process 5.1 Matching resources to revised strategies

Each ranked business opportunity should be analysed more closely to see how it can be resourced. Resources may come from stretching existing resource and standard processes, or may have to have the addition of new types and quality of resource from new sources.

Business opportunity[a]	Current sources and matches[b]	Resource gaps[c]	Potential sources[d]
Spin off the new product department for natural, healthy and fair trade formulations to attract investment in the new products and protect the image and revenues of current products			
Resource requirement[e]			
Better information on CSR issues and trends	Conventional competitor and market tracking data	Lack of early intelligence on emerging CSR and related consumer factors	– Corporate Affairs to set up active links to CSR websites, and circulate digests – Marketing department to prepare CSR/CSO tracking function

Process 5.1 **Matching resources to revised strategies**

Business opportunity	Current sources and matches	Resource gaps	Potential sources
New CEO for the spun-off business	Senior executive team experienced in established company operations	Current executive team not experienced with entrepreneurial start-ups	- More junior management identified for fast track promotion, with accelerated executive training - External recruitment, with intensive induction - Advent CEO to join DTI working groups on CSR/CSO and seek advice on potential recruits and sources - From headhunters
Expertise in international procurement	Current purchasing team have strong relationships with developed world suppliers and purchasing discipline experience	- Current purchasing team inexperienced with sourcing from small suppliers in less-developed countries	- Form partnership with relevant NGO to advise current purchasing team - Find third-party sourcing organisation - Headhunters do search on relevant NGOs for candidates with fair trade experience - Consider joining Ethical Trading Initiative
Finance for investments	Current capital and revenue budgets are fully stretched	Possible requirement for $10m to $20m over short to medium term	- The bulk from investors who could be persuaded that the initiative is both protecting current values and investing in future - Some government incentives available for Fair Trade initiatives - Some costs could be shared by existing suppliers and distributors

Process 5.1 **Matching resources to revised strategies**

Business opportunity	Current sources and matches	Resource gaps	Potential sources
More sophisticated product-labelling expertise	Current marketing and legal know-how is based on mandatory labelling requirements only	Advent need to develop a greater understanding of a whole range of labelling – from more sophisticated allergy warnings to fair trade branding	– Suppliers or key staff in world-famous fair trade cosmetics and personal care products retailer – Get Advent TQM team to address labelling requirements from CSO perspective
The need to get all of Advent Foods' stakeholders on board and in tune with the new product line	Current stakeholders have years of experience in working to the 'old' Advent way	– Risk of routine behaviours by groups such as supplier management, obstructing the new product line – Lack of regular dialogue with some stakeholders	– use of cascaded workshops such as the Advent Sunday Directors' event to gain more insights, and build skills, consensus and support – Company-wide communications programmes – Consider a bespoke CSR course – Consider a CSO session in all staff courses
Marketing and product development capacity aligned to new 'aware consumer' trends	Marketing and product development based on appealing to traditional markets	Lack of skills in predicting consumer trends and in rapid development of new formulations and packaging	– Faster moving sectors such as fashion – Consumer-protection bodies – Establish formal links or membership of an appropriate CSR business group – Contact CSR-aware companies for their advice/contacts

Process 5.1 **Matching resources to revised strategies**

Business opportunity	Current sources and matches	Resource gaps	Potential sources
Part-time and flexitime working allows longer hours and more effective usage of capital. More flexible working improving staff quality, performance and company reputation			
Resource requirement			
Capability to manage older, more experienced staff	Warehouse and factory management experienced in logistics management	– Need to move from young unskilled to mature and skilled – Need for better management skills	From same population as target recruits
Capability to specify, procure and manage sophisticated handling equipment	Manufacturing staff have this capability	Logistics staff are only used to labour-intensive, low-tech operations	Manufacturing staff could be seconded to logistics operation
Finance for new equipment	Capital budget does not include this type of spend	$10m to $20m	– Investors – Government incentives and grants – Target ethical investor funds

Process 5.1 **Matching resources to revised strategies**

Business opportunity	Current sources and matches	Resource gaps	Potential sources
The need to get all of Advent Foods' stakeholders on board and in tune with the flexible employment strategy	Current stakeholders have years of experience in working to the 'old' Advent way	Risk of routine behaviours, such as those of supervisors obstructing the new option	– Use of cascaded workshops such as the Advent Sunday Directors' event to gain more insights, and build skills and consensus – Company-wide communications programmes – Consider bespoke CSR course – Consider CSO session in all staff courses
Need to align all employment practices around CSO	Human resources policies based on conventional good practice	Lack of awareness of emerging CSR employment practices	– Personnel Director to join relevant DTI, NGO or business working parties, to share information and best practice – Contact Business in the Community, IBLF or the ILO
Partly align staff reward schemes around implementation of CSO initiatives	Current senior executive schemes are based on P&L performance against targets only	Bonus schemes do not encourage time spent on new activities	Check via employers' groups for any good examples of CSR-linked incentive/reward schemes

a   This is done for each of the highest-ranked business opportunities still being carried through for analysis.

b   For each of the key resource requirements, derived from the CSO impact on the business opportunity, note the current sources of resource and how they match the new situation. The current resources may be within or external to the organisation.

c   It is likely that changes in the business opportunity with its CSO implications create gaps between the required and the current resources. The gaps may be in the type, quantity, quality and availability of resource.

d   The strategy cannot be delivered if it cannot be resourced. This column summarises where new resources may come from, including from other parts of the organisation. It may be that current resources may be diverted to meet new requirements. Such resources may include finance, training or recruitment.

e   The main resource types for each business opportunity are summarised here.

Step 6 in action
Engaging stakeholders

5:00 pm...

▶ Step 6, Processes 6.1: engaging stakeholders — necessary roles

Facilitator: Now we're refreshed it's time to address Step 6: engaging stakeholders. This step is supported by two processes: Process 6.1, on stakeholder roles and their own desired roles *vis-à-vis* the business, and Process 6.2, on necessary actions. We're going to look at the following stakeholders [*sends list to screen*].

- Customers
- Staff
- Investors
- Local communities
- Partners
- Suppliers
- Distribution channels
- Opinion-forming groups
- Government
- Intergovernmental agencies
- NGOs
- Influencers (media, etc.)

Facilitator: In summarising the impact of the new business opportunities on your stakeholders, you are going to identify new roles for those stakeholders.

Sales Director: I fail to see how some of these so-called stakeholders have any stake in our company at all . . .

Finance Director: As far as I'm concerned, suppliers are simply a group that we negotiate with — toughly — fair-trade or otherwise.

Facilitator: Let's just start looking at these stakeholders, one by one.

Corporate Affairs Director: I wonder whether we might benefit from entering into some long-term international supply partnerships . . .

Finance Director: There would be an opportunity there to attract shared investment in new infrastructure . . .

Corporate Affairs Director: Perhaps government development agencies and intergovernmental agencies are potential partners? They may be able to help us seek out new sources of supply.

Marketing Director: They may help with identifying potential suppliers. If we are going to get fair-trade certification we need to be able to verify that. There are NGOs who would do regular audits for us, I think.

Corporate Affairs Director: You're right. When I was studying for my MBA we learnt about the Ethical Trading Initiative. There are quite a few major UK companies among its membership. Some of them do, in fact, use NGOs for supply-chain verification. If we joined the Initiative we could learn from the examples of those companies?

Facilitator: [*Name of Assistant*], record the suggestion.

Chairman: It seems to me we may have to rethink who our stakeholders are, who are the most important to our future and how we should or should not be engaging with them to go forward together.

[*Nods of agreement.*]

Finance Director: Can we look at the new workforce option? We've mentioned that our current younger staff will increasingly be working alongside more mature colleagues . . .

Personnel Director: I think there's terrific potential in that kind of environment for the mature colleagues to encourage greater learning — even perhaps to mentor the younger members of staff.

Process 6.1 Engaging stakeholders (stakeholder roles)

Responding to new CSO-derived business opportunities requires fully engaging stakeholders and securing their support for the new opportunities. It is important to identify the roles and understandings stakeholders should have in order to drive the initiative forward. The impact information is derived from Step 2, 'Scoping the issues'.

Business opportunity[a]	Impact on new and current stakeholders[b]	Desired stakeholder roles[c]
Spin off the new product department for natural, healthy and fair trade formulations to attract investment and protect image and revenues of current products	**Customers**	
	Increasing dissatisfaction on current mass commodity buying in unfair trade	- Opportunities to become more responsible buyers and consumers - Turn activist customers into promoters of Advent's strategy
	Increasing parental concerns over the growth of obesity levels and possible connections to snack foods	Include parents and schools in communicating the messages about healthier snacks
	Staff	
	Sense of belonging to a new, pioneering operation	- Enthusiastic, contributing ideas to improve operations - Ambassadors for the new approach in their communities
	Investors	
	Growing concern over viability of their investment in Advent in the long term	- Opportunity (requirement) to invest in new start-up to secure long-term viability of the company - Places for new type of investors on the board of Advent

Process 6.1 **Engaging stakeholders (stakeholder roles)**

Business opportunity	Impact on new and current stakeholders	Desired stakeholder roles
	Local communities	
	– Removes emerging resistance to Advent sponsorship of food donations	Goodwill towards Advent for initiative
	– Local church groups support shift of some sourcing to less developed countries	
	Business partners	
		Shared investment
	Suppliers	
	Existing: loss of some future supply contracts to Advent	– Agree to change some growing practices and workplace practices to meet new specifications
		– Shared investments in new supply infrastructure
	New: new business opportunity	To meet new specifications
	Distribution channels	
	Threat of loss of some markets	See opportunity of access to emerging fair trade market
	Opinion-forming groups	
	Need evidence of positive moves to motivate other organisations	Promotion of Advent initiative
	Brand editors' need to understand and support the new Advent approach	Brand editors' to use Advent Foods as a good example of a changed company
	Government	
	Inter-government agencies	
	Advent currently unknown to them	Potential financial contributors and providers of technical support

Process 6.1 **Engaging stakeholders (stakeholder roles)**

Business opportunity	Impact on new and current stakeholders	Desired stakeholder roles
	NGOs	
	Campaigning NGOs will be monitoring Advent's move into natural, healthy and fair trade formulations to see if it is just PR	Enlist NGOs to help identify potential suppliers in less developed countries, help to identify good practice and potentially verify performance.
	Influencers (media, etc.)	
	Increasingly informed consumers interested in fair trade stories	Good-news stories on Advent's new products
Part-time and flexitime working allows longer hours usage of capital More flexible working improving staff quality, performance and company reputation	**Customers**	
	Staff	
	Current younger staff working alongside more mature staff	– Youngsters need to adapt to working alongside older workers – More discipline and respectful environment – Older workers potentially to mentor younger workers
	Investors	
		Providers of additional investment
	Local communities	
	Creates new jobs for locals	Spread message of Advent as employer looking for more mature staff

Process 6.1 **Engaging stakeholders (stakeholder roles)**

Business opportunity	Impact on new and current stakeholders	Desired stakeholder roles
	Business partners	
		Share some new equipment investment for access to cost savings and more dependable deliveries
	Suppliers	
		Share some new equipment investment for access to cost savings and more dependable deliveries
	Distribution channels	
	Demand from Advent for 24/7 service	*Provide Advent access to growing 24/7 customers*
	Opinion-forming groups	
		Communicate Advent's new employment strategy
	Government	
	Positive demonstration of commitment to voluntary push for less age discrimination in the workforce	*Provide some investment and employment incentives*
	Inter-government agencies	
	NGOs	
	Provides good case study for 'Age Concern' and ARP NGOs	*Commendation of Advent for employment practices*
	Influencers (media, etc.)	
		Good-news stories on Advent's new employment strategy

a The opportunity from the previous stage.

b The impact of the highly ranked strategy options are reviewed from the perspective of each type of stakeholder. The impact on each stakeholder is listed under each of the identified stakeholders. The information comes from the earlier Step 2, 'Scoping the issues'. As with many of the stages, the consideration of the newly required stakeholder roles and understandings may throw new insights into how they are impacted, which in turn may require updating the information on Step 2.

c Here is summarised the individual roles each stakeholder should or could play, and the required understanding of the issues and the roles they must have. It is important to think of stakeholders as partners in the new business opportunity, not pawns!

▶ Step 6, Process 6.2: engaging stakeholders — necessary actions

Facilitator: We're now aiming to turn intentions into actions.

Stakeholders won't play the desired roles without appropriate communication, dialogue and incentives. And some of the stakeholders themselves may wish to play different roles. You have to be prepared to modify your own positions in the light of stakeholder dialogue. It cannot just be a one-way street.

Personnel Director: I think we should involve staff in contributing ideas for the new product markets.

Marketing Director: [*Name of former colleague, at leisure-sector company*] mentioned the use of management cascading and team briefing. He said it was important for us to listen, not just to 'broadcast'. His words were: 'Be on receive as well as transmit mode'.

Corporate Affairs Director: Have you been to any of the recruitment roadshows [*Company name*] run each year? Perhaps we can do something similar for investors, to keep them more informed and to bring the investment in? Perhaps even the analyst who made the comment about obesity might be interested. Perhaps we could get her involved, even, as she's always 'on the ball'?

Marketing Director: What about 'brand editors'? Groups such as Friends of the Earth, the media, socially responsible investors and so on. They gather large quantities of information on complicated issues and boil them down into simple messages or league tables about brands — and customers respond to these. If we can communicate to them the good things we are doing with our products we might get some positive coverage or at least send the message that we are making a genuine effort to change our way of doing things.[1]

Facilitator: I think we've achieved some significant breakthroughs in this session. For the final hour I suggest we move on to concentrate on Step 7, 'Measuring and reporting'.

---

1   On brand editors, see *Financial Times*, 'M&S checks out a healthier shopping list', 4 December 2003.

Process 6.2 Engaging stakeholders (actions to achieve desired roles)

The long-term commitment of stakeholders to new business opportunities depends on a real understanding on their part. This requires effective and consistent engagement, dialogue and communication by the company and its leaders.

Stakeholders[a]	Desired stakeholder roles and understandings (C/F)[b]	Actions to achieve[c]
Spin off the new product department for natural, healthy and fair trade formulations to attract investment and protect image and revenues of current products		
Customers	Opportunities to become more responsible buyers and consumers	Marketing campaign to promote impact of CSR-friendly, fair trade products
	Include parents and schools in communicating the messages of healthier snacks	
Staff	– Enthusiastic; contributing ideas to improve operations – Ambassadors for the new approach in their communities	– Recruitment advertising sells Advent as a responsible company – Add CSR elements to induction – Staff publications feature new products and background stories – Management cascading, team briefing, management education stresses CSR issues – Create employee volunteering opportunities in new fair trade suppliers' communities in less developed countries
Investors	Opportunity to invest in responsible new start-up	Promotion of the Advent new product strategy at investor roadshows

Stakeholders	Desired stakeholder roles and understandings (C/F)	Actions to achieve
Local communities	Goodwill towards Advent for initiative	Support 'twinning' of operating communities with new supplier local communities in less developed countries
Business partners		
Suppliers	Existing: – Agree to change some growing practices and workplace practices to meet new specifications – Shared investments in new supply infrastructure New: – Meet specification	Provide capacity-building incentives and support for existing suppliers to transfer some growing and production to new formulation – training, international trips to other producers, etc Research potential new suppliers – partner with NGOs and collective action projects
Distribution channels	See opportunity of access to emerging fair trade consumption market	Present business case arguments and examples; take current distributors on international trips
Opinion-forming groups	Promotion of Advent initiative	Share information in appropriate formats, secure third-party endorsements and independent verification reports
Government		
Inter-government agencies	Potential financial contributors and providers of technical support	Research and network with business intermediaries who have links with multilateral development agencies – invest jointly in local enterprise development schemes and micro-enterprise projects in developing country suppliers
NGOs	Enlist NGOs to help identify potential suppliers in less developed countries, help to identify good practice and potentially verify performance	Open dialogue with key NGOs; consider using business intermediary to facilitate Involve NGOs in finding suppliers, transferring expertise
Influencers (media, etc.)	Providers of good-news stories	Cultivate relationships with key journalists and update on progress

Stakeholders	Desired stakeholder roles and understandings (C/F)	Actions to achieve
Part-time and flexitime working allows longer hours usage of capital. More flexible working improving staff quality, performance and company reputation.		
Customers		
Staff	– Youngsters need to adapt to working alongside older workers – More discipline and respectful environment – Older workers potentially to mentor younger workers	– Communicate clear expectations on behaviour – Provide training where necessary – Build new teams, create mentoring scheme – Support the organisation of appropriate social events
Investors	Providers of additional investment	– Investor roadshows – Communicate benefits of strategy in briefings
Local communities	Spread message of Advent as employer looking for more mature staff	Spread message through local community groups and the company's employee local citizenships councils
Business partners	Share some new equipment investment for access to cost savings and more dependable deliveries	Present business case arguments
Suppliers	Share some new equipment investment for access to cost savings and more dependable deliveries	Present business case arguments
Distribution channels	Provide Advent access to growing 24/7 customers	Liaise with distribution network and negotiate access
Opinion-forming groups	Communicate Advent's new employment strategy	Create platforms for dialogue to share information about new practices
Government	Provide some investment and employment incentives	Research potential incentive and tax benefits; apply for grants
Inter-governmental agencies		

Process 6.2 **Engaging stakeholders (actions to achieve desired roles)**

Stakeholders	Desired stakeholder roles and understandings (C/F)	Actions to achieve
NGOs	Commendation of Advent for employment practices	Invite NGO campaigns on the elderly to comment on best practice in workplace processes; invite NGO leader onto an advisory group
Influencers (media, etc.)	Communicate Advent's new employment strategy	Keep briefed with plans and results

a From previous analysis.

b Carried forward 'key' desired roles.

c The actions begin to address how to share new understandings with the stakeholders, and how to agree with them and equip them for new roles.

Step 7 in action
Measuring and reporting

▶ Step 7, Process 7.1: tracking information — integrated action plan

Facilitator: Thank you for staying with us. The final step is about measuring and reporting impacts. Our task now is to summarise the key information needs we identified during the day — we have been capturing notes as we went along. Secondly, we are going to identify the key actions following from each of the seven steps, assign broad responsibility and set some provisional target deadlines for completion. These actions will then be included in Process 7.3, which we use to measure progress against agreed actions subsequently.

Chairman: And remember, we must not over-commit ourselves because of today's intense involvement. We all have our day jobs to do as well.

[The needs for Step 7 are projected onto the screen.]

- Information needs
- Actions and accountability
- Time-frame

Facilitator: OK. Let's discuss which people are to provide which types of information . . .

Marketing Director: There are some obvious tasks for me and my team: market size, packaging needs for the older customer, and labelling . . .

Personnel Director: And my human resources department will take responsibility for issues such as flexitime working and staff surveys.

Corporate Affairs Director: I will organise to provide information on investor concerns, opinion-forming groups and the successes in CSO of other organisations.

Process 7.1 **Tracking information (integrated action plan)**

A truly informed CSR plan must be based on relevant and constantly monitored information about all factors affecting the opportunities within CSO. Therefore, measurement of the integrated action plan begins with tracking the gathering and maintenance of the guiding information.

Step and issue[a]	Information needs[b]	Who provides?[c]	Last updated[d]
Step 1: Identifying the trigger			
Relevant trigger events impacting emerging CSOs	Status of food lawsuits	Legal department	
Advent CSOs	Media track of consumer food concerns	Marketing	
	Competitor response to consumer concerns	Marketing	
	Price comparison of fair trade food sources with current	– Production – NGO input	
	Share price track against food story scares	Finance	
	NGO strategies	Corporate Affairs with NGOs	
	Costs of lost deliveries	Production	
Step 2: Scoping the issues			
(B2B) Airline business risks	Superfly Air positioning in food compared to industry	– Marketing – Sales with Superfly Air	
staff shortages	Recruitment costs and labour availability	HR	
Market feedback, B2B and B2C	Customer service complaints analysis	Sales	
stakeholder perceptions	Tracking of current and emerging views	Marketing and Corporate Affairs	

Process 7.1 **Tracking information (integrated action plan)**

Step and issue	Information needs	Who provides?	Last updated
Step 3: Making the business case			
Market size for new formulations	– Current and projected sales – Competitor sales	Marketing	
	Competitor brand values for fair trade and healthy eating strategies	Marketing	
New packaging for older customers	'Grey groovers' market projections	Marketing	
	Packaging cost implications	– Production – Finance	
Flexitime implications	Best practice	HR	
	Costs of flexitime	HR with employers' federation and TUC	
Step 4: Committing to action			
Current value sets must change	More relevant and more frequent staff attitude surveys	HR	
Perception of current Advent board and senior executives' roles and values	Updated staff survey	HR	
24/7 working	Ongoing staff and other stakeholder consultation	Line managers, facilitated by HR	
Step 5: Integration and gathering resources			
New spin-off CEO	Competitive salary and package rates	HR	
New product labelling	Forecasts of legislative trends	Legal	
	Assessments of consumer needs and reaction to labelling	Marketing	

Process 7.1 **Tracking information (integrated action plan)**

Step and issue	Information needs	Who provides?	Last updated
Step 6: Engaging stakeholders			
Investor concerns over food investments	Current and projected investment strategies	Corporate Affairs with corporate bankers	
Opinion-former groups' perceptions of Advent	Current and future perceptions	Corporate Affairs	
Step 7: Measuring and reporting			
Benchmarking against other CSO successes	Information-gathering strategies of other CSOs	Corporate Affairs	

a This column should summarise the top-level CSO issues giving rise to specific information needs within each step.

b This process should concentrate on the new, or newly important, information necessary for an emerging CSO strategy. It should not duplicate normal company reporting. Indeed, part of this analysis should lead to this type of information becoming part of normal company reporting.

c The aim should be to use normal accountabilities where possible. This avoids duplicating information gathering, and the 'battle of the sources'.

d The value of information to some extent depends on how current it is. This column shows when the information was last updated.

▶ Step 7, Process 7.2: action targets — integrated action plan

> *Facilitator:* This process is about assigning responsibilities and beginning to put a time-frame on necessary actions.

The process was readily completed, as there was general consensus about what were the urgent requirements, and what required more intensive research and development and consultation. The group also began to consider how they were going to manage the process going forward, and how their own functions and roles might be impacted.

> *Corporate Affairs Director:* Under the 'identifying the trigger' step, I suggest we add quarterly reviews to the board agenda, to make sure we don't fall behind the issues. We should set up formal processes, with formal information sources.

> *CEO:* And maybe, Chairman, we should add new non-executive directors who bring us some of this new knowledge? I was wondering for example whether we really have enough solid science-based knowledge of nutritional issues among us? Anyway, I will take action for the board agenda.

> *Finance Director:* I will take an action on developing further risk analysis on this year's budget.

Process 7.2 Action targets (integrated action plan)[a]

The basis of effective measurement is having a baseline against which performance can be compared. The baseline for implementing new business opportunities driven by CSO is the integrated action plan.

Process 7.2 **Action targets (integrated action plan)**

Step and issue[b]	Action description	Actionee?	By when?
Step 1: Identifying the triggers			
Overall	1. Establish Board-level quarterly reviews of CSR, to prevent Advent Foods falling behind, as it is currently	CEO	First month of each quarter
	2. Establish formal processes to track global forces and identify impacts on Advent strategies		
	3. Formal information sources to be established on CSR/CSO issues		
	4. Consideration of adding new non-executive directors with knowledge both of the wider CSO issues and of the new options		
Identified projects	1. Form project teams for each project	Project teams	Within one month
	2. Project teams to review the initial trigger list, and document the main factors for constant review		
Stakeholders	Establish phased briefing plan for all stakeholders covering succeeding 12 months and beyond	Corporate Affairs	Within one month
Step 2: Scoping the issues			
Impact of triggers	Develop risk analysis of current year's budget based on trigger analysis	Finance Director	Within one month
	Formal risk analysis update. Strategic Three-Year Plan developed, based on project team, input, reviewed and signed off	Board	Within three months
Stakeholder impacts	Set up formal stakeholder involvement and consultation process, phased with briefings	Corporate Affairs	Within two months

Process 7.2 **Progress plan (integrated action plan)**

Step and issue	Action description	Actionee?	By when?
Step 3: Making the business case			
Marketing plan implications	Develop costed marketing plan based on preferred options	Marketing Director	Within four months
Business case	Formal update to Strategic Three-Year Plan developed and accepted	Board	Within six months
Business case	Agree any necessary variations to current-year operational and finance plan	Board	Within six months
Step 4: Committing to action			
Advent values	Work alongside project teams to identify and validate any necessary changes to Advent core value sets and leadership requirements	HR	Within three to six months
Advent governance	Approve changes in governance processes	Board	Within six months
New leadership requirements	Develop senior leadership change programme	HR with Board	Within six months
New procurement practices	Develop new commercial practices for new types of international suppliers, based on Project Team input and requirements	HR plus Operations Director	Within four to eight months
New employee types	Develop new flexible employment standards and conditions, based on Project Team input	HR plus Operations Director	Within four to eight months
Reward schemes for new businesses	Define new senior executive remuneration package for start-up operations	HR plus Board Remuneration Committee	Within four to six months

Process 7.2 **Progress plan (integrated action plan)**

Step and issue	Action description	Actionee?	By when?
Step 5: Integration and gathering resources			
New spin-off business	Recruit new spin-off business CEO	CEO with HR	Six to nine months
New supply sources	Recruit and integrate new procurement staff	HR with Operations Director	Six to nine months
Stakeholder input	Involve current staff with outside input to developing new flexible work practices	HR with Project Teams	Six to nine months
Step 6: Engaging stakeholders			
Active stakeholder input	1. Develop detailed plans for stakeholder involvement	Project Teams	Nine months onwards
	2. Involve current staff in inducting new types of employees		
	Involve external suppliers in Advent strategy conference	Operations Director	Nine months onwards
Step 7: Measuring and reporting			
Information needs	Establish formal information-gathering and resources to support CSR information plan	Board with Project Teams	Within one month
Progress plan	Involve Project Teams in refining Board-developed action plan	Board with Project Teams	Within one month
	Set the Project Teams for each option to define demanding but realistic milestones for measurement	Board with Project Teams	Within one month
Progress measurement	1. Review top-level plan with Project Teams	Board with Project Teams	Within one month, and ongoing
	2. Communicate progress to stakeholders		

a This is a checklist, against which actions from previous steps, and actions derived from reviewing these actions, are used for actionee and date assignment, and subsequent checking. This checklist addresses the options developed in Steps 1–6. It also includes top-level actions to spread CSO across the whole company.

b This is an action plan for delivering a new CSO-derived strategy. The actions are noted here from all the previous analysis. It is very likely that delivering the whole new business opportunity will require more general action plans, such as in product development and market testing. These actions will be planned and managed in the normal way for the organisation. However, there should be links at the top level of these other plans to this CSO plan.

Later

Facilitator: And with regard to progressing Step 7 itself, who should be responsible?

CEO: I will be happy to take this on.

Chairman: Or maybe I should?

Facilitator: My experience of other companies turning corporate social responsibility into corporate social opportunity is that the whole board should hold the responsibility at board level. Progressing these actions should become core to running the whole company by all managers.

Chairman: Agreed — we will brief the full board.

Facilitator: Everyone has done very well, and I hope you too are pleased with the output?

Corporate Affairs Director: I'm very pleased with what we've achieved. We've finally got things onto our agenda that have been needing attention.

Marketing Director: Yes, I think we've got some good ideas starting. I'm keen to get the rest of the board and my team involved — and our stakeholders. I'm actually quite excited about the possibilities.

Chairman: We've certainly got plenty to keep us busy and plenty of food . . . healthy food . . . for thought

Facilitator: While you are having dinner [*Name of Facilitator's Assistant*] will be tidying up the forms he has been completing as we have gone along. You will each be presented with this document as a record of what you have been discussing during the day.

Chairman: I think to capitalise on what has been achieved we should institute at least one special action team to take the output from today and extend the action plan. We'd need at least one of us who was here today to provide input and interpret the results.

Corporate Affairs Director: Yes, I'd like my number 2 to take a look at the output from today. She'll have some good ideas on what we need in the performance measurement charts. When she took her MBA she went deeper into the CSR aspects as she opted to take a dedicated module on the subject. I've got a meeting booked with her. I'll brief her on today and see what comments she has.

Chairman: I'll get on to [*Company Secretary*] to sort out some times for us to have regular reviews. I think we can feel confident that we are going in the right direction for the future of our company — not a bad achievement for a wet Sunday in November! I think we'd all like to thank [*Name of the Facilitator*] and [*Name of the Facilitator's Assistant*] for their time and input. Thank you.

[Everyone applauds.]

At 6.55 pm on the November Sunday evening, this seemed a good note on which to end. The day's formal sessions were over, leaving the facilitator and his assistant to include the agreed actions onto the form for **Process 7.3: progress measurement — integrated action plan** for sharing with the Advent team later. The completed

7.3 form became the main progress document for regular board and review. It was also used by the working party subsequently formed to link their own activities to the board review.

The success of the seven-step approach and the workshop process had convinced them that CSR did have implications for business strategy, and that in some instances could lead to corporate social opportunities.

Process 7.3 **Progress measurement (integrated action plan)**[a]

This does not just include measuring financial performance. Planned changes in financial performance are the consequence of the implementation of the whole range of actions against a regular review of their continued relevance.

Seven steps[a]	Expected outcome[b]	Actual outcome and impact[c]	Corrective actions[d]
Step 1: Identifying the triggers			
Overall	1. Establish Board-level quarterly reviews of CSR, to prevent Advent Foods falling behind as it is currently	1. Done	
	2. Establish formal processes to track global forces and identify impacts on Advent strategies	2. Done	
	3. Formal information sources to be established on CSR/CSO issues	3. Partial progress. Insufficient budget	3. Get approval for additional budget
	4. Consideration of adding new non-executive directors with knowledge both of the wider CSO issues and of the new options		
Identified projects	1. Form Project Teams for each project	1. Done. Insufficient representation from Operations	1. Operations Director to review secondments to project, and release three staff
	2. Project Teams to review the initial trigger list, and document the main factors for constant review	2. Done	
Stakeholders	Establish phased briefing plan for all stakeholders covering succeeding 12 months and beyond	Done	

Process 7.3 **Progress measurement (integrated action plan)**

Seven steps	Expected outcome	Actual outcome and impact	Corrective actions
Step 2: Scoping the issues			
Impact of triggers	Develop risk analysis of current year's budget based on trigger analysis		
	Formal risk analysis update. Strategic Three-Year Plan developed, based on Project Team input, reviewed and signed off	Analysis done within three months. Update to Strategic Plan late. Delays to Strategic Plan. Delays operational budget	Allow one further month maximum
Stakeholder impacts	Set up formal stakeholder involvement and consultation process, phased with briefings	Staff, investors, and local supply chain done. International supply chain proving harder to identify	Seek help from international trade NGOs and specialists within one month
Step 3: Making the business case			
Marketing plan implications	Develop costed marketing plan based on preferred options	Delayed by Strategic Plan update	Apply more marketing resources; work in parallel with Strategic Plan update to make up lost time
Business case	Formal update to Strategic Three-Year Plan developed and accepted	Delayed by Strategic Plan update	Apply more marketing resources; work in parallel with Strategic Plan update to make up lost time
	Agree any necessary variations to current-year operational and finance plan	Not yet due	
Step 4: Committing to action			
Advent values	Work alongside Project Teams to identify and validate any necessary changes to Advent core value sets and leadership requirements	Started. Finish due subsequent month's report	

Process 7.3 **Progress measurement (integrated action plan)**

Seven steps	Expected outcome	Actual outcome and impact	Corrective actions
Advent governance	Approve changes in governance processes	Under way	
New leadership requirements	Develop senior leadership change programme	New values agreed. Leadership coach identified. Personal commitment by senior executive team not complete, delaying visibility across Advent	CEO to review individuals' commitments to change
New procurement practices	Develop new commercial practices for new types of international suppliers, based on project team input and requirements	Just started. Check momentum at next report	
New employee types	Develop new flexible employment standards and conditions, based on project team input	Working party set up. Project Team input received. On track.	
Reward schemes for new businesses	Define new senior executive remuneration package for start-up operations	Board Remuneration Committee briefed. Terms of reference agreed.	
Step 5: Integration and gathering resources			
New spin-off business	Recruit new spin-off business CEO	Job description agreed and input to Remuneration Committee. Headhunters appointed.	
New supply sources	Recruit and integrate new procurement staff	Delays in contacts with international supply expertise	See above action on international supply chain stakeholders
Stakeholder input	Involve current staff with outside input to developing new flexible work practices	On track	

Seven steps	Expected outcome	Actual outcome and impact	Corrective actions
Step 6: Engaging stakeholders			
Active stakeholder input	– Develop detailed plans for stakeholder involvement – Involve current staff in inducting new types of employees	Not yet due	
	Involve external suppliers in Advent strategy conference	Not yet due	
Step 7: Measuring and reporting			
Information needs	Establish formal information-gathering and resources to support CSR information plan	Completed	
Progress plan	Involve Project Teams in refining Board-developed action plan	Completed	
	Set the project teams for each option to define demanding but realistic milestones for measurement	Completed	
Progress measurement	– Review top-level plan with Project Teams – Communicate progress to stakeholders	Ongoing	

a As before, this is an action plan for delivering a new CSO-derived strategy. The actions are noted here from all the previous analysis. It is very likely that delivering the whole new business opportunity will require more general action plans, such as in product development and market testing. These actions will be planned and managed in the normal way for the organisation. However, there should be links at the top level of these other plans to this CSO plan.

b The expected outcomes of actions should be defined at the beginning. This sets the base for measurement.

c The actual outcomes will be measured repeatedly during the implementation. The report should identify the date on which each action was reviewed and reported on.

d This column should identify actions to correct any shortfalls between the planned outcomes at a point in time and the actual outcomes. It may be reasonable that progress to date may require adjustment of the original action or original expected outcomes.

After the Management Retreat

The success of the first Advent Foods' 'seven step' workshop led to three tracks of activity. First, the board started a company-wide series of workshops to involve more stakeholders in identifying necessary changes for Advent. Second, the two options identified at the workshop were refined by selected teams, using the seven-step model, to inform the more established professional processes of market and product planning. Third, and at least as important for the long-term future of Advent Foods, the board decided to commit regular time each quarter to review the company's overall stance on corporate social responsibility (CSR).

Top-down, board-driven reviews would complement activity led by the manage-ment team — and show top-level commitment to the 'new' Advent Foods.

Some of the real breakthroughs came in a series of workshops with younger managers from across the company and some of the younger members of the Advent salesforce. They talked about their hopes and fears as young or prospective parents, about healthy eating and living. Some were almost evangelical about staying fit and in their attitude about what they put into their bodies. It became apparent to senior Advent managers that if they did not move to establish the company as a responsible food manufacturer, they would start to find it harder to attract and retain talented managers — and may have to start paying a wage premium to counteract a negative image.

Afterwards, it was hard to pinpoint who had first suggested the idea of setting up a new venture that would reflect the ideals and the passions of these young man-agers. The Christmas Project, as it quickly became known ('what comes after Advent? — Christmas!') rapidly moved from an after-work pub discussion to a board-approved development project.

Advent's Chairman knew that matters were getting serious when he found that the young brand manager put in charge of the Christmas Project had spent an entire weekend with her team, pulling down the dividing walls between the offices assigned to the Christmas Project and creating a bright, airy open space with designated quiet and creative areas. She explained she was trying to emphasise new ways of working for a new business.

A regular review of Advent's school vending-machine business was transformed when one member of the management team described a dinner-party conversation with her brother-in-law — a full-time official with one of the teaching unions, whose union annual conference had voted to back campaigns against school fund-raising campaigns linked to 'junk food' — about the rising anger among teachers about the behaviour of some food companies.[1] So it was possible that new fair-trade products could end up in school vending machines.[2]

For Advent itself, one of the trickiest moments in its journey came when there was a further board discussion about ethical trading. One non-executive director, the family member on the board, was implacable:

> *Non-executive Director:* My grandfather created Advent to be an ethical busi-ness. We've always paid our bills on time. We've always treated our suppliers fairly. We didn't cut and run in the bad times. We didn't wriggle out of agreements when it would have been convenient to do so. But we never went around telling people how ethical we were — and we certainly did not need any NGO to tell us how to be ethical!

Over time, the Chairman, although not changing the mind of the Non-executive Director, was able to convince him that today, ethical trading meant more than it did in the past, including issues such as conditions on suppliers' farms and factories, as well as the price paid to subsistence farmers in Africa and Central America from which the company sourced significant amounts of its raw materials for Snackotreat and other products. Those members of the board that could see the need for Advent to become a responsible business were able to persuade the dissenters that the company had to be consistent in every aspect of its activities.

Finding the right NGO to work with on the company's ethical trading programme was also problematic. The Advent purchasing team initially believed they were being asked to hand over the running of their department to 'some NGO types'. (Actually, most of the references were rather more colourful!) Their worst fears seemed realised when one of the staff from the first NGO with which they partnered leaked an unflattering first draft of a pilot review of Advent's main supplier farms. The situation was retrieved only when the entrepreneurial director of another NGO volunteered to train the purchasing team in the key things to look out for on their field visits. She was an ex-teacher and was so dynamic and enthusiastic that her passion and obvious integrity won over even the sceptics. She was able to demon-strate how a number of commercially successful multinationals such as Starbucks

---

1   *Financial Times*, 29 April 2003. According to this article,'Teachers are to campaign against the increasing number of company-backed schemes that help boost school finances, especially those linked to "junk food". Members of the National Union of Teachers were told yesterday that the NUT [National Union of Teachers] would support members who refused to co-operate in schemes backed by companies such as Tesco, Walkers Crisps and Cadbury.'

2   According to the *Financial Times* (5 August 2003), school boards in the USA are reviewing their lucrative contracts with soft-drinks and snack companies after George Washington University law professor John Banzhaf wrote to the Seattle school board raising the prospect that board members might be held liable for breaching their responsibility to children if they renewed a $400,000 (£250,000)-a-year contract with Coca-Cola. Similar attitudes are emerging in the United Kingdom, where the Food Commission — which has attacked Cadbury Schweppes over its scheme to give sports equipment in exchange for empty chocolate wrappers — joined the US-based Centre for Science in the Public Interest in seeking a ban on marketing 'high-energy, low-nutrient' foods in schools.

had successfully implemented ethical sourcing practices and 'the roof had not fallen in on their business', as she put it.

Ethical trading continued to be problematic for Advent. The Sales Director was provoked at an ethical trading business conference into making a series of negative comments to an NGO activist who then spent several months hounding Advent on its slow progress.

It was only with the publication of Advent's first environmental and social report, with a series of positive endorsements from development experts and suppliers — and, more practically, some positive data on improving conditions in the pilot farms — that the waters began to calm.

Meanwhile, Advent's factories had quietly been experiencing a revolution of their own. In the initial brainstorming workshop, the long-serving Production Director had, as he later put it, been 'fighting for air-time' to explain 'his' problem — namely, that persistent staff shortages were forcing heavy overtime costs and meant that the Advent factories could not fulfil all their orders on time.

> *Production Director:* Among all the excitement about new products, markets and brands no one seemed very interested in how we were going to keep our factories running. I'd been working alongside the factory managers for the previous 18 months — so I knew they were not slacking. Besides, I'd worked with the three of them for years and we trusted each other. It was just getting harder and harder to get staff with even basic levels of numeracy and literacy and half a head on them! And when we did find some really keen young person, they didn't seem to last five minutes. What really got my goat was when one of those clever young ad agency people suggested that the factory staff were leaving because they had concerns about making unhealthy food!

Indeed, that was not Advent's problem. It was a much more basic reality of supply and demand! Even though Advent had located two of its main factories in the 1970s in areas of high unemployment, its traditional pool of new recruits — young, unskilled people on their first job — was contracting as the population aged. The decision to change Advent's recruitment policies and to try to recruit older workers was an entirely pragmatic move. As a no-nonsense man, the Production Director was quick to disabuse journalists and others who later suggested that the move had been an integral part of Advent's move to embrace diversity.

As time went on, Advent's commitment to being a responsible business and the commercial success that that generated led it to become increasingly involved in a number of industry-wide initiatives and partnerships. Continuing debates about food safety and healthy eating led the food industry into new forms of collective action to build an understanding of the issues and of the tools available to tackle those issues. Over time, Advent became one of the leaders in the food sector in engaging different stakeholders to advance common agendas. One of its most successful was a long-term partnership with campaigning and service NGOs working with families.

Signposts

Throughout *Corporate Social Opportunity!* we have been referring to relevant newspaper articles, reports, books and websites. Here, we summarise some key new resources since the publication of our earlier book, *Everybody's Business* (Dorling Kindersley, 2001).

▶ Books

There are a number of excellent books describing the global forces for change. These include:

- J.F. Rischard, *High Noon: 20 Global Problems; 20 Years to Solve Them* (New York: Basic Books, 2002).

- Peter Schwartz, *Inevitable Surprises: Thinking Ahead in a Time of Turbulence* (New York: Gotham Books, 2003).

- Philippe Legrain, *Open World: The Truth about Globalization* (London: Abacus, 2002).

Useful resources on global CSR initiatives include:

- Claude Fussler, Aron Cramer and Sebastian van der Vegt, *Raising the Bar: Creating Value with the UN Global Compact* (Sheffield, UK: Greenleaf Publishing, 2004).

- Malcolm McIntosh, Sandra Waddock and Georg Kell, *Learning To Talk: Corporate Citizenship and the Development of the UN Global Compact* (Sheffield, UK: Greenleaf Publishing, 2004).

- Deborah Leipziger, *The Corporate Responsibility Code Book* (Sheffield, UK: Greenleaf Publishing, 2003).

▶ Other sources and resources

Free daily or regular e-newsletters on corporate social responsibility

Both our organisations provide a daily e-mail digest of media stories on CSR. Among others we use:

- Sustainable Business News, from Sophie Hooper (sophie@onetel.net.uk)
- DiversityInc.com (newsletter@diversityinc.com)
- Philanthropy Update (update@philanthropyroundtable.org)
- EurActiv Update (updatemail@euractiv.com)
- Articulate — Article 13's newsletter, from Lucy Shea (lucys@article13.com)
- Business Respect CSR Newsletter (Business_Respect@mallenbaker.net)
- RADAR — Sustainability, from Kizzi Keane (keane@sustainability.com)

Journals

Key CSR journals are:

- *The Corporate Citizenship Briefing* (Oliver Balch, oliverbalch@corporate-citizenship.co.uk)
- *Ethical Corporation* magazine (Tobias Webb, newsletter@ethicalcorp.com)
- *Ethical Performance* (www.ethicalperformance.com)
- *The Journal of Corporate Citizenship* (Greenleaf Publishing, www.greenleaf-publishing.com/jcc/jccframe.htm)
- *AccountAbility Forum* (Greenleaf Publishing, www.greenleaf-publishing.com/af/afframe.htm)

Websites

Addresses for major CSR websites (and parts of them most relevant to your interests and concerns). Again, both our organisations (BITC and IBLF) have invested heavily in building up informative and accessible websites:

- Business in the Community: www.bitc.org.uk
- International Business Leaders Forum: www.iblf.org (this includes a regularly updated listing of conferences, workshops and events around the world)

- World Business Council for Sustainable Development: www.wbcsd.org
- David Grayson: www.davidgrayson.net
- Mallen Baker's CSR website: www.mallenbaker.net
- A new UK government website devoted to CSR: www.csr.gov.uk
- For small firms, see: www.smallbusinessjourney.com
- The European Union's Multi-stakeholder Forum on CSR: http://europa.eu.int/comm/enterprise/csr/forum.htm
- The Challenge Forum website provides excellent scenarios, at www.chforum.org, and is particularly relevant to Step 2
- www.conversations-with-disbelievers.net: a web-based collection of practitioner tools to engage sceptics on the business case for CSR is run by AccountAbility and the Boston College Center for Corporate Citizenship, and is particularly relevant to Step 3

Others can be accessed through a global CSR portal, such as:

- www.csreurope.org
- Davos World Economic Forum Knowledge Navigator, at www.weforum.org/site/knowledgenavigator.nsf/Content/KB+Home+Page

▶ Suggestions for getting involved

Joining business-led CSR intermediaries where you have a significant business presence, and getting involved with working parties and leadership taskforces associated with the CSR issues most pressing for you, is a further way to build corporate CSR knowledge and capacity. If a company chooses this route, it is important to ensure that employees who are involved in this way are aware of, and encouraged to compare notes with, their company counterparts in other countries who are similarly getting involved in such taskforces and projects. By concentrating on a few key themes and working on these in different markets and with different CSR national organisations — and capturing these experiences — the company will more effectively start making 2 + 2 = more than 4!

Conferences

You might build up a team of committed advocates and champions across the organisation — dividing responsibility between them for attending the major CSR conferences and reporting back on key lessons and insights for the company and building the new information into the knowledge-management system.

Among the major CSR conferences each year, there are: The Conference Board's Global Corporate Citizenship Conference (New York, February); Boston College Center for Corporate Citizenship (which moves around major US cities in March); Business in the Community (London, July); and Business for Social Responsibility, which alternates between the east and west coasts of the USA (November). All these tend to be business-led and practitioner-focused. The European Union's rotating presidency is now running an annual stakeholder-led CSR conference in November, and the UN Global Compact has established a Learning Network which, *inter alia*, has an annual meeting in December. For a regularly updated listing of conferences, workshops and events around the world, see the IBLF website (www.iblf.org) or the Corporate Citizenship Briefing website (www.corporate-citizenship.co.uk).

▶ Resources for 'bottom of the pyramid'

- Sustainable Livelihood Project, World Business Council for Sustainable Development (www.wbcsd.org)

- Schulich Sustainable Enterprise Academy, which runs Business Leaders Seminars (www.sea.schulich.yorku.ca)

- Digital Dividend, Part of the World Resources Institute (www.digitaldividend.org)

- Centre for Sustainable Enterprises, Stuart Graduate School of Business, Illinois Institute of Technology (www.stuart.iit.edu/cse/home.html)

▶ Training resources and materials on corporate social responsibility

- The European Academy of Business in Society (EABIS) is a unique alliance of academic institutions, companies and other stakeholders committed to integrating business in society into the heart of business theory and practice in Europe (www.eabis.org)

- The Aspen Institute for Business and Society has a free, password-protected website (www.caseplace.org)

- The World Resources Institute website provides links to and information on the location of materials for designing in-house courses (www.wri.org/wri/enved)

- The UN Global Compact has a Learning Network, bringing together signatory companies, academics and non-governmental organisations to develop and present case-study resources (www.unglobalcompact.org).

- National institutes of company directors such as those for Australia and the United Kingdom, offer courses, run conferences and workshops and produce publications on CSR (www.companydirectors.com.au; www.iod.co.uk).

- The Conference Board offers a range of conferences, seminars and research reports on corporate citizenship and sustainable development (www.conference-board.org).

- World Business Council for Sustainable Development (www.wbcsd.org).

- Jonathan Porritt of the UK-headquartered Forum for the Future runs five-day courses for business leaders on sustainable development (www.forumforthefuture.org.uk).

- Managers from Statoil are trained to appreciate human rights issues by representatives from Amnesty International (www.amnesty.org).

▶ Materials on CSR reporting

For those readers who want to delve deeper into reporting trends, there are an increasing number of studies available, including:

- SustainAbility, 'Global Reporters 2000', Global Reporters 2002', www.sustainability.com (these reports analyse trends identified from an examination of what SustainAbility believes to be 50 of the best CSR reports internationally).

- Context and SalterBaxter, 'Directions I: Trends in CSR Reporting 2001–2002', 'Directions II: Trends in CSR Reporting 2001–2002', 'Directions III: Trends in CSR Reporting by 2002–2003'.

- Addison Corporate Marketing Ltd, 'Smoke and Mirrors? Corporate CSR Reporting — Claims and Reality'.

- New Economics Foundation, 'The Troubled Teenage Reports of CSR Reporting'.

- Ashridge Centre for Business and Society, 'An Anchor Not The Answer: Trends in Social and Sustainable Development Reporting'.

- CSR Europe, 'Impacts of Reporting'.

- AccountAbility in association with Ashridge 'AA1000 Conversations: Lessons from the Early Years — 1999–2001'.

▶ Following up this book

We hope that you have enjoyed our book and have got something useful out of it. You and your business may get even more from it by also booking a Corporate Social Opportunity presentation, seminar or workshop.

1. Presentation: given by one of the authors. This is customised to the audience but typically covers the heightened expectations of business; why CSR is now part of the mainstream business agenda; the dangers of over-emphasising the costs, burden, risk-minimisation aspects of CSR; why it is better to be focusing on the more positive opportunities side; and how to achieve this.

2. Seminar: half-day with one of the authors. Again, this is customised to the audience, but, in addition to the presentation, offers more opportunities for questioning and debate. The seminar also has a breakout session to encourage participants to explore CSR issues they have faced, are facing or may face — and how to handle them better.

3. Workshop: running for 1–1.5 days with both authors or one of the authors plus another experienced facilitator. The workshop is highly participatory. Like the participants in the Advent Foods management retreat described in Part II, attendees get to work through the seven-step model and accompanying diagnostic tools real-time and compile a list of the most promising corporate social opportunities for their business to pursue. They will also generate considerable raw material to help them follow up these leads after the workshop.

Member companies of Business in the Community and International Business Leaders Forum may organise any of these through their BITC or IBLF account managers. For all other inquiries, please contact David Grayson (david.grayson@bitc.org.uk) or Adrian Hodges (adrian.hodges@iblf.org) direct.

Acknowledgements

A project like *Corporate Social Opportunity!* only happens because of the hard work and generosity of time and ideas of many different people. We deeply appreciate the patience and encouragement of family and friends whose innocent question 'how's the book?' all too often produced a torrent of questions and challenges from one or other of us.

Many of those friends and colleagues have commented on sections or all of the manuscript, and have helped to develop crucial insights for us. They include: David Alcock, Kay Allen, Geoffrey Bush, Erik Bruun Bindslev, Henk Campher, Damian Carnell, Viki Cooke, John Elkington, Penny Hawley, John Heaslip, David Irwin, Andrew Jackson, Pen Kent, Paul Laporte, Ed Mitchell, Paul Monaghan, Noel Morrin, Jane Nelson, Eric Peacock, David Prescott, Andy Roberts, Andrew Summers, Mike Tuffrey, Catherine Turner, Gerry Wade, Bob Wigley, Ed Williams, John Williams and Andrew Wilson.

A number of business leaders and executives gave us personal interviews and invaluable raw material, including Edward Bickham, Elena Bonfiglioli, Mike Clasper, Crispin Davis, John Drummond, Harry Fitzgibbons, David Gregory, Gail Johnson, Kevan Jones, Peter Kilgour, Justin King, Jerry Marston, Clive Mather, Vince McGinlay, Branka Minic, Mark Moody-Stuart, Gaetan Morency, Graham Oakley, Laurel Powers-Freeling, Charles Pender, Robert Smith, Terry Thomas, Kevin Tutton, Luc Vandervelde, David Varney, Peter White and Jeff Zalla.

Julia Cleverdon at Business in the Community, Robert Davies at International Business Leaders Forum, and David Vidal at The Conference Board as well as being long-term friends and mentors have given both their personal and their organi-sational support — and we are enormously grateful for their backing. Colleagues at BITC who have provided many insights and leads include Mallen Baker, Catherine Carruthers, Caroline Cook, Peter Davies, Gail Greengross, Geoff Lane, Patrick Mallon, John O'Brien, Patrick O'Meara, Catherine Sermon, Charlotte Turner and Lucy Varcoe. Colleagues at IBLF including Amanda Bowman, Zuzana Bragoli, Nick Claridge, Georgina May, Mike Patterson, Joe Phelan and Leon Taylor have supported us at critical moments, and we are grateful for the assistance of Randall Poe at The Conference Board.

John Stuart at Greenleaf has backed *Corporate Social Opportunity!* since we first made contact more than 18 months ago, patiently slowing down the schedule as we fell behind on our timetable; and then sanctioning a breakneck compression of the Greenleaf processes to take our manuscript to market in a fraction of their normal time. As laymen in publishing, we did not realise the amount of midnight oil this would require — not just for ourselves but for Greenleaf colleagues led by Dean Bargh and including Rachael Catt and Sarah Norman — whose good humour and professionalism must have been sorely tried by authors who were also trying to hold down day jobs, which as a result, at times, has involved simultaneously communicating between several different countries and time zones.

We are immensely grateful to Jeremy Pelczer and Richard Aylard of American Water and RWE Thames Water, and Hank McKinnell, Nancy Nielsen and Gill Samuels of Pfizer for their support and encouragement, and for access to information and insights into how their businesses are managing the challenges of corporate responsibility and good corporate citizenship. They were generous with their time and extremely open about some of the dilemmas they face in pursuing a values-based management philosophy. They all believed enough in what we were trying to do that they provided vital financial sponsorship. That finance did not go to us personally, but rather allowed us to contribute to the costs of accessing expertise in the technical development of a diagnostic business tool, in which we were lacking.

That expertise came from two colleagues with a wealth of business and marketing and sales experience: Harvey Dodgson and Kevin Gavaghan. Both have been marketing directors in FTSE 100 businesses as well as founders of small businesses. As well as showing great patience in helping us to turn our ideas into reality for Part II of the book, Kevin's and Harvey's sharp commercial acumen and depth of business knowledge added value throughout the writing process; they have given help way beyond their contractual call of duty — and have been great fun to work with. (Even if — despite travelling in a train driver's cab, David still can't tell Harvey why trains hoot as they exit tunnels as well as when they enter!)

We are very grateful, too, for those organisations and institutions who gave us permission to quote material from their work, without the inclusion of which this book would be the poorer.

As we gear up to find channels to publicise the book, we are in discussion with a network of colleagues who have offered to help, for which, in advance, we give thanks. A particular mention must be given to Eric Gagnon and Daniel Gagnier of Alcan Inc., who as well as being generally supportive have made a donation to help us spread the word.

Finally, a personal word of thanks from Adrian to his partner, Neil, who has provided on cue without any prompting and when needed words of encouragement and hugs. Thank you.

Sins of omission and commission rest with us.

David and Adrian

Partners in Corporate Social Opportunity

Business in the

Community

▶ Business in the Community

www.bitc.org

Business in the Community is a unique movement in the UK of over 700 member companies, with a further 1,600 participating in our programmes and campaigns. We operate through a network of 98 local business-led partnerships, as well as working with 45 global partners.

Our purpose is to inspire, challenge, engage and support business in continually improving its positive impact on society. Membership of Business in the Community is a commitment to action and to the continual improvement of a company's impact on society. Together, our member companies employ over 15.7 million people in over 200 countries worldwide. In the UK our members employ over 1 in 5 of the private-sector workforce.

Our members commit to:

- Integrate, manage and measure responsible business practice throughout their business

- Impact through collaborative action to tackle disadvantage

- Inspire, innovate and lead by sharing and learning

▶ International Business Leaders Forum

www.iblf.org

IBLF

THE PRINCE OF WALES
INTERNATIONAL BUSINESS
LEADERS FORUM

The International Business Leaders Forum (IBLF) is a not-for-profit organisation, founded in 1990 by HRH The Prince of Wales and a group of international CEOs in response to the emerging social challenges that accompanied economic growth and changes in the global economy. IBLF's mission is to promote international leadership in responsible business practices, to benefit business and society. IBLF has a corporate membership of 80 multinational companies from around the world and works strategically with leaders from business, civil society and the public sector in order to promote social, economic and environmentally sustainable development.

THE CONFERENCE BOARD

▶ The Conference Board

www.conference-board.org

The Conference Board is the world's leading research and business membership organisation. Independent and not-for-profit, The Conference Board connects more than 2,000 companies in 61 nations. Its twin missions are to help strengthen business performance and help business better serve society.

The Conference Board has been a leader in corporate governance, corporate citizenship, business ethics and a wide range of other critical management practice areas. Its widely watched economic barometers and reports often move the financial markets. The Conference Board produces the Leading Economic Indicators for the United States and eight other countries, the Consumer Confidence Index and other major barometers. The Conference Board's Board of Trustees include business leaders from throughout the world.

Corporate partners: transparency statement

RWE Thames Water and Pfizer Inc., two companies quoted in the book, provided financial support for the research and development work undertaken for *Corporate Social Opportunity!*

Index

UNIVERSITY OF WALES, NEWPORT
LIBRARY AND INFORMATION SERVICES
ALLT-YR-YN